PERSONALITY DYNAMICS

A
Biosocial
Approach

PERSONALITY

In a series under the editorship of
WAYNE HOLTZMAN and GARDNER MURPHY

DYNAMICS
A
Biosocial
Approach

G. M. GILBERT

Long Island University

with the assistance of
Gardner Murphy

HARPER & ROW, Publishers

New York, Evanston, and London

Contents

Preface

This textbook is an attempt to combine the psychodynamic and scientific requirements of personality study, using a biosocial theoretical approach as its integrating theme. We have, therefore, knowingly sacrificed a more thorough review of the existing experimental literature to the overriding consideration of exploring issues and gaining insights into the behavior of human beings living real lives as members of society. We have, on the other hand, felt free to cite relevant research from any of the behavioral sciences, for we regard the study of personality as necessarily interdisciplinary, cross-cultural, and historical in its dimensions.

In preparing what is admittedly a first attempt at such an ambitious task, we wish to acknowledge the helpful criticisms of numerous colleagues who read chapters of the manuscript pertaining to their respective specialties: Dr. Harry L. Shapiro, Dr. Harriet Commoss, Dr. Carol Bare, Dr. Jean Mundy, Dr. Adel Mahran, Dr. Wayne Holtzman, Mr. Robert Gilbert, Mrs. M. S. Gilbert. We are indebted additionally to Dr. Donn Byrne for his thorough critique of two earlier drafts of the manuscript. Above all, we are indebted to Dr. Gardner Murphy, who not only gave critical readings of each earlier draft of the manuscript over a period of several years, but contributed material incorporated into several of the chapters. Nevertheless, the responsibility for the general conception and final product, along with any errors of omission or commission, must remain the author's. We invite correspondence to correct such errors or to clarify some of the positions taken, in future editions of the book.

Above all, we hope that students will find this presentation scientifically credible, coherent, and *relevant* to the human interests of the times.

G. M. GILBERT

January, 1970

PERSONALITY DYNAMICS

A Biosocial Approach

I

The Biosocial Approach

The Science of Personality   The variability, unpredictability, and apparent willfulness of human nature have been so obvious all through history and in all of our own lifetimes, that it may seem rather futile for psychologists to attempt a scientific study of personality. We would grant at the outset that it would be overambitious to try to apply rigidly formulated and quantified laws of cause and effect to every behavioral process and reaction of the human organism in the same way that exact measures of mass, time, and distance can be applied to the movement of bodies in physics. The early attempts of the psychophysicists (those who attempted to work out such exact equations between stimulus and response in sensation) ended in a total blind alley as far as a science of personality was concerned. The basic reason for this failure is that by mimicking the methods and concepts of physics, we neglect completely the *essential properties* of animal life and, beyond that, the more complex properties of human life that have emerged in the course of millions of years of evolution. These properties of animal life include such functions as awareness, communication, motivated and choice behavior, learning from experience, and group cohesion and interaction—before we even get into the more complex and symbolic behavior of human social interaction, motivation, and values.

The laws governing the motion and changes of inanimate matter were simply never intended to apply to the special properties of higher forms of life, least of all to human personality.

That is not to say that the laws of physics do not apply to human beings; it merely means that for the most part they are quite irrelevant to what a psychologist wants to know in understanding human behavior. If, for example, a man jumps out of a thirtieth-story window, it is quite irrelevant to note that the distance fallen is governed by the physical law of falling bodies as expressed in the formula: $d = 16t^2$. What the psychologist wants to know is: Why did he want to commit suicide? That is a question of motivational and emotional conflict, which is practically impossible to measure. It may require going back into the man's whole case history and assessing his subjective emotional reactions on the basis of expressed feelings and frustrations in his life goals and relationships with other people. In other words, in the behavioral sciences we are dealing with natural phenomena of a higher order of complexity. At that level, the *subjectivity* of many behavioral processes is a basic reality which frequently eludes quantification and reification (i.e., making an object out of an abstract concept), but which must be dealt with as scientifically as possible.

SATISFYING SCIENTIFIC CRITERIA

What, then, are the basic criteria of scientific inquiry by which even the psychology of personality should be bound if it is to be called a science—even that special brand called "behavioral science"? First of all, there must be a degree of *objectivity*, or at least *verifiability of observations*, even in dealing with subjective reactions. If data such as attitudes or motives are essentially subjective, that does not mean they are nonexistent or incapable of verification as data of research. Repeated observations of even the most subjective data may become validated by confirmation or by "consensual validation" of many observers, or by the internal consistency of various criteria of the particular behavior being observed. Thus if a student says he is tense and worried about his exams, and he looks tense and worried, and furthermore acts tense and worried just before exam time, and his teacher and classmates ask him *why* he is so tense and worried, we may reasonably conclude that he *is* tense and worried. Any conclusions we may wish to draw about how emotional tension affects performance on tests may be verified by other researchers by using similar subjects under similar circumstances, provided we have defined our terms and the circumstances exactly. That does not mean that different individuals will always react in the same way to a given situation. Quite the contrary. Persistent and consistent differences in reaction to similar situations may give the very clues to differences in thinking and personality that we are looking for.

Fortunately, the study of personality does not have to be confined to the subjective interpretation of subjective data. Under certain circumstances, and for certain functions of overt behavior, it is possible to measure quite objectively and accurately the responses of the human organism to exactly specified conditions. An example would be the measurement of performance efficiency of different individuals on certain intellectual or mechanical tasks under specified conditions of distraction, pay incentive, competitive performance, etc. Under other circumstances a quasiquantitative value may be assigned to even subjective reactions, such as checking off numerical positions on an attitude scale from one extreme to another, or reporting the gross frequency of specified behavioral symptoms (e.g., "I [never] [sometimes] [often] lose my temper when criticized or contradicted.") Such quasiquantitative and categorical introspective reports are subject to many pitfalls, as we shall see; but an undercurrent of verifiable objectivity frequently comes through when research is done on large-enough samples of well-defined populations that permit one to even out subjective distortions of the actual facts. When it is relevant to study the physiological components of emotional or attitudinal reactions to specific stimuli, these factors may be recorded and measured with a high degree of accuracy by instruments such as the polygraph (popularly known as the "lie detector" because it can sometimes detect emotional reactions to guilty knowledge which is denied). For many purposes, however, the study of the behavior of people, with all their complex motivations and adjustments in real life, requires qualitative or historical analysis, devoid of observer bias as far as possible.

The second requirement of any science is *systematic organization of empirically derived data and establishment of lawful relationships* among these data. Science is based on the assumption that there is order and relatedness of events in the universe and within the microcosms that constitute scientific areas of investigation. The orderliness is somewhat more elusive in the behavioral sciences, because of the emergent properties of animal life we have referred to, but it is still there. It is the behavioral scientist's task, like that of any other scientist, not only to make verified objective observations but also to discover the orderly relationships among them. This is what enabled Charles Darwin to formulate the theory of the evolution of animal species and the ascent of man from lower animals. He did not experiment. The experiment had already been carried out in nature and was still progressing. He simply observed and classified modern animal life and some fossils, noted similarities and differences among species in the course of geologic time, and took note of the struggle for survival in the animal world as well as the relationship of morphology to environment and food supply. Finally, he was able to reconstruct a theory of natural selection and evolution of species that accounted pretty well for all the facts observed in spite of some missing data.

Psychology proceeds from the now well-established theory of evolution of the human species and makes its own observations and classifications relevant to its subject matter. Basic human characteristics and cultural variations are noted by cross-cultural comparisons. Personality development from childhood to adulthood is observed under different environmental conditions and different degrees of consanguinity (blood or family relationships). Variations of normal behavior are described and patterns of behavior disorders diagnosed, while similarities in past experience of individuals with similar behavior syndromes are duly noted. In more detailed analysis, distinctions are made among cognitive (intellectual or perceptive), affective (emotional or attitudinal), sensorimotor, and integrative responses of the total personality. Some of this organization of observations is purely normative and descriptive, allowing for the use of statistical analysis of individual differences. Because many biological functions and structures are distributed in a given species in accordance with the "normal distribution curve," individuals may frequently be compared with respect to their position in such a distribution of intelligence, personality traits, aptitudes, or psychomotor development in the population of their age bracket, sex, or ethnic group. Measurement always imparts a degree of objectivity to observed data. However, many aspects of individual and group behavior and their interrelationships can only be classified or meaningfully related by other abstract concepts. Particularly in the field of psychodynamics, which is our concern in this book (i.e., motivation, growth, conflict, and adjustment of personality), our integrative concepts as well as our original observations will necessarily be largely of an abstract and subjective nature. Even so, it is the task of the scientist to assure a measure of objectivity by defining his concepts and excluding any personal bias or wishful thinking from the interpretation of the data.

From this array of quantitative, quasiquantitative, and largely qualitative data and abstract concepts of related behavioral phenomena, it is but a short step toward fulfilling the third general requirement of science. That requirement is the *formulation of empirically derived laws* of cause and effect or correlation of events, which allows for a measure of prediction. In behavioral science we must generally be satisfied with rules or principles of conduct which show tendencies and probabilities, but must always allow for exceptions. The reason for this is simply that human beings are far too complex and full of subtle individual differences, too subject to the vagaries of environmental influences, and too subject to the flux of their own ideas that trigger decisions to make the prediction of behavior an exact science. It is this quality, perhaps more than anything else, that distinguishes behavioral science from the preorganic natural sciences. The wonder of it is that we are able to formulate principles and predict anything at all, even with a fair degree of probability, considering what a variable creature we are dealing with. However, there are certain gross relationships of cause and effect that, on the basis of empirical observation and experimentation, have been established at various levels of behavioral organization. Many basic principles have been formulated on the relationship between physical stimulus variables and perceptual response, and the ways in which these responses are influenced or distorted by past experience and attitudes. More and more of this research is shedding light on the relationship between habits of perception and personality traits. Some general guiding principles have been worked out (though under differing theoretical formulations) on the normal developmental sequences of behavioral norms and capacities from early childhood to adulthood, and the effects of different childhood environments on later personality adjustment. We can also predict from IQ level in childhood the approximate limit of educability of each child under optimum environmental conditions, and the extent to which the IQ itself may be accelerated or retarded by environmental conditions. And, of course, in collaboration with physiology and medicine, a good deal of cause-and-effect relationship can be established between drugs or stress or brain damage and the behavioral changes that are likely to take place in the individual personality.

In all of these sequential relationships and correlations implying cause and effect, there are margins of error for individual variability that generally increase as we go from simply physiological functions to the more complex psychosocial ones. However, some degree of consistency or predictability of individual behavior under defined conditions may be obtained, because there is a certain degree of consistency to personality in spite of its variability. If this were not the case—that is, if human beings were completely capricious, free-will agents—there would simply be no basis for behavioral science. As it is, we must be content with a science that deals in qualitative analysis, approximate measurements, and predictions of probable behavior.

Finally, there is the requirement of *internal and external consistency* of all science. Even if behavioral science often has to deal with a complexity of phenomena that do not lend themselves to the same thoroughly objective, accurately measureable, and invariable laws as we have in physics, it must always be consistent with relevant laws or principles already established in other sciences. In other words, psychology cannot contradict the laws of physics or chemistry or biology; it can only apply them insofar as they are relevant. There are such overlapping areas of investigation: for example, applying the laws of biochemistry to nerve conduction and the effects of hormones on sensorimotor and emotional behavior. But emergent structures in evolution bring new functions into play. The very appearance of living organisms like amoebae in the oceans of this planet billions of years ago was such an emerging complexity. It involved functions of growth, nutrition, reproduction, and heredity which went beyond the laws of inorganic chemistry that had ruled the universe until then and still apply universally—where they are applicable. Newer laws that are consistent with the laws of physics but go a great deal beyond them are required to explain and organize the data of the life processes. The emergence of bisexually reproducing coelenterates like jellyfish, in the evolution of marine life, brought about still more complex phenomena, requiring still more complex laws of natural variation and heredity. Then a truly revolutionary evolutionary development came about when new wormlike species evolved with primitive brains and nervous systems, bringing about new capabilities of learning and adaptation that went far beyond the simple biochemical responses to the immediate physical environment. Then the emergence of human life from the lower vertebrates, with complex brains and nervous systems, brought about still higher complexities of thought, self-awareness, adaptation by reasoning and problem-solving, complexities of innate and acquired motives, and the transmission of cultural values. In short, the very stuff of which personality is made was but a recent product of the evolving complexity of life on this planet, and it requires the formulation of new principles which are, nevertheless, consistent with the already established principles of biology.

We can think of no better way of defining our subject matter and opening our inquiry into the nature and principles of human behavior than by briefly reviewing the highly relevant evolution of the human species from his apelike ancestors.

Human

Evolution[1]   By the time of the Paleocene and Eocene epochs of recent geological time, some 40–70 million years ago, the evolution of mammals with increasingly large brains had arrived at a high level of development and specialization in the forests of Central Asia and Africa. The most highly developed of these forms was the *primate* order of mammals, with a number of genera (collections of species) that lived in the trees and occa-

---

[1] This section is based on a synthesis of numerous authorities on human evolution, the chief references being: Bordes (1968), Darwin (1871), Howell (1968), Howells (1967), Montagu (1962, 1965, 1969), Roe and Simpson (1958), Shapiro (1956), and Tax (1960).

sionally foraged for food on the ground. Their way of life demanded long, prehensile arms and legs as well as intricate brains and neuromuscular systems that provided a high degree of split-second sensorimotor coordination, binocular (stereoscopic) vision, acute hearing, and the ability to communicate with meaningful sight and sound signals—for these creatures were the first aerial trapeze artists who "made a living at it." The picture of adaptation to life in the trees is not altogether clear, but contributory evidence from fossils, from embryology, and from contemporary zoology also indicates that it demanded a further refinement of the cohesive family life and sexual division of labor these primates had already inherited from their lower mammalian ancestors. This facilitated the protection and feeding of the young, self-defense, and defense of territory to preserve food supply.

PROTOHOMINID BEGINNINGS

It was not until some time between the late Oligocene and early Miocene epochs, some 30 million years ago, that some of these species with more anthropoid characteristics began to descend from the trees and take up more permanent residence on the ground. This may have been a gradual adaptation to changing conditions of ecology (physical environment and food supply) throughout Asia and the rest of the world. As great upheavals of the earth's crust formed mountains and valleys, and as forests and swamps gave way to open plains through millennia of comparative drought, all of the giant reptiles became extinct. Many other species were forced to compete and modify their living habits, or follow the receding forests into Africa, generation by generation. The changing ecology placed high premiums on the ability to adapt for survival, by gradual constitutional changes which made the necessary behavioral changes possible. In each generation, or in the course of millennia, those species and those members of species which displayed genetic variation better suited for survival in that changing environment were better able to survive and reproduce. When adaptation was too slow or the population too dense for the available food supply, decimation and extinction of the less well adapted resulted. This is what is known as "the survival of the fittest" or *natural selection*, which Charles Darwin first postulated as the basis for the evolution of species in 1859.

For some anthropoid apes who survived the transition, adaptation to life on the ground and open plains required an ability to hunt for game over considerable distances, in addition to picking fruits from the ever-scarcer vegetation. This gave distinct survival advantages to those species and variant subspecies who could achieve an erect posture, hold weapons while running or walking (e.g., in stalking game), and could communicate with their fellows to cooperate in hunting large animals, rather than be hunted down singly by them.

Through the millions of years of such natural selection and adaptation during the Miocene and Pliocene epochs, new species diverged from the anthropoid apes, developing fully erect posture, greatly increased manual dexterity and coordination for better grasping and manipulation, and probably the beginnings of a more articulate sound signal system than their tree-swinging forebears were capable of. This enabled them to use tools and weapons while standing or running, to communicate and cooperate in hunting and mutual protection against predators, and to improvise crude shelters that life in the open country demanded or afforded. Most important, natural selection favored those with better-developed brains to mediate the increasing demands of sensorimotor coordination, verbal communication, the use and the making of crude tools, and the planning of cooperative effort to solve many of the problems of daily living. As some individuals and subspecies developed a little better manual dexterity, language facility, and reasoning ability, along with their more highly developed brains and hands, they were better equipped to survive and to pass on their genes to succeeding generations. Those who, in addition to the family cohesiveness of their apelike ancestors, also developed a capacity for and satisfaction in cooperative behavior and social interaction, had a distinct survival advantage when it came to the acid tests of hunting dangerous game and making common defense against predators of their own or other species.

At all events, there is increasing fossil evidence accompanied by archeological artifacts to indicate that many species and subspecies of erect, protohominid "family men" came and went in the course of this struggle for survival through the development of adaptive skills and living habits, which were predicated on gradual constitutional changes through natural selection. We know of definite offshoots from the early protohominid line or evolutionary network who flourished for a time during the early and middle Pleistocene epoch of 2,000,000 to 500,000 years ago, and then became extinct or were selectively absorbed into the heritage of *Homo sapiens*.

The earliest group of these varieties of ape-men, apparently, was the genus known as *Australopithecus*, who inhabited Africa from about 2,000,000 to about 600,000 years ago. One of the earliest subgenera of these early ape-men (or of a closely related line) was *Zinjanthropus*, a rather small-sized and small-brained creature, discovered in the Olduvai Gorge of what is now Tanzania by Louis S. B. and Mary Leakey in 1959. This discovery and some earlier remains were found in association with chipped stone implements and the bones of small animals in what appears to have been a permanent living site. Tests by the potassium-argon method show *Zinjanthropus* to be about 1,750,000 years old.[2] His powerful crushing molar teeth and smaller incisors and canines show that he was accustomed to grinding vegetation in his powerful jaws, but not to shearing flesh as carnivorous animals do. However, the chipped pebblestones and fossilized remains of small animals bear witness to the fact that he had already acquired the ability to make and use stone chopping tools, so that he could supplement his diet with raw meat from the small animals he could kill and butcher singlehandedly. What is remarkable about this find is that evidence of tool*making* (a decisive criterion for ape-man) should have been found so early in protohominid evolution from the ape, while his cranial capacity was still only 530 cc. Tool-making is distinguished from the mere use of objects, such as throwing stones that happen to be handy, by requiring a little more imagination, planning, and skilled execution of a concept, to modify the object's shape for a specific future use. This planning and execution, involving an element of abstract thinking, is just one significant step beyond the momentary "flash of insight" in a concrete present situation that Köhler (1925) reported in his studies of apes (e.g., putting two sticks together to reach food). It should be noted that the brain of *Zinjanthropus* was appreciably larger than that of present-day chimpanzees, whom he approximated in size.

The australopithecines flourished in Africa for over 1 million years. The remains of some of the later specimens (*Australopithecus africanus, Australopithecus robustus*) show evidence of evolutionary changes in constitution and modus vivendi even within this genus. There is simultaneous enlargement of the cranial capacity, refinement and diversification of toolmaking ability, and signs of cooperative hunting with greater dependence on a meat diet. These later or more advanced australopithecines were rather ingenious at converting antelope bones, teeth, and horns into tools for chopping, scraping, and dressing hides, besides chipping stones for use as tools or weapons as their ancestors did. Since they are known to have hunted the comparatively large baboon for food, and baboons then (as now) traveled in troops, it is assumed that *Australopithecus* must also have been able to attack in pairs or groups to overcome his quarry, even with the aid of stone or bone weapons. This would indicate an early form of cooperative hunting, which also implies a degree of planning, foresight, and cooperation early in man's evolution. Much has been made of the australopithecine use of bone clubs (e.g., femur of an antelope) to crush

---

[2] The dating and the genealogy of protohominid fossils is somewhat in dispute, but the general course of human evolution is not. We have, therefore, made use of the most recently available data of physical anthropology, while seeking to present a cohesive picture of the *evolution of human behavior*.

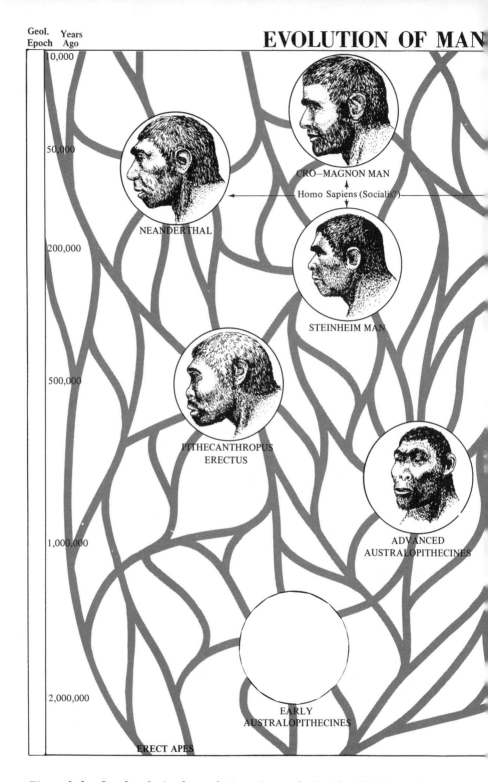

Figure 1–1. Landmarks in the evolution of man during the Old Stone Age. *Portrait sketches of ancient hominids based on reconstructions of fossil skulls by H. L. Shapiro at American Museum of Natural History, New York*

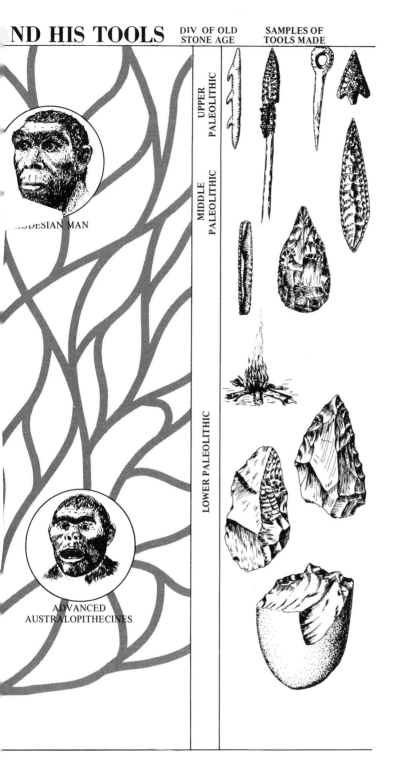

ND HIS TOOLS

	DIV OF OLD STONE AGE	SAMPLES OF TOOLS MADE

UPPER PALEOLITHIC

MIDDLE PALEOLITHIC

LOWER PALEOLITHIC

RODESIAN MAN

ADVANCED AUSTRALOPITHECINES

City, shown in approximate time sequence, but lines of ancestry not known. Sketches of approximately contemporaneous tools copied from various sources.

the skulls of victims as proof of man's innate aggressive barbarity (Dart, 1953; Ardrey, 1961). However, as Montagu and others (1965, 1968) have pointed out, this is jumping to rather drastic conclusions from the fact that hominids became hunting creatures early in their evolution; it ignores the increasing cooperativeness of man as he evolved in the million years since then.

Somewhat later (about 500,000 years ago) came *Homo erectus* (or *Pithecanthropus erectus*), whose remains have been found as far apart as Indonesia and North Africa. What was distinctive about the varieties of *Homo erectus* was their ability to devise different kinds of tools for different kinds of hunting and shelter in different parts of the world—a sign of the growing adaptability of the protohominids through toolmaking and problem-solving. This is further enhanced by the evidence that Peking man, a variety of *Homo erectus*, could make controlled use of fire. He was, therefore, not only able to warm his cave or campsite in cold weather but probably also roasted his meat after separating it from skin with the stone tools he had chipped or ground for that purpose.

A particularly ingenious instrument found at a higher level of the Olduvai site (in association with specimens of *Homo erectus*) is the three-stone bola. It was apparently used as gauchos use it today in Argentina, twirling it above their heads and throwing it at the feet of fleeing animals to bring them down. These stones were found with stone hand-axes and the crushed bones of large animals at a level dated as approximately 500,000 years old.

Nevertheless, it is not certain just how and why each of these earlier Old Stone Age species became extinct. In some cases, it was probably a failure to develop communication and cooperative problem-solving to a degree sufficient to meet the changing demands of their environments or the competition from encroaching species who were developing these capacities faster. In other cases, they may have developed too much or too little aggression to protect themselves from each other. We can only speculate that "optimum aggression" was necessary for survival, but too much or too little might have been self-defeating. Less speculative would be extermination "due to circumstances beyond our control"—such as disastrous floods, drought and famine, pestilence, or the advance of freezing weather during the Ice Age. Undoubtedly, the onset of the Ice Age about 1,000,000 years ago provided a crucial test of all animal species' adaptability to changing climatic and geographic conditions in the northern hemisphere. The four successive waves of advancing and receding icecaps at varying intervals brought about a great upheaval in the survival and distribution of animal species. Only the most adaptive and ingenious of the hominids was destined to survive and eventually spread over the face of the earth.

Just which one or which combination of ancestral lines led directly to modern man we are still not sure; but it was probably part of a closely related group of toolmaking, cooperative, inventive, socially cohesive, yet aggressive hunters, some of whom are known to have existed in the latter part of the Pleistocene epoch or Middle Paleolithic (Old Stone Age).

Some time after the ascendancy of *Homo erectus*, about 300,000 to 200,000 years ago, came larger-brained, even more dexterous and prolific toolmaking hunters like Swanscombe man of England and Steinheim man of Germany, who are generally thought to represent an early edition of *Homo sapiens*. Though it is not known whether these advanced ape-men emerged from or displaced *Homo erectus* from a parallel line of development, they displayed distinguishing characteristics which evidently represented functional advantages in the struggle for survival and the pressures of natural selection. Their reconstructed skeletal structures and the associated archeological finds show that they had larger frontal lobes and could make and use a larger variety of stone and bone tools. They also could live and hunt in groups and make use of fire and shelter, all of which points to an early form of communal living.

The cause-and-effect rationale of this gradual selective pressure toward more intelligent and social (i.e., inventive and collaborative) ways of life is exceedingly complex and the evidence exceedingly sketchy. In general, various structural and functional variants having superior survival value tend to operate in circular fashion, affecting each other's chances of hereditary transmission, rather than evolving as independent effects of environmental pressures. Thus the ability to walk erect and run fast undoubtedly facilitated hunting, but so did the reshaping of the hands for skillful toolmaking and manipulation. One was not much good without the other, so that, in time, every slight advance in one function forced a corresponding advance in the other. But brain development was also necessary for the deliberate shaping of tools and their appropriate use in the cooperative stalking of game. Thus every slight adaptive variation in each function (of brain, hand, and foot) increased the selective possibilities and pressures on every other function; for the cooperative hunter's way of life could not effectively impart a survival advantage unless all functions were operative in some degree of coordination. As this modus vivendi of the species progressed, selective pressures to adapt to it or perish increased, further favoring fleet-footedness, manual dexterity, intelligence, and probably also verbal communication, in optimum combinations, from millennium to millennium. At the same time, behavioral characteristics which obstructed intelligent and cooperative behavior would tend to be eliminated in the struggle for survival.

A variety of surviving cooperative hunters represented by Neanderthal man about 100,000 to 40,000 years ago (?) proved to be sufficiently inventive and adaptable to remain in Europe during the last glacial advance, after wandering north from Africa during the third interglacial period. With the invention of flint-pointed spears and chipped flint handaxes, rudimentary fur clothing, and controlled fire with which to withstand the glacial weather in his cave shelters, the Neanderthal gradually gained ascendancy all over Europe and Asia during this period. His skeletons, tools, and remains of his game show that he was equally adept at hunting, fishing, gathering of fruits and small animals in season, cooperatively hunting down the huge cave bear, or stalking the mighty mammoth in organized hunting parties and making use of its tusks, pelt, and meat. The degree of social cohesion and cultural tradition he had attained can only be guessed at from the variety of tools and weapons he left behind, the signs of group organization and cooperation in the hunting of big game, the evidence of long-enduring family-group life in the caves he inhabited, and the suggestions of quasireligious ritual in the burial of his dead.

During this long progression of increasingly organized and inventive behavior, the hominid brain developed in size and complexity along with the invention of tools for clothing, hunting, shelter, self-defense and attack; the evident ability to plan and work cooperatively; and presumably also the growing facility for symbolic communication through language. The brain capacity of the various fossil specimens from protohominid beginnings shows a gradual increase in size from the 530 cc. of *Zinjanthropus* to the approximately 1,550 cc. of the average Neanderthal, which approximates that of modern man (Table 1–1). Judging from the shapes of the skulls and the contributory evidence of embryology, the development was mostly in the cerebrum, which controls speech, memory, perceptual discrimination, sensorimotor coordination, and above all, the capacity for abstract thinking.

Although there is not an exact correlation between brain size and intelligence (body size and microscopic structure are complicating factors), there is evidently a broad sweep of development in the size and complexity of the brain accompanying the growing complexity of behavior in man. This is true, in fact, for all of vertebrate evolution. For man, this increase in brain size, accompanying the narrowing of pelvic bone structure (as a result of erect posture), presented an obstetrical problem early in his ascent from the ape. Nature's solution (by natural selection) was to let most of the brain growth in the newborn take place after birth. Thus babies are born while their brains are only one-fourth of adult size, before speech and locomotion can be learned, and even before the digestive enzymes for breaking down solid food have been developed. This premature birth and prolonged dependency of the human infant, and the

Personality Dynamics

Table 1-1 AVERAGE CRANIAL CAPACITIES OF SOME APES, FOSSIL APE-MEN,
AND MODERN MEN
(After Montagu, 1965, and Day, 1965)

Chimpanzee (*Pan*)	400 cc.
Orang-utan (*Pongo*)	416 cc.
Gorilla (*Gorilla*)	543 cc.
Zinjanthropus (Australopithecine)	530 cc.
Australopithecus africanus (Australopithecine)	600 cc.
Paranthropus robustus (Australopithecine)	650 cc.
Australopithecus prometheus (Australopithecine)	715 cc.
Homo erectus (Pithecanthropus) *erectus II*	775 cc.
Homo erectus (Pithecanthropus) *robustus*	900 cc.
Homo erectus (Pithecanthropus) *erectus I*	940 cc.
Homo erectus (Sinanthropus) *pekinensis*	1,043 cc.
Steinheim man	1,117 cc.
Rhodesian man	1,305 cc.
Neanderthal	1,553 cc.
Cro-Magnon man	1,590 cc.
(European)	approx. 1,450 cc.
(Mongoloid)	approx. 1,500 cc.

long period of learning and maturation of the skills needed to function as
an adult, have broad implications for the evolution of man as a social
animal.

Female hominids became more and more occupied with the rearing of
their long-dependent children, while the evolution of a hunter's way of
life required the male to assume a greater burden as family provider and
protector. Through the use of language and imitation and increasing
reasoning ability, each succeeding generation of children presumably
learned the sex-related skills, use of tools, role expectancies, and rules of
communal family life from their parents. The more successful learners
and the more cohesive families and bands evidently flourished and multiplied.

With the development of these functions and the brains and constitution to sustain them, *Homo sapiens* emerges during the latter part of the
Old Stone Age as a fairly well-confirmed family man, an increasingly skillful toolmaker and improviser, and with an increasing ability to adapt his
skills to any kind of geographic environment and to hand down his skills
and family traditions from generation to generation. Thus gradually,
almost imperceptibly, a new species-specific modus vivendi had already
emerged in nature—the adoption of *cultural tradition* as a means of
adaptation for survival. The question of man's inherent predisposition to
behave as a socially cohesive and culture-making animal deserves our special
attention at this point, in view of the subject's significance for a biosocial
view of personality.

The transition from herbivorous ape to omnivorous hunter had several repercussions that enhanced the social cohesion of the emerging ape-man. The act of hunting itself was facilitated by cooperation and communication, by the use of weapons and tools copied from parents or from each other, and eventually by the division of labor according to strength and skills in the complicated process of hunting large game and making use of the carcasses. Sharing the kill with their families was also a long altruistic step from the feed-yourself habits of herbivorous apes. Who taught the ape-man such altruism? In the long run, the pressures of natural and sexual selection. A "selfish ape" might have lived to a gluttonous old age, but surely no female would have him and his genes would be lost to posterity. Sexual selection, a recognized factor in evolution, not only favored females with sex appeal and nurturing tendencies but also bred males who were strong, skillful, virile, and *good providers*. We have already mentioned the division of labor and familial cohesiveness forced by female preoccupation with long-dependent children, while the mate hunted to "bring home the bacon" (or mammoth steak!) and fought off predators. But it was not anything as vague as a sense of moral obligation that made a homebody of the caveman. A crucial change in the sexual function, that had long been in the making, helped to cement the family bond.

The female hominid was no longer sexually attractive and available only during a period of the estrous cycle or during a mating season. She became more or less continually available sexually, while the male became, if anything, even more sexually excitable than the ape. For both, the whole sexual function ceased to be a cyclical routine under endocrine control (in which genital changes and smell played a part in setting off an automatic instinctive reaction), but became instead a more voluntary act whose initiation and consummation was under direct control of the cortex of the brain. This not only made the female more accessible but also allowed for something like mutual attraction and desire, a more communicative mating process, an enduring emotional attachment—something akin to a primitive beginning of love. Without injecting notions of romantic marriage into the picture (which is far from universal even now), there is sufficient circumstantial evidence that the hunting economy, child dependency, and corticalization of the sexual function combined to produce a fairly cohesive nuclear family in hominid evolution as "the cradle of civilization."

The evolutionary development of man's toolmaking and group-hunting skills, in coordination with erect posture, cerebral enlargement, and manual dexterity, is fairly well substantiated in the fossil remains of early skeletons and artifacts. Even the elaboration of primate family life through sexual differentiation of self-maintenance functions, prolonged dependency of offspring, and durable mating of parents through corticalization of the sex drive is supported by archeological, embryological, and anatomical evidence. But physical anthropology cannot tell the whole story of the gradual evolution of *Homo sapiens* as a socially interacting organism with a socially cohesive way of life.

We know practically nothing, for example, of the development of capacities for *verbal and emotional communication* that were indispensable to this evolutionary process. It has frequently been remarked that "behavior leaves no fossils." We can, therefore, only speculate on just how human language, for example, might have developed from the primitive grunts and cries and gestures that apes still use as signaling devices and were presumably used by our common ancestors back in the Miocene epoch. It may be that slight modifications of the vocal cords, lips, and tongue made articulate speech possible. More significantly, the expression of meaning, feeling, and intention, and all the abstract thinking that goes with it had to be paced by the development of speech centers in the brain and the involvement of a more developed cerebrum. Here again, the development of structural changes could only have proceeded by small increments through natural selection and in reciprocity with the survival advantages of the speech function itself. Cooperation for survival through verbal communication would become more likely for those who inherited and used these functional increments. As the modus vivendi of the species changed in keeping with the evolution of communicative capacities (i.e., became more socially cohesive), survival pressures would increase to eliminate those who lagged behind in the inheritance of such capabilities. We can only assume that this selective process took place very gradually over hundreds of thousands of years, though there may have been periods of ruthless acceleration of the selective process under severe environmental stress. It certainly had to be well on the way by the time the Neanderthals were able to engage in their cooperative hunting efforts against the mighty mammoths and maintain their sheltered and clothed family life in the caves of Europe during the last Ice Age.

Perhaps even more significant than the cognitive aspect of communication that left no fossils would have been the tremendous elaboration of emotional expression and feeling that we know man possesses today and which we may well regard as indispensable to his evolution as a socially cohesive animal. That is, it would be indispensable if the species *Homo sapiens* was to become inherently social in its basic animal functions, drives, and modus vivendi, as we maintain, rather than a species depending on the recognized expediency of cooperation for survival. What we are suggesting is that a species that manifestly depended on social cooperation for its survival would have had to develop more than an intellectual capacity to communicate and cooperate; it would have had to develop a *need* to communicate and to relate *emotionally*—to develop something approaching emotional interdependence.

We have exceedingly sparse evidence for the evolutionary development of such emotional communication, even though common sense tells us it must have taken place long before recorded history, if it had survival value. Contemporary students of primate behavior have shown that there are crude emotional expressions of excitement, danger warnings, anger, seduction, dominance, and submissiveness among some of the great apes. Such emotional expressions seems to have protective and procreative value, while maintaining a degree of cohesiveness in the ape family or troop. It may be assumed that similar emotional capabilities existed among the common ancestors of man and ape and that these factors contributed to the survival of both in later stages of evolution. But somewhere in the course of evolution, *Homo sapiens* developed (presumably by natural selection) capabilities of admiration, bereavement, pride, disappointment, jealousy, humor, nostalgia, aesthetic appreciation, friendship and loyalty to individuals and ideals, along with shame and guilt. What is more, these capabilities must have developed as emotional experiences and sensitivities extensively integrated with cognitive processes and their symbolic expression, for that is how they function today. In short, there had to be a stage of evolution when *shared values and reciprocal feelings* came into play as mechanisms of social cohesion.

Indirect indications from archeological finds give only the sketchiest evidence that such an emergence may have begun at least by the time of the Neanderthals. Numerous burial sites and caves unearthed in Europe and Central Asia from the Middle Paleolithic Age show that some of the Neanderthal types buried their dead with considerable ceremony. The bodies are frequently bound and buried with artifacts that may have had some religious or superstitious significance, while other evidence suggests tribal religious ceremonies and mourning for the dead. In one such burial site in the Shanidar Cave in Iraq, traces of pollen grains and other parts of flowers were recently detected by microscopic analysis. The evidence strongly suggests that this 60,000-year-old Neanderthal was laid to rest on a litter of flowers as an added touch of tender affection or homage to the dead. Just what these evidences of ritual burial portend for the emotional and social development of the Neanderthal can only be surmised in the absence of writing or other concrete evidence of "the behavior which leaves no fossils." Similarly, when anthropologists or archeologists find the skulls of cave bears in Middle Paleolithic caves inhabited by Neanderthal-type cavemen, and these skulls are placed in what seem to be recessed sanctuaries, they can only speculate on the possible ritualistic worship of this symbol of the caveman's sustenance. Limited as we are to traces of imperishable materials to provide clues to behavior, it is extremely difficult to infer from these scattered bits of artifacts whether man had already begun to develop some forms of religious ritual in connection with the burial of his dead and an appeal to the symbolized forces of nature. The cave paintings of mammoths, bison, and horses in cave sanctuaries came thousands of years after this period and represent art and religion already well developed in Cro-Magnon man.

But Neanderthal remains do give tantalizing suggestions of the early emergence of an aesthetic interest and possible symbolic ritual. In one cave in France, where the earth pigment, red ocher, first made its appearance, a limestone slab with hollowed-out cup-marks was also found. Just what that early Neanderthal dauber used this pigment and palette for is unknown, but in the absence of cave paintings it is speculated that he may have used it for body decoration or ritualistic burial or some other symbolic marking before anyone thought of painting animals on the walls of the cave. Also during this period, we find the first remains of collections of natural objects with interesting shapes, such as mollusk shells, coral, pyrite blocks, collected for no apparent purpose but their aesthetic or symbolic use.

It would be reasonable to speculate, then, that by the time of the Middle Paleolithic period some early versions of *Homo sapiens*, represented by Neanderthal man, had developed, along with cooperative hunting behavior, some emotional attachments to family or tribe, so that the loss of loved ones often caused feelings and expressions of bereavement and gave rise to quasireligious rituals in the burial of the dead. At the same time, a sense of orderliness and meaning in life may have prompted the handing down of these quasireligious rituals from generation to generation, just as the pointed spear and other tools were copied and used generation after generation for thousands of years. Though the emotional and value-sharing aspects of man's personality evolution are necessarily more speculative than the concrete evidence of his developing mechanical skill, one generalization can safely be made: it was probably during the Middle Paleolithic age that *Homo sapiens* began to develop some definite signs of becoming a socially cohesive and value-transmitting species, as well as a tool-making one, and he may well be entitled to the name *Homo sapiens socialis* from this time onward.

By the time of the appearance of Cro-Magnon man (about 20,000–30,000 years ago), definite signs of social organization and planned cooperative effort appear. There are evidences of large-scale seasonal hunting roundups and mass killings of horses for food and hides at the site where the bones of 100,000 horses were found at the bottom of a cliff near Solutré in France. Such industry could have been accomplished only by the planned cooperative effort of a large number of able-bodied men culled from the tribes of the entire country-side. This also implies division of labor and leadership. There are paintings on the walls of caves and images chipped or ground out of stone, which suggest both the emergence of an artistic urge and an attempt to exert some magical influence over events, on the part of some more imaginative individuals.

There are by now more definite signs of the beginning of quasireligious ceremonies. There is evidence of burial ceremonies with votive offerings of food, hunting tools, adornments, and amulets interred with the deceased, presumably to accompany the spirit of the dead to an after-life. Cave paintings and signs of ceremonial feasts and rituals, which employed stone figurines and talismans, suggest ceremonies connected with hunting, fertility, and puberty rites. Toolmaking and craftsmanship have by now advanced to a high level of skill and specialization, with knives and chisels of beveled flint, utensils of bone and stone, clothing of hides sewn together by needles and using leather thongs, even jewelry for adornment. The diversity of skills displayed suggests a high degree of social organization and division of labor—probably the beginning of well-defined adult social roles in a cooperative society.

At any rate, definite signs of community life with increasing populations for centuries have been found at various sites throughout Europe and Asia, indicating highly developed social organization and standardized cultural implements handed down from generation to generation. Thus, by the end of the Old Stone Age, prehistoric man had developed sufficient brain-power, practical skills, and functions making for social cohesion for him to be able to create definite patterns of culture and social organization, and to gain a distinct survival advantage because of it.

By the time the Mesolithic (Middle Stone Age) cultures had sprung up in the wake of the retreating last glaciation (about 10,000 years ago), still more advanced tools and technology as well as social organization had enabled man to adapt, multiply, and spread over the entire face of the earth. Inventions such as the bow and arrow, harpoon, and clay pottery enabled him to exploit and even to store an increasing seasonal or geographic variety of food supplies. Finally, with the development of agriculture in the Neolithic cultures that followed, he was able to control and balance his food supply as well as to settle down to some semblance of stable community life and social regulation of needs.

By that time man had already developed some racial differentiation of superficial physical characteristics (skin color, hair texture, facial features) as adaptations to climate or the result of genetic drift. There is little doubt, however, that all the races of mankind shared in approximately equal variety the common human heritage of the species from our common ancestors. That includes a variety of temperaments, intelligence, skills, and drives singularly adapted to survival under all kinds of living conditions through social cohesion and the learning of cultural patterns of coexistence. Indeed, it has often been stated that, in the case of the hominids, cultural evolution took over where morphological (structural) evolution leveled off as the principal means of adaptation to the environment. But if this is so, *Homo sapiens socialis* had already developed the constitutional capabilities that rendered him *inherently* a culture-making species, and unique as such throughout the entire animal kingdom.

Our main thesis, therefore, is that any true-to-life scientific approach to the dynamics of human behavior must be consistent with this basic fact of nature—must, in short, be *biosocial*.

Implications
for
Behavioral Science

Several considerations emerge from this sketchy review of the evolution of man, the historical background of our domain in the natural sciences. One is the fact that human behavior has much in common with that of the lower animals from which he ascended, while at the same time displaying more complex characteristics which are unique in nature. Feeding, elimination, bisexual reproduction, and vital reflex functions are much the same as in lower primates and mammals generally; but social behavior and communication through symbolically expressed ideas and the transmission of patterns of culture go far beyond anything displayed by any other species in the animal kingdom. We are, therefore, clearly dealing with *levels of complexity* in human functioning, and may properly speak of "higher" and "lower" levels of functional integration (or "advanced" and "primitive") in man's heritage from emergent evolution.

The fact that functional emergence is clearly related to morphological evolution up to the culture-producing level is immediately evident upon an inspection of the brains and nervous systems that have evolved in the animal world. The very simple nodule at the cephalic end of a worm's elementary nervous system merely served to mediate simple locomotion for feeding and avoidance of noxious stimuli. Sensorimotor discrimination evolved with increasing complexity up to the high level attained by thousands of species of insects. Here a new level emerges with highly specialized sense organs like eyes, feelers, taste sensors, signaling devices, and built-in group behavior mechanisms. Behavior is still at a pretty automatic, reflexive level, however. With the evolution of the higher vertebrates like the mammals, a more complex brain makes possible something more in the nature of learning by experience and memory, with crude choice behavior on the basis of such learning. Finally, among the primates, we get a high degree of sensorimotor coordination coupled with the learning of "principles" from generalized experience, and even the beginnings of "insight" in problem-solving among the higher apes. But it is only with the advent of man that we get symbolic reasoning and communication of ideas, the invention of tools for planned uses, complex long-range planning and problem-solving, and the transmission of social values. For this he required a highly developed cerebrum and some elaboration of the autonomic nervous system along with complex sensorimotor networks and cortical control.

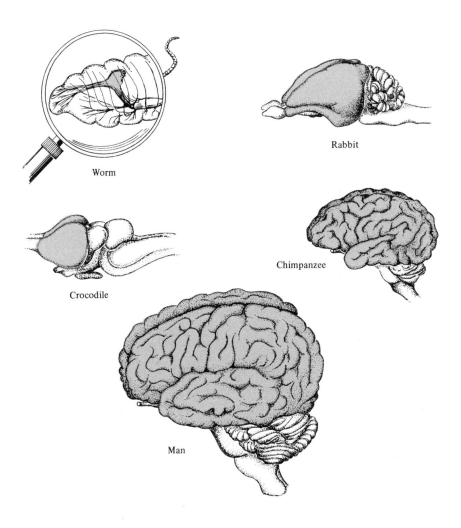

Figure 1–2. Evolution of the brain. (Not drawn to scale.)

Thus we see that evolution is not just a matter of gradually developing morphological refinements to produce quantitative increments of skill in dealing with the environment. It is a matter of *emergent, qualitatively new levels of functioning* in the course of long stretches of time, as the gradual increments make new levels of functional integration possible and the insufficiencies are gradually eliminated in the struggle for existence. We have seen that man's culture-making potentialities evolved very gradually from Miocene to Mesolithic times, but ultimately emerged as something qualitatively and categorically different from anything that exists in the rest of the animal world. Human language is not just based on a "little more schooling" than chimpanzees get; rather, it reflects a new function in the speech centers of the brain. The social values such language conveys can never be taught to any animal, no matter how cleverly we teach circus animals to do tricks in fancy dress. Nor can culture itself be dismissed as something that is "merely learned" by man; one must consider the elaborate evolution of the nervous system that it took to learn it and the evidence that it is universally motivated. But before we get into the confusion of innate and learned functions in personality development, we had best clarify this matter of levels of complexity in the manifestations and analysis of behavior.

LEVELS OF ANALYSIS AND INTEGRATION

In order to discuss laws of cause and effect, or even systematic observations of behavioral functions intelligently, we must recognize that the discussion may take place at any of several levels of analysis, corresponding to the levels of complexity and integration of human behavior. At the most rudimentary level of behavioral processes, as far as psychology is concerned, there are *physiological* processes involving specific tissues and organs. These, as we have already pointed out, are not very different from analogous processes in lower animals. They include processes of digestion, nutrition, and growth, reflex reactions to painful stimuli, maintenance of body temperature and metabolism in a state of equilibrium (homeostasis), reproductive functions, conduction of nerve impulses to the brain from sense organs, etc. This is the level of analysis ordinarily used by medicine and physiology in establishing detailed knowledge of the basic organic life processes and in correcting malfunctioning or "disease." This level of analysis is sometimes considered to be too limited even for certain aspects of modern medicine, which finds it necessary to "treat the whole person" in curing a disease.

At the level of integrated behavior of the total *individual organism*—the whole person seen just as a behaving individual—psychology would be particularly interested in the *psychological* functions mediated by the

wise psychology would only be another subdivision of zoology. In other words, the evolution of a species that could adapt to any environment and maintain a variety of cultures made individual differences inevitable in spite of cultural uniformities. The process of adaptation and personality development obviously has different outcomes if you are strong or weak, irascible or easy-going, bright or dull. To be human is to have a wide latitude in inherent temperamental differences, intellectual and physiological differences, and the way in which these constitutional predispositions interact with an extremely variable environment.

Nevertheless, as we have also pointed out, individual personalities tend to maintain a certain individual consistency as they develop into adulthood, and certain characteristics of the species are universal. People learn different languages and different ways of using (or butchering) the same language, but everybody learns *some* language; it's the human thing to do. Some people are oversexed, some are inhibited and frigid in marriage, some are promiscuous in or out of wedlock, some are homosexual, and a few dedicate themselves to celibacy. One way or another, everybody has to adjust his sexual needs to the social mores and his chosen role in adult life; that is also the human thing to do. That does not mean that everyone is equally well adjusted. On the contrary, the differences in adjustment and maladjustment of needs to social expectations constitute one of the main dimensions of variability of personality and a distinctive feature of the human condition.

Our task in analyzing the dynamics of personality, then, will be to analyze the complex biosocial processes by which individuals develop distinct personalities while at the same time displaying the generic trends of human modes of adaptation. This involves the scientific analysis of both the hereditarily given and the socially derived aspects of human functioning at all levels of integration, in the normal modus vivendi of the species, which is social interaction. In other words, personality theory *has* to be biosocial, because the individual personality exists as a point of convergence and interaction of what the evolutionary process and heredity have provided as generic predispositions in the first place, and what the individual interaction with the environment provides to cultivate it, specify it, and make it operational in the world of social realities. That means that it will not always be easy to distinguish between the forces of heredity and environment, or learning and maturation, in analyzing individual personality development. We may discover, in fact, that there are developmental forces which combine both kinds of processes in the differentiation of personalities, while at the same time expressing the basic human qualities that make man at least potentially superior to all other animals that have evolved on earth.

This brings us finally to a consideration of the scientific implications of man's outstanding emergent function in evolution: abstract thinking, accompanied by symbolic communication of ideas and incorporation of social values into the entire cognitive-affective operational system. It is this network of symbolic functions which makes possible, indeed makes inevitable, the social organization which was man's salvation all through the ages of vicissitudes of nature and competition with other species as well as his own kind. This brings us squarely up against the problem we merely hinted at right at the beginning of this chapter: Is there a place in science for abstract ideas, social values, and human "feelings," all of which are subjective reactions of individuals, and highly variable ones at that? Our hypothetical scientific critic might say, "This is a good basis for humanistic philosophy; but is it science?" To that, our unequivocal answer would be: "It is sound behavioral science. If it is also humanistic philosophy, then there can be no behavioral science without it."

This position rests firmly on the facts of emergent evolution. We have already shown how the evolution of a new species, whom we chose to call *Home sapiens socialis*, represented a new modus vivendi in nature, based on abstract thinking and the communication of values and feelings as well as the cooperative coping with their common human needs. This emergence of symbolically communicated, socially cohesive, and value-oriented behavior is just as real a functional biological innovation at a higher level of integration as the emergence of "brainy" worms, "sexy" jellyfish, and living amoebae were at *their* stages of evolution. As we pointed out at the outset, successively higher levels of complexity and functional integration in the evolution of life on earth require the recognition of new and more complex properties as they emerge. This in turn requires the application of scientific concepts that may have been irrelevant to the analysis of simpler forms of life or of inanimate matter. We are thus forced to face up to the fact that the study of personality as a new and complex emergent biosocial reality in evolution must introduce equally innovative and complex concepts into the realm of natural science. This involves the analysis of human values, symbolic and socially cohesive behavior, along with all other subjective reactions of this complex organism, as part of the *subject matter itself.* If we find that the species we are studying lives, grows, strives, and dies in the context of a social modus vivendi and a self-imposed or communicated set of cultural values, then we cannot ignore this palpable reality merely because it may involve questions of humanistic values or philosophy, which may be irrelevant to *lower* forms of life.

Actually, we do not have to get involved in questions of value judgments and social motives if we are dealing with processes at the simple psycho-physiological level of integration. As with the protohominids before social organization and cultural values emerged, we can think of primitive speech as a mere signaling device not much different from gestures. It could be used to free the protohominid from the restrictions of dealing with objects (food, etc.) in the concrete, here-and-now situation. But it is at the psychosocial level of elaboration and integration that gradually emerged that symbolic communication had its greatest impact in qualitatively changing the modus vivendi of the species (or making that change possible, in coordination with changes in the brain). It facilitated social cooperation and organization; it helped to transmit the products of growing hominid inventiveness in making tools and mastering the physical environment; it helped in cooperative action and planning; it defined social roles in the division of labor and concepts of right and wrong in individual and group behavior; it was a means of seeking to understand and to appease unseen forces; it eventually became the indispensable tool of science, religion, law, and commerce. All of this involves abstractions, symbols, values—but these functional qualities are as solid and substantial realities as anything in nature. We can study their manifestations in personality with the tools and concepts appropriate to a behavioral science, at the psychosocial level of analysis.

We shall recognize that human personality is not only a product of its earlier animal heritage but is also deeply involved with its emergent functions of abstract thinking and goal-orientation; with social values and role expectancies; with issues of good and bad, better and worse, lovely and horrible, right and wrong. We shall study the ways in which the human organism, so constituted and functioning, develops into an adult member of its own society, whatever that society happens to be.

But we must not only recognize values; we can go further, if we wish. We can *evaluate* values. Scientific objectivity does not obligate us to indulge in blind "cultural relativism"—merely noting that one social code or set of values affects people one way, another affects them another way, but it's all relative and "Who is to say which is right and which is wrong?" Without indulging in preconceived moralistic dogma, we can at least recognize that all societies do not have equally sound or healthy value systems. Some societies get all cluttered up with unworkable rules derived from anachronistic traditions; others collapse in the holocaust of their own simplistic totalitarian dogmas and ideologies. It is not true that all societies are equally effective in providing the basis for human living and need-satisfaction or are devoid of gross discrimination among their sub-cultural groups in this respect. There is still a great deal of the tooth-and-claw, a great deal of primitive ignorance and superstition and animal-level

Personality Dynamics

existence which persists from precivilized ways of living. But there are also highly developed social systems and technologies which may have gone beyond their optimum as means of human self-regulation and self-fulfillment. We are undoubtedly still undergoing the trial-and-error aspects of cultural evolution since evolving our culture-making apparatus.

We can scarcely analyze personality dynamics at the psychosocial level without evaluating the impact of different social value systems on different personalities and drawing some value judgments from those observations. We shall not attempt to prejudge these issues, but merely to remind the reader that in talking about evolution as "adaptation to the environment" with the emergence of symbolic behavior as the supreme mode of adaptation, we do not imply that man's present state is his final state of perfection. We are saying rather that human personality must be regarded as a complex and rather fragile expression of life which has arisen under certain biological and social conditions, and that to preserve it and give it strength and beauty, or even just begin to understand it, is going to take a careful study of its origins, its modes of expression, and the basic conditions of its continued healthy existence.

Requirements
of a
Psychodynamic System
We are thus already committed to an analysis of personality within the limits and special dispensations of a behavioral science, with analysis-in-depth at different levels of complexity and integration, and the use of a biosocial approach based on evolution—with a humanistic flavor. If this seems like a tall order, it is at least a forthright attempt to do justice to our subject matter as it appears in nature. It is time, therefore, to proceed from general considerations of the philosophy of science to a program of specific considerations of the psychodynamics of personality as viewed from the standpoint of biosocial theory.

These specific considerations stem from our conception of the human being as a highly evolved, motivated, adjusting organism in constant interaction with the environment, particularly its own social environment. It does not merely respond mechanically to stimuli, but is constantly striving toward goals and creating its own self-stimulation, while seeking out the stimulation of others. The process of growth to maturity and old age involves not merely physical maturation but also the shaping of motives and potentialities by complex integration of generic tendencies and individual experiences. It also involves patterns of adjustment and defense of the self, which may become patterns of maladjustment or psychopathology.

An understanding of the psychodynamics of personality should provide a key to the development of normal and abnormal behavior and the maintenance of mental health.

Basic motives. The core of any psychodynamic system, whether approached from the biosocial, psychoanalytic, or any other point of view, is a consideration of the wellsprings of motivation of behavior. This reflects the basic conception of human nature of any theoretical approach, or of "just what makes human beings tick"—and how that applies to the individual personality. We shall presently show that there is something more than mere identity with the primitive hungers of lower animals in man, just as we have already broadly hinted at the emergence of higher cognitive functions.

Developmental sequence. Since neither structure nor function nor motivational expression is fully developed at birth, the course of personality development from infancy to maturity must be traced as a lawful sequence. This also reflects the biosocial conception of human nature. One based on a simple mammalian conception of man would trace development of basic animal functions up to maturity at puberty. The biosocial viewpoint does not regard man as fully mature until far into adulthood or even old age.

Conflict and adjustment. Since there is more than just one overriding motive in the complex structure of human personality, and since any motive may be frustrated or in conflict with other motives, conflict and adjustment are the order of everyday life. Furthermore, social interaction presents the likelihood of conflict with other people's motives as well. The mechanisms of long-range effects of adjustive and learning processes, as well as their maladaptive outcomes under certain circumstances, must be studied.

Psychopathology and therapeutic rationale. Implicit in the etiology of maladjustment is the etiology of neurosis and a rationale for psychotherapy. This would take us beyond the scope of the present textbook on personality and will not be dealt with here.

Social behavior. Interpersonal relationships and interactions, conformity to social mores and values, and cooperative and competitive behavior are often thought of as the products of environmental influences imposed from without, rather than intrinsic expressions of the nature of man. Our position will be, as we have already intimated, that social behavior is very much an inherent characteristic of the human personality and is deeply involved in the entire motivational, developmental, and adjustive systems of personality dynamics. Our scientific foundation for this lies, of course, in the very nature of man's evolution as a thinking, communicating, culture-making species—*Homo sapiens socialis,* as we have preferred to call him.

*Methods
of
Study*   The ambitious program we have outlined for a comprehensive study of personality dynamics from a biosocial-humanistic point of view inevitably raises some questions about the scientific methodology available for such a study. Recognizing that our subject matter is a highly complex product of evolutionary change in which highly subjective and symbolic aspects of behavior have emerged, it is not surprising that the range of methods needed to study it must go beyond the strictly objective and quantitative methods of natural science. We have already pointed out that whereas subjective value judgments and motives have no place in the basic laws of matter, energy, space, and natural forces, these subjective characteristics are inherent in the subject matter itself when living matter has evolved into human behavior. There are, nevertheless, several methods of experimentation, observation, and direct elicitation of mental processes which make it possible to approximate the scientific requirements of objectivity and verifiability of results or interpretations. The principal methods generally used in personality study are as follows: (1) controlled experiment, (2) clinical examination and testing, (3) controlled observation, and (4) survey and factfinding. Although these methods overlap to some extent, each has distinguishing characteristics not shared by the other methods, as well as distinct advantages and disadvantages.

Controlled experiment.   This is the method par excellence of all science, and by far the method of choice when such choice is feasible. As used in personality study, it usually requires groups of subjects to average out individual differences and rather artificial conditions to isolate one variable and to keep the experimental conditions constant from subject to subject. A classical experimental design is to compare the reactions of a group of individuals (experimental group) before and after the application of a stimulus or change in the experimental situation (independent variable). This change of reaction is then compared with the change of reaction of the control group, which does not have the stimulus or change of experimental situation applied to it. In this way, if the control group's reactions remain essentially unchanged, it is possible to infer that the change in the experimental group's reactions was caused by the introduction of the stimulus or changed condition. An example of the controlled experiment would be the demonstration of the effect of suggestion on perceptual judgments. In such an experiment a group of subjects of known background (let us say, all males and all college freshmen of approximately the same age in an urban community) might be individually asked to estimate the number of men at a "rock" festival. One-half of the subjects (experimental group) are then asked to estimate the number again in the presence of two "stooges" who deliberately underestimate the number by a wide margin (independent variable). The other half of the subjects (control group) are then asked to estimate the number again, but without the benefit of "stooges." If there is no significant change in the estimates of the control subjects but a significant change in the estimates of the experimental subjects (in the direction suggested), we may attribute this change to the experimental variable of suggestion. The extent of such change in each subject may be furthermore taken as a measure of "suggestibility" in each subject, and further research may be done by comparing highly suggestible (gullible) subjects with highly resistant subjects, and so on.

There are many variations on the theme of the controlled experiment, but all are designed to give objective evidence of cause and effect or at least correlations between isolated variables. Though limited in scope because of the isolated variable approach in necessarily artificial settings, controlled experiments have a cumulative effect in establishing scientific principles of behavior and frequently serve as a means of checking hypotheses developed through other methods.

Clinical examination. The clinical method is designed to attain a better understanding of the individual personality, rather than to generate principles of cause and effect derived from experiments on impersonally categorized groups. Nevertheless, it frequently benefits from controlled experiments in the development of some of its instruments and principles and indirectly in the tempering of the clinician's subjective impression with a degree of disciplined objectivity. (For that reason, it is generally conceded that training in experimental psychology is a valuable part of the training of every clinical psychologist.) On the other hand, clinical judgment can be based only in part on objective facts and experimentally derived principles. It must also be based on the subjective impressions and insights of a trained and sensitive human being to the needs, characteristics, and conflicts of another human being—a pattern in which no two human beings are ever alike. There are three basic methods of obtaining data for the clinical examination, which the clinician uses, with varying proportions of fact, scientific principle, and clinical impression: (1) interview, (2) psychological tests, and (3) direct observation.

Interviews may range in structure from completely informal or casual conversation to the highly structured series of questions designed to elicit a complete case history. Beyond that, it may involve the prolonged and revealing interaction of personalities that takes place in counseling or psychotherapy. Some interviews are semistructured with a view to eliciting particular information for a particular purpose, such as qualifications for a position of responsibility, source of marital discord, or reason for under-achievement in school. From the more structured type of interview to the more structured type of personality test is but a short step. The questionnaire type of test is in effect a written formal interview, but it is a highly standardized one that enables the examiner to rate the subject on a given trait or pattern of behavior characteristics. Group testing is sometimes considered a method outside of the clinical sphere. Quite different are the so-called projective tests of personality; they do not use direct questions with a choice of definite answers, but are based on the interpretive or imaginative responses of the subject to more or less unstructured stimuli. Such instruments would include material such as inkblots on the Rorschach Psychodiagnostic Test, incomplete sentences to be completed, pictures to be drawn or interpreted, and the like. Clinical observation may accompany interviewing and testing, but may be carried out more extensively outside of the examination situation. We shall discuss these clinical methods more extensively in Chapter 10.

Controlled observation. Though frequently used as an informal and incidental tool in the clinical examination of individuals, observation of a somewhat more controlled and systematic variety finds wide application as a quasiexperimental and quasiclinical method that deserves some attention in its own right. Systematic observation under carefully controlled conditions, accompanied by measurement, description, or tallying of observed behaviors, has long found fruitful application in the field of developmental psychology. The studies of Gesell on child development in the observation dome at Yale, of Shirley on the motor sequence, and of Lois Murphy, R. R. Sears, and others on the social and emotional development of children are but a few of the normative studies of development carried out by systematic observation. The environment and range of stimuli is controlled in these situations by the psychologist making the study. Different children can then be compared in the same environment for a controlled range of stimuli or for spontaneous behavior when together, alone, or with an adult, etc.

Of special interest is a form of controlled observation known as *participant observation.* Though long used by anthropologists and sociologists to study the habits, mores, and social structures of various types of communities, it has been given scant attention by psychologists until recently. This technique involves the firsthand observation of the behavior of people in their actual everyday activities, or as participants in a situational crisis, but

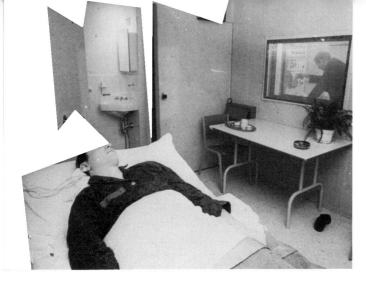

A

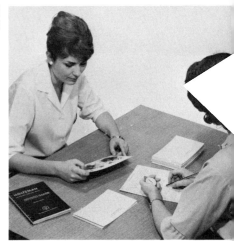

Figure 1–4. Three different methods of personality study. *In stimulus-controlled room (A) a subject's physiological reactions before, during, and after sleep are being recorded in a controlled experimental design. The clinical method concentrates on face-to-face testing and interviewing, as illustrated in photo (B). The participant-observer method is illustrated by the author's discussions with the Nazi war criminals while serving as prison psychologist during the Nuremberg war crimes trials (C). (Photo (A) courtesy of New York University Research Center for Mental Health; (B) courtesy of The Psychological Corporation.)*

B

with the observer as a natural coparticipant in any case. That is, the investigator's presence must be inherent in the situation or historical event, or as an acknowledged member of the community in some recognized role, rather than as an intrusive "inquiring reporter" or a foreign visitor taking notes on "native customs."

Among the classical studies by anthropologists that have yielded valuable data about personality dynamics by using this technique, the studies of Margaret Mead on sex relations in different societies (1955), and of Oscar Lewis on individual families in Mexico and Puerto Rico (1959, 1966) have yielded vivid portrayals of personality interactions in different cultural

Personality Dynamics

C

settings. A study of the leadership of an aggressor nation was afforded by the Nuremberg trial of the major Nazi war criminals when the writer served as prison psychologist there (Gilbert, 1950). Festinger, Riecken, and Schachter (1956) conducted a participant-observer team study of a cultist group prophesying the end of the world and then reacting to the disproof of their convictions. We shall have occasion to refer to some of these studies, too, in the course of our discussion.

Survey and fact-finding methods. Finally, we come to the methods that the layman is most familiar with, and which do not, at first glance, seem to have much to do with the scientific study of personality. These are: the public opinion poll, the marketing research survey, and institutional and demographic statistics. A moment's reflection will suggest, however, that it *can* be useful for a student of personality to know how people of different socioeconomic and educational backgrounds feel about leading social issues of the day (or whether they reply "don't know" or "don't care"); how the divorce rate, crime, and drug addiction are distributed by ethnic group and how those rates have changed over the years; how the frequency of different types of sexual outlets are related to sex, age, religion, education, and socioeconomic status. Much of this is of more direct interest to the sociologist and political scientist; but the psychologist cannot escape these realities of modern life if he is to study the human being as a living and interacting species in the human civilization of past, present, and future. We shall, therefore, also have occasion to cite some demographic statistics to illuminate a point here and there as we discuss the adjustment problems of man in the modern world.

Summary   The evolution of inferred human behavior from the early australopithecine ape-men of two million years ago to Cro-Magnon man of relatively recent times reveals a steady progress of tool-making ingenuity, problem-solving, and social cohesion as the means of adaptation for survival. We therefore prefer to call the human species *Homo sapiens socialis*—the thinking social man, or culture-making species. The important thing to note is that culture is not merely learned as a localized environmental artifact, but that this type of learning is itself part of man's nature—his evolved biosocial way of life.

As a culmination of this long process of biosocial evolution, the human personality must be dealt with as a complex biosocial behavioral phenomenon with subjective, purposive, symbolic, and value-oriented characteristics. Analysis may also be made at different levels of integration, such as the psychophysiological, the organismic or psychological, and the psychosocial.

A comprehensive analysis of personality dynamics would require a discussion of at least the following aspects of human behavior: (1) human nature and its basic drives; (2) developmental sequence from infancy to adulthood; (3) motivational conflict and adjustment; (4) psychopathology and therapeutic rationale; (5) social behavior. All but (4) will be dealt with in this volume. The scientific methods available for such study include: controlled experiment, clinical examination and testing, controlled and participant observation, and survey fact-finding.

2

Human
Nature
and
Basic
Drives

Some Problems
in

Motivation Theory   When anyone says, "It's only human nature to act that way," he clearly implies that there are certain motivated behavior patterns with which human beings are commonly endowed, regardless of their individual or cultural differences. Such a proposition is scientifically tenable, but unfortunately it is usually used by laymen to justify acts of aggression, selfishness, or lust—as though human nature was not very different from that of predatory animals, underneath the veneer of civilization. We have already hinted that there may be more to human nature than that; but in any case the question of basic drives or motivational forces in human behavior actually constitutes the key issue in any psychodynamic theory of personality. Motivation is not only the key issue in psychodynamics, but it is also one of the most complex, intangible, and confusing concepts in the entire realm of psychology. Any attempt to approach it from a simplistic, physiological-reflex point of view only renders it more so, and inevitably fails to come to grips with the vast richness and diversity of purpose in human experience.

Thus it was once a simple and plausible generalization to state flatly that "tissue needs are the source of all drives." One could investigate the various local physiological tension states in various parts of the body and conceive of drive-satisfaction as essentially tension-releasing mechanisms which incidentally serve a biological need—the so-called drive-reduction theory. This seemed obvious enough for basic animal functions of nourishment, reproduction, self-preservation (avoidance of pain and danger), and it mattered little whether one called these things "instincts," "dependable motives," "basic drives," or simply "unlearned behavior."

Much experimentation and theorizing has sought to distinguish between inherent and learned motives, between primary organismic needs and means to an end, between nature and nurture in the development of motivated behavior patterns. But the question of motivated behavior has become increasingly recognized as immensely complicated in man—too complicated to lend itself to simple distinctions of inherent tissue needs and secondary elaborations, between maturation and learning. This is so for the very reason that *Homo sapiens socialis* is *inherently a learning and problem-solving, culture-creating-and-transmitting animal*, with an immense capacity for symbolic behavior and symbolically conceived desires. What is more, all of these behavior patterns and their attendant motivations are subject to widely varying differences in individual predispositions and experiences.

We are, therefore, constantly confronted with such questions as: Is mother-love learned by social indoctrination, or is it innate? Is studying history or math or crap-shooting an expression of inherent intellectual curiosity, social conformity, or just a means to an end, ultimately serving the hunger drive? What explains the differences in temperament, interests, and character among members of the same family—to say nothing of people brought up in different cultures—if there are basic motives common to the human species? What kinds of emotional and motivational conflict produce neurotic reactions in some people under some circumstances and not in others under the same circumstances? Is there *any* basic formula for "what makes people tick," or is it just a matter of individual training and experience? Indeed, some people ask, is any useful purpose served by acknowledging such an elusive and subjective force as "motivation" in the first place, when we can simply describe the diverse behavior patterns of different individuals as we observe them, and let it go at that?

As far as the last question is concerned, the answer is that we can never establish any meaningful psychodynamic principles of behavior or cause and effect if we simply confine ourselves to descriptions of observable motor responses and fail to recognize that virtually all of human behavior is *motivated* one way or another. That is, it is goal-oriented, satisfaction-seeking, conflict-avoiding, self-enhancing (or unintentionally self-defeating), socially communicative, and adaptive. Behavior doesn't just happen in random fashion; there is always some motivational rationale, even when it is irrational or pathological, for just about everything we do, whether conscious or unconscious, obvious or subtle, or even impervious to detection. The behavior of the human species is, like any other, an outgrowth of evolutionary adaptation to needs, and the life process is a continual process of adjustment to inherent needs and their elaborations. The character structures, habits, values, preferred activities, and patent desires of adulthood are the logical outcome of preexisting motives modified by experience in the life history of the individual. They have been shaped by maturation and social interaction during adolescence, by childhood development before that, and childhood character formation was, in turn, largely an outgrowth of basic motivational forces that were already functional or latent in infancy. Both the underlying consistencies and the individual differences in human personality are in large part the differences and consistencies of *motivational* patterns. The problem is not whether human behavior is in fact motivated, but just how we can systematically identify the raw material of biosocial animal drive and trace it through the multitudinous shapes it assumes in civilized living.

This brings us to the other basic question of whether there can be any basic formula for a scientific approach to human motivation or "what makes people tick." Previous theoretical formulations have varied from one extreme to another: from recognizing nothing but a few reflexive behavior patterns similar to those of lower primates, all the way to postulating a multiplicity of drives and instincts to explain any behavior that seemed commonplace among civilized humans. The former position was prominently advocated by the early Behaviorists (Watson, 1925). This mechanistic view of human behavior did not recognize motivation as such, but postulated three basic reflexive patterns of motor behavior observable in infancy. They were labeled (for convenience only) love, fear, and rage. All so-called "emotional" or "motivated" behavior could be derived from those reflexes by a process of conditioning (see Chapter 6). The psychoanalysts of the early Freudian school, on the other hand, regarded much of human behavior, conflict, and neurosis as stemming from instinctual psychosexual needs, which often took devious forms. Hunger and later aggression were also recognized by Freud as independent instincts, but that was about all. With hunger not usually a problem in civilized society (said Freud), all of human conflict could be traced to sex and aggression. We shall be referring to both of these reductionistic views of human motivation in later chapters. At the other extreme of over-fragmentation were the long lists of instincts or "inborn connections" drawn up by some educational psychologists following the lead of Thorndike (1913). This ad lib and ad hoc explanation of any and all prevalent habits by instinct theory without integrative rationale soon earned the ridicule of other psychologists, who subsequently "threw out the baby with the bath water":

Man is impelled to action, it is said, by his instincts. If he goes with his fellows, it is the "herd instinct" which actuates him; if he acts alone, it is the "anti-social instinct"; if he fights, it is the instinct of pugnacity; if he defers to another, it is the instinct of self-abasement; if he twiddles his thumbs, it is the thumb-twiddling instinct; if he does not twiddle his thumbs, it is the thumb-not-twiddling instinct. Thus everything is explained with the facility of magic —word magic (Holt, 1931).

Other psychologists, recognizing that learned behavior often manifested motivational properties in its own right, sought to make distinctions between primary and secondary drives, the latter serving as a means to an end represented by the former. Thus courtship behavior and self-adornment could be seen as secondary motives serving the sex drive, while working for a living was fundamentally a learned form of satisfying the needs of hunger and shelter. The strength and persistence of such "secondary drives," even when the primary drive was already satisfied or no longer relevant, caused Allport to postulate the concept of "functional autonomy" of such learned motives. In the classical example, the miser who started to earn money just to satisfy his hunger need continues to make money for its own sake, long after his physical needs are well satisfied and secured for life. Allport believed that this illustrated the "functional autonomy" of a learned motive which was once a means to an end and then became a motive in its own right. The trouble with the concept was that there was no satisfactory explanation for how functional autonomy of a learned motive came about, or what happened to the original drive, or whether such learned motives are really nothing but a means to an end in the first place. Allport's (1961) later exposition of different degrees and kinds of functional autonomy does point to levels of complexity in the purposive nature of man, and the transformations that motives undergo in the course of personality development and adjustment. Freud also speaks of the vicissitudes of libidinal energy (sex drive) in pathological symptom formation and "Freudian slips"; but he never quite succeeds in explaining how the vast complexities of social behavior are motivated by transformation of sexual and aggressive drives, though he makes some provocative suggestions (1930).

Much of the confusion revealed by the questions we have raised and the viewpoints we have skimmed over would be relieved, it seems to us, if we could find a coherent way of (1) defining basic *generic drives* and relating them to the multitudinous forms they assume in different cultures and among different individuals under different circumstances; (2) clarifying the relationship between *learning and maturation* in the development of motivated behavior; and (3) incorporating *levels of complexity* of be-behavior into the motivational system, or vice versa.

GENERIC, CANALIZED, AND SECONDARY MOTIVES

We prefer the term *generic drives* for those wellsprings of human motivation that have variously been called "instincts," "primary drives," or "dependable motives." We would define generic drives as *motivational forces that are universally inherent in any species, having evolved through natural selection as being conducive to survival*. They are transmitted from generation to generation through the inherent constitutional structures of the species. Their normal functioning in the natural habitat insures the adaptive behavior that natural selection has "programmed" for the species, at some level of integration. These constitutional predispositions may vary from simple reflexes present at birth to highly complex functions of the total organism, requiring maturational processes from birth to adulthood, with environmental interaction that helps to make a latent drive fully operational. In a highly complex organism like that of man, these generic patterns of motivated behavior may take widely different forms among different groups (societies) and display wide individual differences; but they are generic in the sense that the underlying motivation or drive is common to the species and transcends all cultural and individual differences. Such drives are therefore generic not only in the sense of being characteristic of a species or genus of animal life, and being genetically transmitted through the genes, but also in the sense of being categorical types of behavior which may take on different specific forms.

The "catch," of course, lies in making allowance for different forms of development of the same basic drive in accordance with environmental interaction of different individuals with their culture and individual life experiences. This clearly implies an incorporation of learning processes into the concept of maturation of basic generic drives, which seems to obliterate any distinction between innate and learned drives. Is there perhaps a "thumb-twiddling instinct" after all? We have said that the old distinction between the innate and learned is no longer tenable, especially for a species that is *inherently a learning animal*, but we do not advocate complete anarchy in the scientific approach to human motivation. What is needed here is a concept that bridges the gap between inherent generic drives and the various forms it takes in the course of maturation and learning.

Let us take the undisputed basic animal drive of hunger. All humans get hungry; so presumably do cows and monkeys. But how do we account for the enormous variety of human tastes for different foods—the literal revulsion of some people for certain foods that are eaten with relish by others? (The author confesses to having gulped some fried maguey worms in Mexico, rather than offend his Mexican hosts, who considered the worms quite a delicacy.) One can be hungry for meat and undertake great risk to hunt for game to obtain it, while another (say, a Hindu) would rather starve than kill a sacred cow. A Mexican child will salivate at the sight of a stick of sugar cane; an American child at the sight of an ice cream bar; an Eskimo child at the sight of whale blubber; yet one child may not even recognize another's delicacy. Is it enough to say that tastes are simply acquired by learning experiences and therefore constitute secondary drives? In this illustration, it could hardly be questioned that we are merely showing how the basic drive of hunger can be shaped and led into different channels by experience, but it is still a generic drive, transcending all cultural and individual differences.

We have, in fact, already illustrated the concept which helps to bridge the gap between the learned and the inherent in motivated behavior: it is called *canalization*. Adapted from the French word *canaliser*, it invokes the analogy of formless quantities of rain water drenching the hillside and running off through the channels formed by streams and riverbeds, becoming more structured in form and direction as it flows out to sea. So even our basic animal drives and appetites, as well as our more malleable higher functional propensities as human beings, may be thought of as being constantly molded, taking shape, becoming habits or personal preferences, even motivating values, as they find expression through individual experience. The point is, however, that they do not thereby necessarily become secondary or learned motives pure and simple—means to an end, so to speak, but not the real thing. They remain in a very real sense individual expressions or *canalized forms of the original basic generic drive*.

This useful concept, we think, helps to resolve much of the confusion about what is truly inherent in human nature and what is "merely learned." It renders concepts such as "functional autonomy" rather superfluous and admits the whole realm of man's higher functions to consideration as being possibly inherently motivated, rather than relegated to secondary habits because they often involve learning. Does the miser necessarily continue to hoard money because it once served the purpose of providing food and shelter but has since become a habit? That would be one way of looking at it, if indeed making money served only as a means of providing food and shelter and the means then became an end in itself. We might then call it a secondary or learned motive. We might also argue that the hoarding of money was a symbolic substitute for the hoarding of food like a squirrel, and thus represents but a canalization of the hunger drive with its food-gathering behavior. But the old skinflint might never have been hungry a day in his life, and hoarding against a rainy day to avert starvation the farthest thing from his mind. Could his behavior be a canalization of an entirely different generic drive, such as a need for power and social prestige? Are there basic generic drives underlying much of social behavior, or is it all learned secondary motivation? Where do art appreciation, playing of games, joining a club, learning a trade, falling in love and getting married, hating or admiring foreigners, feeling guilty for committing a sin, fighting for an ideal, and a thousand other common practices of human beings fit into the picture of motivated behavior? Clearly, we have to establish some kind of relationship between human motivation and *levels of integration* of behavior before we can hope to understand the forces underlying the surface manifestations of either individual or social behavior.

Inherent Motivation
and
Levels of Integration
We are now in a better position to summarize the biosocial viewpoint on human motivation and to chart a course for a survey of its ramifications in the psychodynamics of personality development: The human being, as an adaptive, integrated biosocial organism, embracing psychophysiological, psychological, and psychosocial functions at one and the same time, behaves as a *pervasively motivated organism, with motivational and adaptive mechanisms evident at all levels of integration as well as in the integrated personality as a whole.* Some of these motivated functions are direct expressions of basic generic drives, some are dependent on canalization through experience, and some are secondary products of environmental influence, only indirectly related to basic drives. Those generic drives that are necessary for the survival of the individual or the species have inherent activating or motivational mechanisms (e.g., reflexes, lowered thresholds of response, and felt needs and satisfactions) that assure the practice of these functions under normal circumstances in the natural habitat of the species (society). It can be seen that the bio-social position stems directly from its conception of man as a biosocial emergent in evolution, whose social behavior and learning ability are inherent in "the nature of the beast," not something just tacked-on for practical purposes. The "activational motivation" hypothesis merely recognizes that functions vital to survival must be "programmed" into the development of the organism—that these functions become canalized in

different ways through interaction with the environment, but ultimately pervade the behavior of the entire organism. In other words, human behavior cannot be conceived of as partly motivated and partly random, and while much is left to experience, nature leaves very little to chance.

The rationale of this principle is evident at once when one considers the long-range demands of natural selection for adaptation and survival. Any variant that tended to favor survival (let us say, the manipulation of tools for hunting and problem-solving) would not be very effective in favoring survival if it depended on pure chance or accidental impulse to be exercised. At least, we would expect that those individuals who were born with not only a little better potential for manual dexterity and neuro-muscular coordination with foresight but also with an *urge* to manipulate objects for problem-solving would be more adaptive to environmental stresses and challenges than those who had similar potentials but no interest in exercising them. We would suggest that in the long history of human evolution it was not only the dumb and clumsy brute in the family but also the highly gifted and *unmotivated underachiever* who passed out of the evolutionary parade. His get-up-and-go caveman cousin developed his capacities in childhood for the sheer thrill of controlling his environment, and eventually found that this gave him the edge on longevity and passing his gene structure on to his progeny. We admittedly know practically nothing about the genetic transmission of temperament, and very little about the genetic transmission of skills, but we can be reasonably certain that if there were no such thing as cognitive needs and achievement drives, there would have been no emergence of problem-solving skills. At least, an unmotivated species would sooner or later have succumbed to a well-motivated one, just as variants with sex organs but no sex urge would soon die out. We would say that the same applies at every level of behavioral integration, and shall now proceed to explore this thesis.

Basic Generic
Drives—

Psychophysiological The most primitive animal drives of the species, and the most indispensable to the survival of any form of animal life, function at the psychophysiological level of integration. This includes such basic drives as hunger, sex, avoidance of harm, and the exploratory or activity drive, all of which have been demonstrated as being common to all mammals, including man. The difference is that in man even these basic drives are subject to wide individual differences, divergent canalizations through experience, and considerable modification by integration with psychosocial needs.

We have already used the development of culturally determined tastes in food as an example of the canalization of a generic drive into specific manifestations of that drive. Actually, we can carry the illustration far beyond the acculturation of taste and refine the canalizations down to the food preferences of regions, families, and individuals. The American child who has learned to like ice cream and candy because the culture makes them readily available to satisfy that universal "sweet tooth" of children may nevertheless prefer one flavor over another. In time his tastes change, partly as a concomitant of maturing appetite and nutritional needs, partly as a result of combined habit and novelty in taste satisfactions. He may grow up on a diet of hominy grits and farm produce as a southern farmer's child, or spaghetti and pizza if he is an Italian immigrant worker's child. But given a little breadth of social interaction and an improvement in socioeconomic status, either one may well develop a taste for esoteric French or Oriental cuisine and a discriminating palate for fine wines and liquors. Yet the deeply canalized satisfactions of childhood diets will usually remain far into late adulthood, unless they have been associated with very unappetizing feeding habits and a miserable childhood.

However, it is not only in the canalization of tastes in food that the adaptability of the basic hunger drive manifests itself. There is the socialization of the entire feeding process, even though the assuagement of hunger and the hunger itself constitutes a basic psychophysiological need. Every culture provides not only a particular variety of foods but also some rather formalized, even ritualized prescriptions for the manner, timing, circumstances, use of utensils or following of ceremony in the feeding process, for each meal of the day as well as for special occasions. These prescriptions and rituals are learned and maintained in fairly uniform fashion, at least within each particular class of a given culture, even though the patterns themselves may vary considerably from one class or culture to another. The growing child in every family is weaned and fed in accordance with practices established by local custom, though naturally limited by the demands of its mammalian heritage. The child soon becomes accustomed to the regular (or irregular) family diet, but also learns when, with whom, with what to eat, and what kinds of rituals (such as saying grace, or licking the plate clean, or burping in appreciation) are expected to accompany the mealtime as a part of the day's social experience. He may, in the course of his lifetime, have to adjust to periodic fasting or feasting as a matter of religious observance or the vicissitudes of food supply, and he may find occasions when he must delay or grossly alter customary hunger satisfaction to conform to the demands of a given situation (like eating fried maguey worms). There is much, in short, that every individual in every culture must learn about satisfying his hunger drive; but no one ever has to learn, in any absolute sense, to *be hungry* and to want to eat. The hunger drive may be canalized and socialized, but as a psychophysiological need it can never be satisfied by anything but food. Moreover, as a generic drive for obvious survival purposes, its universal presence in the species transcends all individual and cultural differences.

The same may be said for the sex drive—only more so. Sexual as well as intellectual maturity is delayed until after puberty in the human species. Since the regulation of family life and reproduction is the cornerstone of the most rudimentary social life as it evolved in humans, the sex drive is subjected to even more restraint and acculturation influence than any other basic psychophysiological drive. That is undoubtedly what led Freud to say that psychosexual conflict is the principal cause of frustration, maladjustment, and neurosis. Without going into the ramifications of the Freudian position at this point, we can readily agree, from abundant clinical evidence, that the delay and ritualization of sex drive gratification presents a more widespread source of motivational conflict than any ritualization of the hunger drive is likely to cause—except for those segments of humanity that find themselves periodically on the verge of starvation. Society does, after all, give you a chance to eat every day, no matter how ritualized the eating procedure may be. Many societies prevent their children and adolescents from enjoying any direct sexual gratification for many years until marriage; and then they enforce strict taboos against incest, somewhat variable taboos against adultery and homosexuality, and variable opportunities for and prohibitions of birth control, all of which inevitably affect sexual behavior. Then there are the individual differences in the strength of the sexual drive and its cognitive-affective or aesthetic accompaniments, which raise problems of individual adjustment and compatibility of mates. Indeed, it is this involvement with psychological functions through cortical control of the brain that makes the human sex drive a complex *psycho*physiological function, and ultimately a biosocially integrated one, rather than the seasonal hormonally-induced one that it is in lower animals. As summarized by Etkin (1954):

In lower animals sexual behavior is predominantly under endocrine control, operating through lower nervous centers. In higher mammals more cortical control independent of the endocrines appears, particularly in the male. In the human this trend is strikingly accelerated, both male and female showing predominance of cortical rather than endocrine control of sexual behavior (Beach, 1948, Ford and Beach, 1951). It is here suggested that this shift in mechanism is part of the behavioral shift whereby sexual behavior became part of the socializing mechanism of the higher mammals, particularly canines and primates. That this shift then is greatly advanced in the human may be one of the results of the selection pressure consequent upon the sociology of the hunting protohominid necessitating family organization and division of labor. Cortical expansion in the human is thus related to sexual behavior control as well as to the intellectual functions. (p. 141)

Thus the restraints, selectivity, and adaptability of the sex drive are built into the constitution of the human being, and need not be regarded as merely learned behavior imposed upon a predatory animal by society. So when a coed complains that her date "acted like an animal," she may be right, but the chances are that he merely failed to exercise the degree of cortical control that she felt was called for in the situation, knowing perfectly well that humans are supposed to be capable of self-control in keeping with the proprieties of a given situation. People are, in fact, quite capable of making lifelong adaptations and canalizations of the sex drive in keeping with a sense of personal dignity, selectivity of affection, and cultural prescriptions of courtship, marriage, and family life. They ultimately integrate their sex and hunger drives and all other drives into adult social-role behavior, sometimes subordinating one urge for the satisfaction of another, modifying and canalizing it in accordance with the social mores and individual need or suppressing it altogether if need be (i.e., the biosocial level of integration and analysis.) Nevertheless, the universal presence of a physical sex urge of varying intensity transcends individual and cultural differences in man and bespeaks the basic generic nature of the drive. It provides a potent source of conflict and adjustment, but is also subject to modification by other basic generic drives in the biosocial integration of personality.

ACTIVITY DRIVE

Another basic generic drive which seems to operate at the psychophysiological level of motivation is the activity drive, sometimes referred to as autonomous or spontaneous activity in animals. It may be readily observed in all mammals as well as in human children. Mice, monkeys, and babies may often be seen creeping or thrashing about, manipulating objects, or simply "snooping around" for no apparent purpose other than keeping active. Controlled experiments with small animals show that they will spontaneously undertake extensive periods of running exercise on the "activity wheel" (a kind of ferris wheel which the animal turns as it runs inside of it) even when there is no hunger or other incentive involved. A study by Hill (1956) showed that this activity was correlated with the length of time the animal was deprived of activity by being closely confined in his cage. As for babies, it was pointed out even as far back as Watson's (1925) work that the surest way to get an anger response from any infant was to restrict its movements. The exploratory creeping and toddling of children as soon as they can creep or toddle, may be compared with the rough-and-tumble, playful chasing and "playing tag" by bear cubs or baby seals as constitutionally impelled behavior. It is as though some basic neuromuscular stress conveyed the message to each mammal: "Don't just lie there; do something, see something, live it up!" Without indulging in such allegorical allusions, we can test our hypothesis by the criteria of basic generic drives.

General activity and exploratory behavior is apparently universally present among many higher vertebrate species as a means of facilitating *all* vital functions. Our activational-motivation hypothesis for natural selection applies perhaps *most* generically to the general activity drive. It is this drive which would have the effect of bringing all sensorimotor, neuro-muscular, circulatory, and every other system into play. Physiologically, we know that the lymphatic system of mammals must be circulated by general neuromuscular activity in order to nourish the tissues of the entire organism and support metabolic processes. It is, therefore, advantageous for survival in the sense that it facilitates tissue growth and vital functions. When applied to exploration and interaction with the environment, it may likewise facilitate the operation of other basic drives such as hunger and sex and higher functions at the psychological and psychosocial levels of integration. Our "tip-off" or lead to higher levels of integration of exploratory behavior comes from the evidence of *curiosity* in both monkeys and babies. To explore this lead and the complex repertoire of human drives more fully, we must examine motivational behavior at the psychological and psychosocial levels of integration.

Basic Generic
Drives—

Psychological At a more complex level than sheer rough-and-tumble activity for muscular exercise and metabolic homeostasis are the intrinsically motivated activities that are principally cognitive in nature. Psychologists have been slow to recognize that basic psychological processes such as perception, reasoning, problem-solving, and understanding relationships are not only essential to the implementation of basic drives but that they also function as inherent or generic motivation in their own right. That is to say, we not only use sight, hearing, smell, and taste to satisfy hunger but there is also such a thing as "cognitive hunger" or intellectual curiosity—the need to exercise our senses and to "make sense" out of our surroundings. *Homo sapiens* (and to some extent the higher primates generally) has not only evolved the capacity to solve problems and master his environment in the service of sex and hunger but he has also been found to be highly motivated to solve problems and gain mastery-through-understanding for their own sake. The human urge to explore, to discover, to invent, to solve, and to create has long been known and honored by society, but has until recently been regarded by experimental psychologists as "learned behavior" undertaken as a means to an end. Problem-solving in monkeys, mice, and pigeons could easily be demonstrated in the laboratory as simply a more primitive form of learning to satisfy a basic drive (such as hunger). Since 1950, however, a series of experiments by Harlow, Berlyne, Butler, Fowler, and others has shown that monkeys, children, and college students exhibit exploratory-curiosity-manipulative behavior and preferences for sensory complexity even in the absence of food or other "basic-drive" incentives. This has not only dealt a severe blow to the drive-reduction theory of motivated learning, but has opened the way for a recognition of basic generic drives at the psychological (cognitive-affective-problem-solving) level of integration.

CURIOSITY-EXPLORATION-MANIPULATION

Probably the initial finding in this series of studies was one by Harlow (1950) in which he followed up a previous lead that suggested that monkeys might be impelled to solve mechanical puzzles for the sheer satisfaction of solving them, rather than as a means to obtain food. Two rhesus monkeys spent considerable time learning to undo a fairly complex bolt-hinge-hasp puzzle without food or other incentive. "Over 250 learned responses were elicited from each animal over the 10-hour workday, a frequency of response which one might well be pleased to obtain under hunger-food motivation conditions." Butler (1957) summarizes some of the subsequent animal experiments which

suggest that a curiosity motive is operative in the behavior of higher animals. For example, when monkeys are permitted to manipulate objects to explore the surrounding environment, these animals engage in this type of behavior for prolonged and repetitive test sessions (Butler and Harlow, 1954; Butler and Alexander, 1955; Harlow, 1950). Other researches have demonstrated that discrimination learning can be established when the only apparent reward is the opportunity to engage in manipulatory or exploratory behavior (Butler, 1953; Harlow and McClearn, 1954; Montgomery and Segall, 1955). There is also evidence that the motivational strength of exploratory behavior varies with the differences in incentive conditions (Butler, 1954).

Butler then goes on to describe an experiment in which rhesus monkeys were deprived of seeing what was going on outside their cages for varying

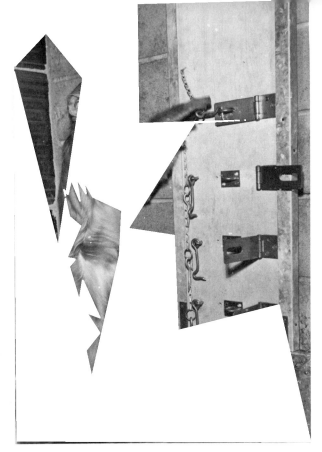

Figure 2–1. Exploratory-manipulative motivation *is exhibited by one of Harlow's rhesus monkeys working sedulously at a hook-hinge-hasp puzzle when not hungry and with no other reward in prospect. (Courtesy Wisconsin Regional Primate Research Center.)*

lengths of time from 0 to 8 hours. It was found that the longer they were deprived of the apparent curiosity satisfaction, the more frequently they pushed against a plexiglas window which briefly opened a view of the outside world. The increase tapered off between 4 and 8 hours of deprivation. Thus curiosity-drive strength seems to increase with deprivation—like any other drive, at least up to a point. Other studies show that satiation sets in after a while and new stimulation is required to claim the animal's attention. Similar results have been found with children.

Leube (1955) and Hebb (1955) have pointed out that such experiments clearly indicate motivation that *increases* stimulation of the organism up to an optimum point and then creates withdrawal or tension-reduction responses as an overstimulated or anxiety state is reached. That is, both monkeys and men tend to explore the environment when the activity state is low (boredom) and withdraw when it is too high, as in fear of strange or threatening objects or overstimulation by their own curiosity. This would seem to have adaptation-for-survival value, if one thinks of the need to master the environment on the one hand, and to avoid danger or nervous exhaustion on the other. Hebb has also suggested that a part of the brain known as the reticular activating system (RAS) could function to mediate this adaptive response to new stimulation. (The RAS is a network of nerves at the base of the brain whose function is to alert the organism to new or sudden changes in sensory stimulation. It is also capable of becoming attuned to stimuli of special significance—such as the baby's cry, which alerts the mother at any time of the day or night.) It is, therefore, not merely a matter of optimum intensity of stimulation, but of an alerting quality of stimulation that may be at least partly learned and is certainly subject to discrimination and feedback from the cortex of the brain. (See Fig. 2–2)

Whatever the neurological arrangements may be, the optimum arousal level of a curiosity-exploratory-manipulative (problem-solving) drive seems to fit the facts of both experiment and common experience better than a tension-reduction-instrumental conception. We all know that we get bored when we have "nothing to do" or are forced to do the same thing over and over again. We long for a change of scenery or routine, a vacation, or something new to challenge our interest. Anything from solving crossword puzzles to gambling or engaging in dangerous sports may be indulged in to increase the cognitive-affective-psychomotor stimulation that our organism seems to require. But no matter how welcome the change or the diversionary activity, we can become bored or satiated with that, too, if it is kept up too long without further variation.

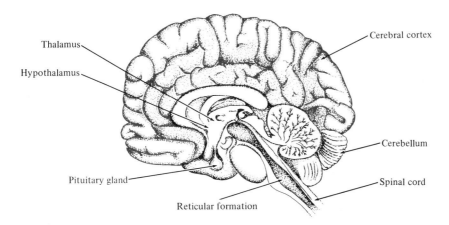

Figure 2–2. Middle cross-section of the human brain, *showing some of the structures involved in cognitive-affective integration and control of behavior. (Limbic system and speech areas not shown.)*

Different individuals will, of course, canalize their exploratory and curiosity needs differently and will have different tolerances for boredom or excitement as well as for degrees of cultural deprivation and stimulation. However, experimental as well as observational evidence suggests that almost any child in almost any culture will exhibit curiosity-exploratory-manipulative behavior at an early age and will continue to express this interest and seek its satisfaction in more and more specialized ways as they grow older. Piaget (1952), for example, has shown that a four- to five-month-old infant will not only study a rattle, toy, or watch to find out "what makes it tick" but will also resort to various devices "to make interesting sights last," and will go on from month to month trying to figure out cause-and-effect relationships even before it can ask questions to satisfy its curiosity. Observations of children's curiosity-manipulative behavior is so commonplace in societies around the world that it is common practice to keep fragile objects out of reach until the child is old enough to understand what it "must not touch." Cultures that go in for child guidance books, like our own, often warn parents not to misunderstand the child's tendency to tear things apart or manipulate them until damaged; it isn't a destructive instinct, just healthy intellectual curiosity.

In any event, both experimental and observational evidence indicate that curiosity-exploratory-manipulative (problem-solving) behavior is manifest in monkeys and men, that it does not depend on association with hunger or sex, that it transcends individual and cultural differences among humans, and that it has a probable base of functional mediation in the known neuroanatomy of the brain. We would, accordingly, be fully justified in recognizing this complex of motives as one of the basic generic drives at the organismic or psychological level of integration.

This psychological extension of the activity drive (or activational-motivation principle) to the realistic apprehension of the environment and coping with its challenges has wide ramifications at both the psychological and psychosocial levels of adaptive behavior. As an exercise (literally) in the use of cognitive and sensorimotor functions, it activates and promotes the growth of reality-testing and adaptive intelligence within the given cultural framework. As an agent of productivity or adeptness in the control of the environment it promotes achievement on the one hand (cf. McClelland, 1961) and self-actualization on the other (cf. Maslow, 1962). Since the latter two motivations are intimately involved with psychosocial needs (social approval and goal fulfillment, etc.), we shall consider them under that heading presently. A connecting link to all of these factors would seem to be the evidence we have cited of an apparently universal and inherent need to understand, to solve, and to cope effectively with the environment.

On the basis of such evidence, White has made a convincing case for the recognition of *efficacy motivation* as a basic drive, even though it does not fit the description of more primitive tissue-deficits and appetites. "This behavior includes visual exploration, grasping, crawling and walking, attention and perception, language and thinking, exploring novel objects and places, manipulating the surroundings, and producing effective changes in the environment" (White, 1959). He further suggests a *competence-motivation* model for human development (1960). The behavioral manifestations clearly go beyond curiosity and suggest a basic generic drive of *efficacy-competence* at the organismic (psychological) level of integration. Although learned skills may eventually become involved, it is apparently a basic organismic need that is satisfied by such behavior. The monkey who gets the window shutter open to see what's outside; the baby who follows the swinging watch with his eyes, then grabs at it, tastes it, and then bangs it on the bars of his crib; the child who plays with matches to see things go up in smoke, or takes his toy apart to see what makes it run—all these activities involve motor manipulations of the environment; but it is essentially a cognitive hunger that is being satisfied. The ramifications of efficacy needs go beyond simple understanding of structures and processes in the environment and involve more complex integration such as achievement motives and social effectiveness motives. At the organismic (psychological) level, however, it manifests itself as a need to understand and to deal effectively with the immediate physical environment.

Further support for the hypothesis of inherent cognitive needs is given by research such as that of Festinger *et al.* (1954) and many others on "cognitive dissonance," which postulates a basic or generic need for cognitive consistency. That is, when people find that their perceptions of reality are inconsistent, or differ from their expectations, or just "don't make sense," they find it very disturbing and they resort to all kinds of cognitive adjustments or manipulations of the elements in the cognitive field to eliminate the inconsistency. We shall discuss this further in the chapter on cognition, but a simple illustration will suffice for the time being. An experienced poker player, knowing that there are only four aces in any poker deck, would certainly experience "cognitive dissonance" (to say the least), if he thought he saw a fifth ace turn up in another player's hand, particularly if that player won the pot because of it. He would most likely try to resolve the dissonance by finding out whether (1) they had been playing with a defective deck, (2) he had counted wrong, or (3) the other player was deliberately cheating. If the social amenities prevented him from resolving this doubt, the cognitive dissonance would persist and create a good deal of uneasiness, because "it just didn't make sense" and because he could not bring himself to believe that his friend was a card cheat. (Of course, when there are no such social amenities, someone might get shot, and that, too, would resolve the cognitive dissonance, if the prevailing laws of cause and effect called for it.)

Evidence such as the foregoing points to a generic cognitive need or drive that may be canalized in many different ways. We would call this a *generic need for cognitive clarity, consistency, and novelty*. Basically, this merely means that the human being has an inherent drive or need to exercise his intelligence to some degree, just as lower animals presumably have a similar drive to exercise theirs. The evolutionary rationale is not hard to see. It stems directly from our basic thesis of activational motivation of the organismic functions that have survival value. If the use of human intelligence with its complex cognitive functions and problem-solving competence were to serve adaptation and survival functions, natural selection would favor the variants that experienced an urge to comprehend the environment, to seek constant interaction with it, and satisfaction in coming to logical terms with it. The point has long been overlooked because it is easy to think of hunger pangs and sex urges as creating needs which will be satisfied when specific organic tensions are relieved; but it is difficult to think of any organic tensions being relieved by seeing connections or solving a problem. Nevertheless, empirical evidence points to the existence of satisfactions on a purely abstract or *ideational* level of brain functioning in *Homo sapiens socialis*—probably the only creature for whom that is true to some extent for most of the population of the species, becoming one of the absorbing interests of life for some. We know, of course, that there are vast differences in the presence and canalized forms of intellectual interests, some of which are set by the limitations of individual intellectual capacities at birth, some by the stimulating or stultifying influences of culture or situational factors. But we do suggest that the presence of intellectual needs, as expressed by the generic need for cognitive clarity, consistency, and novelty, transcends both individual and cultural differences and are in their way just as necessary for the survival of the species as the more primitive drives of hunger and sex.

If one needs further confirmation of this opinion that is based on research and experience, it is of interest to note that even such a rigorous experimentalist in cognition as Helson has stated (1966):

I would go even further in maintaining that cognitive processes per se may generate as strong and even stronger drives than such basic drives as hunger and sex. The drive to find a solution to a problem may keep an individual at work for days and nights to the exclusion of all other considerations. Who has not heard how Newton forgot about meals and hours of the day while engrossed in a problem, and of workers in other fields who persist for days and weeks until an intellectual task is finished? . . .

Men who have been creative, whether in science, the arts, literature, politics, or industry, have often been excited to a far greater degree by ideas than by food, sex, and sleep. The satisfaction of so-called basic needs is necessary but not sufficient for a full and truly satisfying life. It is time that the driving power of *conscious perceiving and thinking* be recognized as much as the driving power of tissue needs, which was so fully exploited by the medical psychologists during the first third of this century. I believe we now have the basis for an experimental approach to the motivating power of perceiving and thinking. Let us therefore get on with these sources of motivation, which are responsible for man's unique position among all living things.

We would, of course, wholly agree with the positions of Helson and others, and believe that as more direct and indirect evidence of cognitive drive accumulates, there will be less reluctance to recognize it as a basic or generic drive in human behavior. In the meantime, its place and rationale in the biosocial framework of psychodynamics are fairly clear and consistent.

Basic Generic Drives—

Psychosocial   It was William James, the last of the great philosopher-psychologists, who, among others, called attention to the powerful force of "club opinion," or self-esteem as a function of social approval, in motivating, guiding, and restraining human behavior. Was this just an upper-class New England custom, borrowed, perhaps, from the *noblesse oblige* of Victorian aristocracy? We have all heard the expression "keeping up with Joneses" and have no doubt seen it and even practiced it in our own communities. Is this just an incidental game developed by the competitive, materialistic habits of a capitalistic society? The practice of dueling to settle an insult persisted in many European and Latin American countries right into the twentieth century, although universally outlawed and commonly recognized as a mere formality. The Kwakiutl Indians of the American Northwest accomplish the same purpose by the "potlatch ceremony" in which one gains status by destroying or giving away much of their property as a sign of contempt and superiority. We know that Japanese and Chinese people, at least up to World War II, would invariably go to great lengths to "save face" and might even commit suicide in the event of failure or humiliation. We also know that various rituals and customs are practiced throughout the world, interpersonal and group relationships and loyalties are formed, and cultural patterns are maintained generation after generation. Are these but habits of expediency learned in childhood to facilitate feeding and reproduction of the species? Are they the products of social coercion to maintain some order in society?

Or is there a common generic drive which expresses itself through a variety of social ego needs and motives, which are in turn canalized by experience in the social milieu?

Let us consider the proposition that there are certain generic needs that come into play at the psychosocial level of behavioral integration and provide powerful motivation for such behavior throughout most of our lives. These would include such common needs as affection and acceptance, recognition and status, and group affiliation or "belonging." We shall avoid the trap that previous theorizers have fallen into by refraining from regarding each of these needs or motives as a separate instinct or drive that must exist independent of the social learning process if it is to be recognized as a basic drive. Such analogies to simple animal reflexes do not, as we have already seen, do justice to the complexity of the developmental process, particularly in the realm of human motivation. We must consider, instead, whether there is a cluster of generic needs that is common to the human species, operating at the psychosocial level of behavioral integration, with a common core of constitutionally inherent motivation that might be designated as "social drive," in spite of the various canalized forms it may take in different individuals and in different cultures.

In other words, we shall not look for simplistic specific-reflex mechanisms such as an automatic "herd instinct" to explain why people "follow the crowd" in tribal warfare, political rallies, or mass recreation. Nor shall we find it crucial to our investigation to decide just how much learning enters into the face-saving behavior of most Orientals, the competitive materialism of Western businessmen, or the cooperative sharing of many underdeveloped societies. What we do wish to explore is the evidence for a basic generic social drive for belonging-acceptance-social-interaction, which reveals a diffuse need to relate to one's fellow-man as its common motivating force, but allows for a great variety of canalized expressions. These expressions include conformity, status-seeking, cooperation and competition, group identification and affiliation, dominance and submissiveness, friendship and rivalry, introception of social ideals and self-restraint, and even life goals and self-concepts that are largely defined in terms of social desirability. All of these varieties and effects of the hypothesized social drive obviously bear witness to individual differences, cultural differences, and varieties of functional expression. They also clearly involve some learning through experience. But, as we did in considering hunger, sex, efficacy, and cognitive needs, we have to consider whether there is not an underlying generic drive that transcends all these variations and is universal in the human species. We must also consider further just how this function served the evolution of the human species on the strength of its survival value as a cohesive force in adaptation to the extreme varieties of environment encountered by the protohominids.

Finally, we have to consider just how this complex of motivated functions at the psychosocial level of integration is related to and inherent in the organic constitution of the species, and how it unfolds in the course of maturation in its natural habitat.

If all these criteria of a basic generic drive are met, we can the more readily recognize the diverse learned elaborations and specifications of the social drive as *canalization of a basic drive* or secondary elaborations of the same, rather than incidentally learned means to satisfy the more basic psychophysiological drives. This will give meaning and substance to our conception of man as an *inherently social learning animal*, a conception which we regard as crucial to the psychodynamics of personality.

MAN AS A SOCIAL ANIMAL

The groundwork for this conception of man was laid by no less an authority on evolution than Charles Darwin himself, about 100 years ago.

Every one will admit that man is a social being. We see this in his dislike of solitude, and in his wish for society beyond that of his own family. Solitary confinement is one of the severest punishments which can be inflicted. . . . Although man has no special instincts to tell him how to aid his fellow-men, he still has the impulse, and with his improved intellectual faculties would naturally be much guided in this respect by reason and experience. . . . Instinctive sympathy would also cause him to value highly the approbation of his fellows. Consequently man would be influenced in the highest degree by the wishes, approbation, and blame of his fellow-men, as expressed by their gestures and language. Thus the social instincts, which must have been acquired by man in a very rude state, and probably even by his early ape-like progenitors, still gave the impulse to some of his best actions. . . .
In order that primeval man, or the ape-like progenitors of man, should become social, they must have acquired the same instinctive feelings which impel other animals to live in a body; and they no doubt exhibited the same general disposition. They would have felt uneasy when separated from their comrades, for whom they would have felt some degree of love; they would have warned each other of danger, and have given mutual aid in attack or defense. All this implies some degree of sympathy, fidelity, and courage. Such social qualities, the paramount importance of which to lower animals is disputed by no one, were no doubt acquired by the early progenitors of man in a similar manner, namely through natural selection, aided by inherited habit. When two tribes of primeval men, living in the same country, came into competition, if (other circumstances being equal) the one tribe included a greater number of courageous, sympathetic, and faithful members, who were always ready to warn each other of danger, to aid and defend each other, this tribe would succeed better and conquer the other. . . . A tribe rich in the above qualities would spread and be victorious over other tribes; but in the course of time it would, judging from all past history, be in its turn overcome by some other tribe still more highly endowed. Thus the social and moral qualities would tend slowly to advance and be diffused throughout the world. (Darwin, 1871, pp. 480-498)

It can be seen that even Darwin regarded it as highly plausible, on the basis of evidence then available, that man had evolved as a social animal from "ape-like progenitors" who had already inherited some social propensities from their mammalian ancestors, by natural selection. Whatever psychological qualities make for group cohesion (e.g., sympathy, loyalty, and mutual defense against danger) are assumed to have survival value and are transmitted in increasing degree by natural selection. The underlying intellectual and emotional functions of the nervous system, whose variability is implied by Darwin, would determine this course of evolution by natural selection. Darwin did not touch upon the importance of symbolic behavior and culture as both the products and directing forces of the evolutionary process, but these influences are now much better understood by contemporary anthropologists and evolutionary theorists.

It is now generally agreed that, whereas man's mental capacities and brain size (see Chapter 1) have undergone little change since his emergence from the protohominids about a quarter-of-a-million years ago, his development of *culture* has introduced a new dimension of adaptation for survival. From a behavioral viewpoint, culture has continued human evolution to new levels of complexity above the plateau at which his morphological evolution seems to have leveled off. That is to say, once the protohominids had developed their crude social capacities to the point where some sort of social regulation was possible through symbolic communication, such social regulation or culture became the chief determinant of survival from that time on.

Thus it did not remain for each new generation of early cavemen to discover anew the survival advantages of using fire, tools, clothing, and weapons, of regulating cohabitation and reproduction in family units and tribal cooperatives, of growing and storing food, of developing technologies for the fabrication of materials and construction of buildings, or of formulating laws for the protection of life and property and the welfare of the community. These practices and principles were transmitted instead through the symbolic communication and introception of social mores and cultural values. But if survival was truly dependent on such social learning, it could not be left to incidental association with hunger and sex, or the recognition of its survival value by each individual. Still less could the mere existence of social mores force their observance upon virtually all members of all societies throughout all of human history. Nature, as we have said, takes no chances on functions vital to survival, unless the chances are clearly stacked in her favor. To restate this principle in operational rather than allegorical terms: Natural selection operates in a manner to insure automatic activation or inherent motivation of all functions necessary for the survival of a species. What was clearly required for the evolution of *Homo sapiens* as a social animal was a *constitutionally motivated propensity to social learning and cohesion—* that is, a generic social drive expressed by a variety of social ego needs. We have already mentioned some of the principal social ego needs: affection and acceptance, recognition and status, group affiliation and "belonging." Add to the emotional (affective) components of these social ego needs the power of reasoning and communicating abstract ideas, and you have a species singularly adapted to creating and transmitting *culture* as its modus vivendi.

ORGANIC BASIS

The survival value of such a generic drive for social cohesion and cultural transmission is not hard to understand. Its emergence in evolution as an inherent function of the organism—which makes use of, but is not created by, social learning processes—is not at first so obvious or plausible. This is due largely to the fact that we are still accustomed to thinking of basic drives as being functions of tension states and automatic response mechanisms of specific organs. Certainly this is true of hunger and sex. Yet we could hardly point to any specific organ that would embrace such functions as social sensitivity and sympathy, symbolic communication, introception of social mores, restraint of emotional impulses, cooperative planning, and mutual defense. But we have already encountered highly cogent arguments that cognitive functions may have their own inherent need systems without being related to any specific organic tensions. These needs function at a higher level of integration than the strictly physiological hungers, although they obviously involve some processes in the brain.

Psychosocial motivation would have to operate, by definition, at a still higher and more complex level of integration than the psychological or psychophysiological. There is an organic basis for such inherent motivation, to be sure, but it is the *entire organism* rather than any specific organ. This may appear to be begging the question, since anything that people do or learn to do may be referred to the entire organism. How can we relate social behavior and motivation to the actual inherent functions of the organism, rather than leave it dangling as a conceptualized by-product of incidental social interaction, which may be learned, and then again, may not be? If social drive and social ego needs are highly integrated functions of the organism, just what is being integrated? When framed in that form, the question is more easily answered.

There are at least three key functions of the organism which are performed by very definite organic structures and are indispensable to the integration of motivated social behavior. These are: (1) the organs of intercommunication—speech, hearing, and vision; (2) the organs of feeling and empathy—principally the autonomic nervous system, the vital organs and endocrine system it regulates, and the hypothalamus which regulates it; and (3) the organ of thinking, particularly of abstract conceptualization, and sensorimotor coordination—the cerebrum. Through the use of speech and perceptual process governed and integrated by a brain capable of abstract thinking and emotional involvement in those concepts, man is able and indeed impelled to function at a level of complex social interaction such as no other animal in nature could conceivably do. That is the kind of "constitutional equipment" we referred to in our previous discussion of evolution (page 21) when we said that "*Homo sapiens* had already developed the constitutional capabilities that rendered him *inherently* a culture-making species." The logical functions of self-other awareness, abstract thinking, empathic feeling, and verbal and emotional communication are the kinds of functions we say are being integrated at the psychosocial level of integration to implement the generic social drive.

It is our thesis that an organism equipped and predisposed to exercise such functions because of their survival value will inevitably develop, canalize, and integrate them into a modus vivendi that is highly social. The young of such species will inevitably seek to communicate and interact with the members of their immediate families—imitating, demanding attention, and establishing emotional ties from infancy onward. This progressive exercise and integration of functions will be limited only by the maturational progression of the relevant organic functions we have mentioned, although much learning will enter into the developmental process. As abstract thinking and emotional refinements develop, the growing child will actively seek approval and identity as a member of its social group by introcepting the social mores and ultimately the values of its culture. Concern for the feelings and opinions of one's fellows, as well as the need for acceptance through conformity and recognition through self-assertion will all grow naturally out of an integration of basic empathy, abstract thinking, symbolic communication, and the perceived significance of action. Perceived rejection or inferred guilt will give rise to a subjective state of maladjustment known as *anxiety*. So will frustration of any social ego needs or conflicts between competing needs (as between acceptance and self-assertion, when the latter tends to produce rejection). The neurological state that underlies anxiety may never be fully understood; but clinical observation will leave no doubt that conflicting or frustrated social ego needs may give rise to such a state quite as readily as the frustration of psychophysiological needs.

It can be seen that much of our thesis of evolutionary constitutional emergence of psychosocial motivation needs to be "checked-out" through an examination of developmental and adjustive processes. In the meantime, we can regard it as being at least highly plausible and consistent with known principles of biology and anthropology that man evolved with a constitution that had the necessary ingredients for a psychosocial level of motivated behavior. In other words, the evolutionary refinement and integration of simpler biological functions led to a qualitatively new emergent function which did not require a new organ, but only interaction with the very social milieu which that emergent function gradually created—the social milieu or culture.

LEARNING, CONFORMITY, AND CULTURE

In the social milieu or culture lies also the key to the paradox of having social behavior and values at one and the same time a product of learning and a product of universal predisposition in man. We know that all the social formalities, amenities, and values and the very language of communication have to be learned by each individual in every society around the earth. The learning content differs with every culture and subculture and is subject to wide individual differences of experience and preference. But the universal predisposition to social learning transcends all such individual and cultural differences. Whether we are dealing with the elaborate "face-saving" rituals of pre-war Japan, or the conformity to "club opinion" in William James' New England, or the Kwakiutl Indian custom of gaining status with a potlatch ceremony, the underlying motive is the universal one of safeguarding social acceptability. As in the learning of a language, it is the language or local dialect of the culture that is learned; however, the *ability* and the *desire* to express oneself through language is inherent in the functioning constitution of the human species. In a similar manner, we have to learn the code of social rituals and values by which we gratify our need for social acceptance and other social ego needs. But the point is not merely that we learn these cultural patterns, but that we *always* learn them and *always* maintain some degree of social cohesion as a result. Even the nonconformist is usually a conformist in disguise. He has usually learned to canalize his need for belonging and acceptance by conforming to the rituals and values of a nonconformist or revolutionary group. An historical example of a revolutionary group movement is the Communist movement, which demands rigid adherence to its dogma and strategy in defying the values of other Western or Oriental cultures. Even criminals, the legally defined nonconformists of any society, are known to conform very rigidly to the code of their local underworld, which usually places high value on personal loyalty and "honor among thieves."

There are, of course, individual differences in this universal tendency to conformity or prescribed nonconformity. But the only individuals who are totally oblivious to any social standards of behavior and seem devoid of any social ego needs are the mentally deficient and the psychotic. Even the seriously maladjusted are usually found to be reacting to the frustration engendered by some conflict between their social ego needs by seeking compensatory social ego gratifications.

Thus upon closer examination the argument that social mores are always learned turns out to be an argument for a *universally inherent generic drive to learn* the modes of social interaction and cohesion. It is the form and not the underlying drive, of course, that is learned. The means-to-an-end hypothesis, which assumes social conformity only by virtue of expediency or coercion to satisfy more primitive animal needs, does not hold true except in an evolutionary sense. It was by *natural selection* that the human species learned by trial and error, so to speak, that social regulations and cohesion through the maintenance of social mores had survival value and provided a more effective way of satisfying other basic needs. Those families and tribes which produced more variants of cognitive and affective functioning required for social interaction, as well as the inherent motivation to integrate them in this manner, were simply better able to survive. The fact that human beings have not been found to exist anywhere on the face of the earth without at least some primitive form of culture is highly corroborative evidence that the mechanisms and motives of social cohesion became inherent in man through natural selection, rather than their being dependent on an unbroken chain of fortuitous or expedient learning experiences all through human history.

In short, despite the fact that cultural patterns are learned, *it is not the cultural pattern which creates and perpetuates social ego needs, but social ego needs which create and perpetuate cultural patterns!*

THE PLACE OF AGGRESSION

The age-old philosophical question of whether man is inherently good or evil has recently been couched in more sophisticated terms: Considering man's animal heritage through evolution, is he not basically an aggressive, predatory animal, whose primitive drives are only thinly camouflaged by artificial social restraints? This was essentially the position taken by Freud later in his career, when he moved to the conclusion that aggression was an independent instinct in man. It has recently been popularized by behavioral scientists such as Lorenz (1966), while being stoutly denied by others (e.g., Montagu, 1968). We have, of course, taken cognizance of man's evolution as a socially cohesive animal with a propensity to social conformity and a need for affection and approval. We did acknowledge that "optimum aggression" (not too much and not too little) was probably necessary for human survival, but what does aggression actually mean? Precisely in that semantic ambiguity lies the source of much misunderstanding as to whether aggression should be recognized as a basic drive in man.

The basic position of the evolutionary-aggression theorists is that individual and group aggression had obvious survival value in the struggle for existence and that this must be a basic characteristic of man. A history full of wars and hostile competition attests to that fact, and the ready resort to hostile behavior by both primitive and civilized man bears witness to its contemporary innateness. Indeed, aggressive behavior is regarded as being normal, inborn, and necessary as a basic law of survival.

There are at least two crucial fallacies in this line of reasoning: (1) aggression covers a multitude of sins and virtues; (2) the opposite of aggression (cooperation) is also demonstrably normal, inborn, and necessary—only more so for human survival!

On the first count, "aggression" cannot be sustained as a necessary motivational force for survival except on the basis of *activating aggressiveness*—what we have called the activating-motivational ingredient in all functions necessary for survival. This is applicable to all generic motives at all levels of integration and takes various forms. It may, as in the case of hunger, take the form of killing an animal, climbing a tree, or simply seeking out a carcass left by another hunting animal. On the other hand, it may require active cooperation in hunting, as it did at least as far back as *Pithecanthropus erectus*, if not with the early protohominid australopithecines. In the case of the sex drive, it may require the active pursuit and overpowering of the female by the male; on the other hand, aggressive pursuit of the goal generally requires mutual attraction and gentle seduction or submission to be successful in *Homo sapiens*. At the psychosocial level, activational motivation may involve competition and hostility; but it may also involve active cooperation and compliance with social mores. Thus the *activational and adaptive aggressiveness* that is logically necessary for survival does not necessarily imply the *destructive aggression* that the innate-aggression hypothesis attributes to man.

The second serious fallacy is the implication that destructive aggression is natural, but that social restraint and cooperation are learned—cultural artifices, so to speak. The facts and plausible interpretations of human evolution, as we have outlined them, point to quite the contrary. It is only because man developed an extraordinary capacity for cooperation, social cohesion, and conformity that he survived at all. (Indeed, group hostilities only provide an anomalous illustration of cooperative aggression.) It makes far more sense to posit uncontrolled destructive aggression as a *negative* selective factor than a positive one. Then why has aggressiveness not been selected out of the human emotional makeup altogether? We would suggest again that an optimal minimum of aggressiveness *is* necessary to activate all generic drives and to provide for defense against physical or psychosocial threat. To the extent that aggression becomes destructive or maladaptive to the individual or society, to that extent it must be considered pathological rather than a normal expression of the modus vivendi of the species. Even if there is fossil evidence that *Australopithecus* did on occasion bash each other's heads in, it would be contrary to principles of natural selection and adaptation to assume that nothing has changed in a million years. On the contrary, it would be plausible to assume that the head-bashing tendencies of certain australopithecines and of the species who came after them tended to eliminate them from the human hereditary pool. Capacities for understanding and cooperation through communication, empathy, and desire for affection and acceptance would have had far greater survival advantage. But even these socially cohesive tendencies would have benefited from optimally aggressive, activational tendencies. Families and tribes and their territory must be defended. The social mores cannot be preserved unless their violation is punished or deprecated. The development of cooperative and adaptive skills can benefit from active competition, striving for superiority, a zest for adventure and achievement. As selective pressures proceed, aggression will manifest itself less and less as a sadistic delight in the slaughter of one's fellows, until it becomes, as we maintain now, a pathological tendency among the frustrated or deceived. *Both* the forms of social cohesion and their aggressive control become learned canalizations of a generic drive; but destructive or maladaptive aggression must still be regarded as an aberration of the activational component in any generic drive, rather than as a generic drive in its own right.

Summary The evolution of the human personality as a complex bio-social organism forms the basis of our conception of motivated human behavior. It is hypothesized that all functions conducive to survival are inherently motivated and are universally manifested by members of the species. These functions constitute basic generic drives which operate at all levels of integration in human behavior, but may be canalized in a variety of manifest needs and subjected to innumerable secondary elaborations. Basic generic drives may be identified not only by their survival value and emergence in evolution but also by their transcendence of cultural and individual differences, their inherence as functions of organismic constitution or integrations of these functions, and their regular appearance in individual development and adjustive processes.

An examination of motivational phenomena at each level of integration suggests the presence of the following basic generic drives or needs:

Psychophysiological—hunger; sex; activity; avoidance of pain.

Organismic (psychological)—efficacy-competence; cognitive clarity, consistency, and novelty; curiosity-exploratory-manipulative behavior.

Psychosocial—social drive, as manifested by a cluster of social ego needs, variously expressed as need for belonging, acceptance, affection, recognition or status, self-esteem, group affiliation and participation.

It is further recognized that social learning is an inherent predisposition of the human organism, which serves to canalize the social drive, and that culture is a product as well as a canalizer of social ego needs. Aggressiveness, in the sense of activation-motivation, is regarded as a component of all basic drives; but destructive aggression is regarded as a pathological reaction to frustration or to situational conformity pressures, rather than as a universally inherent characteristic of man.

3

Child
Development
in
Social
Interaction

Evolution
and
Child Development Our review of human evolution as an indispensable foundation for the scientific study of personality has given us a basic conception of man as a complex product of natural selection, with behavioral capacities and motives ranging from physiological self-maintenance to social cohesion and transmission of culture. We have also taken note of the fact that only a tiny proportion of this vast and complex range of capacities is functionally operative at birth in the newborn infant, and that human offspring undergo a much longer period of growth, maturation, learning, and dependency before achieving adulthood than do members of any other species.

The story of that continuity from infancy to adulthood and the interplay of biological and social forces in the course of its development is a vital part of the closely integrated biosocial approach to the dynamics of personality. This is so for at least two good scientific reasons. One is the *essential continuity* or the *biosocial causality* of personality development throughout the life cycle. That is to say, the constantly evolving personality is a continuous product of previous experiences and motives constantly modified by emerging capacities in social interaction at all times. The experiences of childhood affect the developmental processes of adolescence and these changes cumulatively affect character formation, adjustment, and social interaction far into adulthood. That is why psychologists are fond of quoting and give scientific credence to the poet Wordsworth's observation that "the child is father to the man." That is, childhood experiences and living conditions may have a profound impact on the adult personality. Even in assuming the parental role, for example, it makes a great deal of difference whether a mother was loved or rejected when *she* was a child, or whether the father was deprived or overindulged and what his model was for authority and fatherhood when *he* was a boy. Even the causes of mental breakdowns in adulthood, as clinicians know, may have their roots in the anxieties and emotional conflicts of childhood.

Another basic reason for the study of developmental processes from childhood to adulthood lies in the close relationship between the evolution of the species and the unfolding of the functional capacities of the individual. The higher vertebrate species generally display considerable functional and structural immaturity at birth and require varying periods of growth to achieve adult status, which is generally defined as the stage of maturation of all the essential maintenance and reproductive functions evolved by the species. In the case of man, as we have noted, prolonged immaturity and dependency are at a maximum, presumably because the evolution of higher rational and biosocial functions in *Homo sapiens socialis* has prolonged the developmental process in the individual specimen. This is especially true if we consider that full biosocial maturity is not reached in man at the age of puberty, but some years later, say around 16 to 18, even if we ignore the legal age of adulthood as being 21 in some contexts. In the course of this prolonged period of ontogenetic development (growth of the individual) there is bound to be a gradual maturation and learning of the functions which were acquired by natural selection in the course of evolution: erect locomotion and manual dexterity, speech, abstract thinking, social cooperation and planning, and development of value systems and cultures. This does not mean that there is a highly specific programmed sequence of developmental stages built into the human organism and corresponding exactly to the course of phylogenetic evolution (evolution of species) up to Cro-Magnon man.[1]

---

[1] The biological principle that *ontogeny recapitulates phylogeny* (i.e., that development of the individual member of a species reproduces the stages of evolution of that species from lower species) has been established, with some limitations, as applying to the *embryonic* development of the individual specimen. It has also been found to be roughly applicable to the human embryo and fetus, but no attempt has been made recently to apply it to development through the human life cycle. G. S. Hall's "biogenetic stages" (1916) proved to be too forced a recapitulation.

Nevertheless, it will be seen that there is a certain biological inevitability about the developmental sequence, which starts with an immature organism at birth that develops the simple, primitive, life-sustaining functions at first and proceeds to more and more complex stages of autonomy and social competence. This is much the same sequence in which behavior evolved in the course of human evolution. We call this gross correspondence or parallelism between personality development and evolution inevitable because the laws of organic growth require that simple organic structures and functions develop before they can be integrated into more complex and more highly integrated structures and functions. Thus the child's capacity to develop basic interpersonal relations and communication cannot emerge until basic perceptual, conceptual, and affective capacities have been developed. The adolescent's urge for social competence and identity cannot be satisfied until certain cognitive, communicative, affective, and psychomotor functions have been differentiated and integrated at a preliminary level of social interaction.

The delineation of these normative sequences of biosocial development will not only provide a frame of reference for biosocial causality and continuity but will also serve to emphasize the highly cohesive nature of the biosocial approach to personality.

RATIONALE OF PSYCHOSOCIAL STAGES

Before entering into a discussion of stages of personality development from infancy to adulthood, we might offer a word of explanation for entertaining any "stages" at all, and what our rationale is for offering the ones we have. To be sure, behavioral change and growth takes place in any individual or in any hypothetical group norm by infinitesimal increments or degrees from week to week and from year to year. Moreover, these changes are never exactly the same from one individual to the next. Nevertheless, these gradual changes in degree do, after a time, emerge as distinctly perceptible and more or less common differences in kind, quality, or category of behavior. At some ill-defined point it becomes appropriate to speak of a new stage of development. This is especially true when a new phase of biosocial integration of behavior has taken place—one that transcends the infinitesimal increments in functional capacities that have taken place from week to week and transcends individual differences. Thus rambunctious little schoolboys playing tag and yelling excitedly at each other are behaving at a categorically different level from the solitary creeping and poking into mother's closets they used to indulge in just five years earlier. The problem is only to conceptualize or categorize these two different levels of behavior and to designate the approximate age of transition as a biosocial norm. Furthermore, a mere descriptive catalog of behavioral changes from year to year for each sex and for each specific function would not serve our theoretically integrated purpose. In fact, it would not even give a realistic picture of the development of the integrated personality. We are, therefore, disposed to designate stages of development, but to apply a rationale that preserves the *biosocial integrity* and *causal continuity* of the developing personality from birth to maturity, as well as reflecting the most *salient* aspect of the total personality. We believe that an epigenetic scheme of *psychosocial* stages of development serves these criteria best, while representing an *integration* of organismic capacities that transcends individual and cultural differences.

Ego Emergence
and
Dependency

Having already described the evolution of human complexity of function as one that necessitated, among other things, a prolonged period of parental dependency, it is not surprising that the first stage of psychosocial development should embody this dependency. This dependent relationship remains, to a diminishing degree, from infancy all through childhood and adolescence. What we refer to here is the basic dependency on the mother or a caretaking surrogate, during the first two years of life, for sheer physical survival and the activation of basic biosocial functions. However, dependency has both active and passive aspects, and the term does not adequately convey the emergence of self-awareness and curiosity; the need for affection, attention, and communication; or the drive for efficacy and self-assertion—in short, the emergence of *ego*, before any frankly social interaction can take place. We shall, therefore, refer to this initial stage of biosocial development as *ego emergence and dependency*.

The first few weeks of life are necessarily devoted primarily to the maintenance of vital functions in the infant's still-unrecognized dependence on the mother for sheer survival. To assure the activation and satisfaction of its needs, the infant is endowed with sucking, grasping, and other reflexes, as well as vocal and motor distress reactions to discomfort. The crying, sucking, and general agitation when hungry, followed by contented imbibing of milk as soon as the mouth encounters a warm nipple, constitute an innate reflexive pattern of behavior which human infants display in common with all mammals, except that the crying is more vociferous and is accompanied by tears. The infant does little more than alternate between periods of suckling, sleep, and elimination for the first few weeks of its existence. This period might be designated as essentially vegetative, but there are signs of growing awareness of the environment even during these first few weeks.

Bowlby (1969) has recently summarized the considerations for recognizing *attachment* as the dominant and instinctive mode of infantile behavior. These considerations include the similarity to primate clinging behavior and the separation anxiety that is universally manifest during the first two or three years. Bowlby properly points out that these cannot be explained as secondary (learned) means of satisfying hunger, because it happens even with mother-figures or siblings who do not feed the child. (Harlow's monkeys, in fact, displayed clinging behavior to the nearest approximation of a mother-figure or live companion, regardless of who did the feeding. See Fig. 3–1.) In any event, our use of the broader term "dependency" is intended to include Bowlby's concept of attachment.

NEED FOR AFFECTION, ATTENTION, AND COMMUNICATION

It is notable that the human infant requires not merely the sensations of physical comfort and body contact that Harlow (1958) and others have shown to be a basic need in primate infants, but *comforting* as well. That is, it requires the human vocal and physical caressing that a mother ordinarily gives along with the nursing of the infant. The baby requires it, thrives on it, and deteriorates when it is not provided. It has been shown that it makes a great deal of difference whether an infant is caressed frequently, fed with some show of affection, and lulled to sleep by the "mothering one" as Sullivan (1953) calls her or the "caring figure" as we shall refer to the mother or mother-surrogate. It is this constant need to be *cared for* physically and psychologically that represents the first crude but direct expression of the social drive in the emerging ego.

The fact that such caring or mothering is a vital need in the child's early development is shown by a number of studies of maternal deprivation (reviewed by Casler, 1961). Infants deprived of this mothering for any of a variety of reasons often develop a condition variously described as hospitalism, marasmus, or deprivation syndrome, even though they are fed and diapered routinely by busy nurses or caretakers. Such infants become emotionally, physically, and even intellectually retarded, as well as more susceptible to illness and infant mortality. The fact seems to be well supported that the human infant simply does not function and develop normally if he is deprived of the fondling, baby talk, comforting, and everpresent protectiveness that a fond mother is able to communicate. Moreover, the baby is able to "sense" this protectiveness of the caring figure in early infancy.

We would regard this caring need as presocial rather than presexual, because it leads directly to dyadic and primary group interaction and not to sexual behavior. We shall deal with the remoteness of the psycho-sexual interpretation as we go along. However, we should have no diffi-culty recognizing both components in the situation: (1) insofar as oral stimulation and cuddling provide a pleasurable sensation, it may be re-garded as a forerunner of sexual gratification and may even be later directly associated with it; (2) insofar as it is part of a pattern of physical contact and communication with a caring figure, it is clearly presocial and leads directly to frankly social interpersonal relationships.

The fact that something more than physical or direct sensory satisfac-tion is involved in the infant's relationship to the mother or caring figure is shown by other studies and the daily observations which one can make on the infants in any culture. After the first two or three months, as the vegetative beginnings are overtaken by emerging consciousness of self and environment, emerging psychological needs such as curiosity, cognitive clarity, and efficacy begin to manifest themselves. The infant does not merely respond in reflexive fashion to hunger pangs and nipple and then go to sleep when its tummy is full. It begins increasingly to study the environment, the mother, and its own limbs with great interest. It be-comes attracted to the sound of the mother's voice and shows signs of elation when it discovers that it can make sounds, too. What is more, it readily "catches on" that these sounds can be used to establish two-way communication with this significant figure in its environment. Soon this need to communicate becomes a demand for attention and affection. Flirtatious communications are carried on and attention is demanded through a thousand signals that mother and child intuitively understand. Without any stimulus that can properly be called psychosexual or alimen-tary tension, the infant is able to respond with definite signs of self- and other-consciousness and a need to interact, by the latter half of the first year. The infant begins to respond with giggles or smiles to signs of affectionate attention and is able to convey, even with its limited reper-toire of facial, vocal, and other motor expressions, that it demands such attention and is fully appreciative of it. Indeed, a normally alert infant with a normally fond mother will establish a limited dyadic interrela-tionship on the basis of nonsense syllables, singsong patter, looking, and touching.

A highly demonstrative mother will, of course, afford ample enrich-ment of the infant's need for this emotional security and cultivate an enrichment of the child's own emotional responsiveness. A highly con-stricted, rejecting, or absent parent will soon stifle the emotional enrich-ment which is every infant's birthright in the sense that it is born to demand this emotional comforting. For the infant not only responds with

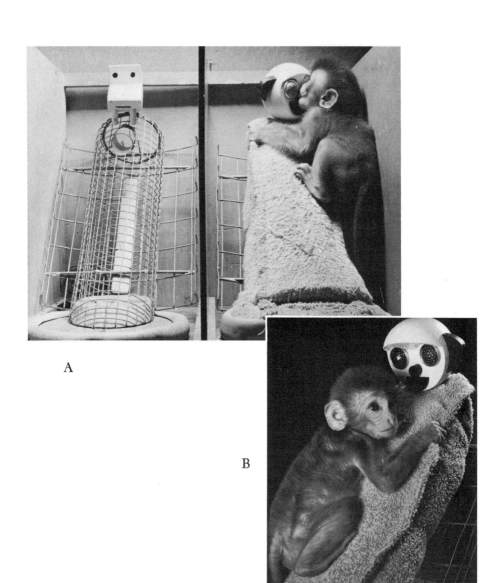

A

B

quite obvious signs of pleasure when so treated, it also gives very unmistakable signs of frustration when neglected; symptoms of maldevelopment appear if this neglect is prolonged. Individual babies will differ in the strength of these early dependency needs, and different cultures will provide varying degrees of facilitation or restraint of these responses. But there can be no doubt that infants everywhere hunger for this comforting and loving attention and that their sense of security and hence emotional development thrives on it just as surely as their bodies thrive on mother's

C

Figure 3–1. Harlow's infant monkeys illustrate the primitive need for physical comforting and succorance which is common to all primates. Given a choice between a wire-frame and a cloth "mother" (A), infants cling to the latter (B), and seek body contact with each other (C) when possible. Most monkeys brought up with such a "deprived childhood" never do grow up normally, while those who get their full share of normal mothering (D), thrive on it. (Courtesy Wisconsin Regional Primate Research Center.)

D

milk. Thus a mother soon learns to judge whether her baby is crying from hunger, from discomfort, or from sheer demand for attention. (It is a wise mother who gives in to the latter just enough to enhance the baby's feeling of security, but not so much as to make her a slave to the baby's whims and egocentric demands.)

However, the infant's relationship with the caring figure in these early months can still be based on little more than a pervasive demand for physical comfort and for pleasant stimulation in its self-centered little world. Neither the development of cortex nor the observable behavior gives any reason to believe that the infant is normally capable of developing a stable concept of "mother" and of reacting to her as a person with

A

B

any clearly conceived set of expectancies that permit participation in a truly social interrelationship. The relationship is undoubtedly much more of a one-way stream, as far as the infant is concerned. The mother, as a caring figure, is at first only a barely recognizable dependable satisfier of immediate physical needs, both visceral and sensorimotor, which include the first crude experience of being loved. It is in that sense that this stage may be referred to as essentially narcissistic or egocentric. However, we prefer to think of it as a presocial stage of ego emergence, not ascribing any more sophistication or romance to the newborn infant than the data would reasonably seem to warrant. Being able first to feel, then to see, and finally to remember a certain caring figure as a giver of pleasant

C

Figure 3–2. Ego emergence and dependency. *From America to Scandinavia to Ghana, a child's sense of security depends on both physical comforting and a sense of being cared for psychologically, which is communicated by the mother even before the infant understands language. (Photo (A) Fujihira from Monkmeyer; (B) and (C), Ken Heyman.)*

sensations, attention, and affection is but a prelude to a truly reciprocal dyadic relationship between two people. It represents at this early stage little more than a process of ego emergence with dependency on the caring figure.

It is even a moot point whether the baby's smile or giggle in response to adult prattle is a truly social response as early as the age of four to six months, though some authorities think it may be (Spitz, 1946; Gesell and Ilg, 1943). Such behavior may be at this early stage just a reflexive kind of reaction to a pleasing sensory stimulus, just as crying is an automatic response to pain or discomfort. We say it is a moot point because for most infants, throughout most of the first year, the emergence of ego manifests itself first in increasing awareness of the self as distinct from the rest of the physical environment, expressing the spontaneous egocentric need for affection, comforting, and efficacy. Memory, perceptual discrimination, and a sense of object relationships are just beginning to develop. Only toward the end of that first year would the average child have developed a sufficiently well-structured and continuing sense of self-and-environmental relationships to have a meaningful conception of "mama and me and what we mean to each other," even though the language for expressing it may still be at the crude monosyllabic stage. Indeed, Piaget (1952), on the basis of exhaustive studies of the development of cognitive capacities of his own children, designates the first year-and-a-half of childhood as essentially the *sensorimotor stage* of cognitive development. The infant is not yet able to conceive of objects as having enduring reality of their own, but perceives them as existing only as long as seen or felt. Nor is the infant capable of thinking of symbolic representation of objects or their qualities or functions, much less of their functional interrelationships. Considering that the infant operates on the principle of immediate and direct sensory apprehension without symbolic significance, and "out of sight out of mind," this early stage of ego emergence scarcely provides the cognitive basis for any truly social interaction.

CURIOSITY AND EFFICACY

If this stage of fleeting sensorimotor, cognitive, and affective response is still too ephemeral and diffuse to provide a basis for true social interaction, it nevertheless provides a sufficient basis for the implementation of efficacy motivation. Indeed, it is the latter which fulfills its biological function of instigating exploratory behavior and attention from early in the very first year of life, so that both psychophysiological and psychosocial development may be enhanced by reality-testing experiences. The work of Piaget is replete with detailed observations and elicitations of infant behavior that not only illustrate the sensorimotor stage of intellectual development but also give unmistakable evidence of efficacy motivation and satisfaction. This is well illustrated by Piaget's observations on Laurent in the fourth month of infancy:

After Laurent has learned to grasp what he sees, I place the string, which is attached to the rattle, in his right hand, merely unrolling it a little so that he may grasp it better. For a moment nothing happens but, at the first shake due to chance movements of his hand, the reaction is immediate: Laurent starts when looking at the rattle and then violently strikes his right hand alone, as if he felt the resistance and the effect. The operation lasts fully a quarter of an hour during which Laurent emits peals of laughter. The phenomenon is all the more clear because, the string being slack, the child must stretch his arm sufficiently and put the right amount of effort into it.

[Two days later] Laurent is subjected to the following experiment. I attach to the rattles (hanging from the bassinet hood) my watch chain and let it hang vertically until it almost reaches his face, in order to see whether he will grasp it and thus shake the celluloid balls. The result is complete negative: when I put the chain in his hands and he shakes it by chance and hears the noise, he immediately waves his hand (as in the foregoing observation) but lets the chain go without understanding that he must grasp it in order to shake the rattle. The following day, however, he discovers the procedure. At first, when I place the chain in his hand . . . Laurent waves his hand, then lets the chain go, while looking at the balls. Then he strikes great blows at random which shake the chain (and the rattle) without his grasping it. Then, without looking, he takes hold of the sheet in front of him (doubtless to suck it, as he does part of the day) and at the same time grasps the chain without recognizing it. The chain then moves the rattle and Laurent again is interested in this sight. Little by little, Laurent thus arrives at discriminating tactilely the chain itself: his hand searches for it as soon as the outer side of his fingers strikes it, he lets go the sheet or coverlet in order to hold the chain alone. Then he immediately swings his arm while looking at the rattle. He therefore seems to have understood that it is the chain, and not his body movements in general, that shakes the rattle. At a certain moment he looks at his hand which holds the chain; then he looks at the chain from top to bottom.

That evening, as soon as he hears the sound of the rattle and sees the chain hanging, he tries to grasp it without looking either at his hand or at the lower end of the chain; . . . as soon as he made contact with the chain he grasped it and shook it. After a few moments of this, he resumes sucking his fingers. But when the chain touches him lightly, he at once removes his right hand from his mouth, grasps the chain, pulls it very slowly while looking at the toys and apparently expecting a noise: after a few seconds during which he still pulls the chain very gently, he shakes much harder and succeeds. He then bursts into peals of laughter, babbles and swings the chain as much as possible (Piaget, 1952, pp. 162-163).

Other observations by Piaget (1952, 1954) show that these sensorimotor explorations into object reality, space relations, and cause and effect proceed by very gradual stages throughout the first year as intellectual matura-

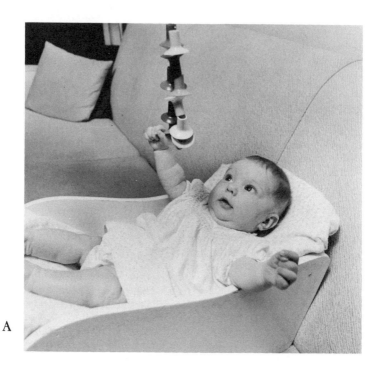

A

B

Figure 3–3. Efficacy
motivation *manifests
itself during early ego
emergence as curiosity and
an urge to manipulate
(just as monkeys do); it
gradually emerges as*
competence motivation
*during primary group
interaction stage of
development* (C). *(Photos
(A) and (B), Merrim,
(C) Zelinka, all from
Monkmeyer.)*

C

tion and experience continually merge in building up the infant's conception of reality. Throughout most of the first year the infant gives evidence of not being able to conceive of the continuing existence and reality of objects unless seen or felt, and only *as long as* they can be seen or felt. Only toward the end of the first year do Piaget's own bright children start to look for objects that have dropped out of sight or out of reach when they "wish to make an interesting sight last" or continue a game of magical influence (efficacy) over the environment. Although he is interested in these phenomena primarily for their significance in tracing the development of the cognition of reality, Piaget incidentally recognizes the efficacy motivation involved. He thus takes efficacy motivation for granted in speaking of the "magicophenomenalistic" conception of causality which the infant seems to be applying throughout the entire middle period (about three to nine months) of the sensorimotor stage of cognitive development.

As soon as the child finds himself in possession of a gesture whose efficacy is revealed in the course of a typical circular reaction he applies it to everything. Thus Laurent, having learned to shake the string attached to his hand in order to shake the bassinet top, waves his empty hand in order to continue the movement of a rattle. Similarly, Jacqueline pulls the string hanging from the top to continue the movement of a book or a bottle, etc., which I swing at a distance. Or again, gestures such as shaking the hand (gesture of farewell), tapping the edge of a bassinet, shaking the head from side to side, shaking the legs, arching oneself up, etc., are used to make some interesting sight last (objects which are moved in front of the child, noises and sounds, etc.).
It is clear that causality of this kind can be interpreted only through the union of efficacy and phenomenalism. On the one hand, the child endows his own gesture with efficacy, independently of any physical or spatial contact. But on the other hand, it is always when this gesture coincides with an internal effect that the subject endows his own action with efficacy (Piaget, 1954, pp. 237-238).

We have suggested that neither the cognitive nor the affective potentialities of the organism provide sufficient basis for truly social behavior during the first few months of life. What does seem to take place is a gradual emergence of ego functioning from the soporific vegetative stage of the newborn to the first quasisocial relationship that becomes crystallized in the conscious mother-child dependency relationship toward the end of the first year. This ego emergence is a complex process of gradual self-awareness, structuring of external reality through transactions with the environment, and the investment of special emotional significance (security-dependence) in the perceived caring figure in its newly discovered self-centered world. During this period the infant does not merely wait for "stimuli" to evoke or condition responses from a fixed repertoire of reflexes. It is actively impelled by a variety of constitutionally based drives to seek certain satisfactions whose ultimate function is to assure survival and growth into adult membership in the species. It cries when hungry and actively seeks the mother's nipple with a ready-made sucking reflex, to be sure. But within a few weeks it is also actively exploring and manipulating the environment, *evoking responses from the environment*, so to speak, to find out what makes *it* tick! Indeed, one is likely to get the impression from Piaget's detailed protocols of infant behavior that the infant acts like a scatterbrained scientist, testing by trial and error and jumping to wild conclusions, laboring under false illusions of magical powers over the environment, achieving fleeting insights which it cannot integrate, being alternately puzzled, distracted, triumphant, and frustrated —but enjoying the quest for its own sake with immeasurable intensity, and learning its first lessons in reality-testing in the process.

The underlying motive for all of this self-generated interest and activity is *efficacy*—the constitutionally based motive that assures the struggle for competence of adaptation and for the *development of the organism's capacities through interaction with the environment.* At this stage it serves to set ego emergence into motion and to assure the development of intellect and affect to the point at which the more complex integration of social awareness and interaction can take place. We shall defer for the time being the question of how learning or exercise is related to maturation of natural functions. What we do posit here is the thesis that simple cognitive, affective, or sensorimotor functions must be developed by some combination of maturation and/or learning before more complex integrations can take place, and that efficacy motivation serves to facilitate the initial development of these functions. Thus, as we have said, the infant must develop perceived distinctions between self and environment, between people and other objects, and some conceptions of time, space, motion, action, cause and effect, etc., before it can establish meaningful relationships between itself and mother. The need for affection can, of course, be satisfied on a more primitive level from the very beginning of infancy, but it will take most of the first year for cognitive-affective integration to produce a truly inter*personal,* dyadic relationship with the mother.

COMMUNICATION AND MOTOR CONTROL

During the second year the basic organismic functions begin to mature to a degree which enhances ego development and interaction with the environment, though the infant is still basically dependent on the caring figure for nourishment, affection, and protection. During this second year most normal children in most cultures advance from creeping on all fours to walking after a fashion, or "toddling." Self-feeding with the utensils and solid foods common to the child-rearing practices of the culture makes its appearance, usually with some help from the caring figure. Typically, this takes the form of "spoon feeding" in Western societies, with the child more and more interested in grasping the spoon himself. In Oriental societies, it typically takes the form of mother and child alternately or optionally conveying rice from the rice bowl to the infant's mouth with the fingers. Toilet-training makes rapid progress during this year, but is usually not fully accomplished until the third or fourth year. All of these functions of motor control and coordination are accompanied and facilitated by verbal communication, which is also undergoing rapid development at this time. Studies of language development in American children (summarized by McCarthy, 1960), show that vocabulary growth takes on a rapid spurt from about three words at age one to about 250–300 words on the average at age two, to about three times that number in the average three-year-old. Much depends, of course, on the nature of the home environment. At the same time, simple sentences of three or four words, including a subject and a verb (present tense), make it easier for the infant to express his needs, feelings, actions, or just to indulge in the satisfying ability to communicate. Verbal restraints, approval, and directions from the caring figure are increasingly understood and immeasurably enhance the socializing effect of this dyadic interaction on the most basic organismic functions. The growing achievements in locomotion, speech, control of feeding and elimination all serve to satisfy the ever-present demands of efficacy, affection, and attention. Though still basically dependent on the mother or other caring figure, the baby's ego enhancement and transactions with the environment progress during this year from the presocial sensorimotor reactions to the first incipient social relationship of dyadic interaction and dependency.

Primary
Group
Interaction

By the third year (give or take a year for individual and/or cultural differences) basic organismic functions have usually matured sufficiently to allow for the integration of these functions into more generalized patterns of social interaction. This takes place when (1) growth and neuromuscular control of bodily functions have matured to include easy erect locomotion, manipulation of objects in the environment, and a degree of control over feeding and toileting—so that basic dependency is reduced and a measure of autonomy is introduced into the daily business of living; (2) cognitive, affective, and verbal interaction have been sufficiently developed to enable the child to establish an appropriate range of interpersonal relationships with the members of the immediate environment. These interactive functions would include perceptual discrimination of individuals, events, and objects, day-to-day memory and stable conceptualization of object relationships, a capacity for sympathetic reactions, and the ability to communicate and understand feelings, intentions, and actions through speech. These are, of course, the same functions that make for social cohesion which we described as emerging during man's long evolution from the lower hominids.

In accordance with our biosocial conception of progressive psychosocial integration of organismic functions, we shall want to designate this stage of personality development by its appropriate level of psychosocial behavior, rather than by any of the organismic functions which make it possible. An appropriate designation for the face-to-face verbal, motor, and emotional interaction and ego elaboration through interpersonal relationships, which take place from about the third year onward, would be *primary group interaction.* We shall postulate a transition to this level of psychosocial behavioral integration during about the third year, continuing to develop largely within that context until about the seventh or eighth year, when more complex symbolic behavior normally begins to appear. Before analyzing this development, let us consider the significance of the term "primary group," which we have deliberately borrowed from its traditional context in sociology.

SIGNIFICANCE OF THE PRIMARY GROUP

The concept of the primary group was introduced by the American sociologist, C. H. Cooley, over sixty years ago. It has become a key concept in the study of social organization and the relationship of personality to culture. What has been generally overlooked, we think, is the appropriateness of this concept for the designation, in operational terms, of the range of processes and interpersonal relationships that take place in the second stage of child personality development. Let us first consider the significance of this concept, as first defined by Cooley (1902), not only for sociology but for personality development:

By primary groups I mean those characterized by intimate face-to-face association and cooperation. They are primary in several senses, but chiefly in that they are fundamental in forming the social nature and ideals of the individual. The result of intimate association, psychologically, is a certain fusion of individualities in a common life and purpose of the group. Perhaps the simplest way of describing the wholeness is by saying that it is a "we"; it involves the sort of sympathy and mutual identification for which "we" is the natural expression. One lives in the feeling of the whole and finds the chief aims of his will in that feeling.

It is not to be supposed that the unity of the primary group is one of mere harmony and love. It is always a differentiated and usually a competitive unity, admitting of self-assertion and various appropriate passions; but these passions are socialized by sympathy. . . .

The most important spheres of this intimate association and cooperation—though by no means the only ones—are the family, the play-group of children, and the neighborhood or community group of elders. These are practically universal, belonging to all times and all stages of development, and are accordingly a chief basis of what is universal in human nature and human ideals. (Cooley, 1902 [1956]).

We can see from the above, and from a mass of psychological and sociological literature on the subject, that primary group interaction does provide a universal basis for the socialization of the ego through group identification and interaction. It is universal because the family is universal to begin with. Peer groups and community groups follow in due course, not merely under the pressure of circumstances that are necessary for food and shelter and eventual reproduction, but under the pressure of a variety of basic motives, including (especially) social ego needs. We have already made the point that it was natural selection that converted this socializing tendency from a fortuitous means to an end to a constitutionally motivated end in itself. We now merely recognize that the first stage of development of this emergent function of human nature, after an initial or presocial stage of ego emergence, is the stage of primary group interaction.

Another way of putting it would be to say that the biosocial potentialities of the organism (which we discussed in Chapter 2) will undergo development and canalization through primary group interaction in early childhood because that is the level of social interaction that the organism is capable of at this stage. This means that the human personality, having developed beyond the stage of crude ego emergence through sensorimotor contact with the environment, now continues to develop through communication, emotional involvement, and other behavioral transactions with the significant figures in the immediate environment. It will not be ready for more complex social interaction until the end of this period. The basic reason for the limitation of personality development to primary group interaction and identification during these years is that the cognitive functions and reactive capacities of the child are still principally concrete, overt, here-and-now reactions to overt stimuli in the immediate environment, with little capability of value judgment or abstraction. The human family or its equivalent provides the necessary and sufficient social milieu for these concrete cognitive and related affective functions to develop.

The primary group need not be a clearly defined nuclear family group as we know it in Western civilization. There are numerous variations of extended families, communal interfamilial arrangements, and even special housing conditions which may take precedence over "blood" relationships. There are many African tribes in which the rearing of children is jointly shared by adults of the community. In the Israeli *Kibbutz* (cooperative settlement) the nuclear family is replaced in large measure by a nursery group arrangement under the supervision of a caretaker called the *metapelet*. The child's primary group then becomes an enlarged peer group consisting of the children of many families with the *metapelet* as the chief caring figure, supplemented by intermittent mothering and fatherly attentions by the child's real parents. This, according to Bettelheim (1969), obviates much of the oedipal conflict and sibling rivalry so prevalent in Western society, and fosters a more cooperative peer interaction.

A unique style of communal housing determines primary group interaction and identification among certain tribes in Borneo (Sarawak). There, along the banks of the Rajang River, Iban and Kayan tribesmen live in "longhouses" which accommodate an entire community in one long house.

The longhouse, which accommodates one loosely defined family in each of its multipurpose rooms, is essentially a communal living arrangement that predetermines all social interaction for the thirty or forty families that inhabit it. The children of the entire "housing project" play together in sex-peer groups, while the women all perform their daily chores, gossiping together on the long veranda of the longhouse. The men go out in groups to hunt, fish, or cultivate rice for the longhouse community. The family unit is very fluid and unstable, not readily identifiable except by the fact that a roughly defined family unit occupies one room of the longhouse. Children of one family are often informally adopted or borrowed by other families in the same or another longhouse as a matter of friendly relations or convenience. Divorce of a spouse is a simple and easily accomplished procedure by declaration of divorce to the *pengulu* (tribal chieftain) and payment of a small fee. Under these circumstances, the primary group is really the longhouse population of loosely defined and intermingled families.

However defined, the primary group in which the child is reared provides the medium for the first stage of psychosocial development beyond ego emergence and basic dependency. The child's sense of selfhood, its need to be cared for physically and emotionally, to communicate its wants and to communicate just for communication's sake, to expand its sense of efficacy in coming to grips with the environment, and to receive attention and affection—all of these are further cultivated by interaction with the primary group. In this way the diffuse social ego needs become canalized in terms of emotional attachments within the primary group as well as certain behavioral operations that provide outlets for these needs. This involves learning, from experience and daily repetition, who is who and what may be expected from each significant member of the group, and what they expect in turn; what is right and wrong by the opportunistic criterion of bringing approval or disapproval; how to modify behavior to win affection; testing the limits for impulse gratification and self-assertion. In short, it involves the first stage of introception of the social mores as defined by the group in concrete operational terms.

UNDERLYING ORGANISMIC FUNCTIONS

All cognitive, affective, and motor development becomes integrated with psychosocial development. Thus the walking and talking which every normal child learns during the second year constitute no mere mechanical achievements of neuromuscular efficiency; nor is increased memory span and perceptual discrimination a mere increase in receptor capacity. All are prerequisites for integrated transactions with the environment by the third year, and the child eagerly undertakes them with everyone and everything in that environment. Some transactions are permitted, some encouraged, some punished or disapproved of, and pleasurable experiences are frequently dependent on "knowing the rules." Certain long-accustomed physical functions, such as eating and eliminating, must now be performed in a certain manner and at times and places apparently insisted upon by the caring figure. The most potent force in inducing control of physiological functions and aggressive impulses is undoubtedly the child's desire for parental approval, which may be communicated by a word, a smile, or just the absence of punishment. The fact that we are dealing with a basic generic need for approval is readily confirmed by the fact that even punishment need not be anything so crude as spanking or withholding food; a mild scolding or gesture of disapproval will do just as well. And if the materialistic observer thinks that the child's call for attention is predicated on a signal for food or comfort, let him observe how often the child demands attention *after* being fed, or when it has no demands other than to "just talk."

From the third year onward the child shows increasing need and capacity to relate to other individuals, especially peers. Various observers (e.g., Marshall, 1961; Stone and Church, 1968) agree that play activities undergo a marked change between the second and third year. Whereas in the second year, children typically play by manipulating objects in solitary exploration, by the third year they are typically playing *with* and talking to each other in genuinely associative relationship. Observations of nursery children show increasing demands for attention and praise from the age of four onward. Affection for adults and peers is noticeable from age one, but increases rapidly throughout childhood, becoming highly differentiated by age four.

Of crucial importance to the emotional and social development of the child is the emergence during this period of *sympathy*—that same sympathy which Darwin recognized as the crucial function whose emergence marked the evolution and survival of *Homo sapiens* as a social animal. Lois Murphy (1937) noted that three- or four-year-old children typically showed sympathetic protective concern for the pain or distress of playmates in a nursery. Even two-year-olds showed some measure of sympathetic awareness and concern under similar circumstances, but were unable to do anything about it. Watching small groups of nursery children for hundreds of hours, Murphy was able to record an average of almost two incidents per hour which clearly met criteria for demonstrations of sympathy. At the same time, a far smaller number of "unsympathetic" responses were recorded. This is highly significant for human character development. What we invariably find during this period of personality development is that the egocentricity of early infancy continues during the primary group interaction stage: "I want what I want when I want it!"

However, it is now very extensively modified by this sympathetic or empathic tendency, which we shall call *primary altruism*—"You are like me, and if anything hurts you, it hurts me a little, too." What we wish to emphasize here is that this primary altruism, while subject to learning in the course of primary group interaction, is not in itself a purely learned function. It is based on man's natural capacity for sympathy, which is subject to canalization through experience.

In most "civilized" cultures, hostile or destructive responses are generally discouraged by disapproval or outright restraint. To the extent that aggression gives way to the desire for approval, there is evidence that the latter is the stronger need. To the extent that aggression spontaneously appears as a method of getting one's way and just as spontaneously gives way to continued friendly interaction, it likewise proves its transitory instrumental characteristic in the total pattern of developing interpersonal relationships. Children will typically fight over a toy or over "who's next" and go right on playing as the best of friends. Even the fighting (up to a point) carries overtones of playful social interaction which is more satisfying than frustrating in promoting vivid, interpersonal experiences. Indeed, the physical interaction among peers may be regarded as largely a continuation of the earlier sensory exploration of the environment on a new plane of interpersonal relationships. Playing with others is simply found to be more fun than playing alone. The "others" may include other "real live people" like cats or rabbits, or imaginary ones like teddy bears and dolls, but there can be no doubt that having other people to talk to and play with is *"really livin'."*

The universal phenomenon of animism in early childhood bespeaks the ubiquitous tendency of emerging human empathy to ascribe human characteristics to animal and even inanimate objects. Chief among these characteristics are voluntary action, sensitivity, and individual personality— characteristics which the child is becoming dimly aware of in himself, and which his empathy leads him to assume are characteristic of all living things as he conceives of them. (For studies of animism see Piaget, 1929.) In any case, interaction with the other living things that populate his immediate environment, and especially with the real people who are so much like himself, provides daily experience in the expansion of the ego to the first truly social level of awareness: primary group identification, with its highly significant manifestation of primary altruism.

A more complex interrelationship of self to members of the primary group constellation develops as cognitive and affective capacities develop during the third and fourth year, and experience makes demands on these capacities. The child learns to expect certain satisfactions and restraints from parents, playful-competitive-sympathetic interactions from peers, protection or torment or condescension from some older figures. Some special relationships like "sibling rivalry" may grow out of particular intra-familial constellations of temperaments with competing demands for attention. By the fourth or fifth year, a highly complex system of inter-personal relationships has developed, in terms of which the child perceives his identity as a function of social interaction: how others relate to him and he to them, what he can and cannot do, what he *may* or may not do, what he can expect from whom, and what this business of daily living with other people is all about.

The development of these interpersonal relationships which help to structure the self-concept and emotional adjustment is greatly enhanced by the elaboration of emotional reactivity along with perceptual discrim-ination. Reactive capacities have passed beyond the primitive emotional reactions which served its dependency needs in the first year or two (cf. Fig. 3–4). From the third year to about the seventh or eighth year, the child is increasingly able to react with specific affection, jealousy, dis-appointment, self-assertion, pride, curiosity, humor—and *sympathy*. He has likes and dislikes of people, activities, and things; he learns how to conform and curry favor in his primary group environment, as well as how to "test the limits" of self-assertion and manipulation of others, depending on his temperamental predispositions and the environmental canalizations of these social ego needs. The highly differentiated emotional reactions and interpersonal relationships are greatly enhanced by the growth of

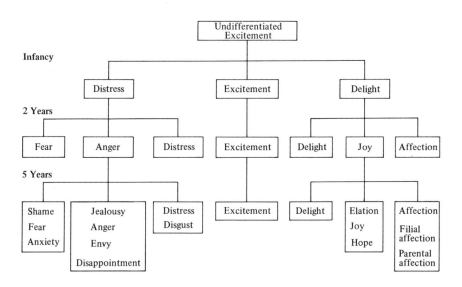

Figure 3–4. Differentiation of emotional capacities in childhood. (*After Bridges, 1932.*)

language and the intellectual development that must support it. The child is thus increasingly able to establish play-companionships, verbal rivalries (boasting contests), interest in adult or peer experiences, stories, or gossip, audiences for his own fantasies, and some immature conceptions of justice and morality (cf. Piaget, 1948).

This is fully and frankly a period of rapid psychosocial development that is distinctly human, making fully integrated use of a wide spectrum of organismic capacities which are fairly well advanced in their phylogenetic development, but are arriving at an early stage of ontogenetic development during this period. As human personality development goes, it is still far from approaching maturity in any sense. It is limited in scope and in its capacity for psychosocial integration by the affective, cognitive, and psychomotor limitations of childhood organismic functioning. Chief among these is the limited capacity for abstract thinking, for self-restraint, and for certain critical refinements of the self-concept which rest heavily on further experiences and the maturation of the organism itself.

Secondary
Socialization
Starting with about the seventh or eighth year of life, psychosocial development of the average child enters a new phase, which is heavily dependent on continuing experiences in the primary group, but involves considerable learning and understanding of social meanings, values, and relationships. Awareness of the environment and relationship of self to others now begins to extend beyond concrete interaction with members of the family and peer groups in the here-and-now situations of everyday life. There is a growing awareness of family and group structures, social custom, similarities and differences among people, rules of right and wrong, and underlying social values. There are many other abstract ideas to be learned and communicated, as well as feelings of others to be understood and their reactions anticipated. Though much of this development is subject to learning and differs with the social mores of the child's subculture, biosocial theory holds that the stage itself is not only possible but inevitable because of the maturation and integration of basic organismic capacities and needs. As it was in primary group interaction, these organismic functions are principally cognitive, affective, and psychomotor. Let us consider the development of cognition first.

COGNITIVE COMPONENT

One essential difference between the three-year-old and the seven-year-old lies in the newly developed capacity for abstract thinking and communication, which is virtually absent in the three-year-old, but reaches a stable and demonstrable level of functioning by the seventh year. An easy way of checking this generalization is to compare the subtests included at the III-Year level and VII-Year level on the Stanford-Binet Intelligence Scale. These are the cognitive tasks that have been found by empirical sampling and testing to be indicative of the mental capacities of the average three-year-old and seven-year-old child in the United States, with comparable results in many other countries.

Standford-Binet Subtests
Year III
1. Stringing Beads
2. Picture Vocabulary
3. Block Building: Bridge
4. Picture Memories
5. Copying a Circle
6. Drawing a Vertical Line

Year VII
1. Picture Absurdities (Interpretation)
2. Similarities: Two Things
3. Copying a Diamond
4. Comprehension (Appropriate Behavior)
5. Opposite Analogies
6. Repeating 5 Digits

It can be seen from the above test batteries that whereas none of the tasks at the three-year-level involves frankly abstract thinking, four of the six tests at the seven-year-level (all except tasks 3 and 6) do involve abstract concepts. By the time the XII-Year level is reached on the Stanford-Binet, virtually all of the tests involve abstract thinking to some degree, mostly on a verbal level. Although schooling and cultural handicaps sometimes obscure individual and group differences in IQ, fifty years of research have substantiated fairly well the fact that the progression of tasks from year to year on the Stanford-Binet is indicative of the sequence of maturation of cognitive and communicative capacities from childhood to adolescence.

This emerging capacity for abstract thinking makes possible a transition from primary group interaction to secondary group (reference group) identifications. It also facilitates the introception of the social mores. In terms of humanitarian or ethical concepts, for example, it makes possible a transition from directly empathic or utilitarian ethics to the understanding and introception of broader moral concepts and rules of fair play as a matter of principle. As a developmental reflection of human evolution, it probably represents the advance from the mental capacities of the group-hunting protohominids of the early Pleistocene epoch to the first organized community life of the Mesolithic age—an advance that took over a million years of natural selection to accomplish. Let it not be thought, therefore, that in designating an advance from primary group interaction to secondary socialization we are merely making use of a convenient sociological abstraction to indicate an enlarged scope of activity and mobility. We are indicating a new frontier of social consciousness and enlarged self-concept, of the channeling of basic motives by the social mores, and of the individual's very conception of his place in human society.

SOCIAL PERCEPTION AND EMPATHY

To be fully effective in facilitating social interaction on something more than a concrete ad hoc basis, the emerging capacity for cognitive abstraction and communication must be integrated with a more sophisticated development of sympathy and interpersonal relationships. We have already noted that sympathy can be observed in three- and four-year-old nursery children (Murphy, 1937). Other studies have shown that this capacity continues to develop with age. Flapan (1968) successfully used sound motion pictures to give a standardized series of close-to-real-life situations for children to react to in terms of their understanding of what the situations conveyed. Though lacking the spontaneity of direct interpersonal interaction by the subjects themselves, this technique did have the advantage of presenting the same series of situations to each subject and getting responses that could be classified in terms of their sympathetic understanding of the feelings, reactions, and intentions of the children and adults portrayed in these little story sequences. Sixty girls of normal intelligence were tested, comprised of groups of 20 in each of three age groups: six, nine, and twelve. All subjects were shown two short movie sequences broken up into shorter segments, each dramatizing an episode in the life of a family, with some interplay of emotions and desires. The subjects were then asked to describe what went on in each film segment, and were queried further to make sure their understanding and empathy had been fully reported.

The results (Table 3–1) showed that all or almost all of the subjects were able to give descriptions of overt situational activity, of verbal and expressive movement behavior by the family members portrayed in the films, and could correctly describe their more obvious feelings and emotions. All of these responses, it will be noted, represent the concrete attitudes, perceptions, and direct empathic responses which we have postulated as being characteristic of the primary group interaction stage of child development. When it came to more abstract interpretations, the results showed that the six-year-olds lagged behind the nine- and 12-year-olds,

Table 3–1 NUMBER OF CHILDREN AT EACH AGE LEVEL WHO, IN THEIR ACCOUNTS OF WHAT HAPPENED IN THE MOVIES, USED STATEMENTS CLASSIFIED IN THE VARIOUS CATEGORIES
(From Flapan, 1968)

Categories of Statements	Number Of 6-Yr.-Olds	Number Of 9-Yr.-Olds	Number Of 12-Yr.-Olds
Reporting & Describing			
Situation-action	20	20	20
Verbal communication	20	20	20
Expressive behavior	16	17	17
Obvious feelings	19	19	20
Obvious intentions	13	20	20
Explaining			
In situational terms	10	19	19
In psychological terms	3	12	14
In terms of interpersonal perceptions	0	6	6
Interpreting-Inferring			
Feelings	0	13	18
Thoughts-expectations	2	13	15
Intentions-motives	2	6	10
Interpersonal perceptions	0	4	7

N at each age is 20.

displaying little capacity for subtler interpretations of interpersonal relations, thoughts, expectations, or intentions. Indeed, understanding the interpersonal perceptions of *others* (explaining or interpreting *their* interpretive reactions to each other) seemed to be little developed even by age 12 in this study, so that further development of these abstract-empathic cognitions into adolescence is implied. The author of this study points out the difficulty of judging children's capacities to react, from their descriptions and answers to questions on interview, because verbal expression may lag behind interpersonal sensitivity and understanding. That is, a child may understand or sense more than it can explain verbally. With that caution in mind, we would nevertheless say that the results are thoroughly consistent with the developmental sequence in psychosocial reactive capacities that we are postulating here.

According to this conception, the primary group interaction, which is characteristic of the concrete, face-to-face, sensorimotor interaction capacities of children from about the third year, begins to enter a new phase of enlarged socialization capacities in about the seventh or eighth year. This stage requires more abstract cognitive capacities, as well as subtle integration of affect and cognition and empathy, so that other people's feelings are more readily understood and anticipated. With the addition of verbal abstractions, values, and rituals, the social mores are more readily formulated and introcepted, and the meaning of social situations better understood beyond their superficial content. There are principles and expectancies underlying behavior, and ways of eliciting approval and satisfaction. Not to be overlooked in the psychomotor sphere is the development of skills which almost every culture offers to preadolescents as outlets for their efficacy and social approval needs. The American child may master his two-wheeler bicycle (with or without the proverbial "Look, ma, no hands!") or show his prowess in classroom or sport. A peasant boy or girl anywhere in the world may help with farm or household chores. Participation in religious ritual may be requisite in some cultures, skill in the "manly art of self-defense" in others, stealing or begging in still others. The preadolescent gang or clique may extend the primary group interaction to formulate a social code of its own in circumvention or in defiance of some aspect of the adult-dictated social mores.

All of this is subsumed under "secondary socialization" which, according to biosocial theory, is predicated on the maturation and integration of cognitive-affective-psychomotor functions that are inherent in the evolution of the species.

REFERENCE GROUP IDENTIFICATION

This growing capacity for first-order abstraction in the form of categorization, generalization, and discrimination, based on primary group experience, probably has its greatest impact on personality through the restructuring of social identification of the self. Identity, as we pointed out earlier, begins universally during the ego emergence and dependency stage as the self that is being cared for by the caring figure, while discovering and manipulating the environment. It continues during the primary group interaction stage to be elaborated as a group membership with varying interpersonal relationships and expectancies with respect to parents, peers, and others in the immediate environment. It also involves such first-order categorizations as being a boy or a girl, little or big. As the capacity for second-order abstractions develops, the child becomes attuned to the social mores and values attached to these and other categories of identification. Being a boy or a girl begins to mean more than a mere categorical physical resemblance. There are vast social implications in being a boy or a girl—in being the same kind of a person as one's mother or one's father. The socially prescribed distinctions in play behavior, treatment by parents, and association between the sexes have already made that clear; further discussion and observation with occasional parental admonition continue to make it clearer.

One thus becomes not only a member of a family group that lives together and interacts daily in face-to-face confrontations but also a

Figure 3–5. Secondary socialization *grows naturally out of primary group interaction as organismic functions (especially abstract thinking) mature to the requisite level. Whether in boys' sports contests or in a girls' gossiping circle, preadolescents begin to understand and put into practice the attitudes, values, and mores of their culture. (Photos by Ken Heyman.)*

member of another kind of social grouping according to sex. This social distinction transcends family lines: it applies to all people everywhere, whether seen or unseen, and it entails vast implications for behavior in terms of social mores. It soon becomes not only evident but also meaningful to the preadolescent intellect that boys and girls are treated differently in all family groups, that their destinies follow the lines of family roles for mothers and fathers prescribed by the culture, that there are rules of approved and disapproved behavior for each sex and for contact between them, and that even the play activities of each group are pretty definitely prescribed by the mores of the adult world. But this requires no deliberate regimentation of behavior into culturally prescribed channels. Social ego needs impel the preadolescent to seek acceptance from both peers and parents just as he did during the primary group interaction stage; but now approval and conformity involve an understanding of social group distinctions and mores. Identification with the parents now involves a growing appreciation of the parental sex role in the family and society as well as the prototypes for aspirations to social competence.

The nature of the sex-role mores as well as the degree of sophistication inculcated in the preadolescent will, of course, vary with the culture and

the individual and situational circumstances. The games played, the folklore heard from adults or transmitted among peers, the rituals observed, the implements and dress used, the behavior approved or punished, all contribute to the boy or girl's growing awareness of the social mores surrounding sex-role behavior in their culture. They not only learn these values verbally and conceptually but also introcept them as part of their own growing system of beliefs and understandings about life, i.e., as part of their own ego structures. This sex-age-group identification and adoption of social mores is predicated on earlier primary group interaction but can now be elaborated by the further maturation of cognitive and other organismic functions.

Most cultures provide other secondary or reference group structures as vehicles for secondary socialization that ordinarily becomes operative at this period. These are the ethnic reference groups that are based on more intangible criteria of group distinctions such as religious, class, tribal, national, or racial affiliations. The child may have picked up the *verbal* family identification of being white or black, Hindu or Moslem, "poor folks" or "better-class people" during the primary group interaction experiences of childhood. However, such nominal reference group distinctions usually do not convey any great significance to the child's self-concept and emotional adjustment until this preadolescent period. For one thing, the limited mobility of childhood deprives him of the necessary breadth of validating experiences in the society at large. More importantly, a capacity for conceptual abstraction is necessary to appreciate the meaning of an intangible reference group and the subtle implications of discrimination and custom that may be involved. Furthermore, a degree of social sensitivity beyond primary altruism is required to appreciate the subtle emotional ramifications of reference group identification. Thus, at some time around the seventh to eighth year (or a little sooner or later, depending on the culture or the individual), the growing social consciousness of the child enables him to become aware of the true social significance of any *reference group identifications* that may apply to him, his family, or "his kind of people." The natural tendency of the perceptually self-centered child upon first encountering these secondary group distinctions is to assume that its own group is "good" or "right" or worthy of his loyalty. We would call this *latent ethnocentrism*, recognizing that identification may take place on the basis of experienced common interest, proximity, familiarity, similarity of values or mores or even physical characteristics as a by-product of secondary socialization. The cultivation of actual ethnocentrism or race prejudice will depend on whether the environmental norms and experiences continue to provide suggestion and reinforcement for the channeling of social ego needs along ethnocentric lines or along humane-egalitarian principles.

What happens to the child who becomes aware of the fact that he is unmistakably identified with a stigmatized or "inferior" group? Frustration of social ego needs inevitably comes into play, with defensive strategies against rejection and self-deprecation resorted to all through adolescence and adulthood. This may range from overt and covert hostility to placid compliance with the expected subservient role. The southern American Negro, for example, has long been expected to behave in an outwardly subservient and slow-witted manner and to show that he "knows his place." Preadolescent Negroes learned this behavior from their elders with increasing resistance, generation after generation, while white preadolescents learned to expect this behavior and the segregation and condescension that went along with it. Current desegregation practices are, of course, bringing about a changing pattern of socialization adjustments for both Negroes and whites in many parts of the country. Nevertheless, many families and groups have always maintained humane-egalitarian relationships regardless of ethnic identification, and preadolescents in these environments have readily absorbed these values as well. The characterological implications of these diverse influences on human relationships are obviously just as great for the child of the in-group as for the child of the minority group.

Membership in stigmatized ethnic groups does tend to accelerate ethnic awareness (Hartley, 1948; Clark, 1963); but even so, there is evidence that full appreciation of its emotional ego-involvements does not ordinarily develop until after age seven or eight. This appreciation of *ethnic identification* with all of its connotations of pride or stigma, acceptance or rejection, is a signficant stage beyond the mere nominal distinctions learned in primary group interaction. As Deutsch *et al.* (1968) state in summarizing research on the development of Negro-white racial concepts in childhood:

Not only is the Negro child racially aware by the age of four of five, but he has already learned the relevant words, concepts, and phrases, used to describe members of his own and other racial (and ethnic) groups. He uses these terms to describe himself and others; however, there is evidence that until age eight or nine his racial conception is somewhat more apparent than real— that is, the child seems to have a "verbal fluency" rather than a conceptual understanding of racial categories . . . In a study of the development of racial concepts in white New Zealand children, Vaughan (1963) found that the actual attainment of racial concepts (categorization) first appears at seven years of age and only after the child has learned to identify and then to discriminate among members of different racial groups. (Deutsch, *et al.*, 1968, pp. 185-186)

We would therefore say that true racial awareness does not ordinarily develop until this preadolescent period and may then become one of the highly significant features of the stage of development we call secondary socialization. Such ethnic awareness with its ethnocentric, group-defensive, or humane-egalitarian attitudes will greatly influence the canalization of social ego needs through reference group identifications. It will help to shape the self-concept, interpersonal relationships, and role-learning adjustments all through adolescence and adulthood. It is, therefore, highly important that we attempt to understand some of the factors that influence incipient ethnocentrism during this secondary socialization stage.

Some authorities regard children's learning of ethnocentric attitudes, like that of all social attitudes, largely a matter of imitation of parents with whom they identify and whose approval they seek. Other authorities, citing extensive studies of prejudice, point out that displaced aggression or "scapegoating" is a predominant feature of prejudice toward minority groups outside of one's own. A study by Epstein and Komorita (1966) suggests that, in the age group we are discussing, identification with parents is the predominant feature of incipient ethnocentrism, even when displaced aggression resulting from punitive treatment is considered. They based their conclusion on a study of 180 American white Catholic children in grades three to five (about nine to eleven years of age, or well within our "secondary socialization stage"). Using an improvised social distance scale[2] for an imaginary group called the "Piraneans," they showed the 180 Ss pictures of supposed Piraneans who were actually Negroes, Orientals, or whites. These people were further subdivided into working-class or middle-class groups (indicated by recognizable features of slum or suburban living conditions). This gave three racial and two socioeconomic groupings, or six groups in all. The children were then rated on generalized ethnocentrism by getting social distance ratings on nine actual ethnic groups. Finally, three weeks later, the children were asked how their parents would rate these groups (first independent variable). As a second independent variable, ratings of parental punitiveness were obtained on a scale the investigators had previously devised. Social distance was found to be greatest for the Piraneans when they were represented as Negroes, or as members of the (lower) working class, regardless of race. There was also a general tendency for the children's ethnocentrism to correspond to the degree of ethnocentrism reported for the parents of each child. But when the parents were divided into high, medium, and low degrees of punitive treatment of their children (i.e., degrees of discipline), it was found that the *medium punitive* (though love-oriented) parental group produced the highest degree of correspondence in the ethnocentric tendencies of their children. The authors regarded the latter result as confirming the studies of Sears and others which show that moderate, "love-oriented discipline" is more likely to lead to emulation of the parent than either permissiveness or excessive punitiveness.

---

[2] Originally devised by Bogardus, the social distance scale measures ethnocentrism by indicating the degree of close association the subject will permit with different ethnic groups: e.g., marriage, visits, etc.

Other studies of ethnocentric attitudes and stereotypes, which we shall refer to again in later chapters, show that such forms of social identification can and do develop, along with altruistic attitudes. Whatever the pattern of social stratification and reference group structure the society may provide, it inevitably influences the growing child's conception of his place in society and the rules for adjusting to it in the pursuit of social ego gratifications. This is widely recognized by students of social learning. We regard such interpersonal relationships and social attitudes as some of the learned by-products of the secondary socialization stage of a species that is biosocial to begin with.

TRANSITION TO ROLE DIFFERENTIATION

In the course of mental and physical growth and cumulative experience in secondary socialization, interpersonal relationships continue to undergo categorization and differentiation. By the time puberty is reached, these differentiated behavior patterns have begun to assume the character of social roles which preadolescents have begun to recognize or impute to each other—at least to the more visible members of the primary group. It will be recalled that Flapan's study, discussed earlier in this chapter, showed that 12-year-olds were far more adept at understanding and interpreting the thoughts, feelings, expectations, and motives of individuals in the enacted true-to-life action sequences than even 9-year-olds. This degree of social sensitivity enables average 12- or 13-year-olds to recognize the distinctive characteristics or behavior patterns of their peers. A study by Peck and Galliani (1962) showed that children can readily agree on character names for some of their peers, which go beyond the indiscriminate use of nicknames that characterize the primary group interaction stage. What is more impressive, the role designations bear some resemblance to the actual behavior characteristics noted by adults, and the intrinsic characteristics (such as intelligence) revealed by tests.

Peck and Galliani illustrated this ability by testing and observing 1,217 seventh-grade boys and girls drawn from three Texas communities. The sample contained a fairly large Mexican minority among the predominantly North American white population, so that it was possible at the same time to test the effect of ethnic bias on the recognition of such primary group roles. The subjects were asked to identify individuals who fit the following roles:

WHEELS—
Name three persons about your age who sort of "make the wheels go 'round." They are boys and girls who tend to run things wherever they are. "They're tops."

BRAINS—
Name three persons about your age who are sort of "brains." They are boys and girls who get their ideas from books. They tend to do what older people want.

AVERAGE ONES—
Name three persons about your age who are sort of "average ones." Outside of school, they run around quite a bit, but they're not "wild."

QUIET ONES—
Name three persons about your age who are sort of quiet. They're often forgotten or just not noticed.

WILD ONES—
Name three persons about your age who are sort of "wild ones." They are boys and girls who could get into trouble.

LEFT OUTS—
Name three persons about your age who are "left out" of things on purpose. They make other people feel uncomfortable.

BIG IMAGINATIONS—
Name three people about your age who have good imaginations. They have new ideas and new ways of doing things.

DAY-DREAMERS—
Name three people about your age who daydream a great deal. The things they dream and think about often do not make sense.

The results showed that (1) there was general agreement among the seventh-graders in designating different classmates for the eight character-roles described above; (2) the character-roles which obviously call for higher intelligence (*wheels, brains,* and *big imaginations*) have a preponderance of higher IQ peer nominations; (3) proportionately fewer Mexicans are nominated for any of the character-roles by both Anglo-Americans and Latin-Americans. The first two results are seen as demonstrating both the character differentiation of pubescent children and their ability to discriminate such character or role differentiation. The last-mentioned result indicates the influence of ethnic bias on the perceptions of the Anglo-Americans and the awareness of minority group status among the Mexicans.

The above study does not investigate, but we may duly note, the fact that by puberty children have developed the ability not only to perceive but to act out peer-group character-roles which reflect their individual temperaments, interests, and gradually emerging values.

CHARACTER DEVELOPMENT

We have already dealt implicitly with one aspect of character development in postulating a latent ethnocentric aspect of reference group identification, depending on the cultural influences present during the secondary socialization stage. The outcome of this always latent possibility in human relationships will usually not become overt, if it does at all, until the adult-role-anticipation stage of adolescence. In preadolescence it may be nothing more than mild xenophobia. On the other hand, primary empathic altruism is likely to continue to develop at least within the reference group framework, now elaborated by emerging conceptions of loyalty, identity, reciprocity, compatibility of interests and temperament, and inculcation of social ideals. Passionate friendships based on reciprocation of loyalties, interest, and favors may be formed, while fantasies run to identification with national or mythical heroes conveyed by whatever media of communication may exist in that particular community. This may vary, of course, from the legends handed down by parents or medicine men in primitive tribes to space-man adventures on American TV. The ability to understand and to empathize with the reactions of others, as well as to anticipate their reactions and the values they share in common, makes this more of a stage of social-interest sharing, reciprocation of loyalties and abiding by consideration of others, than was possible during primary group interaction.

In the realm of moral judgments, Piaget (1948) has postulated a transition from objective (material) damage done to subjective responsibility for *intent*, after about age seven. This development also implies the ability to understand a moral principle at the preadolescent stage. In attempting to test this hypothesis against the alternative theory of social learning by imitation, Bandura and McDonald (1963) tested 78 boys and 87 girls aged five to eleven on Piaget-type moral judgment stories. The experimental variable was the introduction of a confederate model who made a predetermined moral judgment in the objective direction for some of the subjects, but not for the others. The experimenters found that judgments of subjective responsibility (guilt, according to intent or innocence) did in fact increase with age, but that reinforcement by models expressing contrary views could reverse the trend in the experimental situation. The results were replicated by Cowan, *et al.* (1969), who pointed out, however, that predominance of model imitation in a one-shot laboratory situation does not preclude the epigenesis of moral judgment standards in real life, as postulated by Piaget.

We would suggest that the introception of moral standards by social suggestion and imitation is quite consistent with biosocial theory, but that cognitive maturation must likewise be reckoned with. It is understood that different adult cultures may inculcate radically different moral standards in their preadolescents (as, in fact, they do); but it is still not until the preadolescent stage of secondary socialization that normally intelligent individuals begin to understand the *principles* that are being inculcated by precept or example, even though younger children may give lip-service to such precepts and imitate the behavior of adults in specific instances.

4

Adolescence—
the
Adult
Role
Anticipation
Stage

Biosocial Meaning
      of
   Adolescence   Adolescence, the transitional period from puberty to earliest adulthood, cannot be accurately pinpointed as to its age limits, because the onset of puberty varies somewhat with the individual and the assumption of adult status varies greatly with the individual, class, and culture. Nevertheless, the advent of sexual maturity clearly marks a new and highly significant stage of personality development. Formal recognition of this approach or transition to adulthood is contained in the puberty rites or religious "confirmation" ceremonies of some cultures; less formal but equally pervasive recognition is given in the customs of sex-role differentiation from puberty onward in virtually all cultures. Theoretical or empirical studies of personality development invariably treat adolescence as a period of growth with its own special characteristics, although insufficient attention is usually paid to its cultural variations. Freudian

theory, focused as it is on psychosexual development as the key to personality, regards the advent of the "genital stage" at puberty as the culmination of that development, beyond which there are no further essential psychobiological changes. From that point of view, psychosocial development would be regarded as learned sublimations of the psychosexual.

From the viewpoint of biosocial theory, however, it is not sufficient to recognize the maturation of one aspect of psychophysiological development as the key to the maturation of the entire personality, however significant that aspect may be. There are other aspects of organismic functioning, such as the cognitive, affective, and psychomotor, which are also crucial to the development of the total personality. Not only is each of these qualities significant in itself for particular purposes of analysis, but we must also recognize that the *maturation and integration of all organismic functions leads to a more advanced level of integration at the psychosocial level.* New frontiers of interpersonal relations are opened up for exploration; greater refinements of self-concepts emerge along with more extensive introception of the social mores, elaboration of values, attitudes, role-defined skills, goals, and styles of life. All of these facets further delineate each personality as an individual and as a member of society. It is this psychosocial level of functioning, as we have maintained, that provides a more salient and integrative representation of the total personality. We shall, therefore, consider the true significance of adolescence as the stage of development in which the integrated organism is in process of *becoming an adult member of society.*

This presupposes a certain level of organismic maturation and an environmental milieu that is normal for the species. The normal environmental milieu for the human is, of course, the social one, even though its cultural characteristics will vary widely from one society to another. We shall want to see how the organismic changes that occur in the years beginning with pubescence, as well as the awareness of approaching adulthood on the part of the individual and society, bring about a more highly differentiated level of interaction with that social milieu. It might be sufficient merely to designate this stage as "adolescence" and let it go at that, if we were merely writing a descriptive account. We prefer to be more explicit about the aspect of psychosocial development that is most distinctive of this period. As we shall show, it is *adult role anticipation* and its attendant motivated learning that is most characteristic of adolescence. It also provides the most salient and integrative aspect of personality development at this stage, as well as a necessary phase in the continuity of growth toward adulthood.

We believe this to be not merely an incidental or utilitarian learning experience predicated on social circumstance, but rather a universal stage of development of the species that is rooted in the basic needs of the organism at this stage of maturation in interaction with its natural social habitat. To be sure, this interaction with the social environment involves much outright learning apparently imposed by local cultural and situational influences. There are attitudes and perceptual biases to be further differentiated; mores and morals to be further introcepted and reinforced; occupational behaviors to be anticipated in practice; adult goals, values, and ambitions to become identified with; and adult models to imitate with respect to manner, expressions of feeling, situational reactions, and style of life itself. Nevertheless, while learning is intrinsic to the process and varies with the individual and subcultural circumstances, the existence of the process itself transcends individual and cultural differences. The true significance of this stage of growth through anticipatory learning is not that learning is involved, but that this type of learning is *always* involved in personality development as a natural concomitant of maturing basic drives and other functional capacities of the organism. We shall therefore attempt to show that *adult role anticipation* represents a truly significant integration of the unfolding biosocial potentialities of the human organism as well as being the truly salient hallmark of personality development during adolescence.

Sex Drive
and

Sex Role   It is important to recognize in the first place that the significance of puberty lies not merely in the physiological changes that occur with sexual maturation, but in the impact these changes have on motivation, self-concept, interpersonal relations, and social role of every individual.

FEMALE ROLES

The girl who first experiences menstruation, enlargement of the breasts, and secondary sex changes undergoes a change in something more than her body image and functions. Her previous primary and secondary socialization processes have prepared her for the realization that she is now growing into young womanhood as jointly defined by biology and culture, and that motherhood lies ahead, as already exemplified by her own mother. That is to say, she is now ready to learn to *be* like a mother in some of the role's nurturing or caring aspects, and to conduct herself with the probability of eventual motherhood always in mind. This clearly sets her apart from all males and establishes a new relationship between her and her brothers, father, and all other males, which is quite different from that between her and any sisters, her mother, and all other females in the primary or secondary reference groups. It also means that she is clearly entering into a transitional stage from childhood dependence to at least an adult semi-independence and responsibility.

There can be no doubt that much of her increasing interest in sex relations, whether expressed or suppressed, and in marriage and motherhood, whether achieved or not, is a direct expression of the sex drive that comes to fruition after puberty. It also *seems* as if the restraints imposed by the institution of marriage and family, however they may differ, represent artificial restrictions arbitrarily imposed on a natural impulse by social pressure (i.e., fear of punishment). What is all too often overlooked is that this "social pressure" is not an external one so much as an internal one. The adolescent female learns a pattern of behavior and social values associated with her probable role as wife and mother not merely because she is achieving maturation of the sex drive but also because her own social ego needs drive her to seek fulfillment in an appropriate and socially approved role. The fact that the role of mother and housewife is almost universally approved as a proper role for women bespeaks the institutionalization of a natural role for women, a modus vivendi for the female species, rather than the persistence of an antiquated custom from caveman society. (On the other hand, this does not exclude the broadening of the female role and interests beyond the domestic sphere, since the intellectual capacity has always been there.) It cannot be overlooked that for most girls in most cultures, the natural identification with the mother in the primary group, and with the mother's role during secondary socialization, actually precedes the maturation of the sex drive as such and paves the way for the active learning of the domestic or career roles that may be deemed appropriate for women. Sexual maturation accompanied by intellectual maturation (which is also too often overlooked) brings about a new phase of anticipation of adult role behaviors and introception of the values associated with these roles. This awareness of her approaching avenues of self-actualization as a young woman, probably as wife and mother, and in some cultures a career woman as well, necessarily has a profound impact on the young adolescent girl's self-concept, her relationships with peers, seniors, and juniors of her own and the opposite sex, her interests and activities, her development of skills and, finally, her standards of morals. All of this involves a far more complex integration of drive, affect, and intellectual control than sexual maturation itself could possibly account for.

MALE ROLES

By the same token, the boy who begins to experience signs of sexual maturity in his penile erections and emissions, in the new hormonally induced lust reactions to female contact or image, increased strength and growth spurt, voice change and other secondary sex characteristics, likewise becomes aware of something more than a mere change of body image and sensations. He is now more like his father and other grown men, experiencing the same urges that grown men talk about, and is capable of performing many of the same tasks as men, with increasing proficiency. Peer-group relations continue to be predominantly with boys, with more emphasis on "manly" activities than was possible or appropriate at earlier stages. Relations with females are culturally prescribed, ranging from highly permissive sexual relations to taboos against contact with related or unrelated females. To a greater degree than his sisters or female peers, he experiences a transition from childhood dependency to adult independence and responsibility. Year by year he finds himself assuming more and more of the perquisites of the *adult role* appropriate to males in that culture.

Since one of the universally approved roles for men is that of breadwinner in one form or another, he will very likely devote much of his adolescent energies toward developing skills and knowledge that are useful in some occupational role. This may be partly predetermined by a cultural pattern of following in his father's footsteps, by the influences of early education or fantasy-building during the primary and secondary socialization stages, or by the economic circumstances of his adolescent years. In some social classes of some societies the adolescent may not be called upon to learn anything economically useful; in others, he will be engaged quite early, even before puberty, in the family's grinding struggle for the economic necessities of life. Whatever the case may be, the normal adolescent in any culture will readily accept or seek out some anticipatory adult occupational activity, simply because he wants to be recognized and accepted as one who is growing into adulthood. In many societies the distinction between work and play is so loosely drawn that children and adolescents move from playful imitation to useful emulation of their elders, and, finally, into full-fledged adult occupation with little change in the basic motive of achievement for social approval. In societies in which work is considered onerous, or some occupation found to be more so than others, young males will still seek to emulate their elders by trying to prepare for less onerous and more prestigious occupations; but even the more onerous ones will be preferred to the role of the indolent and useless member of society.

As for preparing for the responsibilities of fatherhood and head of a family, there is less evidence that adolescent males anywhere in the world look forward to fatherhood with as much eager anticipation as females generally look forward to motherhood. This is undoubtedly due to the fact that the sex drive is more intimately tied up with the functions of procreation and nurturing in the female, so that there is psychobiological predisposition as well as cultural learning involved in this pervasive sex difference in role anticipation. However, there is reason to believe that the natural and cultivated male interest in exhibiting occupational competence may achieve the same purpose indirectly, since it inevitably involves the role of family provider or breadwinner. That this pattern of male behavior has long cultural tradition behind it, if not a constitutional basis in evolution, is indicated by many anthropologists who comment on man's cultural evolution. Thus Etkin (1954) comments: "The development of a hunting economy can occur in an anthropoid only if the male cooperates in feeding and care of the young." Margaret Mead (1955), goes on to say:

In every known human society, everywhere in the world, the young male learns that when he grows up, one of the things which he must do in order to be a full member of society is to provide food for some female and her young. Even in very simple societies, a few men may shy away from the responsibility. . . . But in spite of such exceptions, every known human society rests firmly on the learned nurturing behavior of men. . . . The division of labor may be made in a thousand ways . . . but the core remains. Man, the heir of tradition, provides for women and children. We have no indication that man the animal, man unpatterned by social learning, would do anything of the sort. Which women and which children are provided for is entirely a matter of social arrangements, although the central pattern seems to be that of a man providing for the woman who is his sexual partner and whatever children she may happen to have.

Mead's conjecture of a continuous chain of learning handed down from the earliest protohominid family life overlooks the likelihood that (1) such behavior may have had survival value and thus translated itself into some constitutional mechanism to assure its perpetuation, through natural selection, and (2) even if paternal nurturing behavior is not specifically constitutionally predisposed, it might have become an easily and frequently learned expression (channeling) of a basic drive. We strongly suggest, of course, that the latter is the case. A natural and common enough expression of male social ego needs would seem to be the learning of adult competence in nurturing a family, as part of the general pattern of learning to be an accepted member of society. Thus, while this and many other socially desirable patterns have no specific basis in innate motivation, they illustrate the way in which cultural evolution has carried on the survival functions of organic evolution, simply because of the crucial drive for social acceptance.

For the adolescent male, perhaps more generally than for the female, the cravings of the ripening sex drive provide a strong new focus of affect and interpersonal relations much more immediate than any anticipation of future family roles. Does not this favor the Freudian conception of a "genital stage" or a psychosexual interpretation of the "adult role antici-pation stage" advanced here? The answer lies in the fact that young men, unlike young baboons, do not resort to automatic satisfaction of any physical urge without some regard to the adult mores and morals inculcated in them. For this reason Freud had to postulate a superego as a "precipitate of early parental influence" which served to inhibit sexual satisfaction, ever since the repression of the Oedipus complex. We find it less of a theo-retical strain to see the adolescent boy as having undergone the gradual maturation of a social ego drive which predisposes him to strive for social acceptance and to modify all gratifications or physical appetites to be in accord to some extent with the social mores. His sexual appetite will likewise be automatically restrained or satisfied in accordance with the degree of permissiveness granted by the culture. This will be deter-mined in large measure by the degree of permissiveness granted adult males, more particularly unmarried adult males. If a double standard exists for unmarried men and women, it will certainly be reflected in the sexual behavior standards for adolescent boys and girls in that culture. In that way, even adolescent sex-play, intercourse, or restraint become a phase of adult role anticipation.

Before we go any further in our theoretical generalizations, let us com-pare the sex role differentiations of adolescents in two rather different cultural settings: urban-suburban United States and rural Mexico.

A CROSS-CULTURAL COMPARISON

In urban-suburban United States, adolescent sex roles have been largely equalized under the influence of democratic equality of education, civil rights, and economic opportunity. Both sexes undergo compulsory educa-tion to the age of 16 or 17, learn a very similar range of basic subjects, and the brighter ones are almost equally encouraged to go on for higher education. Both are allowed wide degrees of freedom in social activities with some adult supervision and, increasingly, without it. Mixed "dating" is generally permitted, even encouraged, with only perfunctory attempts at regulation and chaperoning during the early adolescent years. Pre-marital sexual intercourse is more or less tabooed, but a subtle under-standing exists that older boys may "sow their wild oats" as long as such escapades are kept discreetly quiet. Less tolerance is accorded the female but, even so, loss of virginity in a love affair tends to be less condemned than formerly, provided the affair remains secret and does not result in pregnancy. Adolescent pregnancy, when it occurs, is generally considered a disgrace, or at least a most unfortunate occurrence which requires the utmost of tact and understanding in weighing the alternative solutions.

More generally, adolescents of both sexes are expected to delay full sexual gratification, and at least in middle-class circles they tend to do so, contenting themselves with substitute activities like "necking to climax," masturbation, etc., until late adolescence for boys (cf. Kinsey et al., 1948. Current incidence of heterosexual experience among adolescents is undoubtedly higher.)

In rural Mexico (and most of Latin America) there are striking contrasts between the roles permitted for each sex and between their sex-typing standards and those in urban United States. A veritable cult of virility (*machismo*) encourages, even *compels* the young boy to try out his new-found virility at a fairly early age and to keep up the practice increasingly into adulthood. He may brag freely of his real or imagined conquests and regard any unattached female as "fair game." Since adolescent girls are at the same time strictly prohibited from exercising such license and continually warned by their parents against the lustful nature of the male, the boys' needs must be satisfied either by prostitutes, older women of loose morals, or girls seduced in spite of parental vigilance. Paradoxically, there is not so much stigma attached to adolescent pregnancy and illegitimate childbirth; at least such an occurrence can soon be "lived down" and absorbed in the home-life of her parents or the patron for whom the girl works. Nevertheless, protection of the adolescent girl against the natural *machismo* of the predatory male is virtually an obsession in most rural Latin American families, and seriously affects the education and role behavior of the female. It is quite commonplace to stop sending a daughter to school after about the fourth or fifth grade, in spite of nominal "compulsory education." This is done not only because such limited education is commonly considered to be "enough for a woman," but also because she is needed at home to fulfill her role as mother's helper (*mamacita*, or "little mother") and because she is safer there from the lust of the adolescent and preadolescent schoolboys anxious to exercise their *machismo*. The adolescent girl thus occupies herself either part-time or full-time with learning and practicing the duties of the mother role—cooking, cleaning, feeding, and washing the smaller children, waiting on father. Like mother, she rarely goes far from home (i.e., a short walking distance) unless it is to go to market, and even then, she is in the company of a parent or other older women. If she obtains employment in another village, usually as a domestic, the new mistress assumes some of the obligations of a guardian. In any case, even conversational contacts with members of the opposite sex tend to be regarded with suspicion, and legitimate courtship tends to be highly formalized. Stealthy or indirect contacts may be made, but engagements are usually concluded, if not initiated, through parental negotiation. For the girl, there is rarely any career other than marriage to look forward to, though a limited amount of domestic trade may grow out of family farming or handicraft. Social activity during the adolescent years and afterward is generally limited to church attendance with mother, local female gossip, and participation in local fiestas.

For the boy, *machismo* involves a lot more than demonstrations or allegations of sexual prowess, however important these may be. It also involves demonstrations of manly self-reliance, ability to hold one's own in any competition for dominance in peer relations, fearlessness in the face of danger, and above all, courage enough to "obtain satisfaction" for any real or imagined insult to the male ego or to primary group affiliations. In the latter respects, Latin *machismo* takes on some of the behavioral characteristics of European medieval chivalry or the fierce tribal loyalties of other cultures that persist to this day in many parts of the world. The Latin American youth may not be required to challenge an offender to a duel, but he must either fight or suffer a measure of humiliation when offended. He will certainly try to laugh off or shrug off a real danger that would at least startle the average United States adult. The writer has seen this manifested in incidents such as: encountering a scorpion or poisonous snake, being sprayed by the hot embers of erupting fireworks, riding in a truck on a narrow mountain ledge overlooking a precipice. Competence in physical, nondomestic labor is likewise highly valued in this concept of manliness. Adolescent boys are everywhere to be seen helping their fathers in ploughing the fields, reaping the harvests, tending livestock, carrying heavy loads, practicing handicrafts, riding horseback. On a more recreational note, boys (but not girls) may be expected to engage in athletic contests, gambling and carousing on Sundays while their sisters are in church, disporting themselves on fiesta days, and even getting drunk on occasion in public, as their fathers are seen to do regularly.

Some of these differences have their pale counterparts among American urban-suburban youth: boys' gangs and cliques that indulge in a certain amount of cutting-up;[1] a code of male courage that brands timid or nonreckless behavior as "chicken"; affectations of adult "smart" behavior requiring spending money for "sophisticated" entertainment, clothing, and driving a car. One important difference between the extensions of *machismo* that prevail in the Latin American mores and those in the urban American mild counterparts is that in the former close interaction with females in public is more or less excluded, while in United States urban society it becomes very much a part of the sophisticated intermingling and equalization of the sexes.

[1] For norm-comparison purposes, we are excluding the more extremely antisocial manifestations of juvenile delinquency in both cultures.

VALUE LEARNING, TEMPERMENT, AND ROLE INTEGRATION

It should now be noted that the learning of adult roles is inseparable from the learning of adult *values*, and that the latter are subsumed under role learning. When the rural Latin American adolescent learns to scorn pain or danger, to act like a Casanova or at least to talk like one, to defer to stronger authority but not to let anyone "push him around," he is also learning the manly virtues of his culture. This is not merely an externally imposed code of behavior, but a system of values he readily introcepts to structure his self-concept and interpersonal relationships as a human being. He will judge and be judged by these values, and more significantly, will judge himself by them. He has been exposed to these values during the secondary socialization of preadolescence, when he learned to understand and aspire to them by verbal conceptualization, fantasy-building, and playful imitation of adult roles. Now they are being more deeply ingrained into his ego structure by acting out or living up to his identification with selected adult models and their values. His motives, attitudes, and beliefs, his very conception of what he is and wants to become is profoundly affected by these values.

When the adolescent rural Mexican girl leaves school to take on more household responsibility, or starts to work as a household maid in the big town, staying close to home, being obedient to her mother or mistress, taking care not to talk to strange men, she is likewise building on values she has been exposed to in childhood and preadolescence. But now flirtation and childbirth are no longer matters for play-acting, and male *machismo* is an ever-present threat to her highly prized virginity. Usually, she automatically accepts the cultural values implicit in deference to one's elders, as well as the dominant role and aggressiveness of the male, his sexual promiscuity, the propriety of domestic servitude and piety for females, including virginity up to marriage and housebound faithfulness forever after. The affective ego-involvement in these role-determining values is usually so deeply ingrained that even the efforts of an enlightened government to improve education for women, or of more cosmopolitan women to set an example in achieving careers and social influence, often evoke resistance and hostility.

Meanwhile, the American urban-suburban youth is learning the virtue of competitive achievement in a materialistic society and the status value of conspicuous consumption. He tends to accept whatever remains of the double standard in sex morals, while female teenagers resent it, and both know it is hypocritical in view of the prevailing social values of democratic equality, romantic love, and the double-edged sanctity of marriage. The youngster will very likely spend his entire adolescence preparing for

A

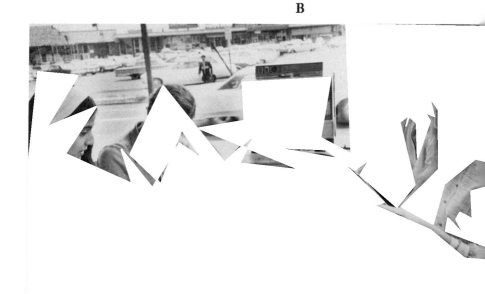

B

Figure 4–1. Adult role anticipation *manifests itself in a variety of ways in the American culture. This may include conspicuous care and use of material possessions, informal (or formal) dating, or the creation of new conventions in defiance of the old. (Photo (A) Strickler, (B) Shelton, (C) Anderson, all from Monkmeyer.)*

a career through formal education, since knowledge is both a practical and social advantage in fulfilling his role expectations. The choice of a field of specialization will be determined by many things, including ability, interest, opportunity, prestige, and material rewards. This involves not only a pursuit of more specific values already learned but also entails the introception of a new set of occupational values in anticipation of his adult role.

Thus an American boy or girl studying for a career in the arts and sciences is more likely to be motivated by a complex of intellectual and aesthetic values and to become more thoroughly indoctrinated in *these* values than the one who goes into business or semiskilled labor with a minimum of schooling to satisfy the material demands of his or her adult role. This is, of course, a very oversimplified distinction, because need and opportunity may diverge greatly from the social values developed by the individual. What we suggest here is that these values become highly significant ingredients of the personality during adolescence, and when the opportunities for social role assumption vary greatly from these values, anxiety and frustration are bound to result.

The creative girl who is forced to submerge her talents to household drudgery and male dominance will either have to find substitute outlets for her creativity, or will rebel if the opportunity arises, or will go on unhappily accepting her role without knowing why she is unhappy. The American college boy with aesthetic inclinations and values, who is thrust

C

into his father's business because circumstances offer him no other choice, will also have to find satisfaction in some aspect of his business or leisure activities, or rebel and take the consequences, or go on grimly resigned to a career that satifies his adult role material needs but leaves him starved for aesthetic or intellectual satisfaction.

What of the Mexican rural youth who is physically and temperamentally unsuited to introcepting the values and role that take the bullfighter as their ideal? He will undoubtedly suffer severe adjustment problems in seeking to cast himself in an acceptable adult role, unless circumstances or change of environment provide the opportunity to cultivate the values and role behavior that are more conducive to his temperament.

In other words, one of the ego-gratifying or ego-shattering experiences of adolescence, after the comparatively easy sex-group identification of childhood, is the discovery that one is or is not suited by physique, temperament, and intellect to fulfill the role expectations of the sex-role types preferred in that particular culture. It therefore cannot be assumed that appropriate adult role learning is automatically imposed on all adolescents in a given culture, any more than it can be assumed that the uniform fact of pubescence automatically bestows virtual maturity on all personalities. Margaret Mead (1949) gives vivid descriptions of these adjustment problems in primitive societies in her later treatment of the problems of sex and temperament, in which she recognizes that individuals differ in their capacities to adjust to different cultural norms of sex-role behavior:

For the children who do not belong to these preferred types, only the primary sex characters will be definitive in helping them to classify themselves. Their impulses, their preferences, and later much of their physique will be aberrant. They will be doomed throughout life to sit among the other members of their sex feeling less a man, or less a woman, simply because the cultural ideal is based on a different set of clues, a set of clues no less valid, but different. . . .
So in each of the societies I have studied it has been possible to distinguish those who deviated most sharply from the expected physique and behavior, and who made different sorts of adjustment, dependent on the relationship between their own constitutional type and cultural ideal. The boy who will grow up into a tall, proud, restive man whose very pride makes him sensitive and liable to confusion suffers a very different fate in Bali, Samoa, Arapesh, and Manus. In Manus, he takes refuge in the vestiges of rank the Manus retain, takes more interest in ceremonial than in trading, mixes the polemics of acceptable trading invectives with much deeper anger. In Samoa such a man is regarded as too violent to be trusted with the headship of a family for many, many years; the village waits until his capacity for anger and intense feeling has been worn down by years of erosive soft resistance to his unseemly over-emphases. In Bali, such a man may take more initiative than his fellows only to be thrown back into sulkiness and confusion, unable to carry it through. Among the Maori of New Zealand, it is possible that he would have been the cultural ideal, his capacity for pride matched by the

demand for pride, his violence by the demand for violence, and his capacity for fierce gentleness also given perfect expression, since the ideal woman was as proud and fiercely gentle as himself.

It can be seen from the foregoing illustration that: (1) patterns of adult role learning may differ greatly from one culture to another; (2) variations in individual temperamental and physical predispositions produce different reactions and adjustments to the range of adult role models available in any given culture; (3) sex-role typing soon reverberates throughout the entire realm of personality development, including occupational roles, maturing social values and interpersonal relationships, and conflicts and adjustments in channeling of motives and self-concepts. Clearly, all this involves a great deal more than the maturation of genital structure and function in which the human being is not very different from the baboon. On the other hand, it is not merely a function of incidental learning depending on social circumstance, because there is a basic universal regularity of development which seems to predispose *Homo sapiens socialis* to this kind of learning and to make it well-nigh inevitable. What is involved here is a natural integrative response of the total organism to its natural environment at this stage of its ontogenetic development, making use of all of the potentialities the species has developed throughout its evolution. This includes its maturing cognitive, affective, and psychomotor capacities, which at this stage are being integrated into the distinctly human level of biosocial functioning which produces both distinct personalities and social organization. It therefore behooves us to inquire further into the cognitive, affective, and psychomotor components of organismic development. We shall have a firmer foundation for calling this a regular stage of personality development if we can show that these organismic prerequisites of adult role learning regularly emerge at a higher and distinctly human level of functioning at the period generally designated as early adolescence.

Biosocial Basis
of
Role Learning

COGNITIVE-AFFECTIVE INTEGRATION

We have already seen that the introception of social mores at the level of adult role learning presupposes a high order of abstract thinking and ego involvement. As we pointed out in the preceding chapters, the beginnings of categorical abstractions are to be found in the primary group interactions of childhood, though the cognitive processes and responses at that stage are largely concrete. However, abstraction of rules of conduct and group identification, some superficial introception of social values, playful imitation of adult roles, a primitive understanding of cause and effect or right and wrong, were all made possible by the normal development of abstract cognitive and reasoning capacities during the secondary socialization phase in preadolescence. We now find that adolescents in widely divergent cultures (and presumably in *any* culture) learn to abstract, introcept, and *begin to live up to* a fairly complex and subtle configuration of social values and mores surrounding their own anticipated adult roles. This involves a growing appreciation of the social proprieties of individual behavior for one's own age, sex, and social status, and for a wide variety of interpersonal relationships—as a matter of *principle*. It also involves the ability to anticipate the consequences of one's own acts, and to prejudge and control such actions in the light of such principles and in the ever-continuing attempt to achieve a degree of social acceptance. Even when this desire for social acceptance and recognition is complicated by the typical adolescent assertion of independence—or when it expresses itself in the seemingly purely emotional "adolescent crush"—there is still a role-related self-concept and the anticipation of social approval that makes these reactions possible.

We find striking confirmation of this point of view in the work of Piaget and his collaborators, who were primarily interested in the development of thought processes from early childhood to adolescence, but recognized their relevance to the development of the total personality:

We take as the fundamental problem of adolescence the fact that the individual begins to take up adult roles. From such a standpoint, puberty cannot be considered the distinctive feature of adolescence. . . . For our purposes, the essential fact is this fundamental social transition (and not physiological growth alone). . . . An adolescent in love . . . generally complicates his feelings by constructing a romance or by referring to social or even literary ideas of all sorts. But the fabrication of a romance or the appeal to various collective role models is neither the direct product of the neurophysiological transformations of puberty nor the exclusive product of affectivity. Both are also indirect and specific reflections of the general tendency of adolescents to construct theories and make use of the ideologies that surround them. And this general tendency can only be explained by taking into account the two factors which we find in association over and over again—the transformations of thought and the assumption of adult roles. The latter involves a total restructuring of the personality in which the intellectual transformations are parallel or complimentary to the affective transformations (Inhelder and Piaget, 1958, pp. 335-336).

What Inhelder and Piaget refer to as "the general tendency of adolescents to construct theories and make use of the ideologies that surround them," is very much of a piece with what is commonly referred to as the introception of the social mores. Their viewpoint confirms the crucial function we assign to abstract thinking in the learning of adult roles and social values and the higher level of cognitive-affective maturation involved. As these authors further state:

If adolescence is really the age at which growing individuals take their place in adult society (whether or not the role change always coincides with puberty), this crucial role adjustment must involve, in correlation with the development of the propositional or formal operations which assure intellectual structuring, two fundamental transformations that adult affective socialization requires. First, feelings relative to ideals are added to inter-individual feelings. Secondly, personalities develop in relation to social roles and scales of values derived from social interaction (and no longer only by the coordination of exchanges which they maintain with the physical environment and other indviduals). . . .

First, we are struck by the fact that feelings about ideals are practically nonexistent in the child. A study of the concept of nationality and the associated social attitudes has shown us that the child is sensitive to his family, to his place of residence, to his native language, to certain customs, etc., but that he preserves both an astonishing degree of ignorance and a striking insensitivity not only to his own designation or that of his associates as Swiss, French, etc., but toward his own country as a collective reality. This is to be expected, since, in the 7–11-year-old child, logic is applied only to concrete or manipulable objects. There is no operation available at this level which would make it possible for the child to elaborate an ideal which goes beyond the empirically given. This is only one among many examples. The notions of humanity, social justice (in contrast to inter-individual justice, which is deeply experienced at the concrete level), freedom of conscience, civic or intellectual courage, and so forth, like the idea of nationality, are ideals which profoundly influence the adolescent's affective life; but with the child's mentality, except for individual glimpses, they can neither be understood nor felt (Inhelder and Piaget, 1958, 348-349).

These studies confirm our contention that around the time of puberty the individual enters into a new stage of socialization through value and concept learning, predicated on the readiness of the organism, both cognitively and affectively, to intcract with the environment on that level. Just how this cognitive-affective reintegration takes place at a higher level of abstraction in the organismic-environmental field is a complex question that has thus far eluded experimental investigation. However, two principles of biosocial development become fairly clear when we put our present knowledge in long-range perspective. First, sexual and emotional maturity is delayed in the human until intellectual development has achieved the capacity for abstraction that is necessary for full acculturation of the individual. Secondly, a significant advance toward personal maturity cannot take place until this cognitive-affective integration and performance capabilities have advanced to at least anticipatory adult-role status in the community.[2]

Since we have attached such crucial significance to the development of abstract thinking in personality development, it would be interesting to note what a standard test of intellectual growth reveals about empirically derived criteria of cognitive maturation at midadolescence. The Stanford-Binet tests found suitable for 14-year and 15-year levels are:

Year XIV
1. *Vocabulary* (to the level of such abstract words as *haste, peculiarity, priceless, tolerate*)
2. *Induction* (including principle from observed manipulations)
3. *Reasoning* (deduction from given facts in hypothetical situation)
4. *Ingenuity* (solving problems of unseen space relations)
5. *Orientation* (imaginative deduction of changing directions)
6. *Reconciliation of Opposites* (abstracting similar elements)

Year XV
1. *Vocabulary* (to the level of such abstract words as *regard, disproportionate, shrewd*)
2. *Ingenuity* (same as XIV, Item 4 above, but 2 out of 3 right)
3. *Differences Between Abstract Words*
4. *Arithmetical Reasoning* (mental arithmetical problem-solving)
5. *Proverbs* (abstracting the commonplace meaning or "moral" of common proverbs)
6. *Orientation: Direction* (more complicated than XIV, Item 5 above)
7. *Essential Differences* (similar to XV, Item 3 above)
8. *Abstract Words* (definitions of *generosity, independent, envy, authority, justice*)

It can be seen from the foregoing battery of test items that by the time the average individual reaches adolescence, significant criteria of his intellectual development may lie entirely in the realm of abstraction, and that this capacity reaches the level of average adult capacity by the time he is 15 years old. Indeed, if we were to designate one of the maturing organismic functions as the hallmark of adolescence, or its most salient feature in personality development, we might very well designate this as the "stage of abstract thinking and behavior." At least we would be hard put to decide whether sexual maturation or abstract thinking was a more significant clue to the emerging behavior capacities of the human being as a social animal. However, neither of these crucial psychobiological functions can be re-

---

[2] The student of psychoanalysis will note that both principles are somewhat at variance with Freudian doctrine. The first does not regard culture as an artificial compact to restrain incestuous impulses, but as a product of human evolution. The second denies that maturity is essentially reached at puberty.

garded as a truly salient clue to the integrated personality. Sex drive modified by principles of social restraint clearly combine with many other aspects of similarly modified psychological development to produce a *socially adapting individual who is mentally and physically ready to find his place as an adult in his society.* It is this global characteristic of human behavior that we regard as the truly integrative and salient aspect of personality development, and it is best signified by the hallmark of "adult role anticipation" (or anticipatory learning, identification, and participation).

To be sure, the Stanford-Binet, a cognitive sampling device empirically derived from samplings of Western cultures, does not purport to illustrate the precise manner in which abstract thinking is applied to the universal introception of the social mores, values, and role behaviors. However, the rationale for such application is not far to seek from some of the clues contained in these tests. An individual who has developed the ability to give the true social meaning (or moral) of a variety of proverbs has evidently developed sufficient understanding of abstract principles to understand principles of social amenities and role behavior, at least at the verbal level. One who can make the finer distinctions between related abstract concepts and define others has at least developed the ability to understand and communicate social values and attitudes on a fairly mature level. And if, in addition to this, he is able to use inductive and deductive reasoning, coupled with the use of mathematical concepts and manipulation of sensorimotor discriminanda, he certainly possesses some of the requisites for learning skills that a wide variety of adult roles call for in a wide variety of social settings.

It might still be argued that these testing instruments, devised by Western psychologists for largely academic purposes, do not necessarily provide a profile of the basic mental equipment for personality development in Oriental or more primitive cultures. Hence, it might be thought that we are merely bolstering the argument for the organismic basis of social role learning by citing intellectual criteria of learning capacity which are in turn the products of learned cultural influences. Our answer would be that *all* cultures require a certain minimum of abstract thinking, reasoning, symbolic communication of values, and behavioral role differentiation *in order for the culture to exist at all.* It should be remembered that while we are being somewhat daring in postulating an innate social drive as inherent in man's evolution as a culture-making animal, it has long been widely understood and accepted that man's intellect had to evolve by natural selection to the stage of symbolic thinking and communication for culture-making to become possible (Tax, 1960; Roe and Simpson, 1958). All we have contributed to this commonly accepted principle is to show how IQ tests reveal the maturation of abstract thinking at about the same time as sexual maturation, and to suggest that this is a universal phenomenon which facilitates full social maturation via adult role learning.

Unfortunately, IQ tests for primitive cultures do not exist at present, and data from culture-free tests are still scarce and unsatisfactory. The principal shortcoming of the latter is their dependence on motor performance and sensorimotor discrimination, with little or no use of language, one of man's chief attainments through evolution. Any cursory examination of the behavioral data from anthropology, however, can quickly disabuse us of any illusion that the technologically more advanced societies of Europe and America have any monopoly on abstract thinking. The religions, laws, customs, and social structures of all underdeveloped or "primitive" cultures give ample evidence of moral principles, conceptions of cause and effect, occupational skills involving planning and foresight, and complex interrelationships of caste, class, sex role and kinship, with their special prerogatives, attitudes, taboos, interpersonal relationships, and styles of behavior. None of this would be possible unless the members of such societies regularly developed and used their capacities for abstract thinking well before adulthood. Although the cultivation of symbolic communication and learning undoubtedly varies from one culture to another (perhaps less in simple and illiterate cultures, or those more depressed by the day-to-day, hand-to-mouth struggle for existence), it is almost inconceivable that any human society could be maintained with any cultural regularities without the regular emergence of a fair capacity for symbolic learning in each succeeding generation. Indeed, those individuals who fail to develop any appreciable degree of such a capacity will fail to make a minimal adjustment to the culture and automatically show themselves to be feeble-minded, just as they do in ours.

Thus the simultaneous maturation of abstract cognition and sexual lust, for those who are normal in both respects, right after puberty (about age 13 to 16), is fraught with significance for personality development. Abstract thinking provides the means for learning verbalized prohibitions and attitudes of restraint or social conformity with respect to sex relations, just as it does in exercising a restraining influence over emotional impulses generally. The stage has already been set for the cultural modification of the sex drive through values inculcated during the secondary socialization stage in preadolescence. Whatever restraints or sex-role prescriptions are provided by the culture are more actively learned and put into practice by the anticipation-of-adult-self motive that dominates adolescence. But it must be stressed that the individual boy or girl does not merely learn to socialize the sex drive by being punished every time he or she violates the social mores. Rather, for most individuals in most cultures, it is the basic generic drive to seek social approval and to guide one's behavior by the growing sense of social proprieties that provides the motivated restraint. This "sense of social proprieties" is not only learned from the parents and other symbolically communicated cultural influences, but it further represents an integration of cognitive and affective functions in the maturing adolescent. Moreover, this restraining, delaying, romanticizing, or at least ritualizing influence on sexual passions is built into the human nervous system. That is what Etkin (1954) meant when he stated: "Cortical expansion in the human is thus related to sexual behavior control as well as to the intellectual function" (cf. Chapter 2).

ATTITUDES TOWARD SEX

There is nothing fixed or uniform about the socialization of the sex drive or the attitudes and behavior it fosters. Individuals and subcultural groups differ and both undergo changes in time. At the present time, American adolescents are undergoing a change in the direction of more liberal attitudes toward sex relations than those which existed in previous generations of youth or are manifest among the present older generation. A study by Reiss (1967) compared the attitudes of about 800 high school and college students with those of a national sample of 1400 adults (80% married) on a 12-item "sexual permissiveness scale." The results showed considerable individual and group differences, as well as male-female differences; but adolescents generally showed much greater permissiveness of attitude than that professed by adults. The greatest "generation gap" appeared on the items pertaining to premarital sex relations when engaged or in love. (Table 4–1)

Underlying the data, of course, are the adjustments that each individual makes between two opposing needs in anticipating the adult role: sexual lust and desire for social approval. The adjustment is complicated by the fact that values of the peer group and adult institutions differ, as do the values publicly expressed and privately condoned. Though the majority of American adolescents seem to advocate much more permissiveness in sex relations than their elders are willing to condone, it is noteworthy that an essentially moral distinction is being made. Sex is OK for couples in love or engaged (at least, "it's nobody else's business"), but the majority of boys and an even greater majority of girls do not condone it "just for kicks." The corticalization of the sex drive is manifest even in the values of the "liberated" American adolescent.

ROLE DIFFERENTIATION AND IDENTITY

The course of neuroendocrine evolution and ontogenetic development in the human thus argues against the designation of adolescence and adulthood as merely the "genital stage" of personality development. What

Table 4-1 PERCENTAGE AGREEING WITH EACH ITEM ON MALE SEXUAL PERMISSIVENESS SCALE
(From Reiss, 1967)

Statement	Adult sample	Student sample
1. I believe that kissing is acceptable for the male before marriage when he is engaged to be married.	95.3	97.5
2. I believe that kissing is acceptable for the male before marriage when he is in love.	93.6	98.9
3. I believe that kissing is acceptable for the male before marriage when he feels strong affection for his partner.	90.2	97.2
4. I believe that kissing is acceptable for the male before marriage even if he does not feel particularly affectionate toward his partner.	58.6	64.2
5. I believe that petting is acceptable for the male before marriage when he is engaged to be married.	60.8	85.0
6. I believe that petting is acceptable for the male before marriage when he is in love.	59.4	80.4
7. I believe that petting is acceptable for the male before marriage when he feels strong affection for his partner.	54.3	67.0
8. I believe that petting is acceptable for the male before marriage even if he does not feel particularly affectionate toward his partner.	28.6	34.3
9. I believe that full sexual relations are acceptable for the male before marriage when he is engaged to be married.	19.5	52.2
10. I believe that full sexual relations are acceptable for the male before marriage when he is in love.	17.6	47.6
11. I believe that full sexual relations are acceptable for the male before marriage when he feels strong affection for his partner.	16.3	36.9
12. I believe that full sexual relations are acceptable for the male before marriage even if he does not feel particularly affectionate toward his partner.	11.7	20.8
N	(1390)	(811)

does seem to be involved is a highly complex emergence and integration of intellectual and emotional functioning in social interaction into a pattern of social adaptation we call role and value learning. The motivating forces that activate this learning as capacity develops involve the whole hierarchy of drives from the primitive appetites of hunger and sex to the social ego needs of community membership and acceptance. That is why the very desire for sexual relations becomes readily subordinated to the desire for self-actualization as a member of society with all its mores, taboos, or double standards, and its prescribed role relationships. This is also what makes the very idea of romantic love both possible and desirable, and the practice of promiscuous sex relations neither as satisfying nor as indiscriminate as it sounds, in societies that do not condone it. It also provides the psychobiological basis for the durability of marriage as a more or less universal social institution throughout man's history, although marriage and romance are still largely separated in most cultures of the world. What we are suggesting, of course, is merely a gross norm based on the constitutional characteristics of the human species. The fact that the specific pattern of this integration is largely molded by the existing culture and social situation does not gainsay the fact that it also is predetermined by the regular emergence of these potentialities during adolescence. Neither, on the other hand, does the regularity of this emergence contradict vast individual differences in temperament, intelligence, and even sexual drive, which bring about quite differentiated individual adaptations to the same environment.

We do not know as much about the genetic differentiation of temperament as we do about the growth and measurement of intelligence, but it is equally important that we attempt to understand its relationship to role learning. While we do not subscribe to any particular system of "types," we do know that temperamental differences can be detected quite early in life, and that these characteristics of individual personality are fairly well differentiated by adolescence. We also know that there are broad developmental forces of motivation and adjustment by which the individual seeks to bring about self-actualization. In adolescence, this manifests itself in the *quest for identity* that is implicit in the learning of social roles and values. Indeed, some authorities, such as Erikson (1959), regard the struggle to achieve personal identity ("identity vs. identity diffusion") as the crucial developmental problem of adolescence. Erikson subordinates "role experimentation" to his concept of developmental crises, but this is quite compatible with our operational concept of role learning. The nature of cognitive-affective maturation and the confrontation of adult roles is such that much of adolescent affect is invested in this quest for identity— for knowing who you are or are becoming, for being recognized as an individual with some acceptable qualities, some reason for being cared for or loved, though no longer a child, and something to care for and identify with—in short, anything to give dignity and meaning to the process of living, rather than to exist as an animal or a nonentity.

Nothing satisfies this need as readily as growing up to be a full-fledged member of one's own society, with a clearly defined and accepted role, enjoying the satisfaction of social participation in some way through the cultivation of interests that are congruent with one's own temperament and the realities of the social context. The temperamental predilections of the individual will certainly help to determine his choice of roles or "style of life" just as much as the social realities will shape, amplify, or stifle his temperament. Indeed, there can really be no such thing as enjoying the exercise of one's own temperament in a vacuum. Society must provide the fulfillment or frustration of a zest for exuberant living, the joy of achievement and the admiration it brings, the calmer pleasures or symbolic orgies of intellectual and aesthetic exploration, the intoxication of dominance and power, or the gluttony of conspicuously consuming material wealth. And if temperamental predilections do not seek fulfillment in any of these role-determining styles of life, there is always the cozy security of unspectacular acceptance by one's peers, primary group, or reference group.

Whatever the mode of cognitive-affective integration, social ego needs will seek canalization through some form of social identification or role. This does not mean that every culture is tailor-made to suit all the possible varieties of temperament. As Mead pointed out, this is not even true of the two sex-role modalities in any given culture. Similarly, some temperamental predispositions will fail to find ideal role canalizations of their needs in their particular culture or subculture and will spend their lives making imperfect adjustments to roles that *are* available to them. Many others will find these very predispositions changed in the course of adolescence and early adulthood by the effect of the subculture's pace and style of life on their psychosomatic functions. Still others will find kindred misfits and create their own little dyads or cliques of nonconformist or deviant personalities which provide their own little island of mutual acceptance or understanding in a hostile environment.

This process gets well underway during adolescence, because organismic maturation brings about a new level of self-awareness in terms of approaching adulthood and social role channeling of ego needs. Adult society provides the models and the milieu for the roles and values through which this channeling can be achieved; peers provide the moral support or socially facilitating milieu through which many of the adjustments and resistances to this process can be "normalized." Thus participation in adolescent clubs, cliques, or gangs provide a shopping or testing ground for the trial exercise of overt role behaviors in concert with peers. The conflict between conformity to adult expectations and to peer demand for independence is notoriously one of the outstanding conflicts of adolescence. It represents a critical adjustment of the individual temperament to the common transitional problem or "developmental task" of transition from childhood dependence and conformity to adult independence and individuality. As we have said, this involves the tentative testing and learning of role behaviors in an attempt to find identities that are congruent with individual biosocial predispositions. But congruent or not, some such role assumption must sooner or later be made. Some societies, like most Western urban societies, provide a wide variety of possible roles and a prolonged adolescence to prepare for the technologically more advanced ones. Some societies are highly restrictive in the roles open to men and allow no choice at all for women, thrusting both sexes into adulthood soon after puberty. But no society can absolve its members, nor can the members absolve themselves of the developmental task of learning certain adult role behaviors and social values, even if only on a tentative, trial-and-error, anticipatory, or resistant basis. The only alternative, in cases of extreme resistance to the maturation of the socialization process, is to cast oneself unwittingly into the role of the immature adolescent and soon into that of the immature, irresponsible, and usually rejected adult. In such cases, explanations in terms of psychosocial pathological processes will not be far to seek, and serve only to underline the normality of the socializing process in maturation of the human personality.

"DEVELOPMENTAL TASKS" OF ADOLESCENCE

One way of looking at the problem of adult role anticipation, therefore, is in terms of "developmental tasks" of adolescence. Some anthropologists have provided data for cross-cultural comparisons of developmental behavior, which have contributed to the developmental task concept. Benedict (1934), for example, contributed rich observations of developmental changes and contrasts between American white and Indian cultures, emphasizing cultural conditioning of role behavior. The major changes which she found characteristic of adolescence in Western societies, though varying with the culture, are:

(1) Responsible vs. non-responsible status role
(2) Dominance vs. submission
(3) Contrasted sexual role

We have already discussed these aspects of adolescent role learning and have cited examples of cross-cultural comparisons of our own and Mead's. However, we are interested not merely in the varieties of cultural patterns but also in the possible biosocial basis for any regularities of personality development.

The developmental tasks for the American (white) adolescent are perhaps best summarized by Havighurst (1953), after long and exhaustive study, as follows:

1. Achieving new and more mature relations with age-mates of both sexes.
2. Achieving a masculine or feminine role.
3. Accepting one's physique and using the body effectively.
4. Achieving emotional independence of parents and other adults.
5. Achieving assurance of economic independence.
6. Selecting and preparing for an occupation.
7. Preparing for marriage and family life.
8. Developing intellectual skills and concepts necessary for civic competence.
9. Desiring and achieving socially responsible behavior.
10. Acquiring a set of values and an ethical system as a guide to behavior.

All of the above developmental tasks of adolescence may be regarded as subsumed under our conception of adult role (and value) learning as the most salient and integrative aspect of adolescent development. Havighurst likewise suggests the biological, psychological, and cultural bases for each of these developmental tasks, even indicating the social class differentials in American society. His presentation thus lends itself to comparison with biosocial theory particularly well. He has no difficulty pointing to psychological and cultural bases for each of these developmental tasks, and a biological basis for most of them. However, he doubts the biological basis for "5" and denies that there is any such basis for "9" and "10."

Unfortunately, when personality development is broken down to specific tasks that are prescribed for the youth of a given society, and the biological basis sought separately for each of them, the biosocial integrity of the behaving and adapting organisms gets lost sight of here and there in atomistic artifacts. We have already shown that there is a definite psychobiological basis for psychosocial development, and that this leads normally to the assumption of social roles and values in adolescence which prepare the individual for adulthood. Among the universal role requirements for males, at least, seems to be some occupational roles, while females generally "have their work cut out for them" in the occupational role of housewife and/or mother. We have already shown that intellectual and psychomotor maturation ordinarily enables the male to learn some occupational role, while his innate need for social acceptance and identification exerts pressure on him to do so. If the culture does not demand economic independence for all of its males, as Western capitalistic society does, then this aspect of occupational roles will not be learned. If it requires all of its females to be housebound and dependent, then such roles will generally be learned by its adolescent females. If a career before or after marriage should become the prestige-giving course of adult role assumption for American females, then *that* will be the course of anticipatory role learning for American female adolescents—as it already is for many segments of our population. The point is, however, that cognitive-affective-psychomotor maturation and integration must and does reach a level requisite for such cultural adaptation by adolescence, for all normal males and females. We need not look for a specific biological basis for each type of role that each society produces, any more than we need look for a specific biological basis for each language.

When it comes to "9" and "10," we would differ from Havighurst in his assumption that there is no biological basis for desiring and achieving socially responsible behavior or a set of social and ethical values. On the contrary, these are impelled by the same social ego needs we have postulated as rooted in the biosocial nature of man. Havighurst's accord with the prevailing "learned motive" viewpoint is couched in terms which almost suggest that there *ought* to be some psychobiological foundation for such tasks. For "9" he claims: "*Biological Basis*. None. This task seems to be entirely due to the influence of society on the individual; unless we wish to postulate a 'social instinct' in man. Also, some have supposed that the observed altruism of many adolescents is a result of sublimation of the sex drive."

Since we do advocate a basic social drive in man and regard altruism as a direct outgrowth of inherent empathy, we had best examine the ethical implications of the biosocial approach to role learning.

ETHICAL IMPLICATIONS OF ROLE LEARNING

We recognized at the outset (see Chapter 2) that man emerged as a social animal when he began to abstract and communicate concepts of social relationships and social control of behavior through speech, while at the same time extending his capacity for empathy and his need for acceptance or interaction with his fellowman. This evolution of the necessary functional capacities of the nervous system for social living has already shown evidence of ontogenetic recapitulation throughout childhood. We now see that the emergence of sexual maturity at adolescence is accompanied by the maturation of a higher order of cortical control and abstract thinking, which lends itself to the social restraint of primitive impulses. This is effected through the learning of social roles and values of adult society during adolescence, largely impelled by the drive for social acceptance, identification, and participation—the postulated social ego drive. What we now wish to point out is that there are inescapable ethical implications of this regular feature of human development.

Most anthropologists have recognized and elaborated upon the Darwinian principle of the survival value of *social solidarity*, with the emergence of sympathy as a key function in the evolution of the nervous system. What some social Darwinists recognized but distorted (Hofstadter, 1944), and most psychologists have completely ignored, is the survival value of *moral sensitivity* in natural selection. The two go hand-in-hand. Abiding by rules of social solidarity, or social mores, implies a willingness to consider the welfare of one's fellowman as an extension of one's own welfare. Wishing to be accepted implies a desire to behave acceptably. Sympathizing with another's pain or pleasure and even anticipating it implies at least some desire to share the avoidance of pain and the seeking of pleasure. We have seen how these expressions of innate social ego needs emerge first as the empathic and identification responses of primary group interaction in early childhood. They then show divergent signs of humane and ethnocentric tendencies during the secondary socialization period of later childhood. Now we see that the social role and value learning of adolescence involves further refinements of social attitudes, behavior control, and interpersonal relationships, in conformity with (or in defiance against) the social mores. One way or another, this profound ego-involvement in principles of behavior toward one's fellow man, one's group, or society as a whole, is essentially a moral issue. Principles of right and wrong, values of what is desirable and undesirable in transactions with the environment, a sense of the proprieties and improprieties of different role behaviors in different social situations—all these will be learned in accordance with the social mores of the given culture. But the point is, they *will* be learned, and they *are* essentially ethical or moral issues. That is to say, in the course of adult role and value learning, one inevitably develops moral, immoral, or amoral values and tendencies which are largely culturally determined; but there is no such thing as *not* developing any moral sensitivity or conflict at all—not unless one is feeble-minded or psychotic. That must be regarded as one of the essential differences between the human being and lower animals, and a direct concomitant of man's evolution as a socially self-regulating species.

All we have done thus far is to admit the issue of ethical implications into the realm of scientific discussion of personality theory. We have not yet dealt with the problem of cultural relativity versus moral absolutism in making ethical value judgments, nor with the admissibility of ethical value judgments as such into the realm of scientific analysis. We shall deal with that problem later.

Returning now to the descriptive analysis of personality development, just what are the particular aspects of role learning in adolescence that are essentially ethical in nature? The specific sanctions of religion, law, and custom, and indeed of socioeconomic status, undoubtedly have their variable influences on the individual's code of conduct and prescribed role behavior in different cultures, while individual temperaments react differently to these same influences. But there are still certain aspects of social role learning which transcend individual and cultural differences. For one thing, there is a further refinement of the humanitarian-ethnocentric dimension which we found emerging during preadolescence. To be sure, these developments are highly susceptible to cultural learning and must now be regarded as secondary elaborations of social ego needs. Thus a religious, familial, and societal influence that elaborates the empathic primary altruism of childhood into humane adult role values would result in *secondary humanitarianism*. This would apply to the adolescents who introcept deep convictions about the dignity of man, service to the community and to society as a whole, and dedication to principles of social justice and social usefulness in one's chosen or accepted role. On the other hand, social influences which serve to intensify the group-centered attitudes of preadolescence into class- and group-centered values and biased role behavior in adulthood could be characterized as *secondary ethnocentrism*. This is the adult-role self-concept introcepted by the racial bigot, the class-conscious snob or rebel, the hostile regional patriot, the political or religious fanatic. This is, of course, an oversimplification, because any degree or combination of these two extremes may occur, and there are times when the extremes are not incompatible (e.g., the humanitarian idealist turning class-conscious rebel against tyranny). What should be quite clear, however, is that such learned attributes and values of social roles can and do determine the individual's relationships to his fellowmen far into adulthood, and these relationships have essentially ethical overtones. They determine the charity or hostility or merely the indifference with which he will treat different individuals or groups, the dignity or rights he will accord them and expect from them, the extent to which he will enrich or restrict his own sphere of social interaction. Such a pervasive influence on interpersonal relations cannot be considered as anything but an ethical one, in the humanistic sense.

The relationship may become clearer if we consider another essentially ethical aspect of adult role learning—the aspect of *social responsibility*. It is our thesis that the assumption of an adult role in any society generally implies the assumption of a certain amount of social responsibility merely by virtue of becoming an adult. This is more clearly articulated in connection with some roles than with others in any given society, and it certainly varies with the type of social organization from one society to another. But we suggest that this, too, transcends individual and cultural differences. If nothing else, the adolescent in any given culture, while learning to assume a role similar to the like-sexed parent or other adults, knows that he is passing from the dependent and largely irresponsible roles of childhood to the more independent and responsible roles of adulthood. This means, for one thing, that he is becoming part of the generation that assumes the responsibility for the care and welfare of the younger generation. Different societies and social groups will vary in the age at which each sex is expected to share in the responsibility of rearing the young, and in some societies this is done collectively. A girl in a Mexican or Indian villager's family will ordinarily start to assume such responsibilities even before puberty, while a middle-class American male may feel exempt from such responsibilities until he achieves fatherhood. However, even in the latter case, there are still other avenues of adult responsibility to which he must respond, such as assuming an occupational role or preparing for one. At the very least, he is expected not to act like an irresponsible child but to show increasing signs of socially responsible behavior. This desire to be regarded as being more competent, more mature, more independent, and more responsible than he was as a child is a normal and highly attractive incentive to adult role learning in the normal adolescent. It is also an illustration of the devices by which social ego needs and competence motivation cultivate the ethical aspects of social maturation.

Thus in cities and villages throughout the world, children first imitate their parents and then, as adolescents, take pride in performing some of the tasks and assuming some of the responsibilities of their parents or other adults in the community. They also generally begin to conform to the moral restraints and social proprieties prescribed for the adolescents and young adults of their culture; but even in rebelling against them, they generally do so in the socially prescribed manner of their peer group. Where extreme antisocial behavior develops and persists, or the learning of adult roles and responsibilities fails to develop at all even in late adolescence, it is suggested that social pathology or psychopathology have disrupted the normal social maturation process at this stage of personality development.

Summary of Child and Adolescent Development

An epigenetic sequence of psychosocial developmental stages has been presented, because it best satisfies the criteria of *salience, integration,* and *continuity* in depicting personality development from infancy to adulthood. These "stages" are not intended to represent sudden leaps to organismic maturity like a butterfly shedding its chrysalis, but rather successive transitional periods of integration of gradually maturing organismic potentialities as they become effectively mastered, modified, and canalized under the common human condition of social interaction and learning. As such, they represent a sequence of successively more complex levels of integration and differentiation toward adult social maturity, more or less paralleling the evolution of human potentialities from early apelike forms to *Homo sapiens socialis.* Although subject to individual and cultural differences, this sequence of developmental stages transcends both. The designations and approximate ages of transition are as follows:

1. *Ego emergence and dependency*: (birth to third year). The infant shows close attachment to the mother or other "caring figure" and complete dependence on her for sustenance, comforting, attention, communication, and healthy stimulation. As awareness of self and environment

emerges, basic psychological needs of efficacy, cognitive clarity, curiosity-exploration, and psychosocial needs of attention, affection, and interaction manifest themselves, expressing presocial and incipient social ego needs.

2. *Primary group interaction*: (third year to seventh/eighth year). As sensorimotor coordination, mobility, speech, perceptual discrimination, and memory reach an early stage of development and integration, more meaningful and deliberate interaction with members of the immediate primary group becomes possible. This period is characterized by playful cooperative-competitive interaction with peers and satisfaction of organismic and psychosocial needs within the immediate familial or community primary group, but is largely limited to concrete here-and-now situational interactions. The emergence of sympathy at age three or four is highly significant and introduces a note of primary altruism into character formation. Acculturation begins to take place through imitative speech and action and the canalization of generic drives on a utilitarian basis, without much understanding of the principles or cultural value judgments involved.

3. *Secondary socialization*: (seventh/eighth year to puberty). By the seventh or eighth year (varying with the individual and the culture), emotional differentiation and abstract thinking have usually developed sufficiently to enable the child to enter into more complex and symbolic (as opposed to a concrete, situational, reactive) interpersonal and cultural interrelationships. This involves ethnic and other secondary group identifications and attitudes, better appreciation of the principles and values underlying the social mores, and better insight into the character, values, feelings and motives of others. Thus the beginnings of social sensitivity, moral code, and socially structured ego identity emerge. Depending on experience and cultural influence as well as temperament, this social identity and attitude formation may take a turn toward latent ethnocentrism and/or more generalized altruism and reciprocity.

4. *Adult role anticipation*: (puberty through adolescence). The simultaneous maturation of sexual, intellectual, and performance capabilities from puberty through adolescence provides a new level of integration and differentiation of organismic and psychosocial needs. This is based largely on a canalization of basic drives through past experience, current learning, and anticipated maturity in the individual's quest for social identity and participation. The predominant theme of adolescence in any culture may therefore be summed up as adult role anticipation. This is manifest in self-actualization and need satisfaction through role and value learning; in tentative exercise of adult behaviors involving adjustment problems of sexuality, social competence, and authority relationships. Though age-sex roles vary with the culture, adolescent female behavior generally antici-

pates the potential role of mother and housewife, while adolescent male behavior generally anticipates some variation of husband-father-provider or self-sufficient bachelor. Ethical aspects of role and value learning include crystallization of attitudes on the humanitarian vs. ethnocentric dimension and the responsible vs. irresponsible dimension.

5

Early Adulthood— Social Role Assumption

The Meaning of Adulthood in Man

The advent of adulthood in humans implies a great deal more in the way of biosocial development than the corresponding advent of maturity or "adulthood" in lower animals. When a zoölogist speaks of a mature salmon or bluejay, he means a specimen that has gone through a series of developmental changes in structure and function and now has fully developed morphologic characteristics that render it capable of performing all of the common functions of species behavior in its natural habitat, including reproduction. In practically all subhuman species morphology is the key to maturation. Not so with the human species. The complex biosocial emergent known as *personality* requires further differential integration of basic functions in social interaction; the human "specimen" cannot be said to have reached maturity until a certain level of such integration has been reached. We have already shown that adolescent development in the human is characterized by cognitive-affective-psychomotor development in social interaction, which brings about a universal type of behavior modification called role learning. This role learning and its attendant introception of social mores, its ego defenses and identifications, and its network of interpersonal relationships, provides an indispensable preliminary stage to the achievement of adult status. Now we shall see that adult status is characterized, in turn, by a further stage of individuation and integration of basic functions, through motivated social interaction, into a pattern of interpersonal and social *commitments,* with all of their behavioral expectancies, ego defenses, and identifications. The most salient and integrative operational concept under which this stage of maturation may be signified is *social role assumption.*

To be more precise, adult maturation in the human is characterized by the assumption of a complex pattern of social role behaviors. Some of these roles grow out of social statuses *ascribed* to him by society in the process of growth, some he *achieves* by his own effort but with social recognition (or nonrecognition), and some roles are *imputed* to him or relegated to him as fortuitous by-products of social situational interaction. Just as some are born great, some achieve greatness, and some have greatness thrust upon them, so the individual gradually assumes his complex of adult social roles through a combination of developmental and situational-social processes.

Whether ascribed, achieved, or imputed by force of circumstance, there is inevitably a large element of outright learning involved in all aspects of this assumption of a complex of role behaviors. Nevertheless, we must not lose sight of the fact that such role assumption represents a regular stage of development of the human organism *as a personality,* which is brought about in the normal course of *inherently motivated* maturation and learning of the inherent potentialities of the species. In that respect, it is just as surely a stage of adult maturation as the spawning behavior of the salmon or the nest-building, hatching, and feeding behavior of the bluejay, even though there is obviously a great deal more outright symbolic learning involved in human maturation. As we have already emphasized, the key to the learning paradox lies in the evolutionary fact that *Homo sapiens socialis* is inherently a symbol-learning and culture-making species, and the criterion of inherence is not whether a function is unlearned, but whether it is *always* learned.

It might be protested that by the time human adulthood is reached, the assumption of social roles and mores is so purely fortuitous and utilitarian that any analogy to the maturation process in lower animals is rather far-fetched. It is true that after cognitive-affective-psychomotor and secondary sex characteristics have matured during adolescence, psychophysiological maturation is more or less complete. However, as we have indicated, the psychosocial level of integration cannot be said to have reached a functioning level that fully represents mature adulthood for the species. There are two principles of biosocial integration which are still operative and which justify the designation of social role assumption as the hallmark of early adult personality development. One is the fact that role assumption is *motivated* in its own right as the canalization of the inherent need for social participation and acceptance. The maturing personality needs to be accepted as a competent member of the family, community, and society, just as he demanded attention and sought curiosity and efficacy satisfaction as a child. The other biosocial principle is that constitutional limitations and predispositions do enter into the learning process, as they always have, on an individual and a species-specific basis. Individuals react differently and selectively to the range of social role influences presented in the same culture, and no culture can maintain role prescriptions that are inconsistent with constitutional predispositions (e.g., sex differences). Thus social role assumption may be regarded as a culmination of the maturation-learning-canalization process by which personalities become differentiated in the course of growing into adulthood. Inherent motives and individual differences help to determine the styles of behavioral interaction that individuals develop, along with the circumstantial learning that inevitably takes place.

We shall, therefore, proceed with our analysis of personality development into early adulthood on the demonstrable assumption that social role behaviors, having been initially intimated during the secondary socialization stage of childhood, and largely learned and anticipated during adolescence, are gradually assumed and acted out by further learning and actual performance in early adulthood, because of the developmental "programming" that is inherent in the biosocial nature of man. We further imply by this that adult maturity has not really been reached until this social role assumption, however defined by the culture, has actually taken place. If this has not taken place at an age that is normal for adult status in that culture, the individual must be regarded as an immature personality or a case of arrested development, no matter how well developed he may be physiologically.

Marital
and
Parental Roles

The modal prescriptions for courtship, mating, and parental role behavior are certainly dependent on the varying structure of the family as a social institution and the social mores surrounding marriage or cohabitation. But even this diversification is limited by the difference of biological involvement of the two sexes in reproduction, and the social awareness or misconception of this difference. This means that the role of the father may be much more subject to cultural variation than the role of the mother, and men's mating behavior in adulthood will vary accordingly. In some primitive tribes of Africa and Australia there is still no awareness of the father's role in reproduction, or it is assumed to be of secondary or auxiliary nature (Boas, 1938). There is no culture, however, which can structure the mother's role on the assumption that *her* part in reproduction is secondary. Even where cohabitation without marriage and illegitimacy of offspring are socially sanctioned up to a point, as in the "consensual unions" of lower-class Latin America, the father's role may become secondary in child-rearing and family cohesion, but the mother's role can never be.

Malinowski (1927) has claimed that a sociological father (whether the real father or not) is a minimal requirement of the nuclear family that provides the basis for civilized living, no matter how primitive. Levi-Strauss (1956), on the other hand, has suggested that family life may exist without a recognized role for the father or father-surrogate. Studies of various cultures may be cited to support either point of view, but they serve to illustrate the variability of the father's role in contrast to the mother's, throughout the variable family structures around the world. Goode (1960) has shown that widespread and socially sanctioned illegitimacy in the Caribbean area, for example, provides a cultural alternative to marriage and legitimate parenthood. The father's role as provider, protector, and authoritative head of the family functions on a tentative basis as long as he chooses to assume the role. He may eventually abandon his family or sanction the bond through legal and religious marriage ceremony. The community simply grants de facto recognition, as it were, to the illicit marriage, which will be legalized eventually if things work out. In the meantime, the father is recognized as the exclusive mate of his "wife" and father of her children, with all the rights, responsibilities, and *machismo* credits thereunto appertaining.

In the absence of legal or religious coercion to enforce the father's responsibilities as head of the family, it is perhaps surprising that so many fathers assume and maintain their roles as heads of their families for as long as they do and eventually do get married. Clearly, the satisfaction of social ego needs provides as much of a motivating force as the sexual. The head of a family always has a more accepted social position in the community than the perennial bachelor; the prestige-giving evidence of virility, so highly valued in Latin America as elsewhere, is directly proportional to the size of the family; the exercise of authority and the exchange of affection within the family brings to a level of mature responsibility the satisfaction experienced in primary group interaction, secondary socialization, and adult role learning. The same motivational arguments could be advanced for enticing free males into marriage anywhere, but it becomes clearer in cultures in which a more or less binding marriage is not necessary for the satisfaction of the sex drive. For the women who become mothers without the security of legal marriage, it may be truly said that both psychosexual and psychosocial fulfillment may be achieved in the very act of assuming the mother role, as long as there is no serious social sanction against unmarried motherhood. With or without the formality of marriage, the children are cared for, family and community life go on in their usual fashion, generation after generation, even if the fathers occasionally abandon their families, or drift in and out, while the mothers provide the stable backbone of family and community life. A study of sex differences in mental health in a Mexican village by Gilbert (1959) showed that women were generally better-adjusted than men. It is apparently easier for women to fulfill their natural ego needs by assuming the role of motherhood than for the men to live up to the inordinate demands of *machismo*. More research needs to be done to relate the variables in these gross sex differences, but it would certainly seem plausible that mental health is related to sex role adjustment.

The wide disparity between Latin American and Anglo-American-European mores guiding family formation and parental role assumption is well illustrated by statistics on illegitimacy in these two vast, culturally different areas. The data in Table 5-1, taken from the 1961 edition of the

Table 5–1 ILLEGITIMATE BIRTHS PER 1,000 LIVE BIRTHS IN LATIN AMERICA, ANGLO-AMERICAN AND CONTINENTAL EUROPEAN COUNTRIES

(Source: *Encyclopedia Britannica*, 1961, vol. 12, "Illegitimacy")

Latin America			Continental Europe		
Argentina	(1958)	240	Austria	(1958)	132
Bolivia	(1955)	208	Belgium	(1958)	20
Chile	(1958)	173	Bulgaria	(1958)	76
Colombia	(1958)	245	Denmark	(1957)	69
Costa Rica	(1958)	235	Finland	(1958)	40
Dominican Republic	(1958)	616	France	(1961)	61
Ecuador	(1957)	351	Germany (West)	(1958)	67
El Salvador	(1953)	613	Ireland (Republic)	(1958)	16
Guatemala	(1958)	716	Italy	(1957)	28
Honduras	(1957)	645	Netherlands	(1958)	12
Mexico	(1957)	236	Northern Ireland	(1958)	23
Nicaragua	(1957)	563	Norway	(1957)	35
Panama	(1958)	739	Portugal	(1958)	105
Paraguay	(1957)	455	Rumania	(1957)	119
Uruguay	(1954)	211	Scotland	(1958)	41
Venezuela	(1956)	564	Spain	(1958)	29
Anglo-American Countries			Sweden	(1958)	100
United States	(1957)	47	Switzerland	(1958)	36
Canada	(1958)	40			
England and Wales	(1958)	49			

Encyclopedia Britannica and listing all of the Latin American and Anglo-American-European countries therein listed, illustrate this gross disparity. The Latin American countries all exceed by far the incidence of illegitimacy in all of the Anglo-American and continental European countries, and some of the former actually report a majority of all births as being illegitimate. Observations by Goode and others suggests that this is principally a lower-class phenomenon. In any case, the implications for adult role assumption (and adolescent role learning) are fairly obvious. A lower-class Latin American male may readily avail himself of the prerogatives of cohabitation and fatherhood without assuming the legal husband role, but the Anglo-American or continental European male must generally choose between marriage and childless bachelorhood. The Latin American lower-class female will more readily allow herself to become a mother and settle for a cohabiting mate; she may even hope for eventual marriage to her mate and father of her children, if she proves to be a good helpmate and mother, and he an aspirant to more middle-class values and Christian morals. However, middle- or upper-class females, as well as those with more devout and protective upbringing, will resist the temptations and blandishments of seductive courtship. She will conform to the inculcated ideals of legitimate married life, even though the double standard of sex morality will give her husband far more latitude in his role assumption than she dare exercise in hers. For that matter, some males will assume their legitimate father-provider roles without availing themselves of the culturally sanctioned double standard, in Latin American communities just as in any other. As always, there are individual differences in temperament and character formation which express themselves in radically different styles of life and adult role assumptions, even within the same family.

There are, of course, numerous sources of error and distortion in such gross sociological statistics: the reluctance to report illegitimacy in some communities, the concealment of illegitimacy through abortion, or marriage after pregnancy, the prevention of pregnancy through use of contraceptive devices, the unavailability of legitimatizing agencies in many remote communities. Nevertheless, the gross cultural differences and individual variations in parental role assumption would still hold true. Perhaps more reliable are the statistics on marriage and divorce in our own country, which also reflect cultural differences that affect individual circumstances in role assumption and change (Fig. 5-1).

What none of these statistics can convey, however, is the human drama that is acted out by the individuals entering upon, by-passing, or dissolving the marital bond; the aspirations, frustrations, and compromises of mating with or without personal attraction, with or without parental approval or social sanction; the eternal dilemma of indulgence in pre-

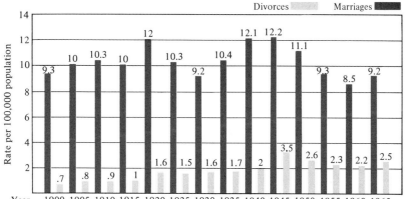

Approx. Ratio
Divorces to
Marriages 1/13 1/12 1/11 1/10 1/8 1/7 1/6 1/6 1/6 1/3½ 1/4 1/4 1/3.9 1/3.6

Figure 5–1. Annual rate of marriages and divorces in the United States, every 5th year since 1900.

marital sex relations when it is not socially condoned, or of resolving jealous rivalries and choices of marital partners even when it is condoned; the practical and religious considerations in choice of mate and in the practice of birth control; the adjustments to the double standard and to gross infidelity or abandonment under varying conditions of social sanction and individual temperament; the strains of adjustment of temperamental differences, sexual compatibility, dominance-submissiveness, and cooperation in family cohesion, with or without the divorce and separation alternatives; and, finally, the delights and exasperations of bringing up children as satisfying fulfillments of the parental role or as the neurotic projection of one's own needs unto the next generation. We do not wish to indulge in script writing for TV "soap operas" but even the most dispassionate personality theorist (if there is such a thing) must take cognizance of the fact that every aspect of marital role assumption, evasion, or dissolution is fraught with impact on the self-concept, ego defenses, interpersonal relationships, and the very meaning of life for every individual—in short, impact on his personality development in the very deepest psychodynamic sense.

Occupational

Roles   The assumption of occupational roles would seem to be even more a matter of outright learning by fortuitous circumstance than is the case with assumption of a marital role. Many a man in every country can point to the purely accidental way in which he obtained a position or was assigned a task that happened to be available at the time that he was there; or he can recall the series of casual contacts that piqued his interest in a certain activity and caused him to experiment with it, until, before he knew it, he was getting involved in that activity as a career; or he can point to the shifts of technological advances, economic prosperity, or social tensions and dislocations that threw him into occupational roles in which he had never before had any interest, or even rendered him unemployed. In educationally advanced countries, the impulsive choice of a secondary school major or the attachment to a teacher may have cast the die; in less developed countries, the absence of advanced education or technical-professional occupations would have limited the range of choices to begin with, or simply have confronted a young man with no choice but to follow in the father's footsteps. The obvious influence of circumstance in the assumption of occupational roles makes it difficult to realize that underlying all the vicissitudes of the working part of life, as of the mating and family-forming part, are certain biological imperatives.

OCCUPATION, NEED SATISFACTION, AND ABILITIES

As in the case of family role assumption, choice of occupation reflects the inherent need to participate in social interaction in some ego-satisfying manner. By the advent of adulthood, this need has long since incorporated the need for efficacy. The drive which made the infant experiment with his father's watch or his mother's beads has by now been channeled into an occupational interest or skill that satisfies both social status and efficacy needs to some degree and manifests itself as a need for social competence. Secondly, there is a selective tendency—faltering though it may be, and limited by social circumstance as it certainly is—which causes individuals to select or get progressively involved in activities for which they have at least the minimal intellectual, psychomotor, and temperamental requirements, and to fail at those activities for which they do not have the minimal requirements. We must reject the thesis expressed by Linton (1936), which reflects earlier attitudes in the history of behaviorism, that "human beings are so mutable that almost any normal individual can be trained to the adequate performance of almost any role. Most of the business of living can be conducted on a basis of habit, with little need for intelligence and none at all for special gifts." Few contemporary anthropologists would insist that a frail and timid child could be taught to assume the role of a Masai warrior-hunter in Africa just as readily as his more robust and aggressive cousin; or that a 'dull child lacking in verbal facility and foresight is just as likely to be groomed for the role of tribal chief as his brilliant, alert, and eloquent neighbor—to say nothing of their chances in European politics or professional life.

The fact is that it requires at least borderline intelligence to assume *any* occupational role with a minimum of adult dependability in any culture. The feeble-minded are, by definition, those who do not possess the requisite learning ability to maintain themselves in any given society or to display the minimal degree of responsibility which adulthood implies. This has been fairly well spelled-out in the legal and custodial institutions of advanced societies, but even in less advanced societies it is necessarily practiced by the demands of plain common sense. At the other extreme, there is the inescapable requirement of high intelligence for the more technically demanding occupational roles or for certain leadership roles which demand a high degree of abstract thinking. These requirements apply more readily to achieved than to ascribed roles, but even the latter tend to show the effects of success or failure in living up to the role expectancies. This is not to say that all "leaders" and technicians are bright and that all of the dull are unemployed everywhere in the world. What we do maintain is that there is a crude, overall selective factor of intelligence and probably temperamental predispositions as well, which influence role assumption in every culture. Beyond that, these individual differences in learning ability and temperament help determine the effectiveness with which the occupational role is practiced, and this in turn affects satisfaction and interpersonal relations. The effects of such social interaction may bring about shifts in social status or role behaviors. One may be recognized as a wise or a foolish chief; the best construction organizer in the community, or a clumsy dolt; a provident and efficient housewife or a scatterbrained and negligent one. Much of the difference will be attributable to the way in which role learning took place in adolescence; but even then, as we have pointed out, individual differences influenced role learning under the same circumstances.

The relationship between intelligence and occupations becomes more evident as technology and social mobility increase. This is well-illustrated by the distribution of group intelligence test scores (AGCT) according to occupation of the millions of enlisted men in World War II (Fig. 5-2).

It can be seen that in spite of the considerable overlapping from one group of occupations to the next, in terms of technical skill required, the interquartile ranges (middle 50 percent) of AGCT scores that prevail among each of the semiskilled occupations (bottom 13) and those of the professional (top 7) do not overlap at all. That means that in our technologically advanced and fairly mobile, democratic society, the average semiskilled laborer does not have the intelligence to learn how to become

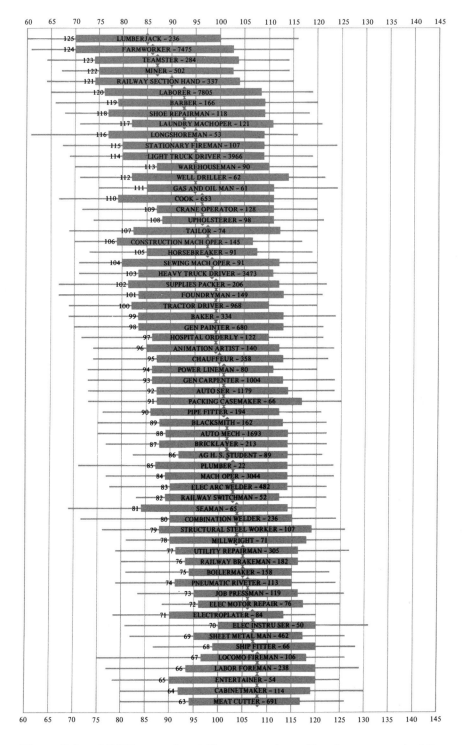

Figure 5–2. AGCT scores for civilian occupations. (Based on scores of white enlisted men only.)

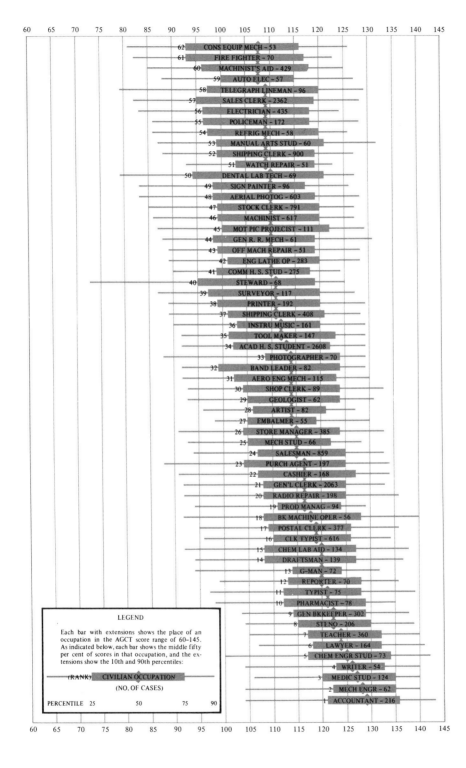

	60	65	70	75	80	85	90	95	100	105	110	115	120	125	130	135	140	145

62 CONS EQUIP MECH – 53
61 FIRE FIGHTER – 70
60 MACHINIST'S AID – 429
59 AUTO ELEC – 57
58 TELEGRAPH LINEMAN – 96
57 SALES CLERK – 2362
56 ELECTRICIAN – 435
55 POLICEMAN – 172
54 REFRIG MECH – 58
53 MANUAL ARTS STUD – 60
52 SHIPPING CLERK – 900
51 WATCH REPAIR – 51
50 DENTAL LAB TECH – 69
49 SIGN PAINTER – 96
48 AERIAL PHOTOG – 603
47 STOCK CLERK – 791
46 MACHINIST – 617
45 MOT PIC PROJECIST – 111
44 GEN R. R. MECH – 61
43 OFF MACH REPAIR – 51
42 ENG LATHE OP – 283
41 COMM H. S. STUD – 275
40 STEWARD – 68
39 SURVEYOR – 117
38 PRINTER – 192
37 SHIPPING CLERK – 408
36 INSTRU MUSIC – 161
35 TOOL MAKER – 147
34 ACAD H. S. STUDENT – 2608
33 PHOTOGRAPHER – 70
32 BAND LEADER – 82
31 AERO ENG MECH – 115
30 SHOP CLERK – 89
29 GEOLOGIST – 62
28 ARTIST – 82
27 EMBALMER – 55
26 STORE MANAGER – 385
25 MECH STUD – 66
24 SALESMAN – 859
23 PURCH AGENT – 197
22 CASHIER – 168
21 GEN'L CLERK – 2063
20 RADIO REPAIR – 198
19 PROD MANAG – 94
18 BK MACHINE OPER – 56
17 POSTAL CLERK – 377
16 CLK TYPIST – 616
15 CHEM LAB AID – 134
14 DRAFTSMAN – 139
13 G-MAN – 72
12 REPORTER – 70
11 TYPIST – 75
10 PHARMACIST – 78
9 GEN BKKEEPER – 302
8 STENO – 206
7 TEACHER – 360
6 LAWYER – 164
5 CHEM ENGR STUD – 73
4 WRITER – 54
3 MEDIC STUD – 124
2 MECH ENGR – 62
1 ACCOUNTANT – 216

LEGEND

Each bar with extensions shows the place of an occupation in the AGCT score range of 60–145. As indicated below, each bar shows the middle fifty per cent of scores in that occupation, and the extensions show the 10th and 90th percentiles:

(RANK) CIVILIAN OCCUPATION
(NO. OF CASES)

PERCENTILE 25   50   75   90

	60	65	70	75	80	85	90	95	100	105	110	115	120	125	130	135	140	145

an accountant, engineer, or teacher. There are, of course, individual and group exceptions, such as those handicapped by immigrant status, racial prejudice, etc. In general, however, intelligence, canalization of needs, and circumstantial learning combine to determine occupational role assumption. We turn now to a consideration of specific occupational role behaviors as they are related to personality.

Business executives. More attention has probably been directed to the qualifications and behavioral expectancies of the American business executive than to any other role in American society. A report by Henry (1949), based on a study of 100 American executives, reveals how intimately related such role behavior is to the psychodynamics of personality.

The participation in this role, however, is not a thing apart from the personality of the individual participant. It is not a game that the person is playing, it is the way of behaving and thinking which he knows best, that he finds rewarding, and in which he believes.

Thus the role as socially defined has its counterpart in the personality structure of the individuals who participate in it. To some extent the personality structure is reshaped to be in harmony with the social role. The extent to which such reshaping of the adult personality is possible, however, seems limited. An initial selection process occurs in order to reduce the amount of time involved in teaching the appropriate behavior. Those persons whose personality structure is most readily adaptable to this particular role tend to be selected to take this role. Whereas those whose personality is not already partially akin to this role are rejected. . . . Individual uniqueness in personality was clearly present, but despite these unique aspects, each executive had in common this personality pattern:

Achievement Desires. All show high drive and achievement desire. They conceive of themselves as hard working and achieving people who must accomplish in order to be happy. The areas in which they do their work are clearly different, but each feels this drive for accomplishment. . . .

The Idea of Authority. The successful executive posits authority as a controlling but helpful relationship to superiors. He looks to his superiors as persons of more advanced training and experience whom he can consult on special problems, and who issue to him certain guiding directives. He does not see authority in his environment as destructive or prohibiting forces. . . . It is of interest that the dominant crystallization of attitudes about authority of these men is toward superior and toward subordinates, rather than towards Self. This implies that most crucial in their concept of authority is the view of being part of a wider and more final authority system. . . .

Decisiveness. Decisiveness is a further trait of this group. This does not imply the popular idea of the executive making quick and final decisions in rapid-fire succession, although this seems to be true of some of the executives. More crucial, however, is the ability to come to a decision among several alternative courses of action—whether it be done on the spot or whether after detailed consideration. . . . The breakdown of this trait (usually found only in cases where some more profound personality change has also occurred) is one of the most disastrous for the executive. . . .

Personality Dynamics

Activity and Aggression. The executive is essentially an active, striving, aggressive person. His underlying personality motivations are active and aggressive—although he is not necessarily aggressive and hostile overtly in his dealings with people. This activity and aggressiveness are always channelized into work or struggle for status and prestige. . . .

The Nature of Their Interpersonal Relations. In general the mobile and successful executive looks up to his superiors with a feeling of personal attachment and tends to identify with them. His superior represents for him a symbol of his own achievement and activity desires and he tends to identify himself with these traits in those who have achieved more. . . . On the other hand, he looks to his subordinates in a detached and impersonal way, seeing them as "doers of work" rather than as people. He treats them impersonally, with no real feeling of being akin to them or having deep interest in them as persons. . . .

The Attitude Toward His Own Parents. In a sense the successful executive is a "man who has left home." He feels and acts as though he were on his own, as though his emotional ties and obligations to his parents were severed. . . . In general we find the relationship to the mother to have been the most clearly broken tie. The tie to the father remains positive in the sense that he views the father as a helpful but not restraining figure. Those men who still feel a strong emotional tie to the mother have systematically had difficulty in the business situation. The residual emotional tie seems contradictory to the necessary attitude of activity, progress, and channelized aggression. The tie to the father, however, must remain positive—as the emotional counterpart of the admired and more successful male figure. Without this image, the struggle for success seems difficult.

Implicit in Henry's description is a confirmation of our thesis that occupational role assumption is both a product and an instrument of personality development at maturity, and that there is both individual choice and social selection involved in a mobile and industrially advanced society. In this case, selection is likely to be done on a fairly deliberate basis after the candidate has become available, while the individual's decision to make himself available is determined by temperamental and intellectual predispositions already channeled in this direction in childhood and adolescence. The social interaction of aptitude and circumstance and of experiential channeling of needs goes on in the very process of occupational role assumption. Society, in this case represented by the employer and the business world, judges the individual by his performance in accordance with its competitive-materialistic values and the particular needs of the industry of which he is a part. The individual must continue to find the style of life and values of his occupation sufficiently satisfying to continue to strive for "success" by its definitions, and to display or develop the aptitudes to assure satisfaction rather than frustration or failure. If both the individual and the role of executive find that they are "made for each other," he will continue to "climb the executive ladder of success," to use business-school and financial-page jargon, and will perceive himself, his fellows, and the world with the eyes of an executive.

There are, as we conceded at the outset, many fortuitous circumstances which determine occupational role selection. In the executive realm, there are men who inherited their positions from their fathers or married the boss's daughter, just as there are women who "succeed in business without really trying" by using their feminine wiles. With or without these bypaths, there is nevertheless a long-range selective process, constantly involving experiential modification of personality, which makes occupational role assumption a truly intrinsic part of personality development and tends to select as well as to cultivate similar character trends among the individuals assuming similar roles.

Scientists. This is further borne out by other studies of personality characteristics of people in different occupations. Of the many studies available, we shall quote from Roe's (1956) summary of her own study on eminent American physical scientists:

The studies of physical scientists included physicists, physical chemists, geophysicists, astrophysicists and theoretical engineers. The study of individual scientists reports clinical analyses and life histories of 22 men who were selected by their peers for their eminence in research (Roe, 1951). This group is subdivided into those doing theoretical and experimental work, since it developed that this difference in orientation is associated with different personality and intellectual factors.

For the theorists, going to college was usually taken for granted in the family, but it was unusual for the experimentalists. The theorists liked school and reading, the experimentalists rarely did. The psychosexual development of all of them was more often retarded than not, and few of them have any genuine social interests now. A striking aspect of the present adjustment of both groups (clear both in interview data and in projective tests) is the nature of their relationship to other persons. For the most part these are not close, and are relatively unimportant to them in the over-all picture of their lives. This does not prevent their being adequate husbands; divorces were fewer in this group than in any other groups of scientists. On the whole the theorists seem to have developed more adequate social contacts. Both groups have normal aggressive tendencies, but these are better controlled with the theorists and less likely to be handled by getting out of the provoking situation, or, if this is impossible, by explosive outbursts.

Attitudes toward their parents now and in earlier years seem to have been an important factor. They are largely free of present parental ties of any strongly emotional sort, and without guilt over this. Although there is frequently present an open or covert attitude of derogation of their mothers, they almost universally respect their fathers profoundly, although they seem never to have been very close to them. This situation may well have been a factor in their adoption of a profession which has more 'masculine' values in our culture than have many of the learned professions. (You will remember that Henry noted in business executives a similar freedom from conflictual parental ties.) (Roe, 1956, pp. 214–215)

OCCUPATIONAL PRESTIGE

Another aspect of occupational role assumption that is particularly germane to biosocial theory is *prestige*. Most societies recognize a hierarchy of prestige in the different kinds of occupational roles they maintain in their social structure. This provides motivation to achieve high-status occupations insofar as they can be achieved and to live up to high-status positions insofar as they are ascribed to the individual. Where there is social mobility it provides incentive to "improve oneself"—that is, to assume successively higher occupational roles in the prestige hierarchy, as we have already mentioned, in "climbing the executive ladder." When the social structure is fairly rigid, it provides incentive to improve one's performance through effort and experience, so that one may gain the prestige differential of being respected or sought-after as a particularly skillful or reliable worker. Even when there is little latitude for self-improvement, or the individual does not have the achievement drive to exert himself for it, he will usually fulfill some easily achieved or ascribed role in order to enjoy a minimum of social acceptance, rather than sink to the role of the useless member of the community, which entails the lowest prestige of all. All of this is easily understood in terms of the basic nature of social ego needs and their canalization through the adult role behaviors of the culture. It cannot be explained on the basis of learned instrumental behavior to satisfy hunger and physical comfort needs, nor as sublimations of the sex drive. This is demonstrated over and over again when individuals choose occupations or positions for less money but more assured prestige, or the lengths to which they will go to protect their reputations when it cannot serve any purpose other than prestige.

Lest we think that the occupational prestige hierarchy is merely a by-product of the industrialized society's wealth-and-power hierarchy, or a relic of the feudal system's class structure, let us remember that even fairly primitive societies have their occupational prestige hierarchies. Herskovitz (1952) observed that among the Tonga of East Africa the occupational hierarchy ran about as follows, from highest to lowest: canoe-builder, cutters of whale teeth, funeral directors, stonemasons, net-makers, fishermen, large house-builders, tattooers, club-carvers, barbers, cooks, peasants.

In larger countries that really comprise several subcultures, where some industrialization has taken place, a variety of complex institutions have become well developed, urban and rural life exists side-by-side along with great technological advances and notable cultural lag in some areas, and the division of labor has reached a truly fragmented state. Thousands of occupations can be listed and defined (as is actually done for the United States in *The Dictionary of Occupational Titles*). Classes of occupations are broken down into kinds of jobs or professions, or areas of interest;

these in turn are broken down into specialties, and these into sub-specialties, and new ones are created every year as technology advances. But in spite of all this fragmentation and innovation, the general outlines of a fairly well-articulated prestige hierarchy of occupations keeps right on developing, differing somewhat among different subcultures, and shifting from time-to-time, but showing a remarkable consistency among different investigators.

Table 5–2 OCCUPATIONAL PRESTIGE RATINGS FOR THE UNITED STATES, 1947 AND 1963
(After Hodge, *et al.*, 1964)

Occupation	Rank 1947	Rank 1963	Occupation	Rank 1947	Rank 1963
U.S. Supreme Court Justice	1.	1.	Building Contractor	34.	31.5
Physician	2.5	2.	Artist—Paints & Exhibits	24.5	34.5
Nuclear Physicist	18.	3.5	Musician—Symphony	29.	34.5
Scientist	8.	3.5	Orch.		
Government Scientist	6.	5.5	Author of Novels	31.5	34.5
State Governor	2.5	5.5	Economist	34.	34.5
Cabinet Member-Fed.	4.5	8.	Official—Int. Labor	40.5	37.
Gov't.			Union		
College Professor	8.	8.	Railroad Engineer	37.5	39.
U.S. Rep. in Congress	8.	8.	Electrician	45.	39.
Chemist	18.	11.	County Agric. Agent	37.5	39.
Lawyer	18.	11.	Owner-Oper. Printing	42.5	41.5
Diplomat-U.S. Foreign	4.5	11.	Shop		
Service			Trained Machinist	45.	41.5
Dentist	18.	14.	Farm Owner-Operator	39.	44.
Architect	18.	14.	Undertaker	47.	44.
County Judge	13.	14.	Welfare Worker—City	45.	44.
Psychologist	22.	17.5	Newspaper Columnist	42.5	46.
Minister	13.	17.5	Policeman	55.	47.
Member Bd. of Dir.—	18.	17.5	Reporter—Daily Paper	48.	48.
Large Corp.			Radio Announcer	40.5	49.5
Mayor—Large City	6.	17.5	Bookkeeper	51.5	49.5
Priest	18.	21.5	Tenant Farmer-Manager	51.5	51.5
Dep't. Head—State	13.	21.5	Insurance Agent	51.5	51.5
Gov't.			Carpenter	58.	53.
Civil Engineer	23.	21.5	Mgr. Small City Store	49.	54.5
Airline Pilot	24.5	21.5	Local Official—Labor	62.	54.5
Banker	10.5	24.5	Union		
Sociologist	26.5	26.	Mail Carrier	57.	57.
Instructor—Pub. Schools	34.	27.5	Automobile Repairman	59.5	60.
Accountant—Large	29.	29.5	Railroad Conductor	55.	57.
Business			Traveling Salesman	51.5	57.
Public School Teacher	36.	29.5	Plumber	59.5	59.
Owner-Factory—Approx.	26.5	31.5	Playground Director	55.	62.5
100 persons			Barber	66.	62.5

Personality Dynamics

Table 5–2 Continued

Occupation	Rank 1947	Rank 1963	Occupation	Rank 1947	Rank 1963
Mach. Oper.—Factory	64.5	62.5	Dockworker	81.5	77.5
Owner-Oper.—Lunch Stand	62.	62.5	RR Section Hand	79.5	77.5
			Night Watchman	81.5	77.5
Corporal—Regular Army	64.5	65.5	Coal Miner	77.5	77.5
Garage Mechanic	62.	65.5	Waiter in Restaurant	79.5	80.5
Truck Driver	71.	67.	Taxi Driver	77.5	80.5
Fisherman—Owns Boat	68.	68.	Farm Hand	76.	83.
Clerk in Store	68.	70.	Janitor	85.5	83.
Milk Routeman	71.	70.	Clothes Presser—Laundry	83.	85.
Streetcar Motorman	68.	70.	Soda Fountain Clerk	84.	86.
Lumberjack	73.	72.5	Sharecropper	87.	87.
Restaurant Cook	71.	72.5	Garbage Collector	88.	88.
Singer in Nightclub	74.5	74.	Street Sweeper	89.	89.
Filling Station Attendant	74.5	75.	Shoe Shine Boy	90.	90.

Comparing the results of such surveys in other more or less industrialized countries, a surprising degree of agreement is found in the prestige rankings for similar occupations. Inkeles and Rossi (1956) give the correlations of ranks assigned to the common core of similar occupations in Russia, Japan, Great Britain, New Zealand, the United States, and Germany (Table 5-3).

Table 5–3 CORRELATIONS BETWEEN PRESTIGE RANKS ASSIGNED TO COMPARABLE OCCUPATIONS IN SIX COUNTRIES
(After Inkeles and Rossi, 1956)

	Japan	Great Britain	New Zealand	United States	Germany
U.S.S.R.	.74	.83	.83	.90	.90
Japan		.92	.91	.93	.93
Great Britain			.97	.94	.97
New Zealand				.97	.96
United States					.96

These very high correlations—in spite of the diversity of cultures and the numerous sources of variability and error of judgment—suggest, for one thing, a basic undercurrent of approximation of social status values among industrialized societies. It also illustrates that there is an underlying recognition of selectivity by competence, especially in more mobile and democratic societies, and an acceptance of social prestige as an incentive for competence motivation.

As with marital and occupational roles, reference group identification often grows directly out of adolescent role-learning experiences. However, the assumption of affiliative roles is subject to varying degrees of awareness or commitment by the individual and of recognition by society. It often changes imperceptibly in the course of ripening values in adulthood; it may change drastically in the process of social change or by deliberate effort on the part of the individual, especially in a more mobile society. This is not so true of such well-defined group memberships as church, race, and nationality. But it often applies to looser reference group identifications, such as socioeconomic class, segments of political public opinion (e.g., "liberal" or "conservative"), avocational-interest groups (e.g., sportsmen, music lovers, literati), or other categories of common interests, values, and styles of life. Most of these identifications grow initially out of the role- and value-learning experiences of adolescence, when maturing social consciousness is channeled into an awareness of social structure and the individual's anticipated place in it. This is further defined by adult experience, changing status in familial and occupational spheres, and the adjustment of emotional needs to and through such group identifications. We shall discuss the psychodynamic aspects of role conflict, change, and adjustment in Chapter 7.

A principal category of group or class identification that is not always clear-cut but is fairly universal is socioeconomic class. Such class distinctions are at a maximum in societies organized along more or less feudal lines with landed aristocracy at the top and peasants or serfs at the bottom, or whatever the hierarchy of power and wealth might be. They seem to be at a minimum in so-called homogeneous societies in which the entire population exists on a bare subsistence level and would be called "lower class" if there were any actual class structure in their society. A closer look at such social units usually reveals, however, that even there some distinctions of socioeconomic status are made. Just as "in the kingdom of the blind, the one-eyed man is king," so in lower-class peasant life the man with a few sheep he can call his own is envied or emulated by the neighbor who has none. Only complete communal ownership of property can eliminate this distinction of socioeconomic status, but then some form of bureaucratic hierarchy is apt to take its place to administer the communal production, distribution, and use of property. Without getting involved in social philosophy at this point, we can only note that some form of social prestige hierarchy exists in almost all societies, not only in occupational roles, as we have already noted, but also in terms of more generalized socioeconomic status.

Since all aspects of social role behavior are interrelated in the integrated functioning of the personality, it is impossible to separate socioeconomic status from occupational status, marital status, or other categories of reference group membership and identification. Occupational status is often used as the best indicator of socioeconomic status. Marriage is most frequently entered into between partners of similar social status, race, and religion. Occupational opportunities are frequently affected by racial prejudices and class distinctions which serve in turn to perpetuate these distinctions.

The close relationship between family role, occupational role, and ethnic or class reference group identification is most clearly illustrated in societies that maintain a rather rigid system of race, class, or caste discrimination. In India, for example, the caste system has dominated social life for centuries, determining reference group identification at birth and setting rather inflexible limits on ascribed (or prescribed) adult role commitments. Rigid rules forbid marriage outside of one's caste; almost as rigid rules prevent eating and drinking together. Discrimination favors some castes and excludes others from certain general occupational classifications. A quite well-understood social hierarchy of status pervades the whole system. In this hierarchy, the Brahmin Hindu caste is generally conceded to be the highest and the Harijan (Untouchables) caste the lowest. Even though the Indian Constitution of 1950 abolished Untouchability and sought to encourage equality, social caste discrimination has continued. This is true even for Indian college students, who approve of equality in principle but still maintain attitudes of "social distance."

A study by Kuppuswamy (1956) showed that the vast majority of 591 Indian college students questioned in the state of Madras wanted to abolish or modify the caste system (Table 5-4).

Table 5-4 ATTITUDES TOWARD CASTE AMONG SOUTH INDIAN COLLEGE STUDENTS
(After Kuppuswamy, 1956)

	N	Abolish Caste System	Modify Caste System	Marry Anyone	Eat With Anyone	Rent To Anyone	Admit To College
Brahmin (Hindu)	188	43	48	29	77	44	97
Non-Brahmin (Hindu)	290	66	31	55	85	55	66
Muslim	36	55	28	45	83	61	56
Christian	77	64	34	29	77	48	78

However, less than half were willing to allow a member of any caste or creed to marry outside of his caste. The data show less discrimination (more acceptance) for renting a house and still less for eating together or admitting to college—but the discrimination is still there. In general, women were more ready to accept the status quo than men.

PSYCHOSOMATIC REPERCUSSIONS

Here, too, it must be remembered that socioeconomic status and ethnic affiliation have more than descriptive significance as interrelated variables in the network of adult role assumptions. They are deeply involved in the individual's sense of identity, of his worth as a human being, in the determination of his style of life, and in the frustrations and satisfactions of his basic needs—from the psychophysiological to the psychosocial. In the interrelated biosocial system of personalities in social interaction, the perception of imputed inferiority or superiority, of belonging to or being excluded from various reference groups, and the different styles of life that these differences entail, can have repercussions throughout the individual's entire personality structure. This will entail not only such psychosocial abstractions as self-concept reflecting the imputed status by society but also the psychosomatic reactions to one's perpetual sense of frustration or well-being, as the case may be. The practice of racial segregation in various countries is, of course, a case in point.

An interesting illustration of the psychosomatic effects of racial discrimination and segregation was carried out by Scotch (1960). He obtained blood pressure measurements of male and female Zulus in an urban and a rural community in the Union of South Africa and compared these readings with other published data showing the average blood pressure measurements of American males and females and the averages for white and Negro residents of a biracial community in Georgia. We have condensed and simplified the data in Table 5-5. This table bears striking testimony to the thesis that any conditions of social stress which provoke tension[1] or anxiety in *any* of the individual's role assumptions will have an observable and sometimes measurable impact on the total personality. It will do so both in the outward manifestations of role behavior and in the psychophysiological state of the organism. According to biosocial principles of levels of integration within a total field or system of interrelated forces (see Chapter 1), such psychosomatic reactions to perceived social discrimination are highly probable. They are just not always easy to demonstrate. In this study, they can be.

We can see from Table 5-5 that Negro residents of the biracial community in Georgia generally have higher average blood pressure in both

---

[1] In individual cases, high blood pressure (hypertension) does not necessarily imply emotional tension or anxiety; however, in group comparisons these exceptions will tend to cancel each other out.

Table 5-5 MEAN SYSTOLIC BLOOD PRESSURES IN ZULU URBAN AND RURAL, REPRESENTATIVE AMERICAN, AND GEORGIA NEGRO AND WHITE RESIDENTS (Adapted from Scotch; *in* Smelser and Smelser, 1963, pp. 324–26)

Age Group	Amer.	Zulu		Diff. (Urban)*	Georgia		Diff. (Negro)*
				MALE			
25–44	127	rural	118	+07	white	123	+15
		urban	125		Negro	138	
45–64	136	rural	128	+13	white	135	+24
		urban	151		Negro	159	
				FEMALE			
25–44	122	rural	116	+12	white	117	+18
		urban	128		Negro	135	
45–64	137	rural	132	+16	white	141	+23
		urban	148		Negro	164	

* Differences below 12 or 13 are generally significant at the 5% chance level, and over 12 or 13 are significant at the 1% chance level.

younger and older age groups and in both sexes than do the whites. Compared to a wide sampling of Americans, the Georgia whites generally run lower and the Negroes higher, showing a great deal more hypertension among Negroes than among whites in the same community. That this is not merely an inherent racial difference is indicated by the fact that rural Zulu natives' blood pressure runs slightly lower than those of the Georgia whites, while the urban Zulus run considerably higher than the rural— though not quite so high as the Georgian Negroes. Selective urban migration is ruled out in the Georgia sample because both racial groups live in the same community, though segregated; it is ruled out in the Zulu sample because many urbanites stated preference for the country life and vice versa. Other possible factors such as diet have likewise been ruled out. The most likely explanation for these differences is the different style of life and role behavior imposed on each group as they are exposed or not exposed to the onus of social discrimination and socioeconomic constriction. In the case of the Zulus, their exposure to degrading conditions of working for their white European masters in the city is compounded by the stresses of urban life for the segregated Negro working class. This is further compounded for women, who occupy a subservient role to the men wherever they are, and by added role conflict in the midst of social change.

Almost all rural informants said that poverty and migratory labor were the major problems of life. In the city, however, respondents went on and on when asked the same question. Not only was there poverty, but degradation and humiliation in the treatment of Africans by Europeans, frequent arrests, high rates of illegitimacy, divorce and separation, alcoholism, and open competition for a few jobs. It is of interest that a significantly greater percentage of city dwellers expressed a preference for living in the country. . . .

In contrast to the dominant position of men in the traditional social structure the position of women is subservient. Whereas the men work hard for only a few months out of every year and spend the rest of the time in relative leisure, looking after cattle and in general supervising the output of the family unit, the women work extremely hard and have relatively little leisure. They are engaged in such matters as working in the fields, fetching water, and chopping and carrying firewood great distances. Women's positions in this society involve difficult and arduous roles, which are nevertheless clearly defined and inculcated during childhood training. . . .

In the city the Africans live crowded together in "locations" that can charitably be described only as slums. The quality of the housing, the sanitation, and the space must be described as poor. The men work for low wages at the most menial tasks and under the most trying conditions. Moreover the men have to travel great distances to work with inadequate transportation. Since the men do not earn enough to support their families, it is customary for the women to take jobs as domestics, and this requires that they too travel long distances and spend the greater portion of their time away from home. Children are either sloughed off on relatives or friends, or left to fend for themselves in the streets of the location. . . .

The position of the women has become less subservient though more ambiguous, and this increases tension between man and wife. Now that many of the women are wage earners they have begun to emerge from their traditionally subordinate position. This is made easier by the fact that in the city a woman is no longer under the domination of her husband's mother and other in-laws, but this emergence is not without attendant difficulties. While working as domestics for European families the Zulu woman learns that she need not be completely subordinate to her husband. She also learns that the European husband and wife share many activities, but when she returns to the location she finds that her husband absolutely refuses to engage in joint activities and maintains tribal tradition to the extent of sharing his leisure with other men (Scotch, 1960).

It may seem that we are overstating the case for biosocial repercussions of social status. May it not be that such differences in high blood pressure (appropriately called hypertension) merely reflect the arduousness of the labor traditionally performed by the different racial groups and the physical severity of their segregated living conditions? The statistical data alone do not give unequivocal proof on this point, but the interview data (obtained by Zulu assistants for the Zulu sample) do lend the necessary qualitative support to our thesis. If one needs further proof that it is the *indignity* of segregation and relegation to lower social status that increases frustration and hypertension, there is more gross and valid evidence in current history than any bookful of statistical data can possibly document.

Witness the abandonment of the "separate but equal" doctrine of segregation in the United States; official abandonment of "untouchable" class status in India; and the continuing revolution against *apartheid* in the Union of South Africa itself. It is often the fate of psychological research merely to confirm in almost infinitesimal scope the human motivations and conflicts that give rise to mass movements and history itself.

AFFILIATION, SOCIAL CHANGE, AND ALIENATION

We have discussed this study in some detail because it illustrates in many ways the significance of reference group identification for the psychodynamics of personality adjustment. We have already commented on the psychosomatic component of frustrating role conflict. The study also illustrates the effect of social change on social identification and alienation, which has broader implications.

It cannot be assumed that all aspects of adult role assumption, particularly the fluid reference group affiliations, are automatic fulfillments of identifications anticipated and learned during adolescence. In some respects, the reference group identifications and attendant value systems automatically learned by introception from parents, peer group interaction, and more formal educational influences do not survive the reality-testing and often disillusioning experiences of adulthood; nor can they avoid the modifying effect of competing value systems and roles brought about by enlargement of the life space and the recognition of social change.

One widespread casualty of reference group identification, either in early or middle adulthood, is religious identification and conviction. We say identification rather than affiliation because the identification may suffer without any change in the nominal affiliation; and we say conviction rather than professed or acquiescent belief because it is easier to give lip service to religious precepts than to believe and live by them. The sincerely idealistic adolescent has often assimilated his parents' religious identification, with its belief system and values, only to be confronted with a number of "cognitive dissonances" in adulthood. Among these are often (but not necessarily): (1) the challenge of science and technology as a dependable basis of reality-testing and belief, rather than faith in religious dogmas or the efficacy of magical powers; (2) the onslaught and prepotency of material need and the demonstrations of power in real life as against the strength of spiritual values; (3) the incompatibility of competitive or exploitative conceptions of self-aggrandizement and "progress" with the altruistic or even self-abnegating doctrines preached by many of the world's greatest religions; (4) increasing skepticism about the moral necessity of different doctrinaire restraints and taboos; and (5) doubts cast on the ethnocentric bias of many religions as being contrary to democratic or nationalistic principles (conflicting loyalties) and inconsistent with experience in social interaction.

The result is often a gradual alienation from religious convictions and identification, even if affiliations are loosely maintained, so that it becomes a less and less salient aspect of the adult-role complex than it was in adolescent role learning. This happens not only to the Zulu turning his or her back on tribal witchcraft and superstition in the face of the efficacy of modern technology and medicine, but it happens frequently among the more educated members of Judeo-Christian societies in Western civilization. Some of the typical forms in which a perfunctory religious reference group identification is maintained are: acknowledgment of family's "religious preference" on records and questionnaires, without the person's having any actual church affiliation; purely social church affiliation with only occasional attendance; use of religious ceremony only at crucial life milestones: birth, marriage, death; perfunctory participation in prayers and other religious rituals only on prescribed public occasions when nonconformity would be too conspicuous (e.g., grace before meals, or Invocation at public ceremonies, or the Moslem call to prayer); lip service to sexual taboos and other religious sanctions, while maintaining the right to do as one pleases, or to do as others do, in one's own private life. This common practice of "perfunctory conformity" is a far cry from the devout religious conviction and identification which many an adolescent has learned from early childhood. Many maintain it as a central anchorage of their adult value systems, but many gradually grow away from it with advancing maturity, sometimes returning to it in later life.

The resolution of the cognitive dissonance referred to above, perhaps more often than people are willing to admit, sometimes goes to the extreme of complete disengagement from any sectarian religious affiliation or belief and to conscious adoption of social value systems which have little reference to the religious group affiliations of the individual's parents. Some drift to other religious group identifications which seem more consonant with their values or their other reference group identifications. Any such "identification drift" away from or toward or between religious reference groups is bound to have some ethical implications in the adult's social role behavior. We say this not because we grant that religious institutions are the exclusive guardians of moral values, but rather because *any* restructuring of one's conception of his relationship to his fellow man has some ethical implications. Even if the humane or ethnocentric bias cultivated during secondary socialization and role learning fades into a socially alienated, amoral hedonism in adulthood, *that*, too, is a system of social role values with ethical implications. If we recognize a modicum of social responsibility and concern for one's fellowman as a universal and biosocially determined characteristic of adult maturity, then we may justly diagnose this amoral hedonism as actually an egocentric regression. In any case, the important point is that reference group identification is not merely a matter of specimen-labeling for group-handling purposes, but a vital approach to the understanding of individual character and psychodynamics.

Psychodynamics of
Role Behavior

We have attempted, in our brief description and illustration of the principal aspects of adult role assumption, to hint at the underlying psychodynamics of personality development in social interaction. In the most basic sense, the concept of self—of who I am and what I want to be, what I want out of life in common with others, and what satisfies me as an individual, and how I behave to protect my self-esteem and acceptance by others—all of these are most intimately involved with the assumption and acting out of a social role-complex in the course of maturation of the organism. This requires a deeper and more psychodynamic conception of role than that of an assigned part in the tragicomedy of life, which one accepts and acts out like a type-cast actor playing the king or the fool in Shakespearean drama. Adult social-role assumption, as we have been using the phrase and will continue to use it, signifies the behavioral integration of all that a person is and strives for, inwardly and outwardly and in his interpersonal relationships, as a member of the society which he and his fellow human beings have created and continually re-create as their natural way of life. It refers not merely to the nominal social statuses implied in each aspect of the role-complex, but to the motives and satisfactions, emotional conflicts and adjustments, both conscious and unconscious, that determine his choice of roles and his manner of integrating them, as well as the personal idiosyncrasies that put his stamp of individuality on the "interpretation of the role." For the part one plays in life and the way in which he plays it reveals in large measure the total character and personality of the actor. It is not merely a legalistic set of facts or a behavior protocol of what the individual did and did not do in a sequence of events.

Thus the *persona* or "player's-mask" concept of social role has little validity for personality theory, because it does not do justice to the integrative-psychodynamic conception of role behavior as an expression of the total personality. The often portrayed clinical picture of "the real inner man" of repressed primitive desires, lurking far beneath the superficial mask he wears for social play-acting, rests on a misconception of the psychodynamics of role behavior. Role behavior is determined not only by the social prescriptions for certain generic roles in each culture but also by the developing character structure and the predisposing tendencies of the individual assuming the role. Thus the very manner of assumption and adjustment to the role-complex may reveal the deepest motives and emotional conflicts not observable to the public, or it may express the most superficial and banal conformity to social expectation without conflict. In either case, the depth of the individual's motivation and the presence or absence of conflict is part of his manner of assuming and playing his complex role in life.

Having sketched the general outlines of personality development from earliest ego emergence and socialization to adult social role assumption, and having laid so much stress on the integrative-psychodynamic nature of social role in personality analysis, we can now review and articulate more clearly some of the psychodynamic principles of role behavior which we have intimated in the course of these chapters.

PRINCIPLE OF PSYCHOSOCIAL CONTINUITY

We have already stated, as a cardinal principle of psychodynamics, that "the child is father to the man." That is, the experiences, emotional conflicts, and character formation undergone in childhood generally determine what kind of an adult that child will turn out to be. Our psychosocial developmental scheme is ideal for psychodynamic analysis in terms of a continuity of stages of ego development from infancy to adulthood. We have seen how social consciousness first develops in the milieu of face-to-face primary group interaction; then becomes more "acculturated" through learning experiences that make use of the child's increasing capacity for abstract thinking and communication within its expanding life space; then goes on through a period of more deliberate individuation and integration in terms of social role anticipation; and finally reaches early maturity through the assumption of a complex of social roles. It is thus easy, or at least rational, to trace back the case history of any adult with a given set of behavioral characteristics and interpersonal relationships to see "how he got that way." We can do so because we have seen how the channeling of basic motives in a particular direction in childhood predisposes the individual to role learning that is either consistent with it or creates some conflict and adjustment, and that in turn largely predetermines the adult's pattern of role assumption and adjustment. The continuity may not be superficially clear-cut in every case, and there are situational as well as cultural circumstances which require abrupt changes of status and role behavior. However, there is a psychodynamic continuity just the same.

Because psychosocial development is, in fact, the most salient and integrative aspect of personality development and provides a realistic basis for the lifelong continuity of ego adjustment, it provides a normative sequence of psychogenic (mental) causation. Moreover, it makes no arbitrary assumptions about the critical period or the level of personality integration at which lifelong anxiety may be generated. As we see it, maladjustment, frustration, and anxiety may be generated at any period of development and through any cause that threatens ego security or interferes with its normal process of development. That could be the lack or loss of a caring figure in childhood, physical injury or disease at any age (especially any disorder that impedes communication), social dislocation or discrimination in adolescence or adulthood, traumatic experiences or an accumulation of them at any age, or the inability to fulfill ascribed roles in adulthood. Any of these and an endless variety of other causes could affect the entire personality from then on, although the effect will be influenced by the ego strength built up, up to that time, and the success of the defenses mobilized from that time on.

We would suggest that much of psychosexual determinism is a misinterpretation of the consequences of earlier psychosocial development. At least, the principle of psychosocial continuity in psychodynamics is more parsimonious and more readily observable than the principle of psychosexual determinism. According to the former, early experiences with parental dependency and the give-and-take of primary group interaction will invariably influence reactions to authority and peer relations in later stages of role learning and role assumption. The reaction may be rebelliousness in one case and submissiveness to authority in another, ready assumption of adult roles, or shrinking from parental responsibility. But in any case, there will be psychodynamic continuity from childhood experience to adult role assumption, as the case history will show. Other sources of conflict and adjustment may not come into play until well after early childhood, because the organism simply is not ready to experience them as meaningful emotional conflicts until further psychosocial development has taken place. This applies to such areas of potential conflict as awareness of ethnic and social-class status, which can scarcely become meaningful before the secondary socialization stage, or to a discrepancy between skills and social competence needs, which may not become acute until the adult role anticipation stage. Such psychosocial adjustments and conflicts will inevitably have a bearing on the social role assumptions and adjustments of adulthood. So will psychosexual adjustments, but these will probably be subordinated to and integrated with the continuity of social role development, which we see as the continuous integrator of the total personality.

Since individuals usually assume their ascribed roles with apparent conformity to a social norm in a given cultural setting, or even achieve them within a narrow set of alternatives provided by the social structure and the learning opportunities that setting presents, it is often overlooked that such conformity may be purely superficial. The failure to probe deeper into individual differences in *adjustment* to any assumed role has led some anthropologists to assume that almost any individual can learn to assume the roles that society ascribes to him or the few that are open to competition. Even ignoring for the moment the limitations we pointed out at the extremes of intelligence, aptitude, and temperament, there is still a question that applies to the vast majority: Even if you can make the average person in any culture assume his ascribed role, can you make him *like* it and feel that he really "belongs" in that role? What we are implying, of course, is that in spite of superficial conformity to social role prescriptions, there are vast differences of adjustment that actually alter the role as played by the individual. The truth is, to give the cultural relativists their due, that most individuals do learn to "like it"—more or less. That is, they learn to accept the roles that come their way without much regard to individual differences, and manage to find some satisfaction or security in filling such roles. The reason for this is the satisfaction of social ego needs that make culture possible in the first place. Every individual needs a sense of belonging and acceptance in his social community—assuming that any ascribed, achieved, or imputed role does at least provide some kind of status in the community.

Yet each individual personality is continuously undergoing a process of adjustment and accommodation in a field of forces including his social and other ego needs, his role expectancies, and the interpersonal relationships that revolve around them. It is in the very nature of the human life process that individuals do seek constantly to adjust, and many do succeed— more or less. But it is that very "more or less" that interests the personality theorist and clinician, even if it is of little interest to the anthropologist. It is a psychological truism that a constant state of perfect adjustment is an impossibility, because every satisfaction brings on its own further need for newer satisfactions. Add to this the tremendous individual variability that is bound to exist among the performers of any given set of roles and the variable impact of cultural and situational demands on those individuals, and we can soon guess how tremendously variable role adjustment must be. What needs to be recognized, however, is that it is not the adjustment of the personality *to* an imposed or chosen role that is involved here, but the adjustment of self *as defined by* the role-complex in depth.

To illustrate this principle convincingly would require the clinical presentation of many case studies of various individuals—showing their unique adjustments and maladjustments to given sets of circumstances and role expectancies. Yet any biography or collection of case studies would illustrate it well enough, as does observation with a clinician's eye in any social setting. For while roles and social situations in a given culture may be stereotyped, individuals never are. All one finds is a gross conformity—more or less—to prescribed behavior in given situations, but never a lifelong, uniform pattern of well-adjusted compliance to all social expectations by all individuals in any given community—not even in any single family.

Without going into such elaborate case studies, it takes very little imagination to see the implications for individual variability of adjustment even in the group data we have presented. We have already referred to the limitless variety of human conflicts and adjustments concealed behind the cold statistics on marriage, divorce, illegitimacy, etc. We have also seen how rebellion against the inferior status of a segregated race is complicated by the rebellion of some of their women against *their* subordinate status. The data presented by Scotch (1960) show the great variability of these reactions, with a few men and women exhibiting far more hypertension than the rest. In contemporary and past history, we also know that some individuals rebel more openly against subjugation than others; some seethe with inner rebellion, and some seem able to comply with almost anything as long as they are accepted and protected for what they are. Gilbert's (1959) study of mental health in a Mexican village likewise showed wide differences in adjustment of the men in the village to the strains of *machismo*, and the women showed similar individual differences in adjustment to their domestic roles. Even then the results are obscured by the selective emigration of young men and women out of the village to the more sophisticated city, when they find the extremes of sex-role behavior patterns intolerable. Indeed, with so much individual variability in adjustment to the prescribed role behaviors in any culture, it is truly remarkable that investigators have ever been able to get statistically significant differences of adjustment indices at all.

PRINCIPLE OF ROLE INTEGRATION

Finally, we must recognize that in spite of the convenient abstraction of considering each part-role separately, it is the integration of the total role-complex that reveals the biosocial integration of the total personality. To hark back to our rejection of the original meaning of *persona*, we reject it whether it means one or several masks that the actor wears on life's stage. What we are dealing with in personality dynamics is an organized (or even poorly organized) *person*, who is eternally aware of the continuity and indivisibility of selfhood and is so recognized by his fellows, in spite of all the gradual changes of growth and the sudden shifts of behavior called for in different social contexts.

We can put this integrative hypothesis to the test by considering whether there is always an inner psychodynamic consistency in the role complex assumed by any individual. Can a man really be a Dr. Jekyll and Mr. Hyde—two radically different and incompatible characters—in his professional and his secret private life? Forgetting the fictitious drug in the original story for the moment, it has been known to happen in certain pathological states known as *dissociative states*.[2] Personality disorganization may also occur in an entirely different way in certain psychotic ("insane") states in which there is no rational consistency to behavior, but rather an inconsistent irrationality. And that is precisely the point. One has to probe into such rare dissociative or psychotic states to find conditions under which the personality apparently loses its integrative cohesiveness. Even then, the astute clinician or psychotherapist seeks to unravel the psycho-dynamic processes through which unfulfilled or frustrated ego needs sought outlet through such pathological conditions or escapes from selfhood.

But what of the apparently inconsistent character traits revealed in different roles assumed by the same individual in everyday life? What of the meek employee who acts like a tyrannical dictator in his husband-father role at home? What of the sweet and obliging coed who makes everybody, including her sorority sisters, love her in college, but who acts like an ungrateful and demanding brat to her mother? What of the Zulu worker in South Africa who resents the daily indignities imposed on him by his white employer, only to force other indignities on his own wife? We already know the answers to these apparent inconsistencies, for they all illustrate the same basic psychodynamic pattern: displaced aggression in reaction to frustration or the strain of excessive conformity.

The study of such personalities and their varying patterns of role behavior shows that there is usually a dynamic reconcilability of the most divergent and inconsistent role behaviors, leaving no doubt about the essential consistency of the total personality. There is indeed an "integrative character" that reveals the basic personality structure more clearly than the enumeration of the various parts of the role-complex assumed by the individual. Is he a regular churchgoer and self-righteous public citizen, but a cheat in business and a faithless husband to boot? Then perhaps "pious hypocrite" keynotes his character better than a description of any of his role behaviors. Is he truly humane, altruistic, and construc-

---

[2] The student should not be confused by the popular misconception that such "split personality" cases are properly diagnosed as schizophrenia. The latter is an example of severe disintegration of the total personality and derives its name from being "cut off" from reality. The "split personality" is a neurotic dissociative state in which each of the dual personality entities retains its ability to function in accordance with reality.

tively productive in all of his role behaviors, deriving his greatest satisfaction from helping others and benefiting society? Then we are dealing with that rare character, the true humanitarian, and that character pattern overrides any and all of his specific roles.

There are also apparent anomalies in the behavior of frankly antisocial characters, but these cases also fit into a consistent psychodynamic pattern. Al Capone, the Chicago gangster of yesteryear, was supposed to have been a devoted family man and a protector of his loyal henchmen. There is really nothing incompatible about these seemingly inconsistent role behaviors. Such ruthless characters often use their different social roles in different ways to serve the same central purpose of unenlightened egocentricity, exploiting or brutalizing those who are objects of or obstacles to their greed, and displaying a purely egotistical patronage to those who accept, admire, or belong to them. In terms of character development, this situation merely suggests arrested development at the primary group interaction stage without the secondary elaborations of primary altruism. Other antisocial role patterns develop along lines of even greater cleavage between primary group identification and out-group or "inferior-group" rejection. Combined with rigid social values that depersonalize or abort any sense of adult responsibility and empathy, such cleavage in social role can bring about truly monstrous results. We found many such anomalies among the Nazi war criminals, whose personalities seemed greatly at variance with the crimes they admittedly committed (Gilbert, 1950). To understand such behavior, it is necessary to examine it in the total context of psychosocial dynamics and social pathology. The enormity of the antisocial behavior can often be understood only as a social magnification of a seemingly minor characterological defect, but there is always such a defect and it does help to explain the individual's role in such actions. We shall deal with antisocial behavior more fully in Chapter 11.

Summary We have designated early adulthood as the *social role assumption* stage of personality development. This is based on the premise that assumption of a complex of social roles and their attendant behavioral prescriptions, adjustments, and responsibilities is the hallmark of adult maturity in *Homo sapiens socialis*. Though social role assumption presupposes a period of learning and anticipatory behavior in adolescence and continued learning and cultural adjustment in early adulthood, it represents an integration of organismic potentialities and needs that transcend individual and cultural differences. Moreover, certain generic roles are more or less universal to the species. These roles include familial, occupational, and (usually) group-affiliative ones, which are inherent in the biosocial nature of man, regardless of their individual and cultural variations. These and other roles and statuses are dynamically interrelated in affecting the self-concept and emotional adjustment of the individual. Therefore, in postulating the assumption of some such complex of social roles as the hallmark of human adulthood, we reject the static "player's mask" concept of role (or *persona*), but conceive of it instead as the operational medium of personality dynamics in adulthood. This may be seen in the mutual interaction of marital, occupational, and reference group satisfactions or frustrations and their impact on the mental health of the individual. Furthermore, there is a certain continuity and integration of individual personality development in the striving for human dignity, identity, social competence and acceptability.

In further elaboration of this concept, we have discussed three principles of psychodynamics in role behavior: (1) psychosocial continuity, (2) variable adjustment, and (3) character integration. These principles provide a basis for the study of individual personality and character development as well as of certain phenomena of social action and interaction.

Illustrative Case History

Throughout this discussion we have emphasized the importance of affiliative satisfactions or frustrations to the personality adjustment of the individual. This is true of both privileged and underprivileged minority groups, and of ethnic differences and social value systems that sooner or later affect every one in this world of changing and impinging cultures. It is, therefore, not to illustrate an unique minority-group problem in America but rather to exemplify a universal one that we turn to the case of an American Apache Indian, growing up and striving to make an adjustment in the transition between two cultures.

PHILIP CASSADORE—APACHE AMERICAN

Philip Cassadore was born in 1933 on the San Carlos Apache Indian Reservation in Arizona, the youngest of four sons of Chief Broken Arrow, and a great-grandson of Chief Cassadore, who negotiated the peace treaty between the Apache tribe and the United States Government. His entire childhood was spent in the reservation-traditional upbringing of an Apache boy—living and sleeping on the floor of the family's wickiup, eating typical Apache food; learning the Apache language, customs, myths, and religion; and becoming accustomed to life in the woods and fields under his father's watchful eye. Though born to a matrilineal kinship system, he recalls his father's influence on his upbringing from early childhood. His earliest recollections are of waking to the sound of his father's chanting of Apache songs and legends and being taken to the woods by him to learn about nature. His father took the general attitude of letting the boy learn from experience, though he might warn him not to touch a poisonous snake and would see that no real harm befell him. Without formal instruction, his father's example and the primary group norms managed to inculcate in him the manly virtues of courage, truthfulness, tribal pride, personal reticence, respect for the person and property of others, and strict separation from the female sex.

His entrance into the reservation's elementary school introduced an element of culture conflict right from the beginning. Apache tradition and religion had been conveyed to him in song, example, and precept at home in the absence of written language, and continued to be. At the reservation school, however, the 3 R's and history were taught entirely from an ethnocentric American point of view. He could not help sharing with his Apache peers a sense of shame and guilt over the backwardness, violence, and treachery imputed to the Indians, and the general assumption that the good, civilized people were Christian Americans. As a result, celebrations at Christmas, Easter, and Thanksgiving usually made the Indian children feel "left out" and rejected, and these holidays were ignored as much as possible. Exceptions to the rule were the converted Catholics from the missionary school, who felt superior to the unconverted Apaches. July 4th was always a happy occasion, because the Indians were allowed to identify as Americans and the British became the enemy for a change. The culture conflict and its attendant frustrations of acceptable identity reached a peak during the preadolescent years and engendered some aggression in the usually compliant Apaches. They could not direct this aggression to the all-powerful and paternalistic white establishment; instead, they tended to berate each other. As a result, many fights broke out among the schoolchildren—a pattern which Philip thinks persists into adulthood for many reservation Indians.

When old enough for junior high school, Philip attended the public high school in Globe, Arizona, along with four other Apaches. In this mixed school population the prejudice against the "dirty, warlike, treacherous Apaches" soon took on a more overt and hostile form and Philip suffered much humiliation on this account. All five Apaches eventually quit the school under the pressure of this harassment and ostracism. Nevertheless, determined to finish high school, Philip earned his high school diploma by taking correspondence courses, as permitted by the rules governing Indian education.

Like many other Apache boys, Philip's first sexual experience was with an older woman, in this case an Apache divorcee, when he was 14. Such experiences were sporadic, however, because of the strict separation of the sexes.

By the time he finished high school, Philip found himself still stranded between two cultures, unable to compete for a job in the white man's world and not content to settle for the dull and poverty-stricken life of a semi-educated reservation Indian. This was increasingly driving his brother and many of his peers to drink and delinquency. The problem of assuming some self-sufficient role in Indian-American society was rendered more acute by the death of his father when he was 19 years old. At about this time he was attracted to the Mormon missionaries by offers of food and sympathy. Recognized as a bright and personable lad, he was given a scholarship to study business administration at Brigham Young University in Provo, Utah. Here the same old problem of ethnic identity raised its ugly head. Though there were many Indian students from tribes all over the country, tribal rivalries and religious identifications insinuated themselves into all aspects of campus life. Being unwilling to change his deeply ingrained Apache identification, Philip was unable to find rapport with either the eastern or midwestern Indians, who had generally adopted the Mormon religion and white culture; nor with the white Mormons, who regarded Apaches as heathens in the first place. Caught in this cross fire of prejudice from both the majority and minority groups, he quit the university in his third semester.

Soon thereafter, at about the age of 27, he married a 24-year-old Apache nurse who had attended the St. John Missionary School and had been graduated from the Albuquerque Nurses Training School for Indians. They married in typical Indian style by parental negotiation and no ceremony. His wife, having been converted to Catholicism and educated as a Catholic, besides becoming familiar with the white man's ways as a nurse, resented this reversion to "primitive custom," although she could do nothing about it. She had secretly wanted a regular Church wedding with a white gown and all the trimmings (instead of being treated like a squaw). The wife's familiarity with the white man's ways in love-making (from observation, movies, woman-talk, and general cross-cultural exposure as a nurse), also proved to be disconcerting in other ways. "She's dissatisfied because I don't kiss her and fondle her all the time like a baby, the way a white man does. But if I did, I'd feel unnatural. An Apache doesn't pay so much attention to his wife's feelings and isn't expected to cater to her the way a white man does. . . . She's also been brain-washed by this psychiatric stuff about sex." Discussing what he meant by the last point, it appeared that psychiatric social workers on the reservation, misinterpreting the cultural sex patterns, glibly attributed latent homosexuality to any Apache who defers to his mother and fails to satisfy his wife. Philip thinks one man committed suicide as a result of this. Many divorces, suicides, and alcoholism result from the cultural clash on sex relations.

His three younger children are being brought up as Catholics by his wife, although no definite understanding or commitment was ever arrived at. Philip is not sure what stand he should take and prefers not to make an issue of it.

Increasingly concerned about the ethnic prejudices and economic hardships bedeviling his people, Philip decided to devote himself to the study and propagation of Apache culture among his own people, to foster a sense of tribal pride and a willingness to help themselves in gaining some control over their destiny. He first worked as a clerk in the tribal trading post in San Carlos, while gaining some recognition as a singer of tribal folk songs. He later took a job as the court clerk in the tribal court, but continued his appearances on radio, at festivals, and other public affairs as an Apache folk singer. This eventually brought him a regular weekly spot on the local radio and some recordings of folk songs. At the same time, he was able to obtain part-time assignments such as getting tape-recordings for an oral history project for the Department of Anthropology at the University of Arizona. Still trying to work out his personal and career problems as an Apache American in a white Christian civilization, he hopes to achieve acceptance and self-help for his people without the violent confrontation that some of his eastern tribal counterparts advocate, or the complete (and impossible) loss of Indian identity that some of his peers have aspired to.

6

Other
Developmental
Viewpoints

In the foregoing chapters we have traced the broad common features of personality development from infancy to adulthood, with some indications of how individual and cultural differences develop and interact. Our theoretical framework was based on the fundamental facts of human evolution and the biosocial complexity of motivated human behavior which it reveals, both in phylogenetic and ontogenetic development. The successive modal stages of integrated and differentiated psychosocial behavior were highlighted by observational, experimental, and statistical data. These data provide reference points and contributory evidence to the general theoretical framework, but require much more extensive confirmation, especially by cross-cultural research. In presenting this developmental program and rationale for *Homo sapiens socialis*, we glossed over some other widely held theoretical formulations for personality development which also take evolution for granted, implicitly or explicitly, and recognize the psychodynamics of personality growth, motivation, conflict, adjustment, and change. Two schools of thought widely discussed as alternative developmental theories are psychoanalysis and S-R (stimulus-response) learning theory. Each school has a number of varying doctrines and dissenting disciples, so we can attempt only a brief commentary on a few of the leading viewpoints. (For a more comprehensive survey of personality theories, see Hall and Lindzey, 1957; for theories of child development, see Baldwin, 1968.)

*Psychoanalytic
Viewpoints*

FREUDIAN PSYCHOSEXUAL STAGES

Freudian developmental theory is predicated on the assumption that instinctive behavior in man is fundamentally the same as it is in lower animals, except that the sex drive[1] in man is modified by the prolonged, immature dependency of childhood and the restraining influences of society. Because of this, as well as the clinical evidence of neuroses originating in the libidinal (psychosexual) conflicts of childhood, Freud conceived of personality development as consisting essentially of stages of psychosexual cathexis (discharge) from infancy to puberty. These states may be described briefly as follows:

Oral stage (first year). The newborn infant derives pleasure from suckling at the mother's breast; later from eating, drinking, and biting. The incorporation of food (oral receptive) and the biting (oral aggressive) aspects of pleasurable oral activity provide the prototypes of character traits that may persist far into adulthood. This pleasurable stage of oral dependency may also represent a retreat or reversion in later life from mature adult heterosexuality, as in alcoholism or homosexuality, or excessive passive dependency.

Anal stage (second year). The pleasurable sensation of elimination is thought to encounter restraint and an imposed self-regulation during toilet training. The child senses this as a means of pleasing or frustrating the mother, and develops habits of retention or elimination as part of its emotional interaction with the mother. Retentiveness, compulsive cleanliness, and impulsive disorderliness are traits that Freudians relate to the habits of pleasure-seeking formed during the anal stage.

Phallic stage (third to fifth year). During this stage the boy becomes aware that he has a penis like his father, and the girl undergoes the traumatic experiences of thinking she is castrated because she has no penis. The boy shows his sexual interest by exhibitionism, masturbation, and sexual fantasies in which he gets rid of his father in order to claim the affections of his mother. This is called the *Oedipus complex*, after the legend of the king of Thebes who unwittingly killed his father and married his own mother, in fulfillment of a prophecy by the Oracle. Without necessarily understanding fully the nature of marital relations (though he has presumably already witnessed the "primal scene" of sexual inter-

---

[1] The German word *Trieb*, as used by Freud, may be translated as either "drive" (its cognate) or as "instinct," as it usually is in psychoanalytic literature.

course between his parents), the boy does sense that his Oedipal fantasies are dangerous and subject to punishment by the threatened father. He imagines (or has heard) that the appropriate punishment for his sexual interest is castration and so he undergoes "castration anxiety." This tends to repress to the unconscious his new-found stirrings of sexual interest. A girl undergoes a somewhat similar experience with psychosexual cathexis and penis envy with respect to the father, but does not experience as complete a repression of sexual interest because she can no longer be castrated. The working through of the Oedipus complex and its repression is considered crucial to personality development in all people. Freud maintained that all neuroses could be traced back to such repressed infantile sexuality.

Latency period (sixth year to puberty). Psychosexual interest remains repressed (unconscious) until puberty reawakens it.

Genital stage (early adolescence). With the reawakening of the sex drive through endocrine changes and mature sexual sensations, the essential maturity of the organism is reached right after puberty. This maturity is expressed by an interest in heterosexual love and sharing, in contrast to the self-centered or narcissistic sexuality of childhood. It implies realistic planning and adjustment to the demands of society in fulfilling the biological function of reproduction. A variety of defense mechanisms may be used, but much depends on whether the psychosexual conflicts of childhood have been resolved or persist in disguised form.

Few clinicians today would dispute the general principle of psychic causation of neurosis which Freud advocated, or the working hypothesis that much of adult maladjustment may be traced back to emotional conflicts of childhood. Many have believed from the very beginning, however, that Freud rather overstated the case for sexuality as the central theme of personality development, adjustment, and deviant behavior. While some of these reservations and antipathies may have been due to Victorian prudery in the early years, studies of child psychology and personality in recent decades have brought the whole Freudian developmental rationale into serious question.

We would question, in the first place, the adequacy of any psychophysiological course of development to represent the complex integration of the total personality. The use of the term "sexual" or "libidinal" may sometimes be stretched to include all emotion, affiliation, and human relationships, but Freud's psychosexual stages of development are quite clearly set at the psychophysiological level of explanation. Even so, it is true that psychosexual development may influence social behavior; but so may cognitive development or any other organismic function influence social behavior (as we have shown). Moreover, the reverse is also true—basic social needs may influence the sexual—and indeed, any function may influence any other in an integrated organism. We have suggested that developmental stages should represent, insofar as possible, an integrated, salient, and continuous course of development for the total personality.

Another deficiency in the Freudian developmental scheme is the lack of correspondence between his psychosexual stages and systematically observed patterns of behavior in later studies. (Freud did not, of course, have the benefit of such systematic observations, but reconstructed child development largely from the memories and fantasies of his patients.) One stage that is generally conceded, even by Freudians, to be in error, is the latency stage. It is strange that Freud should have designated the entire preadolescent period as one of sexual inactivity and repression, when survey data (e.g., Kinsey et al., 1948, 1953) support widespread clinical impressions that this is actually the period when sex interest and activity begin in many children. The data show a continuously rising curve of sex interest and activities (substitutive as well as direct) from preadolescence to early adulthood, with indications of wide individual and subcultural differences. Cross-cultural studies likewise show wide cultural differences in sex play and sexual indulgence, with no "latency." Freud's scheme of childhood psychosexuality with its castration anxieties and Oedipus complex, followed by six years of repressed interest and then a sudden resurgence to maturity is not only at variance with observed empirical data, but seems to put a strain on the rule of parsimony in theoretical formulations.

Finally, Freud virtually ignores the continuous psychosocial development of the child, which most authorities would agree is indispensable to the understanding of personality development, as well as emotional adjustment throughout life.

ERIKSON'S PSYCHOSOCIAL STAGES

E. H. Erikson has sought to reinterpret Freud's essentially psychophysiological analysis of libidinal cathexis as really representing a series of psychosocial crises in which basic attitudes and feelings are brought to a head and resolved to the benefit or detriment of individual personality adjustment. He also fills in the gap in the latency period and extends his analysis through late adulthood. Erikson's thinking reflects not only the advances of several more decades of research in the behavioral sciences since Freud's formulations but also his own direct involvement in child psychiatry, longitudinal child development studies, and the comparative study of American, Indian, and Germanic cultures. The main thrust of this breadth of experience and research exposure on Erikson's thinking was an emphasis on ego adjustment to the realities of the social environment and on the importance of interpersonal relations in personality development. (This illustrates the influence of such studies on the whole movement known as "psychoanalytic ego-psychology," with which Erikson is identified; cf. Rapaport, 1959.) Erikson's "Eight Ages of Man," (1959, 1963) include somewhat psychosocialized versions of the five Freudian stages plus three stages of adulthood. They may be summarized as follows:

1. *Basic trust vs. basic mistrust.* The easy satisfaction of the infant's physical needs (hunger, sleep, elimination) lays the foundation of basic trust of the environment. Gradually he is able to associate human figures with this feeling of comfort, and he gains reassurance from the familiarity of the mother's face and the dependable repetition of need-satisfying routines. The mother's sensitive care of the baby's needs not only creates a sense of trust but also forms the basis for a stable sense of identity in the child. Inconsistent or interrupted care may lay the foundation of lifelong basic mistrust or anxiety. (This corresponds to Freud's oral stage.)

2. *Autonomy vs. shame and doubt.* Autonomy is expressed by voluntary movements such as grasping or the choice of when and how to eliminate. Shame and doubt stem from the sense of being observed "with one's pants down" and exposed to disapproval, often without knowing exactly why. A sense of self-control brings a lasting sense of security. Loss of self-control brings a lasting propensity for shame and doubt. The child's sense of "law and order" is shaped from this time onward. (This period corresponds to Freud's anal stage.)

3. *Initiative vs. guilt.* Autonomy is augmented by a sense of initiative stemming from infantile genitality. Seduction, jealousy, sibling rivalry, quests for privilege, fantasies of power, dreams of being overpowered and punished, all these express initiative, but spill over into areas that are taboo or punishable. Here the stage is set for an anticipation of the child's future parental role or a long-lasting guilt reaction with attendant defense mechanisms and hostility toward the forbidding parent. (This period corresponds to the Freudian phallic stage.)

4. *Industry vs. inferiority.* Sexual fantasies are put aside and sublimated by learning and productivity. The kind of instruction offered children will vary with the culture, but the child becomes aware of the technological ethos of the culture and his identity within it. Failure to measure up produces a sense of inadequacy and inferiority. (This period corresponds to Freud's latency stage.)

5. *Identity vs. role confusion.* With the advent of genital maturity and the recognition of adult tasks ahead of them, adolescents become concerned with what others think of them and how they will fit into society. Role confusion may involve conflicts over sex or group identification, which adolescents guard against by romantic, ethnic, and clannish over-identification. Young people are, therefore, particularly vulnerable to social ideologies. (This period corresponds to the Freudian genital stage.)

6. *Intimacy vs. isolation.* The young adult is now eager to fuse his identity with that of others. The subordination of self to sexual and social intimacies may bring about defensive reactions that lead to self-isolation. The fulfillment of mutual intimacy through sexual orgasm depends to a large extent on cultural and class mores, opportunity, and individual temperament. However, mental health does not preclude delay for the sake of emotional preference or ethical considerations. Furthermore, true adult genitality implies mutual heterosexual love and trust, with a sharing of work, procreation, and recreation. Isolation precludes such adult intimacy and cultural continuity.

7. *Generativity vs. stagnation.* Generativity is primarily the older generation's concern in establishing and guiding the next generation, but also is meant to include *productivity* and *creativity.* Generativity thus includes both psychosexual and psychosocial creativity, and the absence of either leads to a life of stagnation.

8. *Ego integrity vs. despair.* The well-adjusted and creative individual faces the final years with an acceptance of life with all its vicissitudes and limitations, but with satisfaction in his own style of life and personal integrity. Having given meaning to life through his own life, he can face the end with less remorse. To the noncreative person, the thousand little disgusts and disappointments of life culminate in the fear of death, the final testimony to the meaninglessness of life.

From a biosocial point of view, Erikson's stages of ego development through the life cycle are a decided improvement over Freud's psycho-physiological stages of libidinal cathexis. At least they provide some recognition of social interaction, role learning, and the influence of cultural diversity. Within that context, the psychosexual stages are not abandoned, but become somewhat symbolic prototypes of advancing maturity with individual and cultural differences. However, it does appear that Erikson is often straining to achieve a "Freudian fit" to the observable social development and acculturation of the individual, as well as the integration of cognitive processes with other organismic functions in this socialization process.

As a result, Erikson's psychosocial stages may also be questioned on empirical and theoretical grounds. It is not certain that the attitudes or adjustment crises designated at each stage really constitute the most salient features of their respective age periods or places in the sequence of development. Granted that identity is a recurrent theme, we would think that the same may be said for basic trust, autonomy, industry, inferiority, initiative, and guilt; that they do not necessarily come to a head in the sequence or in the paired alternatives given above. Furthermore, it is not clear how the designated stages—which are psychological rather than psychosocial elaborations of psychosexual stages—are integrated into progressive social development (e.g., role learning, role assumption, and the like), although some of this is implied. We have the impression that Erikson was trying to work out a biosocial framework of personality development, but was too committed to the Freudian framework to make it work completely. Further research may clarify this approach or work out a closer "fit" with biosocial theory.

SULLIVAN'S DEVELOPMENTAL EPOCHS

Other latter-day students and practitioners of psychoanalysis also felt that Freudian psychodynamics needed to take more systematic account of the social nature of man and of his social development from infancy to adulthood. A group of these theorists, sometimes designated as neo-Freudians (though that designation could be more appropriately applied to the "ego-psychology" group), concluded that a different approach to psychodynamics and development was necessary, rather than patching up or amplifying Freudian doctrine. Of the psychoanalysts most closely identified with this socially oriented neo-Freudian group, Harry Stack Sullivan was the one who most explicitly defined a new set of dynamic concepts and a developmental scheme based on it.

Sullivan rejected libido theory as the dominant force in personality adjustment and development. Instead, he defined personality as an abstraction of interpersonal relations, and psychiatry itself as "the study of interpersonal relations." It is this essentially social interaction and development that gradually transforms man the animal into man the human being at maturity. Although subject to the maturation of man's unique constitutional characteristics, personality development is largely based on the experiences of developing interpersonal relations common to the species, and their individual variations. (The similarity to the basic biosocial point of view should be obvious here.) The tension states of basic needs as they occur are recognized, but so are the tension states generated by *anxiety*-provoking interpersonal experiences. These tensions undergo energy transformations in the course of experience, in which cognitive and other organismic processes are also involved. The developmental epochs are designated by the commonly used terms, with the insertion of "juvenile era" between childhood and preadolescence. In this section, all direct quotations are from Sullivan, 1953.

Infancy. The child enters life with only fleeting, disconnected sensations, which Sullivan calls the "prototaxic mode" of cognition. However, the infant is dependent on the "mothering one" for sustenance and comfort, and this is signified by the infant's attachment to the mother's nipple. The significance of this attachment, however, is not a discharge of libidinal energy through the mouth, but the first means of establishing an interpersonal relationship—one of dependence on the mother. The nipple takes on object significance as good, bad, wrong, or unsatisfactory, in accordance with the mother's dependability in providing need satisfaction. In the course of learning to make sense out of its environment, the infant advances to the "parataxic mode" of cognition, which assumes cause and effect by association. At the same time, the infant's self-system begins to take shape as it begins to recognize its own body and to learn from experience how to respond to its experienced tensions.

Childhood. Interpersonal relations are enhanced by the learning of rudimentary speech and gesture, and cognition soon advances to the "syntaxic mode." This involves the beginning of logical thinking and meaningful communication. Learning from the environment proceeds rapidly. The self-system begins to distinguish between the sexes and to identify with the parents accordingly. Verbalisms and dramatizations facilitate these processes. Punishment or restraint by the parents in the course of the child's explorations are not necessarily damaging to the self-system. It is the rejection of the child or the withholding of tenderness when needed that brings about "malevolent transformation" in children, making them act as though living in a hostile world. This reactive obstinacy or defiance may trigger a vicious circle of mutual hostility which colors the child's interpersonal relations from that time on.

Juvenile Era. This period spans the middle years of childhood and of elementary school, providing an opportunity to adjust the self-system to a broader segment of society. "Take, for example, the child who has been taught to expect everything, who has been taught that his least wish will be of importance to the parents. . . . Or take the petty tyrant who rules his parents with complete neglect of their feelings. Take the child, on the other hand, who has been taught to be completely self-effacing and docilely obedient. . . . In this culture, where education is compulsory, it is the school society that rectifies in the juvenile era a great deal of the unfortunate direction of personality evolution conferred upon the young by their parents and others constituting the family group. There are two contributions to growth in the juvenile era, the experience of social subordination, and the experience of social accommodation" (p. 228). Much of this restructuring of the self-system takes place in interaction with the peer group, which characterizes the emerging needs of the juvenile era. Adjustment to new authority, competition and compromise with peers, sublimation of needs, social judgments and stereotypes, and orientation in living are among the developments of interpersonal relationships in the juvenile era.

Preadolescence. The need for interpersonal intimacy is expressed in seeking friendships and forming gangs and cliques. Altruistic concern for a pal appears between 8½ and 10 years. "I trust that you will finally and forever grasp that interpersonal intimacy can really consist of a great many things without genital contact; that intimacy in this sense means, just as it always has meant, closeness, without specifying that which is close other than the persons. Intimacy is that type of situation involving two people which permits validation of all components of personal worth. . . . They also, specifically and increasingly, move toward supplying each other with satisfactions and taking on each other's success in the maintenance of prestige, status, and all the things which represent freedom from anxiety, or the diminution of anxiety" (p. 246). Both constructive affiliations and antisocial gang activity represent community influences on the inevitable socialization process.

Early adolescence. The lust dynamism of puberty and the continuing need for intimacy lead simultaneously but independently to a shift of interpersonal interests to the opposite sex. "The change in the need for intimacy—the new awakening of curiosity in the boy as to how he could get to be on as friendly terms with a girl as he has been on with his chum—is usually ushered in by a change in covert processes. Fantasy undergoes a rather striking modification. . . . This interest in members of the other sex also spreads into the area of communication between the chums. . . . If the group includes some members whose development is delayed, the social pressure in the group, in the gang, is extremely hard on their self-esteem and may lead to very serious disturbances of personality indeed" (p. 265). The lust dynamism may thus collide with the socially-defined sense of security, with self-esteem, and with the need for intimacy itself, depending on the prescriptions of the culture and the specific situation. Under favorable conditions, these and earlier dynamisms are integrated into a readinesss for lasting love relationships, heterosexual as well as nonsexual.

Late adolescence. "Late adolescence extends from the patterning of preferred genital activity through unnumbered educative and eductive steps to the establishment of a fully human or mature repertory of interpersonal relations, as permitted by available opportunity, personal and cultural" (p. 297). Both formal education, if pursued to late adolescence, and life experiences contribute to the growth of thinking and adjustment in the syntaxic mode—by consensual validation of social realities, finding one's place in the cultural patterns of living and making a living, and of achieving sympathetic understanding of others as prerequisite to self-respect and a maturing sense of responsibility. Residual anxieties from previous stages of development, or new conflicts in interpersonal relations, may retard the achievement of maturity, or cause regression to childish modes of behavior.

Of the three psychoanalytic viewpoints we have briefly reviewed, it is evident that Sullivan's comes closest to our conception of what the biosocial nature of human development requires. He recognizes that the self-system (ego) or the core of personality itself is largely developed by social interaction, though its progress is controlled by the integration of organismic–motivational and experiential factors. Evidently reacting against Freud's overconstitutionalized and narrow instinct theory, Sullivan is not very explicit about basic drives or the maturation of basic organismic functions from infancy to adulthood. Man is seen as becoming irrevocably a social animal by experiences common to the species, while certain key organismic functions such as speech and sexual lust enter into the development of interpersonal relations at critical periods. Some of the organismic functions like cognitive processes seem insufficiently integrated with development to adulthood. Nevertheless, Sullivan managed to convey the basically valid conception of human social maturity and dignity, or its neurotic and regressive failures, emerging from growth in interpersonal relations, predicated in part on the maturation of underlying organismic processes.

S-R Learning
Theory
Viewpoints Learning may be broadly and simply defined as the process by which behavior becomes modified through interaction with the environment. In the realm of personality development, it would include modification and adjustment of drives through experience, acquisition of skills, assimilation of attitudes, cultivation of interpersonal relations, value systems, roles, and personal identity. We have seen that learning enters into every stage of development we have presented from the biosocial point of view, though we have tried to show the close interrelationship between learning and maturation. The two have often been

considered as fairly distinct processes of development, even mutually exclusive ones. Whereas learned modifications of behavior depend on experience, maturation is presumed to follow a genetically programmed developmental sequence of structure and function. Among the psychoanalysts, as we have just seen, Freud stressed this organismic maturation and cathexis of the sex drive, while Sullivan stressed the learning of interpersonal relations in the course of growth. Learning theorists generally pay little attention to developmental stages of basic drives, but seek to demonstrate experimentally that individuals may serve their basic needs by learning the appropriate means of satisfying those needs.

Right there the relevance of learning theory to personality development runs into several snags. In the first place, learning and maturation can scarcely be distinguished in a species that is "inherently a culture-learning and transmitting animal" to begin with. We have sought to show that basic organismic functions making for social cohesion and learning (e.g., speech, empathy, abstract thinking), etc., have been programmed into the ontogenetic development of the species in such an inherently motivated manner that social learning can be counted on from the very nature of primary group and cultural living in the species. Certainly social mores and situational circumstances will exert their influence on the learning content, but inherent needs and capacities of the species and the individual predetermine the selectivity and direction of behavior modification.

In the second place, the term "learning" itself covers a multitude of behavior-modifying and habit-acquiring processes. We would, for example, consider it essential to distinguish between the immediate (associational or suggestive) processes and the long-range (cumulative or developmental) processes, since it has never been made quite clear just how the former are related to the latter. It would be useful to know, for example, just how these learning processes are distinguished from each other and how the first set is related to the second:

(a) *Immediate (Associational and Suggestive) Learning Processes*
    1. imitation and suggestion
    2. imprinting[2]
    3. classical conditioning
    4. operant or instrumental conditioning
    5. memorizing by repetition
    6. learning by practice
(b) *Long-Range (Developmental or Cumulative) Learning Processes*
    1. canalization (of motives)

---

[2] Imprinting is the fixation of an innate response to the first response-eliciting object encountered after birth or at an early critical period in development; this is illustrated by the "following" response in ducklings (Hess, 1959).

2. acquisition (of language and skills)
3. perceptual individuation
4. adaptation (to stresses and anxieties of way of life)

Of all these variations, the classical and operant conditioning processes have been found most readily susceptible to experimental models for developmental processes, and we shall discuss them presently.

Third, there is much confusion and misconception in the "means-to-an-end" rationale when learning is used to explain how social behavior responses become instrumental in satisfying primary animal drives. We have taken the position that social behavior is programmed for learning by maturational stages for its own sake, and is not merely learned fortuitously as a means of satisfying hunger or sex drive. It may also serve these purposes, of course, and has done so in the evolution of the species, (from cooperative hunting to community life). The means-to-an-end rationale must, therefore, be applied to *phylogenetic* development with natural selection as the instrument of preserving these means for survival and reproduction, not to *ontogenetic* development in the sense of learned behavior for ulterior purposes. We have shown that the survival of *Homo sapiens socialis* and his propagation over the face of the earth was facilitated by the phylogenetic development of language, abstract thinking, and empathy, which could be integrated by learning and cooperative planning to adapt to any climate, any way of life, any culture.

Finally, we must remember that no matter how readily S-R conditioning lends itself to controlled experiment, personality development in real life rarely consists of modifying one mechanical response to one stimulus at a time, or of the summation of such responses. Nevertheless, we must examine these building-blocks of an empirical behavioral science to see how far they can take us and to what kinds of situations they are applicable.

CLASSICAL CONDITIONING

As any student of elementary psychology will recall, it was I. P. Pavlov, the Russian physiologist, who first discovered that a dog's salivation response to the sight or taste of food could be conditioned to respond to an extraneous stimulus such as a buzzer or a flash of light. This happens when the extraneous or conditioned stimulus (CS) is repeatedly presented just before or during the presentation of food. The dog will, after several such paired presentations (reinforcement), salivate upon presentation of the CS without food. However, repeated presentation of the CS without food will gradually diminish the conditioned response (CR) until it disappears (this latter process being called "extinction").

Although first studied in the dog and other animals, so-called "classical conditioning" has been extensively used with infants, children, and adult human subjects. It seems to warrant the generalization that stimuli concurrent with, or just preceding a natural or unconditioned stimulus that normally produces a given response, will come to serve as substitute stimuli to evoke that response (CR). For the purpose of personality study, we are more interested in the way the process may account for the development of affective or attitudinal responses or habits that mark the characteristic behavior of the individual. Fertile ground for such study has been provided by examples of appetitive-conditioned responses (those involving the conditioning of a need or desire) as well as aversive responses (those involving displeasure or avoidance of pain).

Thus J. B. Watson, founder of the Behavioristic school of psychology (1925), showed how various emotional responses of children could be conditioned to various stimuli by associating the latter with the natural stimuli for such emotional reactions. In a classical experiment, he showed how a baby's reflexive fear reaction to a loud sudden noise could be made the CR to the presentation of a furry animal simply by the repeated paired presentation of the two stimuli. If sufficiently reinforced, such a conditioned fear reaction to furry animals could become a long-lasting aversion, and might even be generalized to all furry objects. It is easy to see how the early Behaviorists would explain the development of neurotic reactions such as phobias on the basis of CR to fear stimuli in childhood. On the appetitive side, love of the mother would simply be a CR to being handled and cuddled by the mother, in the course of which the stroking of the skin and genitals would evoke the love response. The idea that there could be anything more to love than a conditioned response to physiological stimulation was anathema to the Behaviorists, who ruled out all subjective responses, all sentimentality, and all "speculation" on motives, feelings, values, inspirations, and even perceptions. Watson's prescription for child care, as you can well imagine, was one of "strictly business" care of necessary physical needs. The t.l.c. (tender-loving-care), caressing, babbling, and playful stimulation which we know to be healthy and necessary for the baby today, were all ruled out for fear of reinforcing the baby's infantile dependency responses. (One often wonders whether the behavioristically reared babies of the 1920s became the overly permissive, compensating parents of the 1940s and 1950s, afraid to deny their children anything.)

The Behaviorist school of training and development on the classical CR model held sway during the 1920s and 1930s and dominated much of American academic thinking about personality development. Since any kind of stimulus could be conditioned to any kind of response, anything was possible; everything but a few native reflexes was just learned behavior, and there was no use talking about stages of development or

Personality Dynamics

inherent differences in temperament, or even learned social values. Responses not only had to be learned by conditioning, but had to be observable in the form of overt motor behavior. Subjective responses might exist, but were not fit subjects for scientific investigation. Even thinking was "subvocal speech." The possibilities for the conditioning of such overt responses was limitless. Watson (1925) even went so far as to boast:

Give me a dozen healthy infants, well-formed, and my own specified world to bring them up in, and I'll guarantee to take any one at random and train him to become any type of specialist I might select—doctor, lawyer, artist, merchant, Indian chief, and yes, even beggar-man and thief, regardless of his talents, penchants, tendencies, abilities, vocations, and the race of his ancestors.

The Behaviorist's mechanistic Utopia was never realized, of course (except in Skinner's fanciful *Walden Two*, 1948), and it was probably not offered very seriously, but it did engender a lot of research. Some of this was rather loosely related to personality development and equally loosely related to the rather rigid mechanical model of classical conditioning. Thus it was easy to show not only that children's fears and affections could be conditioned by manipulation of their environment, but also that styles of behavior and preferences in music and art could be influenced by appropriate conditioning techniques. A study by Razran, for example (reported much later in 1954) showed that preferences for musical excerpts could depend on whether the subjects were hungry or eating at the time they heard them. A study by Gesell and Thompson (1941) showed that anxious rigidity elicited in one of identical twin girls by premature training in the first year persisted well into adolescence. It should be noted, however, that the closer such studies came to dealing with personality development, the more they departed from the Watsonian model. Razran's study, for example, raised the question of cognitive conditioning, something that an orthodox Behaviorist could not entertain. Gesell and Thompson's study involved not only a very complex kind of conditioning but also raised the unorthodox questions of maturation and adjustment in child development and training.

So far, we have discussed conditioning of sensorimotor responses which Pavlov related to the "first signal system" that man has in common with lower animals to regulate behavior. As the human child begins to learn the names for things (presumably by conditioned association of word and object), he is ready to embark on the vast new world of the "second signal system," the world of symbols. As words are remembered and associated consistently with appropriate objects and with acts performed or qualities of objects (nouns, verbs, adjectives), even when not present in the here-and-now, true symbolic communication begins to take place. The child is gradually able to understand and to communicate more and more, and is consequently more and more amenable to complex conditioning by verbal restraint and reinforcement. Child development, as we know, is accompanied by increased complexity of abstract thinking and communication, inculcation of attitudes and values, establishment of interpersonal relations. However, it is not entirely clear how all this develops from S-R conditioning. Granted that the Pavlovians were somewhat more sophisticated than the Watsonians in recognizing the importance of communication of ideas and cultural values, it has never been satisfactorily explained how this sense of values and the expression of ideas through language itself is developed ontogenetically through a conditioning process. In fact, an expert in psycholinguistics (Chomsky, 1969), has recently reported sadly that the early hopes of linguists that language development would eventually be explained by conditioning processes (presumably by showing how the second signal system grows out of the first and reflects the evolution of communication from lower animals) have been effectively dashed by now.

This is not to deny that verbal conditioning, both as CS and CR, may be involved in the development of vocabulary and the affective connotations of words, inflections, and gestures. But that is a long way from the variable expression of ideas to different people in different situations, the combination of words to express new ideas or old ideas in new contexts, or the gradual growth of abstract thinking and discrimination in some people more than in others, regardless of exposure to reinforcement. Nor can one deny that habit acquisition and reversal can frequently be explained by behavior-modification theorists who use "conditioning therapy" to extinguish bad habits by associated aversive stimulation. There have been cases of enuresis, hiccoughs, alcoholism, and even homosexuality which have been relieved by using either shock (first signal system) or moral suasion (second signal system) to inhibit the undesirable response pattern in subjects. But this, too, is a long way from explaining the complex process of socialization of the child, the maturation, social interaction, conflict and integration of a hierarchy of drives, or the preservation of self-esteem—all of which are so pervasively involved in the psychodynamics and psychopathology of personality development.

One obvious defect of learning or behavior modification on the classical conditioning model was that behavior was too narrowly and passively conceived, in keeping with the conditioned reflex model of Pavlov's dog. In actual behavior of both animals and humans, it was gradually realized, the organism performs acts in seeking to satisfy drives, and adjusts to the success or failure (reward or punishment) of its attempts to satisfy the need. Some work along this line had already been done on animal learning by Thorndike and a number of other researchers earlier in this century, and was continuing to attract attention during the Behaviorist era of the

1920s and 1930s. In place of an automatic CR, Thorndike postulated a gradual trial-and-error learning procedure, in which responses which brought satisfaction closer tended to be "stamped in" and those which proved to be errors or blind alleys were "stamped out," until the animal learned the shortest way to reach its goal and satisfy its need (hunger). The guiding principle of this selectivity of responses was called the "law of effect." It smacked too much of subjectivity to suit the Behaviorists, but the reality of reinforcement of effective responses in active attempts to satisfy a need impressed other S-R theorists. Other experimenters like Tolman stressed the essentially purposive nature of learning in animals and men. Out of these studies there emerged a new viewpoint and a body of theory and research which placed crucial emphasis on reinforcement and means-to-an-end behavior in the conditioning process.

OPERANT CONDITIONING

About thirty years ago B. F. Skinner elaborated a procedure of learning through rewards, known as "operant conditioning." It differed from the classical conditioning of the Pavlovian model in stressing that learning took place not merely by association of S_1 and S_2 in producing a CR, but through rewards contingent upon behavior desired by the experimenter. It is, therefore, also sometimes called instrumental or reinforcement learning. Skinner and his followers have done much research on animal learning and some on human subjects as well, which differs in some essential respects from the classical conditioned response procedure. Instead of harnessing the animal or human subject to wait passively for a stimulus to evoke a reflexive response and then to evoke a CR, the subject is allowed to explore freely his limited environment. In the course of the exploratory or trial-and-error behavior, the subject is rewarded for successive approximations to the desired behavior, but not for other exploratory moves. This is called "shaping" the S's behavior. The experimenter has determined in advance which pattern of behavior he wants to elicit, and he successively rewards or reinforces every "step in the right direction." The reward with an animal is usually food; with a human it may be praise or the satisfaction of solving a problem. (Skinner carefully avoids attributing motives to his subjects, describing merely the results of the operational procedure.) Thus through a process of "shaping" one can obtain behavior not originally in the repertoire of the subject. In Thorndike's trial-and-error learning, the subject is left in a static situation, in which it may or may not eventually make a successful goal response. That might suffice to get an animal to run a maze or escape from a puzzle box, but it would never do to teach an animal a really novel kind of behavior.

Let us say we wanted to train a seal to play baseball. We could hardly expect the seal, after trial-and-error exploration, to pick up a bat and then go in search of a baseball. Rather, every movement toward the bat, every movement toward the pedestal on which the ball is placed, would be progressively reinforced with little rewards of food. The animal's behavior would be "shaped" by reinforcing every step in the right direction, thus eliciting a complex pattern of behavior that the animal could never have hit upon by mere trial-and-error exploration or just doing the obvious. This is the method used to train dolphins to shoot basketballs through hoops in the Marineland exhibitions in Florida, California, and Hawaii. Skinner's method could also be used in discrimination training (i.e., making predetermined responses to selective components of the perceptual field). This method was used by Skinner to show, during World War II, how pigeons could be trained to "steer" guided missiles or bombs toward their targets by pecking at the image of a target on an automated panel. (The idea was abandoned because it sounded too bizarre, not because it wouldn't work.)

However, our interest in operant conditioning obviously extends beyond the training of circus seals or making bombardiers out of pigeons. The relevance of operant conditioning to child development lies chiefly in its objective and predictive approach to the modification of behavior through environmental (therefore, cultural) influences. It is as though culture is the experimenter which rewards the child (through food, comfort, etc.) for successive approximations to its standards of behavior. Unfortunately, the Skinnerian reluctance to deal with motives as such limits its usefulness for the psychodynamic study of personality development. A somewhat more relevant application of operant conditioning comes from the Hullian school, which at least recognized motivation or drive as one of the indispensable elements in any learning formula. According to their basic formula, an animal or person, motivated by a basic or acquired drive (which sets up a physiological tension state), learns to respond to cues which produce the reward of satisfying the drive (hence reducing the tension). This has obvious applications to teaching animals anything by satisfying the hunger drive contingent upon appropriate responses to cues. What is more important for personality theory, it is also applicable to the socialization of the child by the mother and the rest of the environment, making use of a variety of motives. A sharp distinction is made between basic drives and learned motives, with social motivation generally regarded as a learned or secondary motive, which is instrumental in reducing the tensions of more basic animal drive. The basic position of the Hullians was probably stated by Dollard and Miller (1950) with respect to socialization:

In the light of the fact that the requisite social conditions for learning exist in the family, it seems reasonable to advance the hypothesis that the related human motives of sociability, dependence, need to receive and show affection, and the desire for approval from others are learned (p. 52).

It is assumed, in other words, that any function which involves learning is ipso facto a learned function and not one that may be regarded as inherent in the species. It also implies that the learning of that function is only a means to an end, presumably the end of getting food and comfort. We have already pointed out the dual fallacy in this kind of reasoning: (1) the assumption of an either-or dichotomy between learned and innate motives and (2) the failure to recognize the means-to-an-end rationale as inherent in the evolution of the species. It has nevertheless become fashionable for contemporary textbook writers in child psychology to accept the neo-Behavioristic rationale, generally adhering to the central thesis that social development is merely learned behavior. Thus, while Thompson ascribes physical dependency to maturational needs in the child, he clearly regards the development of social behavior as an incidentally learned means to an end, reinforced by the tension-reduction of satisfied biological needs.

What are the forces that socialize the egocentric infant who is wholly concerned with the satisfaction of his immediate needs? When does this socialization process begin? Why does the child come to need the company, the respect, the admiration of his associates? . . . Maturational factors make the infant dependent on the mother, or the mother surrogate, for the satisfaction of his physical needs. Since this unique social situation always accompanies the reduction of biological needs, the social interactions of mother and child acquire need-reducing properties. By the learning principles of generalization and secondary reinforcement these social interactions may become needs in their own right. (Thompson, 1962, p. 461)

Unfortunately, the tension-reduction hypothesis, the means-to-an-end implication, and the learned-vs.-innate dichotomy all run counter to empirical evidence and theoretical consistency. We have already shown how the tension-reduction conception of motivated activity has suffered from the results of experimental work of Harlow, Fowler, Butler, and others on animals; the work of Piaget on children, and the theoretical considerations advanced by White (see Chapter 2). What seems to be involved in the operant conditioning interpretation of socialization in children is a confusion of ends and means in motivational reinforcement. When a child or a young monkey shows that it is attached to a mother-figure from whom it has also received some food and comfort, which is the means and which is the end in this tension-reducing behavior? Does the infant cling to the mother and demand her attention only because bodily contact with her has been found to be tension-reducing when he is cold or hungry? If so, why does the child demand attention when not hungry? Why does he babble a blue streak with mother and demand her attention even when fully fed and comfortable? Why does he toy with his milk bottle and keep mother occupied with all kinds of ministrations, if it is only hunger and comfort-satisfying operations that are being reinforced? Why does baby persist in this seductive and attention-compelling behavior even if he is regularly fed by someone else, and why does he extend this sphere of social interaction to his siblings as soon as he is able? The empirical evidence is that the socialization responses of the child are no more a mere instrument of physical need satisfaction than is the puzzle-solving interest of Harlow's monkeys or the what-makes-it-tick curiosity of Piaget's babies. Brackbill (1958) has shown, for example, than an infant's social responses to a familiar adult's face may be reinforced merely by reciprocating these social signals. The frequency of smiling and vocalization by the infant will increase in direct proportion to the adult response of smiling, nodding, or talking. Thus social responsiveness in the infant may be reinforced or shaped by mere reciprocation, as an end in itself, rather than using it as an instrument of physical tension-reduction. In a similar manner, the child's attachment to the mother may be just as readily conceived of as a means of achieving cognitive, affective, and social satisfactions that are not essentially instrumental in achieving hunger satisfaction (except in a phylogenetic sense).

Undoubtedly, there are multiple need satisfactions being sought and simultaneously frustrated or deferred in favor of the more insistent ones all the time. The simple S-R investigation of hunger, sex, or pain (one at a time) in a drive-reduction context is restrictive enough even in rat learning experiments. It proves to be utterly artificial in attempting to understand the psychodynamics of personality development from infancy to adulthood, even though there is manifestly a great deal of "learning" involved.

Because of such discrepancies and inadequacies, some of the leading advocates of S-R reinforcement theory have had to seek new hypotheses and operational models to explain even the immediate associational type of learning that is applicable to the acquisition of habits of the simplest sort. Miller (1963), for example, has suggested a more flexible model of elicitation and conditioning of some hypothetical "go mechanisms" in the cortex of the brain, which activate basic drive responses. These responses may vary in relative strength, and they are not necessarily reinforced by mere repetition. What is most interesting is the idea that these neural mechanisms may be released in a variety of ways, by internal, external, or cognitive stimulation.

A similar approach to a sophisticated neurological model of motivated learning has been carried still further by Pribram (1963). He seeks to relate motivational learning processes as different as efficacy, cognitive discrimination and dissonance-resolution, acquisition of skill, pain avoidance, addiction, and hunger to neurological processes—even though some of these function contrary to the expectations of drive-reduction theory. Research on brain implantation of electrodes in animals and the testing of behavior-triggering functions of the hypothalamus, amygdaloid complex, hippocampal formation, and reticular activation system (see Fig. 2–2) provide the empirical basis for this theoretical structure. Pribram makes note of the fact that in the course of performance differentiation a reversal of means and ends often takes place, which serves to confirm our suspicion that many a basic generic drive has been confused as a "means-to-physiological-tension-reducing-ends" in the first place. He also makes the intriguing and far-reaching suggestion that neural mechanisms involved in adaptation, satiation, and reinforcement of need-satisfying behavior may be directly related to achieving happiness (contentment? feeling of well-being?) in the self-actualizing sense.

It should be noted that the more sophisticated these models become in approaching the complexity of behavioral change and adaptation, the more they depart from the basic S-R reinforcement models of classical and operant conditioning. Even so, little is said that really conveys the picture of personality development from infancy to adulthood, except as an implied summation of acquired responses and modified drives. The work of both Miller and Pribram and a host of other researchers suggests that we may be entering a new era of learning theory.

This offers interesting possibilities of tying-in research on brain functions (particularly the reticular activation system, hypothalamus, and cortex) with research on behavioral changes. This might conceivably strengthen the experimental underpinnings of biosocial theory at the psychophysiological level of explanation. In the meantime, however, the basic inadequacy of any S-R operant conditioning model for psychodynamics still remains. Of the four deficiencies of S-R learning theory pointed out at the beginning of this section, the last (the S-R mechanical viewpoint itself) is probably the least susceptible to "patching up" without destroying the entire model. It is difficult to see how the emergence of ego and its defenses, the lifelong quest for self-esteem and acceptance, the canalization of drives, the almost imperceptible assimilation of cultural values, the successive integration of maturing organismic capacities into more and more socially mature behavior could ever be adequately explained by a system of reinforced S-Rs, no matter how complex. We are inclined to agree with J. T. Spence (1965), who states:

All in all, the empirical events that learning theorists have attempted to explain have little resemblance to those phenomena that we commonly refer to as "personality." What bearing, then, do contemporary learning theories have on personality? In the strictest sense, little or none. While learning theories are in such form that testable predictions may be logically derived from them, none of these predictions are directly related to the type of behavioral events that are the immediate concern of the personality theorist.

Spence obviously had S-R operant conditioning theory in mind. However, it would be rash to dismiss all learning theory as having nothing to contribute to personality theory. We merely suggest that something more global and complex, less mechanical, more cognizant of the complexity of human motivation, and more adaptable to the integration of maturation and learning in human growth is required. Until such a model is perfected and integrated into biosocial theory, we can use the S-R experimental approach in any of its present forms for the purpose for which it was designed—immediate associational mechanical learning of specific responses—and resort to a variety of descriptive and psychodynamic concepts to provide the framework of personality development, adjustment, and character formation.

Summary We have briefly illustrated two other principal schools of thought or approaches to personality development, with recognition of the fact that there are many divergent viewpoints within each, and that many significant viewpoints or avenues of research are not clearly identified with either school. These are the psychoanalytic and the experimental S-R approaches.

The original psychoanalytic formulations of Freud are predicated on the primacy of the sex drive, the libidinal energy of which is conceived of as going through successive stages of organ fixation from infancy to puberty. These so-called psychosexual stages of development are: *oral* (first to second year); *anal* (second to third year); *phallic* (third to fifth year), with its attendant Oedipus complex; *latency* (fifth to twelfth year); and *genital* (puberty). It is suggested that a psychophysiological level of analysis is too restrictive and the meaningfulness of psychosexuality in infancy is still in doubt. In any case, the latency period seems definitely misconceived in view of available data. The importance of psychosocial motives and development is largely ignored, or relegated to learned resolution of psychosexual conflicts. In an attempt to correct these deficiencies, E. H. Erikson has presented eight stages of psychosocial development: (1) basic trust vs. mistrust; (2) autonomy vs. shame and doubt; (3) initiative vs. guilt; (4) industry vs. inferiority; (5) identity vs. role confusion; (6) intimacy vs. isolation; (7) generativity vs. stagnation; (8) ego integrity vs. despair. Although a decided improvement over Freud's stages, Erikson's scheme (we believe) strains too hard to achieve a "Freudian fit" in the early stages. Furthermore, the primacy and polarity of the selected "crises" at each stage of development and their sequence of succession are open to question.

H. S. Sullivan, like other "neo-Freudians," rejected the pansexual approach to motivation and development, and defined personality in terms of interpersonal relations. He accordingly described the development stages in such terms, using familiar designations and empirical clinical observations for each stage. These are: infancy, childhood, juvenile era, preadolescence, early adolescence, and late adolescence. The basic rationale is a development of more and more complex and mature interpersonal relations as the individual's underlying cognitive and affective capacities mature in interaction with the environment. Among the three viewpoints presented from the psychoanalytic schools, Sullivan's conception of development is closest to the biosocial viewpoint.

S-R learning theorists make use of classical and operant conditioning models to show how behavior becomes modified through experience. Little attention is paid to basic drives, which are generally assumed to be the same in man as in lower animals. Social motives and values are generally assumed to be learned by instrumental conditioning in satisfying basic drives like hunger and sex. There are accordingly no "stages" of development; but methods of child-rearing and experiences in childhood are demonstrated to have definite influences on habit formation and later personality development. Recent abandonment of the tension-reduction hypothesis of motivation and increasing interest in brain mechanisms that control a variety of basic drive responses seems to open the way for a better reconciliation of S-R theory and biosocial theory of personality dynamics.

7

Conflict,
Adjustment,
and
Defense

The foregoing chapters should have made it clear that personality development, unlike growth in lower animals, does not involve merely the maturation of body structure and its functions. Nor does it come about by mere accretion of conditioned overt responses attached to physical needs. It involves a dynamic flux of overt, covert, and symbolic transactions with the environment, through which basic drives are channeled and ego needs adjusted to reality (and vice versa). We have concentrated on psychosocial development from early primary group interaction to adult role assumption, because it serves to portray the integrity and continuity of the personality in its most salient aspect. Nevertheless, we have never lost sight of the organismic developmental processes which make such psychosocial development possible in the first place and constantly determine the limits of interaction with environmental conditions. All through this analysis we have repeatedly hinted at adjustment processes or defense mechanisms and strategies in motivational conflict. These are the psychological defenses the organism is capable of mobilizing to satisfy ego needs and to resolve or divert the anxiety generated by any threat to ego security. The time has now come to discuss these mechanisms and strategies in some detail.

We can get a better perspective on these adjustive processes if we regard adjustment as part of the continuous growth and adaptation process of personality, and not just as little tricks that the mind plays on itself every once in a while to get over a major or minor crisis. Furthermore, we shall find it useful to make a distinction between *defense mechanisms* and *defensive strategies*, a distinction which has not been made heretofore. The former may be regarded as cognitive-affective responses to stimuli that serve to adjust ego needs to reality at any given moment, though they may function in a repetitive and cumulative manner and have long-range effects on personality development. Since they are, in a real sense, "all in the mind," they are not susceptible to direct observation, but must be inferred from behavioral changes and the situational context, past, present, and future, in which they occur. *Defensive strategies*, on the other hand, may be defined as long-range changes of behavior patterns, adjusting the style of life, role behavior, or other forms of social interaction to meet the demands of ego security and self-actualization in the total life process. Since they invariably involve overt behavioral manifestations in addition to whatever adjustment mechanisms may be employed, they are susceptible to observation and serve to confirm the reality of the entire process of adjustment of ego needs.

Defense

Mechanisms The psychoanalytic literature from Freud onward has been so truly productive in introducing and elaborating upon concepts of defense mechanisms that it may seem unnecessary to do more than review these mechanisms and show how they apply to our broader biosocial framework. We shall begin by doing just that, but will not automatically and uncritically accept the validity of every concept as formulated. We have already taken exception to the libidinal-aggressive formulations of basic motivation, on which many of the Freudian defense mechanisms rest. In addition, we shall have to go further in introducing new concepts or elaborations on the old ones to clarify psychosocial processes which were either ignored by the psychoanalysts or were of no concern to a discipline that originated in a medical context. However, some of the more special mechanisms relating to particular forms of psychopathology will not be dealt with here.

IDENTIFICATION, PROJECTION, INTROJECTION

These closely interrelated defense or adjustment mechanisms are of central importance to normal personality development as well as to features of deviant behavior. All three are immediately implicit expressions of the innate need of every individual to relate to other individuals. They become manifest from the very beginning of primary group interaction and underlie the secondary socialization process.

Identification, although variously defined in different contexts, basically means a cognitive-empathic response in which an individual experiences a sense of belonging to another person, group, or group symbol. In its earliest form it is a sense of belongingness to the caring figure—hence, identification with the mother, sometimes the father. As "self" and "other" precepts become clearer and similarities between the two are perceived, a closer identification is experienced with the parent of the same sex, and still later with siblings and peers. As primary group interaction proceeds and cognitive-affective maturation develops along with this interaction, a sense of primary group membership further articulates the identification. During secondary socialization, identification becomes more abstract. The child becomes more aware of belonging to or not belonging to different kinds of socially defined groups; of being a child of a given age and sex, from whom certain kinds of behavior are expected or approved, and others are not. Thus our primary and secondary socialization stages are actually also identification stages, and would have been labeled as such but for the needs of conciseness. This becomes all the more obvious in the adult role anticipation and assumption stages, when identification becomes more clearly delineated.

By the time of adulthood one might identify himself with the role and values of upper-class businessman, or middle-class professional and family man, or the blue-collar working-class husband or perennial bachelor of his community. These may be extensions of or reactions against the original identification with the father or mother and the remembered identifications with the primary group. Our entire developmental scheme is, in fact, an historical account of the ontogenetic evolution of ego identification. Its basic function is to implement and give direction to ego development in social interaction, avoiding isolation and nonparticipation, which have in the long run of evolutionary selection proven maladaptive to survival of the species. The adjustive and defensive aspect comes in when these identifications change, undergo conflict, and are manipulated in the struggle for social acceptance and self-esteem. Under those circumstances we may be dealing with various manipulations of affiliation, which will be dealt with under defensive strategies. Both personal and social identifications serve to give the individual some sense of security in knowing who he is and being assured that he at least means something to somebody—that some individual or group cares about him and recognizes him as having something in common or as being "one of us."

If the identification itself is frustrating, as ascribed or imputed roles sometimes are (e.g., rejected son, rejected minority group member), then variations on the identification theme come into play in terms of the affiliative manipulations we have already mentioned. This use of "defenses against defenses that don't work" has scarcely been touched upon in the literature on personality adjustment. We can deal with it here in terms of the complexity of identifications stemming from role complexities, aside from the defensive strategies that we shall discuss later.

Let us take the case of an immigrant worker's child. He would tend to identify with his parents, sharing their sentimental attachment to the "old country" and perhaps even learning their native language. Bilingualism would be the least of his problems. The immigrant's son, growing up among his peers in the adopted country, would have strong identifications with them and assimilate himself to the local subculture, while at the same time maintaining his identification with his father and his culture. He would have to make an adjustment between two nationalistic identifications. This can be managed in a culture that is tolerant of *ambiguous identification*, in which an individual may alternately or simultaneously find acceptance as both a loyal American and a sentimental devotee of the parental "old country." This happens continuously among many Americans of recent foreign extraction, because America is for the most part a nation of immigrants. Thus the loyal sons of Erin go marching proudly up the main avenues of major American cities on St. Patrick's Day, different religious groups observe their own holidays, and no one but ethnic bigots question these people's identification as Americans.

But what happens when a society makes such dual identification difficult or impossible? Take the problem of religious affiliation in Communist Russia, or German membership (citizenship) for Jewish Germans under the Nazis. And lest we forget, what of American identification for native Americans of Indian, Mexican, Negro, or Japanese descent at various periods in our own history? The individual caught in such conflicts of identification may make use of *ambiguous identification* defenses until the defense breaks down under social pressure. Then either rejection of one of the conflicting identifications must take place, or a defensive strategy of social behavior must be resorted to, or a constant state of rejection anxiety will be generated, calling for more pathological defenses against self-rejection.

We submit that such conflicts do not necessarily represent the re-arousal of psychosexual identification conflicts that occurred in childhood. There may never have been any. Psychosocial identification conflict can generate anxiety quite as easily in its own right during adolescence and adulthood as the rejection by a parent in childhood, and even then the identification conflict is not necessarily a psychosexual one. Other sources of later identification conflict stemming from early parental identification may be: inability or unwillingness to live up to parental expectations, or a desire to exceed them; tarnishing of the idealized father-image in the light of observed realities; competitive ego-ideals provided by learning about cultural heroes and idols; and others. Here, too, ambiguous identification may resolve a discrepancy, but it will be difficult to maintain such a resolution if the parental identification and the cultural ego-ideal are diametrically opposed. This would take place in the relationship with a meek father in an authoritarian culture, or a frank "sinner" in a puritanical one.

If ambiguous identification doesn't work, there is always the alternative of *projection* to use as a defense against unacceptable identification. Projection may be defined as a cognitive-affective process by which one attributes one's own characteristics or motives to another individual or group. This usually entails negative projection, as when one attributes to another the undesirable characteristics, inferiority, or guilt that one senses in himself. It may also involve positive projection, as when one individual perceives another to be a "kindred spirit" and therefore attributes some of his own characteristics, interests, or motives to him. Negative or disowning projection is the underlying mechanism involved in "scapegoating"— the kind of prejudice that uses a stigmatized minority group as the scapegoat for projecting and punishing one's own inferiority or guilt. The classical case of negative projection of one's own duplicity, guilt, and inferiority to a scapegoat group is that of Adolf Hitler (cf. Gilbert, 1950), whose obsessive persecution of the scapegoat and attempts at self-aggrandizement had such disastrous consequences for both victim and tormentor. Other examples occur daily in our own culture and in many others among the more rabid advocates of ethnic bigotry, for it is usually those who are more neurotically insecure about their own identifications who *need* scapegoats for their frustrations.

Introjection is one of the adjustment mechanisms by which the individual becomes socialized, particularly in the early stages of the developmental process. It may be regarded as a subprocess of identification, largely implemented by such elemental processes as suggestion and imitation. One identifies with parents in childhood and introjects their admonitions as the beginnings of conscience, assimilates social values all through childhood and adolescence through a similar process of introjection, and anticipates adult role behaviors through introjection from adult models. The socialization process is not a process of forced instrumental learning, but an assimilation and channeling process of basic motives in social interaction. Identification and introjection are integral parts of this process, and empathic responses are closely related to both. The symbolic processes of verbalization and conceptualization make it possible to internalize such external reality.

RATIONALIZATION, DENIAL, SUPPRESSION OF INSIGHT

All of these mechanisms refer to cognitive distortions which protect ego needs by avoiding a frank realization or acknowledgment of perceived or communicated reality, when those implications are damaging to self-esteem. *Rationalization* is familiar to the layman as the common device of "making excuses" for errors, failures, or acts with ulterior motives. The rationalizer either shifts the blame, pleads extenuating circumstances, or professes intent other than the one that implies failure or discredit. A favorite illustration is the "sour grapes" fable, in which Aesop's anthropomorphic fox seeks to rationalize his failure by pretending that he never really wanted the grapes anyway, because they must be sour. This kind of rationalization would be applied in everyday life in such situations as belittling the job one didn't get or the college one wasn't admitted to; or reasoning that one wouldn't have accepted it anyway for one reason or another, so there's nothing lost. In other words, one can pretend that he hasn't really failed to gain the recognition implied in either situation, because he didn't really want it anyway. The catch is, of course, that if the object really wasn't worth gaining one wouldn't have tried to gain it in the first place.

Other illustrations are not hard to find. Unwillingness to appear inadequate or guilty of failure in a given marital or occupational role frequently brings forth the rationalization that the spouse or the boss is really at fault, when he may not be. Or one may rationalize the situational factors to provide a specious excuse for one's own shortcomings (e.g., mother-in-law trouble, working conditions). Most urgent of all are the rationalizations that are used to justify acts that are known to be selfish or improper, because the individual does not want to suffer loss of self-esteem or social approval. This would apply to such commonplace acts in our culture as: driving a hard bargain or indulging in misrepresentation in business, evading or stretching the law (as in minor tax evasions), cheating on exams, taking unfair advantage of another in competition for recognition or power (as in political campaigning), or indulging in premarital sex relations. A typical rationalization for all of these situations might be, "Well, everybody's doing it, so why shouldn't I?" It should be noted that there is an implication of consensual validation in this rationalization of what is right and wrong. If it were true that everybody did it, it would manifestly be an act that is sanctioned by the social norms. Another common type of rationalization is the reversal of an ulterior motive—specious reasoning that makes a selfish act look unselfish. "It's not that I care about these privileges as such," a profligate executive may say, "but it's for the good of the company that my position should be respected and given an aura of prosperity." Another example is the "you-too" argument: "I only did what you would have done under the same circumstances," the greedy manipulator may say or think.

Socially and historically, rationalized aggression has been used repeatedly in the acts of nations when the wielders of power used the excuses of higher social virtues to rationalize their ulterior motives. This has taken place in religious persecution and conversion by the sword under the guise of pious works. Patriotism and self-defense has been the rallying cry of warmongers since time immemorial; "enlightenment" and "protection" the slogans of imperialists past and present.

Denial as a defense mechanism is a little more subtle than conscious denial of a known fact, which is simply lying. It is essentially a semi-conscious kind of self-deception in which one simply refuses to believe what his senses and reason tell him is true. He denies it to himself in situations in which acknowledgment would be damaging to self-esteem. Denying the fact doesn't really make it go away, but it enables the individual to pretend to himself that it isn't really what it appears to be. This may seem to be attributing far more defective powers of observation and reasoning to *Homo sapiens* than he is supposedly endowed with, but the clinical and experimental evidence is that human beings do often practice self-deception.

Perhaps the naturalness of this defense mechanism will become clearer when we remind the reader that denial of having performed a forbidden act is quite commonplace in childhood, as is the refusal to acknowledge a traumatic event like a death in the family. Animism and fantasy persist far into adolescence, which seems to be carrying wishful thinking a little too far for the reality-oriented adult. But a child or adolescent will readily seek to maintain acceptance by parents or peers simply by verbally denying that he did something they don't approve of and convincing himself of this by verbal autosuggestion. This can be done more successfully when the situation itself is rather ambiguous, so that he can convince himself that it is really not what it seems. Thus, the vase really fell and broke by itself; the other fellow started the fight; and Aunt Martha didn't die, she just went to sleep for a long, long time. This is not mere lying, but simply making the least threatening interpretation of a situation that is to the child still in the realm of "ambiguous percepts." The child's conception of reality, cause and effect, and certainly of death, is simply not so clear-cut as it will be in adulthood. Mental images, words, and symbols stand for so many things that are not seen, and so many realities come into being simply by playful pretending, and go away when you stop paying attention to them, that it is small wonder the child wishes away an unpleasant event or implication simply by denying that it is so.

When an adult does so, we must infer either defective cognition or the use of the denial mechanism, in which the need or the wish is father to the thought. The situation must still have an element of ambiguity in it to be credited with semiconscious denial, else we should have to suspect him of deliberate lying. Thus the two drivers in a car collision will each swear to entirely different versions of the accident because they literally remember it differently under the stress of denial of responsibility in a somewhat unclear moment of crisis. If the memory of the situation is clear, but elaborate excuses worked out to justify one's action that, of course, would be rationalization. If the event is so traumatic that all memory of it is erased, that would be repression. Remembering seeing the *other* fellow drive recklessly may simply be a denial of your own responsibility for the accident. But what of more complex situations, such as those involving interpretations of value conflicts which are in turn implied by rational interpretation of available facts? Is there another level of semiconscious self-deception that goes beyond the more primitive form of simple denial?

This brings us to one of the most significant defense mechanisms overlooked in the psychoanalytic literature and scarcely alluded to in psychology: *the suppression of insight*.[1] Although often resorted to as a device by which denial is accomplished, this mechanism has far broader functions and should be considered as a major defense mechanism in the context of rational adult behavior. The suppression of insight serves to inhibit conscious awareness of a conflict by preventing all the elements in a situation (perceived, implicit, rational, affective) from becoming integrated into an insight that threatens ego security. This applies principally to more complex situations and interpersonal relationships, in which interpretive perception of events are involved in drawing inferences that may evoke feelings of guilt or apprehension of danger. When such insight would be damaging to self-esteem or the personal value system, or even call for action that is dangerous to one's role or even one's life, the reasoning apparatus is capable of "suspending judgment"—that is, not thinking the situation through and drawing the logical conclusions that might give impulse to dangerous action. The anxiety generated in the mere process of cognition of some of the elements in such a situation seems to generate inhibitory processes which suspend the processes of rational inference in midair, so to speak. One somehow just does not get to realize the full implications of events and relationships in which he is involved, and manages to suppress the ego-threatening insights that would logically stem from such awareness.

The needed defense may stem from conflicts between two or more aspects of the individual's role-complex and value system, making real

---

[1] Dollard and Miller (1950) mention suppression in contrast to repression, but only as a device for controlling attention, not as a defense mechanism.

integration impossible. If he is a respected leader in the community and a good Christian, can he turn his back on bigotry at his doorstep? He may not be able to rationalize it, but he might suppress insight into the extent of it and his obligation and ability to combat it. If he is a politician and aspiring to responsible leadership, can he ally himself with a government policy that is diametrically opposed to all that he supposedly stands for? Integrity would demand that he resign, try to change the policy, or denounce it and disassociate himself from it. If that proved too dangerous, he might rationalize his position while secretly opposing the policy and "biding his time"—or he might simply suppress insight into the incompatibility of the values which his role prescribes for him. The anxiety would still remain in suppressed form; certain perceptual data would still come to his attention, but he would not allow himself to become quite fully aware of their implications. Sooner or later, of course, the defense breaks down when harsh reality descends upon him and can no longer be suppressed. His reaction then would be, "I guess I knew it all the time, but tried to put it out of my mind." In other words, there are none so blind as those who will not see.

This subtle and elusive defense mechanism is possible because so much of social behavior and knowledge of reality depends on symbolic communication. It takes a good deal of inference and interest to be receptive to the fragmentary information that comes to our attention in the normal course of daily events and to interpret it in terms of our own interest and any professed interest in human welfare. If the implications are unpleasant or ego-threatening, it is quite possible not to pursue the matter as anything of any concern to ourselves, or simply to fail to put two and two together—that is, to leave conclusions suspended in midair, or to divert one's attention to something more pleasant without thinking this particular problem through. If the situation still intrudes itself on the attention too much to have insight obviated by inattention or diverted by a shift in the focus of cognition, then one can still alter its significance by calling it something else.

This means that there are at least three submechanisms by which this semiconscious suppression of insight is accomplished: (1) *diversion* of insight by suspending the process of interpretation and inference before reaching a conscious conclusion, while allowing other stimuli in the conscious field to claim one's attention; (2) *obviation* of confrontation of the conflict by not observing relevant data or thinking about the problem altogether, as may be accomplished by adopting regular avoidance habits; and (3) *semantic camouflage*, which couches the problem in euphemistic terms or deceptive phrases which succeed in obfuscating the issue sufficiently to serve the purpose of self-deception. The latter is the adult's somewhat more sophisticated version of infantile denial, since words continue to represent reality and may actually alter perceived reality in many areas of ambiguity.

The suppression of insight applies to many aspects and incidents of daily life and has a certain adaptive value in preserving sanity or conserving reactivity to manageable proportions. If we allowed ourselves to be constantly aware of all the possible implications of everything that comes to our attention or that could be learned if we were sufficiently concerned, or if we became overly concerned about the possible dangers inherent in everything we do in our daily lives, we could hardly maintain our sanity or live tolerably balanced lives. We would never have respite from the call to arms against all the injustice in the world and the possible or actual injustices to ourselves. We would constantly be calculating the risks of riding in a car or plane or even crossing the street or going to sleep; we would be ever alert to the signs of rejection or critical reaction which any person makes or might make to every act we perform; we would constantly have to speculate on the future outcome of every plan we make and those of others that might affect us. In such behavior lies obsessional oversensitivity and even paranoia. However, there are many situations in which simple adaptive intelligence demands that we observe and interpret facts and their implications in the most rational reality-testing terms available to us. This sometimes requires looking unpleasant facts in the face, drawing the necessary conclusions, and having the fortitude to take the necessary steps to avert impending disaster. It is in those situations that suppression of insight is distinctly maladaptive. Furthermore, there are role demands, particularly those related to adult responsibility and competence, which require some degree of social concern and reality-testing. This is necessary if an individual of some maturity is to fulfill his normal aspirations for self-esteem and social approval. In leadership roles particularly, evasive self-deception and the lack of integrity it implies may become as catastrophic to self and society as the most deliberate destructive aggression. We shall consider such a case at the end of this chapter.

REPRESSION

Repression is the key concept of ego defense in the psychoanalytic interpretation of psychosexual development as well as the etiology of most of the neurotic behavior disorders. It represents one of Freud's major contributions to psychodynamics. Repression may be simply defined as a process of more or less complete inhibition of any behavioral impulse originating in the basic drives of human nature when subjected to conditions of emotional conflict, so that neither the basic motivation nor the conflict associated with it reaches conscious awareness or remains conscious. This usually entails the forgetting or distorting of memories associated with the conflict situation and the inhibition of affective responses appropriate to the situation. This does not mean that the conflict simply disappears without trace. Psychoanalysis has contributed abundant evidence that such repressed conflicts continue to exist at a subconscious level in the mind of the individual and usually find expression in some disguised form. This is illustrated by dream analysis, the famous "Freudian slips," by cases of hysterical dissociation or conversion symptoms, and by numerous studies of hypnosis. Nevertheless, some critics have questioned the ubiquitous explanation of "repression to the unconscious" (e.g., Papageorgis, 1965).

We would question the validity of interpreting the conflict in every case as a psychosexual one, but would not quarrel with the existence of repressive processes as such. The distinction between the psychosexual and the psychosocial may be partly a matter of semantics, but we have already pointed out that it involves a basic difference in conceptions of human nature. Conflict that could logically be interpreted as frustration of social ego needs in childhood, as in parental rejection or cruelty, would most likely be interpreted as "castration anxiety" in psychoanalytic theory, and repressed hostility toward the parent explained on that basis. This would be in keeping with the Freudian theory that an Oedipus complex regularly emerges at the "phallic stage" of ego development in boys around the age of five to six, and that the Oedipal desires must be repressed for fear of the consequences of displacing the father in the mother's affections. From a biosocial point of view, it is quite enough for the child to experience parental rejection for such a basic threat to basic social ego needs to be repressed.

However, there can be little doubt that *any* psychophysiological, psychological, or psychosocial drive may become frustrated and repressed, causing longstanding unconscious conflicts. These conflicts may render one man sexually impotent, thrust another into a state of periodic depressions or religious ecstasies, and cause a third to become a misanthropic hermit. But the nature of the effect is not necessarily parallel to the nature of the repressed need, as if a simple conditioned reflex were being set up. The process of repression finds devious ways of disguising cause and effect in the course of the unconscious transformations that take place—although "depth analysis" can often trace the connection.

Aside from long-range influences on character and deviant behavior, there are the immediate effects of traumatic experiences on behavior. A dramatic example of this is the combat-fatigue reaction which sometimes inflicts partial amnesia on soldiers and pilots who have been subjected to shellfire and loss of comrades in battle. (This is what was mistakenly called shell-shock in World War I, but was recognized as a reaction to psychological shock in World War II.) Such soldiers and pilots frequently repress the details of their experiences and find it impossible to give an account of what happened, even though it may be important to do so in debriefing procedures for military intelligence. Interviews under the influence of sodium pentothal (the so-called truth serum which induces a semiconscious state in which repressed memories may be recalled) sometimes reveal that the amnesic soldier has not only repressed the fear of death that stared him in the face a short time ago but also guilt for having somehow let his buddies die. This often provides a clue to the necessary psychotherapeutic procedures to bring these feelings of guilt and fear to the surface and assuage them (cf. Grinker and Spiegel, 1945).

Repression is the essential defense mechanism that gives rise to other pathological reactions as well. Aside from the dissociative states we have already mentioned in passing (dual personality and amnesia), there are the hysterical conversion states that first led Freud to seek the psychological basis for these strange infirmities. These are conditions in which the conflict is repressed and the anxiety unconsciously "converted" to a functional disability with no organic impairment to account for it. Examples of this would be hysterical blindness, lameness, or anesthesia. The affected organ may be found to function under hypnosis and the nature of the conflict likewise uncovered. These and other deviant reactions would take us too far into the realm of psychopathology. It is sufficient for our purposes to know that there is such a defense mechanism as repression, and that the causes of the conflicts that call for such drastic defense may be frustration of any of the basic needs of the organism.

Defensive
Strategies
In contrast to the defense mechanisms, defensive strategies are long-range adaptive patterns of behavior involving social interaction. They may incorporate the periodic or continual use of the mental defense mechanisms, and may even be the acting-out strategies for such mechanisms or the motives that prompt them; but they are not the same thing. The distinction is usually not made, but we consider it worth making in order to avoid some of the confusion that surrounds the analysis of adjustive processes. A significant step in this direction was made by Lois Murphy (1960) when she distinguished between "coping devices" used by children to overcome stress or meet challenges of the environment and the "defense mechanisms [which] are intrapsychic operations utilized by the child to reduce anxiety aroused by inner conflict." The coping devices of childhood are fairly rudimentary tactics of avoidance, dependence, or mastery. We have in mind here the fairly complex, long-range adaptations of role behavior and social interaction that serve the more

mature needs of self-esteem, social acceptance, self-integration, and self-actualization in adulthood.

Some of the leading neo-Freudian analysts made significant use of what we call defensive strategies in the psychodynamics of personality, without labeling them as such or contrasting them with the defense mechanisms. They generally reacted against the shortcomings of Freudian pansexualism and the whole confusing array of defense mechanisms based on libido theory, stressing instead the importance of intrapersonal relationships as the actual medium of personality adjustment. Perhaps the most articulate in terms of defensive strategies was Karen Horney (1945). In terms somewhat reminiscent of Adler's "style of life" concept, Horney showed how different people adopt different styles of relationships with other people, all for the common aim of seeking acceptance and avoiding rejection. Her now-familiar three styles of relationship are: *moving toward people* (giving affection or acceptance in order to receive it); *moving against people* (hostility or domination to achieve fear or respect, or sufficient power to be immune to rejection); and *moving away from people* (withdrawal from close association in order to avoid the frustration of rejection). These oversimplified styles of interpersonal relationships at least served to show that there is a psychosocial alternative to the defense mechanisms conceived of in psychobiological-libidinal terms. Even Adler's original conception of compensation for feelings of inferiority (though poorly conceived, as we shall see) was an attempt to recognize the constant struggle of the individual to achieve mastery over his environment and defend himself against feelings of inadequacy in his own eyes and the eyes of his fellows. Our own conception of defensive strategies finds a place for these obvious-enough devices, as well as for some of the other psychoanalytic and nonanalytic concepts frequently lumped together with the basic mental defense mechanisms. We shall consider here the main defensive strategies that are commonly employed by individuals in any culture in the course of social interaction in the quest for ego security.

AFFILIATION

Personal and group affiliation represent the overt acting out of the need for identification and belonging. Whereas identification is a cognitive-affective process, often semiconscious in nature, affiliation is an act or commitment of voluntary association with another person or group. It is often a condition or a by-product of primary and secondary group interaction or of reference group identification in role assumption. However, it involves a more overt commitment than identification, such as making and keeping friends, recognizing family ties and obligations, "joining the group," or guiding one's behavior by the standards of a reference group and verbalizing one's commitment to it. Any such act of affiliation reinforces and structures the security of reciprocal acceptance with another person or group, in the normal course of fulfilling social ego needs. However, the defensive aspects of affiliation become manifest when conflict or intense need cause an individual to *manipulate affiliations.* One may affiliate himself with more than one person as a friend and more than one group as a member. One may even be recognized by another as a "brother" in spirit, as in fraternity initiations or tribal rituals. But this process cannot go on ad infinitum. Somewhere along the line arises the question of the compatibility of such affiliations. Different groups may have different values, and different friends may be so hostile toward each other or to the values of some of the friend's affiliations that a real problem of compatibility may arise. In such cases, real alternatives in defensive strategies may become manifest; either *reversible, opportunistic affiliation,* or selective integrity of values and loyalties. The politician may seek to be "all things to all men," but in so doing he betrays a basic lack of integrity in his affiliative manipulations.

Some individuals find it easy to reverse their loyalties or affiliations without any qualms, merely shifting with the winds of expediency. Others take the practical attitude: "If you can't beat 'em, join 'em." On the other hand, some may doggedly persist in personal loyalty or devotion to a cause even in the face of betrayal and unworthiness of that person or cause. The question of integrity versus opportunistic defense in affiliative strategy hinges, of course, on the question of whether there is any principle involved. The integrity of sticking to one's principles may require abandoning an old affiliation or even condemning it; on the other hand, it does not allow one to turn one's back on an old friend just because he is temporarily "in the doghouse," or to forsake a movement one still believes in simply because it has ceased to be popular.

Some affiliations are even more casually opportunistic, or purely nominal. This includes "name-dropping" of people of repute whom one has met most casually, or frequenting "exclusive" establishments and gathering places of the "intellectual" or "influential"—all to imply affiliation with those who are "in." The defensiveness of this minor strategy is in direct proportion to the lack of common interest the individual has with those people and places and the extent to which he finds it necessary to call attention to and exaggerate such contacts. Nevertheless, the insecure may grasp at such straws to give themselves the appearance of acceptability in circles of social prestige. The obvious and persistent social climber is often one who adopts such strategies of opportunistic affiliation to conceal his basic insecurity of identity. It is similar to the device of "conspicuous consumption" described by the economist Thorsten Veblen

(1899) as a means of gaining status. In this case, the striving for status is more direct and does not necessarily involve the use of material resources. We might call it "conspicuous affiliation" for snob appeal, regardless of whether any material wealth is displayed or consumed in the process. This is the strategy often resorted to out of necessity or choice in the intellectual or pseudointellectual world. A wry commentary on this phenomenon was made to the writer by one of the habitués of a Parisian sidewalk café which was supposed to be a hangout for the devotees of Jean-Paul Sartre's existentialist philosophy. "Most of the people who come here," he said, "have no interest in existentialism and can't even understand it. They think that by sitting in the same seat where Sartre sat, they can absorb existentialism through the seat of their pants."

Still another variation on the theme of opportunistic affiliation is that of *hostile or partisan affiliation,* an odd but commonplace combination of affiliation and aggression. This is the strategy of showing someone that you are "his kind of a person" because you hate the same things or the same people that he does. Some affiliations exist on nothing more substantial than such shared animosity or snobbery; but that, too, serves the need for acceptance and belonging for the individuals concerned. The reversible affiliations of the aforementioned political demagogue may, if he has nothing else to offer, take the form of a succession of hostile affiliations with each group he appeals to—providing each with a scapegoat, tailor-made to suit different group interests. Politicians often make strange bedfellows for that reason. History is already familiar with Hitler's appeal for the support of various groups by his successive attacks on capitalists, communists, aristocracy, working-class rabble, Catholics, Jews, Junker (Protestant Prussian) ruling class, depending on whom he was talking to at the moment (cf. Gilbert, 1950; Shirer, 1960). In the laboratory, Aronson and Cope (1968) readily showed that "my enemy's enemy is my friend."

Ironically, the same reversible opportunistic and hostile affiliation may be used as a second line of defense by the very people who are instrumental in creating these group hostilities in the first place, as soon as the hostility backfires and fails to serve its original purpose. Such a situation arose in Nazi Germany after the war was lost, when being an active Nazi suddenly changed from conveying membership in the "master race" to membership in a cruel, defeated, and criminally suspect social movement. Many of the Nazi leaders we examined in Nuremberg (Gilbert, 1947, 1950) protested that they weren't "really Nazis" deep down, but decent Christians and patriotic Germans who just couldn't understand how they had become involved in aggressive war and atrocities in the first place.

AGGRESSION

We have already discussed our views on aggression as a basic motive or drive (Chapter 2) and have taken the position that it is more of an adjustment to the frustration of *any* drive. It is accordingly appropriate to consider it now as one of these adjustive or defensive strategies. We can then get a clearer picture of where the various forms of aggression fit into the picture of psychodynamic processes of personality adjustment.

We must begin by recalling the distinction between destructive aggression and constructive aggressiveness. The latter may be a wholly adaptive pursuit of goals defined by the channeling of basic drives in social interaction, with due account taken of the demands of reality. Destructive aggression, on the other hand, would be a maladaptive reaction to frustration or threat, or an exaggeration of the aggressive pursuit of legitimate goals beyond the culturally tolerable.

What we are concerned with here is the use of more or less hostile relationships to other people as an adjustive strategy. This is what Horney referred to as "moving against people." Many clinicians regard this hostile strategy as the basic problem of personal adjustment and psychopathology. In its simplest form, *reactive aggression* is a primitive defense against injury of any kind. If a child is hit or hurt, even by an inanimate object, he is likely to hit back, unless he has already learned to fear further injury from such reactive aggression. An adult who is rejected or frustrated by another person is also likely to "hit back" symbolically by hostile attitudes or retaliatory behavior that will prevent him from being the "underdog," if he can possibly do so. Group identifications often require the learning of defensive hostility on a more generalized and impersonal basis, such as when forming counterprejudices toward prejudiced groups. Like the employee who says, "You can't fire me; I quit!", the reactively hostile individual may forestall his rejection by his own attitude of hostility toward the anticipated source of rejection. This is the typical "chip-on-the-shoulder" attitude of those who have learned to expect frustration or rejection. It must be remembered, however, that there are other possible reactions to frustration, such as withdrawal; that some people are temperamentally incapable of overt reactive aggression; and that some have learned to disguise their aggression through a variety of "diversionary tactics" against their enemy or source of frustration.

Some of these variations on the theme of aggression are usually discussed as defense mechanisms, but they are really defensive strategies. One is *displaced aggression*, in which the subject employs the strategy of directing the reactive aggression toward a safer target than the one that created his frustration in the first place. We have already seen examples of this in the segregated Zulu who "takes it out on his wife," in the scapegoats of frustration provided by political demagogues, and in the senseless riots of prisoners and teenage gangs. A milder form of displaced aggression may actually be built into the social structure as in the aggressive-submissive patterns of role behavior prescribed for each echelon in an authoritarian hierarchy. Whether in an authoritarian culture or not, displaced aggression is a common strategy for using social role behavior to enhance self-esteem. Among the forms which such displaced aggression may take are: hostile group partisanship, flouting of parental or civic authority, dominance or exploitation of individuals other than those providing the threat, and prejudicial attitudes toward individuals and groups.

Another variation that is discussed in the psychoanalytic literature is *self-aggression* (turning against the self). In such cases, when a sense of guilt or rejection cannot be discharged by reactive or displaced aggression, it turns against the self. We would regard this as a strategy by which the subject's self-deprecation in relations with others serves, nevertheless, to reject the unacceptable aspects of his status. This may be done in a tolerably adaptive manner, if the individual merely resorts to expressed dissatisfaction with his status and attempts to improve it. More often, however, it has a debilitating effect in destroying self-confidence and lowering levels of aspiration in all avenues of social interaction. It may even give rise to masochistic tendencies, in which anxiety can be relieved only by constant self-abasement or suffering. This reaction may stabilize in the role of the self-effacing underling or "penitent sinner," depending on the role outlets available in the culture.

WITHDRAWAL, REGRESSION, RETROGRESSION

These strategies represent a retreat from the demands as well as the satisfactions of social maturation. *Withdrawal* is merely a retreat to comparative isolation, in order to avoid the risks and frustrations of social participation if such interaction shows signs of exposing the individual's inadequacies or subjecting him to rejection. It is, of course, the opposite of active affiliation and overparticipation. The difference in choice of strategy probably lies to some extent in the predisposing temperament of the individual, but will also depend on the pressures and opportunities presented by the situational context. For some individuals *any* kind of social participation is uncomfortable. This may result from an initially sensitive and retiring disposition which becomes more and more fixed in its social detachment through isolated living or exclusion from the needed social participation. It may also be the reaction of the outgoing personality who has been "burned" by continual social rebuff or far-reaching traumatic experience. Such defensive strategies are illustrated by the "loner" in school, who has been teased by his classmates and goes on to become an isolate in adulthood; or the gawky adolescent who never overcomes his or her feelings of unattractiveness and physical awkwardness; or the jilted lover who keeps his or her distance from the opposite sex and from social situations that might expose the individual to "entangling alliances." Whether the withdrawal reaction is partial or complete, temporary or permanent, it involves much more in the nature of overt modifications of role behavior in coping with the environment than a defense mechanism would imply. It does not involve a full retreat from adulthood as such, but rather becoming a withdrawn adult personality.

Retrogression and *regression*, on the other hand, involve a full-scale strategic retreat to prepared defenses in the rear—that is, to the comparative security of childhood defenses. This usually represents a shrinking from the responsibilities of adulthood and its role demands, sometimes even before they are fully experienced. This is possible because adult role-learning behavior in adolescence requires anticipation and incipient practicing of adult role behaviors. Retrogression may take place in a mild form in an adult who shrinks from marital, occupational, and community responsibilities and persists in reverting to the irresponsible and impulsive behavior that he indulged in as an adolescent or preadolescent. This may affect speech, emotional reactions, work, and play activities, and all interpersonal relationships. Refusing to "grow up" or "act your age" constitutes a relative retrogression, since the individual's social development lags behind his age and physical development and alters his relationships with peers and other adults. This is further confirmation of the normative biosocial process which underlies the stages of personality development that we have outlined right through adulthood.

The retrogressive process may go to a more pathological extreme when severe emotional conflict or even psychotic processes bring about a gradual regression to childhood patterns of incompetence, dependency, and emotional deterioration. Such extreme regression, which is characteristic of certain behavior disorders, would have to be considered under the heading of pathological defenses, which we cannot consider here. Indeed, it may be necessary to make a categorical distinction between the defensive strategy of retrogression and the pathological deterioration of the total personality in extreme regression.

COMPENSATION, REACTION FORMATION, SUBLIMATION

These closely related defensive strategies have in common the concealment of weaknesses or unacceptable impulses by adopting behavior patterns that show entirely different or opposite characteristics. Although usually referred to in the psychoanalytic literature as defense mechanisms, they fit our definition of long-range strategies for averting anxiety by modifying overt behavior in social interaction.

Compensation is the strategy of "accentuating the positive" to make up for one's deficiencies. A person may be aware of some weakness or vulnerability in his striving for social acceptance, but would play it down and seek to emphasize or cultivate some point of strength in character, competence, or social desirability. *Reaction formation* would ordinarily involve the denial mechanisms to begin with, and the adoption of a behavior pattern which is precisely the opposite of the unacceptable characteristic. *Sublimation* (to the extent that it is a valid concept) involves the direction of the energy of an unacceptable (and therefore repressed or suppressed) motive into socially acceptable activity or role behavior.

Compensation was originally advanced by Adler as the main defense mechanism or strategy involved in the organism's constant struggle to overcome inferiority feelings. Though neglected since then and "out of style" owing to the oversimplified psychobiological context in which it was then presented, the concept does seem to us to have a definite psychodynamic function in its proper biosocial context. That context is its use as a defensive strategy in striving for satisfaction of social ego needs or efficacy motivation through the adjustment of role behaviors. Organ inferiority is only occasionally the basis for inferiority feelings that Adler thought it was, and sexual impotence is only occasionally the real source of personal inadequacy that Freud thought it was. Yet both situations may give rise to compensatory strategies, just as any other source of threatened self-esteem may do. This is because both physical defect and sexual impotence are likely to interfere with *social acceptance* or sex-role fulfillment in almost any culture, and not because of any physiological self-regulatory process.

In the case of the individual who does have reason to doubt his virility, he may indulge in reaction formation by assuming the role of a powerful executive or a uniformed brute. It was not a mere coincidence that a clique of the most sadistic Nazi Storm Troopers was the homosexual Roehm gang; or that some of history's most brutal rulers have been inadequate, passive-dependent personalities. Such individuals assume their roles and use their power in a reaction formation against the anxiety of betraying personal inadequacy. *Compensatory aggression* is another strategy that involves elements of both aggression and compensation. One may also indulge in compensatory use of physical prowess to make up for intellectual inadequacy, and vice versa. On the other hand, the pseudo-intellectual aspirations of a mediocre intellect, or the athletic aspirations of a frail child, would be evidence of reaction formation. The original cause of the sense of inferiority may be psychobiological, to be sure, but it is the social perception of such inadequacy that precipitates the sense of inferiority. It is the defensive use of role behavior and social interaction that provides the outlet for compensatory or reaction-formation strategy.

Sublimation is a little more difficult to explain, either as mental defense mechanism or as overt defensive strategy. In traditional psychoanalytic terms, sublimation is typically resorted to as a device for diverting repressed sexual energy into an activity acceptable to the superego. It is not clearly understood just how this energy is diverted into an entirely different kind of activity, but plausible examples are readily supplied. Oral sexuality may be sublimated through smoking, eating, drinking, or public speaking, which may even be done to excess. Anal sexuality may be sublimated through working with plastic art materials, or through the hoarding of money. The creative genital urge may be sublimated through artistic creation, philanthropy, and the like.

There is some question about the validity of this concept on both the grounds of pansexuality of motivation and the nature of the motivated-learning process. Unlike conversion states, in which repressed energy finds expression in some pathological process of functional inactivation, sublimation does not seem to release any of the repressed energy and, in fact, does not seem even to repress it. It is difficult to see how painting pictures actually releases energy that would ordinarily require sexual orgasm. And if the artist is leading a satisfying sex life, as most presumably do, just what is being repressed and sublimated? With the exception of the celibate clergy, there seems to be little real evidence that socially dedicated people are sublimating their sexual energy through good works.

The explanation that biosocial theory offers for these activities is much simpler and more susceptible to operational testing, while nonetheless being psychodynamic. For some people, usually those of suitable temperamental predispositions, efficacy motivation and social ego drive are *channeled* during primary and secondary socialization stages into creative or humanitarian interests. If cultural and situational interaction reinforce this direction of canalization and provide the necessary role outlets, the individuals concerned will learn and finally assume the roles that give full expression to these channeled and integrated social-efficacy interests. There need not be any repressed or sublimated sex drive involved, although all motivation is ultimately interrelated in the dynamic integration of personality. The difference is that the sex drive may not have *prime relevance* to the choice of the adult role. The artist or minister or social worker may or may not have a satisfactory sex life, and that may affect his work, just as his work may affect his sex life. But it does not necessarily follow that the energy that is frustrated in one sphere is sublimated in the other. If anything, satisfaction and competence in either sphere may be a *compensation* for frustration in the other, but that is not sublimation. We would, therefore, hazard the suggestion that sublimation of basic drives is possible, but that it is often mistaken for the ordinary channeling of basic social and efficacy drives into socially constructive role behavior.

A much more common and understandable phenomenon, we suspect, is the use of sexual conquest as a defensive strategy to compensate for insufficiencies in other spheres. When such compensatory needs are mutually satisfied, it may become the basis of either "sacred" or "profane" love. It has been found to be true of indiscriminate lovers and even in homosexuals. In such cases, conquest or seduction becomes a means of reassuring oneself of his social efficacy and desirability, not the other way round. We would suspect that even Don Juan, in his overindulgence in sexual conquest, was reacting more to the fear of social ineffectuality than of sexual impotence.

Summary Biosocial theory maintains that motivational conflict or frustration may arise at any level of personality structure (psychophysiological, psychological, or psychosocial) and at any stage of development from ego emergence to adult role assumption. The anxieties thus generated undergo a continual process of adjustment, resolution, or defense. A distinction is made between the cognitive-affective processes that are immediately mobilized as *defense mechanisms* and the longer-range or cumulative *defensive strategies* that involve patterns of social interaction and role behavior.

Among the defense mechanisms, we have described several that are familiar from the psychoanalytic literature: identification, projection, introjection, rationalization, denial, repression. To these we have added *suppression of insight*, with its three submechanisms of diversion, obviation, and semantic camouflage.

In the newly postulated category of defensive strategies we have described various styles of affiliative strategies (manipulative, reversible, opportunistic, and hostile affiliation); various styles of aggression (reactive, displaced, compensatory, and self-directed); various forms of withdrawal (withdrawal, regression, retrogression); and various compensatory strategies (compensation, reaction formation, sublimation). Canalization of social and efficacy drives is considered a better explanation for creative social behavior than is "sublimation of the sex drive."

Illustrative Case History

The somewhat anecdotal illustrations that are commonly resorted to in defining the various defense mechanisms and defensive strategies cannot do justice to the dynamic flux and interplay of motivational adjustments and the course of behavioral adaptations in continuing social interaction. It would, therefore, be highly desirable to see these defenses operating conjunctively and in continuity with the course of a life history in which the subject's role-complex and aspirations were seen in their proper social context. Since historical figures enact roles that are matters of familiar historical record, and since the Nazi leaders were the only historical figures ever subjected to long and intensive examinations by a psychologist, we shall present one of these case studies to illustrate how these defenses operate in real life. We present here excerpts from our case study of Adolf Hitler's foreign minister, Joachim von Ribbentrop (*The Psychology of Dictatorship*, Gilbert, 1950, pp. 176-204). The study is based on a full year's intimate observation, in which clinical and participant-observer techniques were used. The situation (the Nuremberg war crimes trials) required Ribbentrop and his fellow Nazis to review their careers, and to answer for their behavior, motives, and values. Many of the motivational conflicts, defense mechanisms, and defensive strategies we have discussed are illustrated in this case study; so are some of the points we have made about social role assumption and adjustment. The reader may well set himself the task of noting these as we go along.

HITLER'S FOREIGN MINISTER, JOACHIM VON RIBBENTROP

EARLY BACKGROUND

Joachim von Ribbentrop was born in 1893 in Wesel in the Rheinland. He was the second of three children born to a career army officer whose ancestors had been officers for generations. This fact gave the family some social status but was not enough to identify them with the Junker clique, since this branch of the Ribbentrop family had neither aristocratic title nor property. The mother suffered from tuberculosis and Joachim knew her only as an invalid. She died when he was eleven years old. Essentially a weak, passive-dependent child who also suffered from a mild case of tuberculosis, Joachim felt the loss of his mother very keenly. It also made him more dependent on the affections of his father, whom he admired with the awe that was a German officer-father's due. The pattern of Ribbentrop's emotional need gratifications was no doubt set by the early courting of paternal affection and approval from a father with neither the time nor the inclination for demonstrations of affection. At the same time, the father's doubts as to either son's ability to carry on the family-officer tradition (since both contracted tuberculosis at an early age) would necessarily create keen feelings of inadequacy in such a cultural setting. This feeling of inadequacy could be resolved only by identification with the strong authoritarian figure on whose favor the children were now completely dependent.

Joachim's education was sporadic and unsatisfactory, due largely to the father's moving about from one garrison town to another. He received elementary schooling in Kassel and Metz in Alsace-Lorraine, where he acquired some familiarity with French culture. He was considered lazy, mischievous, and not very bright as a student. However, he did show the intellectual capacity to advance in subjects which interested him, such as history and languages. He also acquired some proficiency in playing the violin. A rather personable lad, he was adept at making friendships among his neighbors and schoolmates.

The father retired as a lieutenant colonel in 1908 and remarried at about the same time. This appeared to threaten Joachim's need for paternal attention and affection, and only prompted resentment of the mother-substitute. In a short time the family ties were so strained that Joachim had to be sent away to London, ostensibly to study there. He remained in London for about a year, perfecting his English and acquiring a taste for cosmopolitan living, but he never made any serious attempt to study for a career.

In 1919 his linguistic ability won him an assignment as an aide to General von Seeckt, one of the War Ministry's commissioners to the peace conference. The Treaty of Versailles gave him his first bitter taste of military diplomacy on the defeated side, but it does not appear to have been an unduly traumatic experience to him personally.

THE SOCIAL CLIMBER

Ribbentrop managed to land a job as sales representative of the German champagne producer, Henkell . . .

Once again the struggle for status and security began. Ribbentrop made his choice among the limited possibilities in accordance with the "style of life" that was conducive to his temperament. Not being an aggressive man-of-action or an ideological fanatic, he was repulsed rather than attracted by the revolutionary turmoil. Without Junker background or money there was nothing he could exploit to political advantage. But he could capitalize on his engaging personality, his talents as a "good mixer," and his adeptness at superficial niceties to achieve some financial and social success. Like many a demobilized officer in what remained of the old social order, his trump card was his eligibility. He played this card shrewdly and married the proprietor's daughter in 1920. Although father Henkell expressed some misgivings about Ribbentrop's character, he helped his son-in-law build up a rather flourishing liquor import monopoly.

To enhance his social status, in 1925 Ribbentrop acquired the right to use the aristocratic "von" on a legal technicality.

The "von" Ribbentrops never overlooked any possible occasion to "leave cards" or to wangle an invitation to a reception. They traveled a great deal, "following the calendar" to mingle with the international aristocratic set during the appropriate seasons at the Riviera, London, Paris, and Switzerland. All this proved good for business as well as for social status. Ribbentrop gradually became "accepted" and prosperous by the end of a decade of feverish social activity, in accordance with the well-worn pattern of behavior for businessmen with social aspirations.

. . . Ribbentrop now began to groom himself for political influence. His mansion in the fashionable Berlin-Dahlem section became a center of social activity for the Berlin diplomatic set. However, the depression which descended upon the Western world in 1930 began to throw the entire political and industrial machinery of the country into a state of chaos. Ribbentrop was threatened not only with the frustration of any further social ambitions, but even the loss of the hard-won and dearly cherished status he already had. Lacking the ego-strength, the basic competence, or the basically sound social values to withstand any reversal in his superficial attainments, he could only fall back on the social defenses of the incompetent and insecure. Now he, too, sought scapegoats on whom to vent his aggression and a "dynamic" social movement with which he could identify. The Nazi party seemed to provide both.

. . . Ribbentrop's "style of life" and group identification had kept him aloof from the revolutionary rabble up to 1930, but social disintegration and frustration were now producing similar reactions among all strata of German society. In Ribbentrop's case, the metamorphosis to a "convinced" adherent of Nazism was far easier to undergo than was the case with aristocrats like von Papen. For one thing, his status in the aristocratic in-group was far more tenuous than that of the old landed aristocracy; but more important, the inadequate, passive-dependent, suggestible personality was far more susceptible to such dominance and introjected aggressiveness. Ribbentrop's superficial ego-defenses had started to break down at the first puff of an ill wind, revealing once more the insecure youth courting the protection of an authoritarian figure. The psychodynamic motivations served at least to reinforce the shrewd calculations of the inveterate social climber and facilitate the restructuring of his own identifications. . . . He soon found he had backed a winner. [Playing the game of empire-building in Hitler's retinue with consummate skill, he was eventually appointed German ambassador to the Court of St. James in London. Ribbentrop had finally "arrived."]

HITLER'S TOUGH DIPLOMAT

With his ascendancy to exalted social status, Ribbentrop's personality underwent an external change. A new conception of his own social role evolved out of his passive identification with the aggressive Nazi leader. He was now not merely a top-ranking, wealthy, titled diplomat, but the official spokesman for a powerful dictator who was leading a great nation to its manifest destiny. As his adulation of Hitler's leadership increased, he wasted less and less civility on his social inferiors or on foreign diplomats. This change of behavior was not merely the crude tactic of a political opportunist and social climber who had "arrived"; it was a passive-dependent personality's awkward expression of the intensified sadomasochistic authoritarianism of his culture. The values of moribund Prussian militarism had been reanimated by Hitler's "dynamic new order" and the adaptive poseur threw himself enthusiastically into the role that provided admirable defenses against his own insecurity. If he had failed to measure up to the paternal tradition of militarism in adopting the "style of life" of effete café society, he could now correct any misapprehension over his fitness for his historical role. He accordingly bent every effort to impress Hitler with his "hardness" rather than his *Salonfähigkeit* [social adeptness]. The gracious charm now gave way to a brusque, arrogant manner, punctuated with sharp demands and threats of force. From his underlings he exacted a formal deference and discipline that would have done credit to any petty medieval tyrant, while obsequiously courting the favor of a stern paternalistic Führer. It was not long before Hitler granted him a general's rank in the Elite Guard (SS), and from then on his overbearance knew no bounds.

By the end of 1937 Hitler's plan for hegemony in Europe had become crystallized into a definite timetable for piecemeal aggression, with the calculated risk of war. Ribbentrop was not actually present at the "Hoszbach conference" in November,[2] but he lost little time proving that he was present in spirit. Within a few weeks he sent a memorandum to Hitler confirming the practicality of armed aggression. He too advocated force to bring about a change in the European status quo and to establish Germany's eastern sphere of influence. Europe could be made safe for German expansion if England were discouraged from backing France in any possible intervention. The cold logic of his arguments was little more than the repetition of the strategy divulged by Hitler at the fateful meeting in November. Foreign Minister von Neurath had expressed some misgivings about Hitler's aggressive plans, but now Ribbentrop confirmed their feasibility. Hitler's mind was made up. A month after he had written the memorandum in which he showed such statesmanlike insight, the Führer's "tough" favorite diplomat became Foreign Minister of the Greater Third Reich.

. . . Ribbentrop's role in the series of aggressions which followed in rapid succession was wholeheartedly cooperative, even if secondary to Hitler's and Goering's. Within a few days of his appointment as Foreign Minister, he was echoing Hitler's intimidating threats to Austrian Chancellor Schuschnigg, in preparation for the Anschluss. Two months later he signed the decree of annexation. A short time after Hitler had given the world his assurance that he had only the most peaceful intentions, Ribbentrop was at work in collaboration with the whole Party machinery, fomenting agitation for a "settlement of the Sudeten problem." Hitler negotiated the Munich Pact himself as Ribbentrop sat in rapt admiration of his master's persuasive powers. [Then] Poland was next on the list. But by now Allied forbearance was clearly at an end. The French and British governments gave Hitler clear warning that any further aggression would mean war. President Roosevelt urged peaceful settlement of any outstanding differences. Ribbentrop nevertheless confined himself to deceptive pretenses of negotiating a settlement with Poland and . . . assured Hitler that he need not be deterred by England's guaranty of Poland, because the British "would leave Poland coldly in the lurch" if it came to a showdown.

As the German armies stood poised to strike, Hitler sent Ribbentrop to Moscow to negotiate a nonaggression pact which gave Germany a free hand in dealing with Poland. . . . The invasion of Poland and the declaration of war by England and France inevitably followed. Ribbentrop told us that he suffered an attack of nerves when the news of the Allied declaration of war came, but Hitler was very calm about it. However, the record shows that Ribbentrop soon overcame his attack of jitters and expressed satisfaction that the war had come, because he, too, thought the problem of Germany's *Lebensraum* should be solved in the Führer's lifetime. There could be no turning back from his historical mission, even if his own daring frightened him.

Poland, Belgium, Holland, Norway, Denmark, and France fell in rapid

---

[2] The conference at which Hitler outlined his plans for the conquest of Czechoslovakia, Austria, Hungary, as a prelude to the conquest of all of Europe.

Figure 7-1. Nazi Foreign Minister von Ribbentrop *shakes hands with Prime Minister Daladier of France upon conclusion of French-German Nonaggression Pact. Ribbentrop's case history and examination illustrates the motivational conflicts, defense mechanisms, and defensive strategies of a passive-dependent personality aspiring to greatness in a regime dedicated to violence. (Photo by World Wide.)*

succession, and the Balkans were overrun soon after. In June, 1941, Hitler made his fateful decision to attack Russia in an all-out offensive involving millions of troops. Ribbentrop kept urging his Axis partner, Japan, to attack Russia and to harass the United States to checkmate help from that quarter. At the end of 1941 the Japanese militarists decided they could at least attack American possessions safely.

Through all of this bloodshed and violation of solemn commitments, Ribbentrop's main concern continued to be his share of public recognition and favor in the Führer's eyes. His quarrels with Himmler, Goering, and the General Staff over jurisdictional matters were as acrimonious as they were petty, resembling nothing so much as sibling rivalry in its most childish form. Even in the cataclysmic struggle for Germany's manifest destiny, the Führer's entourage continued to be a house of squabbling egotists competing for status and recognition.

One such dispute with Hitler in 1941 proved to be a highly significant and very traumatic experience, because Ribbentrop referred to it repeatedly after

Hitler's death. Ribbentrop had taken his grievance over some fancied slight to his authority (he was later vague and inconsistent on this point) directly to Hitler, giving vent to petulant recriminations. Only under these circumstances, we gather, did he venture to criticize some of Hitler's policies. When the argument became heated, Hitler flew into one of his furious temper tantrums with marked psychosomatic reactions, screaming that Ribbentrop was taxing his health and menacing Germany's destiny with his petty objections. The device was not unlike that which an hysterical parent may resort to, stirring guilt panic in an ungrateful child, as a weapon of control. At any rate, the effect on Ribbentrop was exactly the same. He begged forgiveness, reaffirmed his loyalty, and promised never again to provoke Fate by challenging the Führer. It should be mentioned that Ribbentrop's father died the same year (it is not certain whether the father's death preceded or followed this scene). If anything was needed to reinforce Ribbentrop's slavish obedience to his father-surrogate throughout the critical war years, Hitler's well-timed threat of collapse turned the trick. Since the suggestible Foreign Minister fully accepted Hitler's identification with Germany's destiny, the appeal to that symbol even provided a workable rationalization for reinforced submission. In the succeeding years, Ribbentrop outdid himself in supporting Hitler's most brutal policies.

. . . In 1944 world-wide revulsion over the discovery of Maidanek extermination camp forced him to make timid inquiries as to whether this was all in order. Hitler reminded him sharply that those things were under Himmler's jurisdiction and none of his business. The Foreign Minister dutifully dismissed the matter from his mind. . . .

OBSERVATIONS AND EVALUATION

It was an extremely confusing world in which Ribbentrop found himself after the death of the Führer. He had, of course, experienced some nervous exhaustion and a severe jolt to his ego in the collapse of the Third Reich, as had most of the Nazi leaders. But the panic and disintegration that Ribbentrop manifested as he went on trial were quite extraordinary. . . .

As we have already seen, the disintegration of the Nazi microcosm produced different reactions in the leading personalities of the Third Reich. The revolutionists fell back on pathological defense mechanisms similar to those that had set their world in motion; the diplomatic and military satellites retreated to their "second line of defense." . . . But after Hitler's death, Ribbentrop had nothing. He had neither the pathological defenses nor fanaticism of the revolutionary mental deviates, and he was cut off from the "second line of defense" of the aristocratic in-group with whom he sought to identify.

Like von Papen,[3] Ribbentrop had sought to aspire to social respectability and had not been driven by a pathological lust for rebellion against the established order. But, unlike von Papen, his social aspirations were not so much the product of deeply rooted in-group values as they were the compensatory needs of an insecure personality. With his lack of basic values or ego-strength, Ribbentrop's ego-ideal had always been "status at any price"—with neither the restraint of the well-bred aristocrat nor the antisocial impulses of the psychopath. The solution for a personality so constructed, in a time of crisis,

[3] Franz von Papen, a Junker aristocrat, was Chancellor of Germany before Hitler, then served as Vice Chancellor and in various ambassadorial posts under Hitler.

had been to identify with a dominant political leader who represented his ego-ideal, to introject *his* aggression, his social values, even his heroic fantasies and plan of action. The strategem had worked magnificently for a time in producing the primary gain. But the inevitable secondary loss of such completely obsequious identification with the dictator had been the utter deterioration of any other ego defenses.

In terms of group acceptance he was neither fish nor fowl; in terms of personal conviction he was a complete nonentity. The aristocrats rejected him as an unscrupulous pretender; the Old Fighters [the vanguard of the Nazi revolutionaries] resented him as a bandwagon climber who had achieved his status without fighting for it; the militarists understandably relegated him to the genus "cheap politician"—i.e., one of those who play reckless politics to maintain their own power and then leave the soldiers to fight it out and take the blame.

As for motives and values to justify his actions, Ribbentrop was completely at a loss. All attempts to get at his basic convictions proved fruitless, for he had no basic convictions. He had attempted the impossible feat of championing the values of polite society and the Nazi New Order at one and the same time and had never resolved the dilemma.

The full extent of his suggestibility in his reaction to the mere image of the Führer had to be seen to be appreciated. When the movies of the Nazi Rise to Power were shown in the Nuremberg courtroom, for example:

> (*December 11, 1945, courtroom.*) Ribbentrop was completely overwhelmed by the voice and figure of the Führer. He wept like a baby, as if a dead father had returned to life. "Can't you feel the terrific strength of his personality?—Can't you see how he swept people off their feet? I don't know if you can, but we can feel it. It is *erschütternd* [unnerving] . . ."
>
> (*Later, in Ribbentrop's cell.*) Still half moved to tears, Ribbentrop asked me if I hadn't felt the terrific power of Hitler's personality emanating from the screen. I confessed I hadn't. Ribbentrop talked as if he were again hypnotized by the Führer's figure. "Do you know, even with all I know now, if Hitler should come to me in this cell now, and say, '*Do this!*'—I would still do it. Isn't it amazing? Can't you really feel the terrific magnetism of his personality?"

Small wonder that Ribbentrop's first reaction to the war crimes indictment had been: "The indictment is directed against the wrong people.—We were all under Hitler's shadow." The Foreign Minister's personality *had* become absorbed in the dictator's shadow, and that was all that was left of it now.

Ribbentrop's explanation of his statesmanship never rose above the level of inane palaver, either in our informal conversations in his cell or in his formal defense before the Tribunal. On such a catastrophic issue as the making and breaking of the Munich Pact, he recalled that Hitler had simply charmed Chamberlain and Daladier with his glowing personality; he was sure because he had felt it himself. Besides, the Pact had not really been broken because Hitler had established a "Protectorate"—after some "sharp talk" to be sure— but then Czechoslovakia had merely been a state created by the Treaty of Versailles, and one must not take "diplomatic language" too seriously. We sought to draw him out on some rationale for signing the Russian Nonaggression Pact after signing the three-power Anti-Comintern Pact, and then attacking Russia two years later. He assured us that he had always been in favor of rapprochement with Russia and had wanted to include her in the three-power pact. The idea of including Russia in an Anti-Comintern alliance did not strike him as presenting any diplomatic difficulties. Besides, "Hitler had great admiration for Stalin. He was only afraid some radical might come in his place."

. . . To analyze his guilt reaction in this state of demoralization, we must first separate the war guilt from the atrocities. Ribbentrop was spared the full impact of guilt feelings about precipitating the war by his inability to comprehend it fully. To some extent, at least, his war guilt anxiety was buried in a maze of confused rationalizations about loyalty, foreign oppression, and "political dynamics." But no amount of confused rationalization could sufficiently obfuscate his moral guilt for unprovoked mass murder. Even in those states that bordered on agitated depression, he felt constrained to make the distinction.

> (*January 5, 1946, Ribbentrop's cell.*) "In the atrocities and persecution of the Jews, our guilt as Germans is so enormous, that it leaves one speechless. There is no defense, no explanation. But if you just put that aside—really, the other countries all have a share in bringing about the war. . . . I know how Germany was being strangled by the Versailles Treaty. . . . How Hitler could have done all those things later, I don't know—I just don't know."

As the atrocity evidence multiplied, Ribbentrop's anxiety increased to panic. On that issue, at least, the impossibility of being Hitler's shadow and one of the socially élite at the same time fully penetrated his consciousness. Indeed, the dilemma had now to be finally resolved with his own life hanging in the balance. The testimony of his brutal ultimatum to Regent Horthy of Hungary —"They [the Jews] must be either exterminated or taken to concentration camps"—shook him even more than his threats to President Hacha of Czechoslovakia. "I *could not* have said such a thing! It is so entirely contrary to my character," he insisted. He had "violently opposed" Hitler's persecution of the Jews. Decent Germans simply don't *do* such things!

It was, indeed, rather strong talk for one who had aspired to be the epitome of social respectability. Such statements, literally taken out of Hitler's mouth, might have sounded more in character coming from any one of the revolutionary psychopaths than from the genteel, would-be aristocrat of Berlin and London salons. We have already indicated that by that time Ribbentrop had completely subjugated his mind to Hitler's. But the traumatic impact of the atrocity evidence involves something more subtle than his realization that he was being held culpable for the role of Hitler's shadow. Our observation was that Ribbentrop acted as if he had *not fully realized* that the mass exterminations were actually taking place while he was implementing the policy of genocide.

We must pause here to consider a crucial question: How was it possible for a political leader, supposedly not a criminal psychopath, however unscrupulous in his ambition, to continue for years to condone a policy of human extermination, unless he did not know that it was actually being carried out? —and how could he have failed to know it?

Let us first cite Ribbentrop's reaction to the testimony of Colonel Hoess of Auschwitz [commandant of the main extermination camp], describing how he himself had carried out this mass extermination on Hitler's orders:

(*April 20, 1946, Ribbentrop's cell.*)   ". . . Tell me, I wasn't in court on Monday.—Did Hoess actually say—that Hitler had ordered the mass murders?—In 1941?—Did he say that?—In 1941?—In '41?—in '41?—Did he really say that? (We confirmed the testimony.)—But Hitler spoke of transporting them to the East or to Madagascar. . . . Did Hitler really order the extermination?—In '41?—in '41?

Ribbentrop held his head in his hand and repeated in a descending whisper, "—'41—'41—My God!—Did Hoess say in '41?" (We again confirmed the details.)

"Stop! Stop, doctor!—I cannot bear it!—All those years—a man to whom children came so trustingly and lovingly.—It must have been a fanatic madness. There is no doubt now that Hitler had ordered it? I thought even up to now that perhaps Himmler, under some pretext—. But '41 he said? My God! My God!"

To understand this reaction, we must first recall that 1941 was the year in which Ribbentrop's father died, as well as the year in which the violent scene with Hitler occurred. Panicked at the threat of losing favor, or of causing the mighty Führer's collapse, Ribbentrop had given his word of honor never to question his judgment again. This had required nothing less than the complete stifling of the last vestige of independent judgment and conscience, since the actual extermination program went into full production that year. That operation was, to be sure, a carefully guarded state secret strictly under Himmler's jurisdiction, but there can be no doubt that the ubiquitous Foreign Minister had, as always, gotten ample indications of what was afoot. Indeed, it was common knowledge among the higher SS officials, and one of Ribbentrop's underlings later stated, that "the Reich Foreign Minister Ribbentrop obviously knew Hitler's intention to exterminate the Jews of Europe." Nevertheless, it is a moot question just how clearly Ribbentrop allowed the *actuality* —the *full realization*—of mass extermination to penetrate his consciousness. The distinction is no mere academic quibble. It is the crux of our observations on the vital question: How could the respectable conformists to the norms of Christian civilization have apparently condoned and even promoted the commission of such fantastic atrocities?

Our psychological reference point, of course, is the functional gap between discreet sensations and the full realization of meaning in social context, with value judgments leading to action. It is a psychological truism, often applied to hysterics, that "there are none so blind as those who will not see." We know that Ribbentrop was a passive, suggestible, inadequate personality who dared not see the evil of the man who so abundantly fulfilled his ego needs and whom he had sworn under traumatic circumstances never to criticize. . . . Yet he could not have done what he did with full knowledge of the consequences. . . .

But between knowledge and ignorance there is the limbo of arrested perceptions and inhibited insights. Between calculated hypocrisy and hysterical dissociation there is semiconscious self-deception. It is possible to look at things without fully perceiving them, to divert one's attention from the unpleasant to the pleasant, from the ego-threatening to the ego-gratifying; to suspend the process of rational inference in mid-air, and to distort one's insights just enough to suppress anxiety. As Hans Frank said, "We did not *want* to know"—and there are none so blind as those who would suppress anxiety by arresting insight.

The question whether Ribbentrop was fully aware of the enormity and actuality of his guilt with respect to the atrocities can be answered only in such paradoxical terms. We can reconcile all of our observations and evaluations only by inferring that Ribbentrop verbalized Hitler's aggressions while blinding himself to their actuality; that he suppressed any full realization of his guilt in preference to sacrificing his only source of security in a chaotic world. . . .

. . . When we speak of reckless political opportunists, we must distinguish at least two extremes of personality variants: the ruthlessly aggressive psychopath who consciously pursues his self-centered goals with a cynical disdain for the social mores; and the passive-dependent, suggestible conformist, who seeks social status at any price but suppresses any insight into the incompatibility of his motives. These opposite extremes may join hands in a political conspiracy to achieve their common material goals—a conspiracy in which the morally halt lead the purposefully blind. This is particularly true in an authoritarian culture, which reaches the epitome of capricious leadership under an ideological dictatorship. In such a conspiracy, the passive, imitative, compensatory aggression of the inadequate personality may become just as disastrously effective as the aggressive lust of the most ruthless psychopath. Such, at least, was Foreign Minister Ribbentrop's function in the Nazi dictatorship.

8

Cognition and Personality

In discussing learning (Chapter 6), we said that perceptual individuation was one of the long-range developmental changes that take place in the course of behavior modification through learning experiences. We implied that such developmental changes were not adequately accounted for by S-R conditioning theory and were all but ignored by psychoanalytic theory. Yet there is ample evidence that individuals learn to perceive their environments differently and, therefore, react differently to the same situation. If we expand the approach of perceptual individuation to include the total cognitive interaction with the environment and society—the modifications of perception, memory, reasoning, social judgment, and even self-concept—we have a truly profound basis for the understanding and assessment of individual differences in personality. The lead to such understanding is so productive of research and applications that we would be well-advised to consider some of those currently being explored. Before we proceed with a sampling of these problems and techniques, it would be appropriate to examine the complexity of the perceptual-cognitive process itself.

The
Cognitive

Process   The act of seeing something in the visual field and becoming aware of what it means involves much more than the registering of an image on the retina and the transmission of a corresponding set of impulses to the brain. There are "intervening variables" between the stimulus and the response which modify the process of perception and bring a large element of subjective interpretation to bear on any cognitive-perceptual experience. It was, in fact, customary for many years to insert an O (for organism) between the S and R of early psychophysics and behaviorism to indicate the intervening variables of attitude, set, and previous experience.

More recently, Solley and Murphy (1960) offered a more detailed analysis of the perceptual process, which lends itself more readily to the task of relating cognition to personality (and indeed to the learning models suggested by Miller and by Pribram). According to Solley and Murphy's analysis, there is first a state of ongoing expectancy, then attention to the new stimulus, and then a moment of "trial-and-check" process before the percept is finally apprehended. Between reception and perception, and simultaneous with the trial-and-check process, there is interaction with autonomic and proprioceptive arousal mechanisms. This serves to screen the apprehended stimulus for its affective and sensorimotor connotations before the percept is finally structured and its meanings (with connotations) understood (see Fig. 8-1).

This is a useful model for analyzing the complexity of a momentary perceptual response. However, as we all know, cognition is an even more complex ongoing process involving modification by past associations and concurrent cognitive-affective influences. For the purpose of application to personality dynamics, we would carry the analysis a step or two further into the dimension of continuing experience in time. We would further-

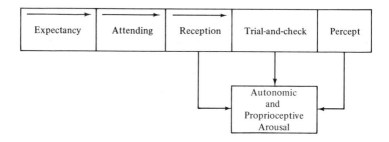

Figure 8–1. The process of perceiving. (*After Solley and Murphy, 1960.*)

more make provision for the continual modification of cognition by on-going cognitive-affective "sets" or canalized motives, as well as the circular process by which the cognitive or behavioral responses themselves become new data of awareness (see Fig. 8-2). It is important to note also that cognition and impulse to behavioral reaction are constantly subject to defense mechanisms which may inhibit or distort both cognition and overt reaction. We have already discussed examples of such defense mechanisms in Chapter 7. The whole process of cognition, therefore, undergoes continuous and cumulative modification in time, as learning influences, canalizations of drives, and maturational changes interact or synthesize. These changes affect the entire personality, but they are some-times most easily tapped by their effects on perceptual individuation.

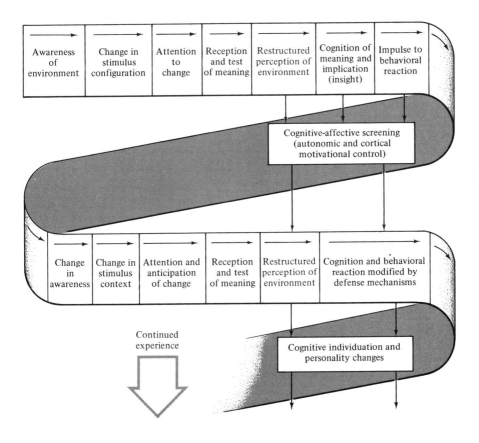

Figure 8–2. The complex processes of cognitive interaction and individuation, extended in time.

Actually, we do not need elaborate diagrams to understand how differently people perceive the same situation, but such schemata do have some utility in illustrating the complexity of certain processes that we ordinarily take for granted. References to subjective variations in perception have been found in literature and drama at least as far back as Shakespeare, and examples of biased "eye-witness testimony" in court cases have by now been reduced to a banality. In our everyday experience, examples of how perceptual discrimination is individualized and acculturated by learning experiences are as commonplace as our own daily activities at work or play. Many a good cook or gourmet can tell you exactly what ingredients went into the cheese soufflé you're eating, and any French wine taster can tell you the exact type and vintage of most wines sampled when blindfolded; yet to the uninitiated or uninstructed, one cheese soufflé or white wine is very much like any other. An experienced art critic or dealer can point out nuances of technique, composition, and color that would escape the novice, and could very likely spot a forgery of the work of a famous artist he is familiar with in a matter of minutes or seconds. A doctor will notice the bit of pallor on your face that escapes the English teacher who just caught your grammatical error, which the attentive psychologist recognized as really being a Freudian slip! But you are oblivious to all this, if you are a young fellow "on the make," because you have already surveyed the company of females present and have spotted the prettiest and best-dressed girl in the room, and have decided that her every gesture, her voice and bearing, her taste in clothes all denote "class." Obviously, individual motives help to structure our individual perceptions, regardless of the amount of learning that has entered into the situation.

The refinement of perceptual discrimination and judgment through experience and channeled motives applies likewise to the common experiences that make for cultural differences. If an American walks along the streets of Tokyo for the first time, he does not see, in the dress and stylized gestures of a cultured people, the meaningful symbols of social interchange which make up cultivated Japanese life, any more than a Japanese would at first see such meanings in a French salon or at a British tea party. The same goes for American Peace Corps volunteers in their first encounters with strange foreign customs and "proprieties" that keep them wondering, "What did I do wrong now?" They soon learn that they have been missing perceptual cues and failing to make appropriate responses, or giving false cues because they have not been sensitized to the different meanings these cues have. Female volunteers often have to be warned that the mere exchange of a friendly smile with a passing stranger in many Asiatic or Latin American countries can invite trouble, even though it is a perfectly innocent exchange of perceptual cues on an American college campus.

The fact is that perceptual cues are not merely seen or heard or tasted. They are selectively *attended to* and *interpreted* in the light of past experience and the sensitivities built up from these past associations. The meaning attached to them invariably reflects the attitudes, values, expectations of consequences, and need arousal that have been conditioned, channeled, or directly taught through such past experience. Some of this perceptual individuation and conformity is culturally determined; some of it is selective because of individual predilection and experience. The perceptual patterns of selective attention and interpretation influence further attitude formation. This circular reinforcement tends to ingrain perceptual biases deeper and deeper, until new experiences and motivation for accommodation to changing environmental relationships bring about the learning of new perceptual habits. Just how this perceptual individuation and change takes place is a very complex question. We are dealing not only with an essentially circular sequence of causes and effects but also with all the forms of associative learning and other developmental effects that enter into the process. Social suggestion, conditioned emotional responses, mere practice and instruction, canalization of motives, adaptation to stress—all enter into it.

Thus it is not possible to say that any particular kind of perceptual distortion or structure takes place as a direct consequence of any particular learning process—or, indeed, as a direct consequence of cumulative learning processes alone. There are undoubtedly maturational processes in cognitive differentiation (e.g., analysis and abstraction) which set limits on perceptual learning capacities at any age. There are also motivational and affective forces which influence cognitive-perceptual individuation and susceptibility to learning. The cumulative effects of learning processes in personality development are not segmentalized, but function in unison to affect the development of the total personality. It is, therefore, not surprising to find the same personality characteristics reflected in verbalized attitudes, expressive movements, affective reactions to personal encounter, interpretations of daily events witnessed or heard about—or of inkblots on the Rorschach test.

Thus we need not look to immediate personal experience alone to explain the rather wide individual differences in perceptual interpretation of similar environmental data. The vast world of prejudice, rumor, propaganda, and conflicting interests is replete with emotional misrepresentation, assignment of absurd meanings to commonly perceived events, imputation of sublime or ulterior motives, and appeals to our own canalized fears and desires. These influences on our perception of the people and events around us, or *as we imagine them to be*, are not limited to the direct modification of behavior by classical conditioning in the first signal system of Pavlov. You don't have to have an unpleasant encounter to "see" blacks as "shiftless." It is quite sufficient to have verbal stereotypes or implicit prejudices of others communicated to you symbolically for your perception of blacks to be distorted by selective association. This is especially true if you *need* to feel superior to another group.

It is easy to see, incidentally, how these cognitive discrimination and individuation processes, interacting with motivational-adaptive processes of the total personality, produce some of the defense mechanisms we discussed in Chapter 7. Identification, projection, suppression of insight, selective association, and semantic camouflage are all mechanisms which imply cognitive distortions or manipulations in the interest of ego defense. When we say that "there are none so blind as those who will not see," or "people hear only what they want to hear," we are only saying that perception is highly selective and can be readily distorted in the service of ego defense. Whether the cognitive defenses as such are learned by some process akin to operant conditioning, or represent merely canalizations of the social ego needs themselves through available means of expression, is a question for further research. In any case, individualized manipulations of the cognitive-communicative processes are frequently resorted to as a means of satisfying ego needs and averting anxiety.

Studies
of Cognitive
Variability

One of the most productive areas of research into individual differences, and the one that actually started psychology as a laboratory science, has been the measurement of differences in sensory acuity and judgment. Hundreds of studies were done in American and European universities to show how individuals differed—and generally differed consistently—in their sensitivity to light and sound, their ability to discriminate minimal differences of brightness, color, size, pitch, loudness, and a variety of other dimensions of sensory stimulation in the various modalities of sensation. It was hoped by the early pioneers in experimental psychology, such as Wundt, Titchener, and Cattell, that a science of individual differences in personality could be constructed, step by step, beginning with minute analyses of sensations, then emotions, etc. Unfortunately, this atomistic analysis of stimulus properties, "the physical dimensions of consciousness" as Boring (1933) once called it, proved to be a very shaky foundation for the study of meaningful perception itself, to say nothing of the complexities of personality. In recent decades more attention has been paid to the subjective variability of perceptual responses, such as influences of attitude, mental set, social suggestion, selective attention and association, and even cognitive styles and habits in determining the conscious content of awareness. This in turn has led to more fruitful approaches to the study of personality through perception.

COGNITIVE STYLES

Following some earlier leads by Sherif, Asch (1951) showed not only that people were influenced by the judgments of others in their estimates of the lengths of lines they were shown, but that different *kinds* of social conformity were involved in this susceptibility to suggestion. Some individuals actually modified their perception of the lines in conformity with the artificial group norms and saw things as others saw them. Some failed to do so, but *said* they did, just to "go along with the crowd." Some independent souls called their shots as they saw them, without succumbing to social suggestion at all. The studies showed not only a wide variability in susceptibility to suggestion but also considerable consistency on the part of the same individuals in the extent and type of susceptibility. It was clearly indicated that "cognitive styles" of highly suggestible or independent perception were individual personality characteristics.

Further exploration of this line of investigation was undertaken by Witkin and his collaborators (summarized in Witkin *et al.*, 1962). In a long series of studies, Witkin investigated the susceptibility of the individual to the confusion of cues or conflicting frames of reference from *his own* perceptual field. Three principal kinds of tasks were used. In the rod-and-frame test (RFT), the subject in a darkened room was presented with a luminous frame which was tilted, and asked to adjust a luminous rod until it was truly vertical, regardless of its position within the frame. In another test, the subject was placed in a tilted room on a tilted chair and asked to adjust the position of the chair until he sat erect. This was the body-adjustment test (BAT). (See Fig. 8–3.) In a third test, the subject was asked to extract a simple geometric figure from a more complex geometric pattern in which it was embedded. This was the embedded figure test (EFT). In each of these perceptual tasks the subject had to divorce one set of cues from the rest of the perceptual field in order to perform the task required. Thus on the BAT they had to distinguish their own somatic cues as to upright or tilted position from the misleading cues of the surrounding tilted room. Witkin found the expected individual differences in sensitivity to bodily orientation and rather consistent differences in dependence or independence of cues from the visual field. Moreover, the same people who showed dependence on the visual field (and were thus easily misled) on one task were also

A

Figure 8–3. Testing field-dependence-independence in perception. *Above, subject in tilted room must adjust body position to vertical in spite of misleading cues from room. Below, subject must adjust rod to vertical position in spite of misleading cues from frame and from own tilted position. (Photos by David Linton.)*

B

generally "field-dependent" on the other tasks. Those who were able to perceive their body positions without being confused by the tilted room in which they were sitting (the "field-independent" ones) were generally better able to judge true verticality on the RFT and to extract the geometric figure on the EFT. Correlations of field-dependence-independence ratings from one task to another generally ran from about .3 to .6, indicating a fair though variable consistency on this dimension of "cognitive style." Some people, at least, were consistently able to control their selective cognition of environmental or internal stimuli in order to make the behavioral adjustment called for in the situation, while others were readily and consistently influenced by distortions of the total field.

Further comparison with the performance of children on certain relevant parts of the Wechsler Intelligence Scale for Children led these workers to conclude that "there is a general cognitive style which runs through perceptual and intellectual functioning" (Witkin et al., 1962, p. 60). The authors also regard field-dependence-independence as the perceptual component of a broader cognitive dimension. This cognitive dimension of style ranges from an extremely analytic to an extremely global (unarticulated) mode of experiencing the environment.

The possible relevance of these cognitive styles to personality dynamics becomes evident when we consider that the individual's sense of identity, his interpersonal relationships, and many of his defense mechanisms involve cognition directly. Studies by the Witkin group and others on the "sense of separate identity," for example, are summarized as follows:

A "sense of separate identity" is the result of development of awareness of one's own needs and characteristics as distinct from those of others. The self is experienced as segregated and structured; stable internal frames of reference are available for self-definition and for interpreting and reacting to the world. In the absence of such inner frames of reference, definition of the characteristics of the self is likely to be determined from without and ability to function independently of external standards limited. The following observable ways in which a developed sense of separate identity might manifest itself were considered . . . limited need for guidance and support from others; ability to establish and, within limits, maintain attitudes, judgments, sentiments without continuous reference to external standards; a stable self-view, despite variations in social context.

It was our hypothesis that persons with an analytical field approach would be more apt to show these characteristics than persons with a global approach, reflecting their more developed sense of separate identity. . . . These studies have used a great variety of situations and methods. Their results give strong, consistent support to our hypothesis (Witkin et al., 1962, p. 155).

Those individuals who use an analytical (or field-independent) approach in assessing themselves and the environment have been found by investigators to be regarded as socially more independent and less influenced by authority. They are also guided by values, standards, and needs of their own, while possibly less sensitive to subtle social cues and needs of others. Both children and adults who use an analytical field approach tend to use isolation and intellectualization as defense mechanisms, rather than primitive denial or massive repression.

The possibilities for investigating psychodynamic processes through cognitive styles and articulation are provocative indeed.

COGNITIVE DISSONANCE

Another provocative area of research in cognitive processes which seems to have relevance to the psychodynamics of personality is one which has recently been called cognitive dissonance. This area has been largely developed by Festinger (1957) and his co-workers, though it has antecedents in Bruner's work on "perceptual defense" and is implicit in Sherif's work on adjustment to social norms in attitudes and perception. It deals essentially with the discrepancies that are encountered in daily life between different aspects of the cognitive field or between expectation and reality. This may come about from the need to deal with opinions that are different from one's own, from failure of anticipated events to materialize, from a recognition of gross inconsistency of appearances in the environmental field, from illogical sequences of cause and effect, or even from inconsistency between one's own behavior and professed values or those of a friend. Under such circumstances, Festinger has shown, the individual tends to make any one of a number of adjustive changes in behavior or cognition to bring the discrepant elements in the cognitive field into more *consistent* realignment with each other. It is implied that there is a *need for consistency* in cognition and behavior which constantly gives rise to efforts to reduce or eliminate cognitive dissonance. This is very much in line with the basic motive of cognitive clarity and consistency which we posited in Chapter 2 as one of the generic motives of *Homo sapiens socialis*. As a result of this need for consistency in cognition-experience, which has stood man in good stead throughout his long evolution as a rational and social animal, a number of adjustive devices may be demonstrated experimentally or cited from daily experience.

Festinger and his followers have designated at least five types of reaction which may be resorted to for dissonance reduction: (1) the subject may alter his attitude, opinion, or evaluation of the situation; (2) he may undergo an actual distortion of perception or memory; (3) he may alter his behavior to conform to the reality of the situation or restore its harmony; (4) he may alter the situation itself to conform to his own cognition or expectations; and (5) he may add new cognitive elements (new information, broader scope) to reconcile opposing viewpoints or discrepancies in the situation. To these reactions we would add a sixth, whereby the subject leaves the discrepancy intact but resorts to defense mechanisms to render it less disturbing to him. Although a defense such as rationalization may be implicit in the first reaction noted, there are others—e.g., suppression of insight, repression of memory, ambiguous identification, etc.—that are not. In another sense, all of the devices noted might be considered to be defense mechanisms or strategies when they are employed to resolve any *anxiety* that may be generated by cognitive dissonance.

We may first illustrate some of the tactics of dissonance reduction in commonplace occurrences that most of us are familiar with. When a person who smokes reads about evidence relating smoking to the incidence of cancer, he may choose to dismiss the evidence as "inconclusive" or "far-fetched," or he may decide to cut out smoking altogether in order not to take chances. If neither the change of attitude nor the change of behavior proves feasible, he may seek out new information showing which brands have the least "tar" and nicotine and thus compromise with attitude and behavior change by switching brands. However, he might also rationalize his smoking by rejecting self-denial of all of life's little pleasures in an uncertain world; or he may simply ignore the threat and suppress insight into the danger to his health that his action poses.

Let us take another illustration from stock market speculation. A person gets a "hot tip" and buys Blue Rainbow stock at 40, being convinced that it is sure to shoot up to 60 because of a planned merger. Instead, it gradually drops to 30. Our subject calls his informant to get further information to correct the cognitive dissonance. He is told that the planned merger has only been delayed, but he would be smart to buy more at 30. He does so, adding behavior change to attitude change and new cognitive elements, while suppressing his suspicion that he is being "taken." If the stock then drops to 25, he may drastically reverse his evaluation of the situation, dumping the stock at the market and blaming both the company and his "tipster," but not himself for naïve cognition in the first place. If he has high frustration tolerance and unwillingness to perceive himself as a loser, he may decide to sit with it until the stock comes back to his average price of 35, no matter how long it takes, just so that he can break even. But, as the stock goes up again to 35, his perception of the situation again changes, and he decides he was right to wait for 60 after all, because the stock is "going up" as he had expected it to. We shall leave him there, before any further dissonance is created between expectation and reality.

In the realm of romance, we have all known or heard of spinsters and bachelors who have put off marriage because of the cognitive dissonance between their romantic ideal and the ordinary people they meet. In the realm of work or study for rewards, we know how often a person is satisfied with his pay or his term grade, until he finds out that someone who didn't work as hard got a bigger raise or a better grade. And so it goes, in virtually every activity in life, since all goal-directed behavior involves cognition and adjustment.

Many similar situations have been tested experimentally, although under highly restricted and artificial conditions. Adams and Rosenbaum (1962) found that workers tend to increase or decrease their productivity when they feel that they are being overcompensated or undercompensated under conditions of hourly pay, but tend to slow down their productivity (and pay) when overcompensated on a piece-work basis. There is generally not only a tendency to recognize that "you only get what you pay for" but also that, in working for pay, "you only produce what you're paid for." When it comes to situations in which success or failure or degree of skill is the determinant of dissonance, we have a setup similar to the older "level-of-aspiration" studies. Here it is found that people tend to perform in conformity with their own expectations, though some people consistently set higher goals for themselves, while others consistently set low goals to avoid frustration or dissonance. Aronson and Carlsmith (1963) showed that subjects who were allowed to do better than they expected managed to increase their failure rate on a repetitive task to keep their level of performance down to a manageable level of expectation. Festinger (1957) and Cohen *et al.* (1959) showed how college students change their gambling strategies when chosen alternatives bring about cognitive dissonance through failure of the "system" to work.

On more vital issues of interpersonal relationships, there have been studies such as reactions to inflicting pain on others, to participation in desegregated housing projects, and defection of American POWs to Chinese communist "brain-washing" tactics. In the case of communist "brain-washing" of American defectors in Korea, it is pointed out by Brehm and Cohen (1962) that it was the reduction of cognitive dissonance by both the communist indoctrinators and the prisoners themselves, rather than any gross coercion, torture, or drugs, that brought about "conversions" to communist ideology among the few prisoners on whom the indoctrination succeeded. The same authors discuss the theoretical issues involved in bringing about *acceptance* of desegregation along with practical measures of implementation like integrated housing projects. A review of several studies suggests that living in close proximity to Negro families creates cognitive dissonance between prejudiced attitudes of whites and the realities of neighborly behavior. This tends to be reduced by a positive change in attitude, the most prejudiced showing the greatest change. The situations studied allow for voluntary choice of desegregated housing. There is some debate on whether forced or directed desegregation brings about similar attitude change.

Although most of the research in this field is undertaken as an exploration into cognitive processes per se, there are two aspects of it that have a direct bearing on personality dynamics. One is the study of individual differences in the arousal of dissonance. The other is a possible relationship between dissonance reduction and defense mechanisms or strategies. Some suggestive studies along these lines are summarized by Brehm and Cohen (1962) but, admittedly, the surface has only been scratched.

DEFENSE MECHANISMS

The dissonance approach seems to be a useful way of testing operationally inconsistencies in values, self-concepts and behavior, and the tactics of maintaining apparent cognitive consistency. As far as defense mechanisms are concerned, we detect some confusion and redundancy in attempting to distinguish between cognition and motivation. It must be recognized that we are dealing with a basic motive of cognitive clarity and consistency to begin with, in keeping with our biosocial concept of a hierarchy of motives in the integrated organism. There is no such thing as cognition without motivation, even if it is unconscious. The same goes for the old argument about "perceptual defense," which bogged down over the question of how one can use perception as a defense when one has already perceived a situation. The answer to both, of course, is that motives affect the very process of perception, memory, interpretation, reasoning, and inferences drawn to instigate behavior. But even though we may separate the component processes of perception and motivation and memory for experimental purposes, and further break down perception into states of attending, reception, etc., these are but artifacts of analysis. In real life the integrated organism undergoes a continual interaction with the environment in which the ebb and flow of motivated awareness of the environment and the effects of this interaction is a central feature of consciousness. In this ebb and flow of integrated cognitive-affective response, any component process may affect any other at any time and alter the total pattern of motivated awareness and behavior.

This is particularly true when *anxiety* is aroused. It is not easy to define anxiety, but it certainly involves a sense of disequilibrium, apprehensiveness, frustration, or conflict in motive satisfaction. Although clinicians generally think of it as a state of emotional imbalance, leading to adjustive and/or maladjustive behavior, it may very well be closely related to cognitive dissonance. In any case, there is no question but that cognitive processes may be mobilized as defense mechanisms when anxiety is aroused, so that ego threats or emotional conflicts may be resolved, obviated, or minimized. In Chapter 7 we gave a clear illustration of how cognitive processes may be used as defense mechanisms in the *suppression of insight*. In the process of integrating cognition and (anticipated) affect, the insight which would instigate guilt reaction and dangerous behavior commitment is simply suppressed. Here we have semiconscious self-deception, with anxiety continuing in suppressed form along with the suppressed cognition at the fringes of consciousness. In the case of repression, we have total obliteration of conscious cognition of the conflict and its anxiety-provoking implications, although the emotional "energy," as Freud would put it, finds its outlet in some pathological symptom.

Just how might cognitive styles and cognitive dissonance be related to defense mechanisms as described either in psychoanalytic or biosocial theory? Only a few suggestive experiments have been performed to date, but they do provide interesting clues. Gardner and his associates (1959, 1968) found some relationships between cognitive style and the type of defense mechanism frequently indulged in by their subjects. People who indulge in repressive mechanisms are likely to be "levelers" in cognitive style. That is, they tend to assimilate past and present experiences, so that if this assimilation proves to be ego-threatening in a given situation, they are more likely to repress it than would a "sharpener," who clearly differentiates successive experiences. However, there are "levelers" who do not indulge in repression.

Gardner found considerable individual consistency in cognitive styles and defenses over long periods of time, and found similarities greatest between identical twins. This suggests a possible constitutional basis for cognitive style and defense, and may eventually provide some basis for understanding problems of "choice of symptom" and "deviant personality types" in maladjustment and psychopathology.

In further applications of dissonance theory to Freudian concepts of defense, Festinger and Bramel (1962) showed how projection of latent homosexuality may be experimentally induced by first providing cognitions of implied latent homosexuality to their subjects. After being indoctrinated on the assumed prevalence of latent homosexuality, and being tricked into thinking that photographs of nude men were "getting a rise out of them," the male subjects reduced their cognitive dissonance by attributing latent homosexuality to many of the subjects whose photographs they were shown. However, according to biosocial theory, *any* socially undesirable trait may be similarly induced to give rise to cognitive dissonance and denial by projection to others. It is the threat to the maintenance of a socially acceptable self-image or social role that requires a reinterpretation of the social environment by showing that one is "no more peculiar than anyone else." Projection of one's own undesirable traits serves the purpose of normalizing or reversing the social desirability relationship. Further research along these lines may well enlarge our knowledge of defense mechanisms and strategies, which until now have been rather narrowly conceived in Freudian psychosexual terms.

All through the previous discussion we have assumed a normal state of consciousness as prerequisite to cognition, regardless of individual differences and detours through defense mechanisms. Defense mechanisms such as repression do point the way to radical or even pathological alterations of conscious cognition; but there are other conditions that are either universal or commonplace alterations of the normal waking state of consciousness under more or less self-controlled behavior. For one thing, let us remember that sleep is an everyday universal occurrence with a strange phenomenon known as dreams, the significance of which has piqued man's curiosity since pre-Biblical times. Alcoholic inebriation in varying degrees, from sipping apéritifs to engaging in drunken orgies, is a very widespread practice in Western civilization and parts of the Orient, with well-known effects on cognition and personality. The recent upsurge of indulgence in "pep pills" and drugs among American youth has stimulant, anesthetic, hallucinogenic, or just soporific effects on conscious cognition, with or without addictive properties. Hypnosis has been experimented with for almost 200 years since the demonstrations of the Viennese physician, Franz Mesmer, who mistakenly attributed the alteration of consciousness to "animal magnetism." The distortions or repressions of perception, memory, and judgment that may be induced by hypnotic and posthypnotic suggestion have often been cited as merely more extreme illustrations of man's susceptibility to social suggestion, but they certainly represent altered states of consciousness. Clues to the disorienting and stultifying effects of lack of environmental stimulation are contained in experiments on sensory deprivation and are implicit in clinical studies of childhood marasmus.

All of these deviations from the normal state of consciousness affect or reveal personality differences through their alteration of cognitive processes. Not all, however, are readily susceptible to experimental investigation. Let us take the matter of the interpretation of dreams. Orthodox psychoanalysis has long maintained that dreams usually contain deep psychological significance in their latent content, beneath the surface of their manifest content. Freudian interpretations are likely to attribute a great deal of sexual symbolism and primitive wish-fulfillment to the latent content of such dreams. Jungian analysts usually find examples of primordial imagery recalling archetypes of man's experience since his cave-man ancestry. The interpretation of such individual reflections of instinctive motives revealed in unconscious cognitive processes requires deep analysis in the course of prolonged psychoanalytic probing. Subjects cannot produce dreams on demand, they are not subject to experimental controls, and there is no way of getting at even the manifest content except through unreliable recall upon waking. Nevertheless, it has been noted that Freudian patients produce "Freudian" dreams, while Jungian patients produce "Jungian" dreams. This is not just a matter of theoretical bias in interpretation. We have heard both Freudian and Jungian analysts describe cases in which the patient came in for a session with an enthusiastic remark like: "Oh, boy! Did I have a dream last night! You'll love this one!" We cannot help believing (as some psychoanalysts have come to realize) that indoctrination by suggestion on the part of the analyst influences thinking and imagery in the patient and induces such appropriate dreams by the patient's sheer desire to be accepted by his analyst! Call it "transference" if you will, but "seeing things as others see them"—even the unconscious imagery associated with one's own emotional concerns—is an example of the biosocial principle of cognitive accommodation to social needs.

Nevertheless, some research is progressing along various fronts to bring dream analysis into some recognizable relationship to conscious experience and personality differences, stripped of their knotty theoretical entanglements. Some results thus far reported by the Research Center for Mental Health at New York University show that different age groups and deviant personality groups give characteristic differences in the types of dreams reported. Adolescents, for example, tend to reflect concern with identity and control of aggression.

From the Research Center we get some suggestive results (Biennial Report, 1963–1965) on the ways in which conscious experience is affected by taking the hallucinogenic drug LSD:

Differences in reaction to the drug are systematically related to personality differences. Thus, for example, those Ss who exhibited the most psychotic-like features—loss of contact with reality, impaired sense of identity, loss of control, and paranoid ideation—tended to be persons who, without the drug, cope inadequately with their problems, and have weak identities, poor defenses, and poorly controlled primary process thinking. Those Ss, on the other hand, whose LSD experience was reported as enjoyable and instructive and whose performance on cognitive tests was not unduly disrupted by the drug generally were people with high self-esteem, sensitivity, and introspective and creative capacity.

It was further found that LSD use tends to impair performance on all cognitive tests such as comprehension, word-naming, and digit-span. However, a subject under the influence of the drug rarely fails to recognize the influence it is having on him as noted by observers, and he is able to report vividly the bizarre cognitive experiences both during and after the experience. These psychoticlike reactions were found to be quite different from the reaction of actual schizophrenic patients, so it would be incorrect to say that LSD reproduces a schizophrenialike condition.

Of considerable interest are the data on sensory deprivation. Interest in this area has no doubt been stimulated by the need to learn more about human reactions to drastically altered environments, such as prolonged reduction of auditory, visual, and gravitational stimulation in space. Subjects were placed in an isolation chamber in the New York University laboratory and compared for their reactions to the sensory deprivation. Comparison of basic skin resistance level and introspective reports showed that isolation was increasingly anxiety-provoking for most subjects. Surprisingly, it was the more extroverted, expressive, and socially oriented individuals who appeared better able to withstand isolation. We may be dealing with a general adaptivity phenomenon, rather than with a psychophysiological threshold of susceptibility to cognitive stimulation.

Many experiments on perception when the subject is under the influence of hypnosis have produced evidence or subjective reports of analgesia, visual and auditory hallucinations, deafness, amnesia, and the like. Some subjects are found to be highly responsive to hypnotic and posthypnotic suggestion, while others were not. Experimenters usually select their subjects for hypnotic induction experiments by finding the most responsive subjects in preliminary response-to-suggestion tests. Personality differences between those subjects who are easily hypnotized and those who are not have not been systematically worked out beyond the observation that some are more suggestible than others. There have been hints here and there that the more suggestible (and, therefore, more easily hypnotizable) subjects are more gullible in such matters as yielding to propaganda or deception, and that they are also more likely to lapse into dissociative states (Jekyll-Hyde split personality or amnesic types) or conversion states (functional lameness of limbs, loss of speech, memory, or sensation, etc.) when they suffer "nervous breakdowns."

There is other evidence, however, that hallucinatory experience may not be a unique property of the "hypnotic trance" state, but may be a fairly general response to suggestion in a large proportion of the population. Barber and Calverley (1964), for example, used both simple task-motivating instructions to one group and hypnotic induction with another group of female Ss to compare their susceptibility to visual and auditory hallucinations. On pretest, both groups and a control group were instructed to produce auditory and visual "hallucinations." About half of all the subjects reported hearing the suggested melody (a recording of "White Christmas") and about one-third reported seeing the suggested object (a cat sitting on her lap). Oddly enough, there was no significant difference between the instructed test group and the hypnotized test group in producing similar "hallucinations" under test conditions. Barber (1967) concludes from such results, as well as the lack of instructional and pretest controls in other studies, that hypnotic hallucinations may be more a matter of instruction, motivation to comply, and test control than anything categorically different from ordinary suggestibility. In other words, when experimenters go to the trouble of "inducing a hypnotic trance," they may not be doing anything more unusual than merely suggesting, to a highly suggestible person, what he should see or hear or forget.

In a similar vein, Shor (1962) has shown that hypnotic analgesia may depend on the elimination of pain-facilitating anxiety or apprehension in the administration of painful stimuli, rather than any change in physiological reaction or sensitivity. By artificially eliminating the "unexpected shock" value of sudden and unpredictable electric shocks, he was able to minimize the experienced pain of Ss even in the waking state. He concludes that the hypnotic state serves the same purpose by eliminating apprehension through suggestion and diversion of attention. Hilgard (1969) confirms this, but shows that physiological reactions conform to hypnotic and waking differences in analgesia. Most workers in the field find that formal induction of hypnosis does produce more extreme alterations of consciousness and even pathological distortions of perception.

Although it is not yet fully clear whether there is a difference in degree or in kind between ordinary suggestibility of perception in the waking state and in the "induced hallucinations" of analgesia of the hypnotic state, there is no doubt about the extraordinary susceptibility of human perception to the influence of verbal suggestion. This susceptibility has a wide range of applications from political propaganda and advertising to "natural childbirth," analgesic surgery, and psychotherapy for symptom removal.

For more detailed reports in the provocative area of altered states of consciousness, the student is referred to Tart (1969).

Developmental
Aspects

It would now be eminently instructive to tie together the various implications we have cited in this chapter for the most salient and integrative aspect of personality dynamics: psychosocial development. Studies of perceptual individuation, cognitive styles and differentiation, and adjustment to social norms and suggestion all show how the cognitive component of organismic integration may be involved in personality development. Some of this susceptibility to differentiation and suggestion may be genetically determined, but a great deal of it is demonstrably due to the cumulative effects of individual experience in the course of growth and social interaction.

We have taken pains at various points in the foregoing discussion to point out that there is subjectivity and motivation underlying man's development of awareness of his environment: it doesn't automatically register "because it's there." In light of the biosocial integration of behavior, one of the motives we discussed in Chapter 2 may influence any other and may, at the same time, influence cognition or be influenced by it. At the psychological level, at which cognition itself operates we are certainly dealing with the basic motives of efficacy and cognitive clarity, and often exploration and need for novelty as well. These are the needs that activate the use of intelligence to "make sense out of the environment," to test reality and manipulate it or adjust to it. There is also input and feedback from the psychosocial level of integration in structuring social attitudes, perceptions, expectancies, self-concept, and interpersonal relations. Going still deeper into the psychophysiological level of functioning, even basic nutritional needs and physical well-being may influence cognitive styles and content. Since all of these needs undergo maturation-learning-canalization as well as differentiation-integration processes from infancy onward, we may well expect that differences in early need gratification will influence cognitive development. We might look for data from longitudinal studies to provide confirmation of this hypothesis. Alternately, we would expect that different cultures provide different kinds of experiences both in the habitual stimuli of the environment and in the motivational systems that influence selectivity of perception. We might look for cross-cultural data to confirm that hypothesis and, if longitudinal comparisons are also available in cross-cultural comparison, so much the better.

Actually, both longitudinal and cross-cultural comparisons of perception have been hard to come by, except in the somewhat anecdotal reports of anthropologists. An example of this is Malinowski's (1927, 1929) frequently cited report that Trobriand Islanders always perceived their children to look like their fathers, but never like their mothers or like each other, because of tribal taboos. This was stoutly maintained, even though sibling and maternal resemblances were obvious to an outsider, and sheer logic demanded that if two brothers resembled their father, they would have to resemble each other. Nevertheless, some recent summations of evidence and programs of experimental investigation have thrown some light on the developmental aspects of perception.

CROSS-CULTURAL STUDIES OF PERCEPTION

In his *Comparative Psychology of Mental Development,* Werner (1957) made note of the accumulating evidence of perceptual and conceptual differences between "primitive" peoples and more literate Western cultures. Subscribing to a general ontogenetic-phylogenetic parallelism, as we do, Werner sought to relate these cross-cultural differences to the evolution of perceptual differentiation in man and its development in the life of the individual. He noted that many primitive tribes tend to conceive of natural forces and events in concretized, reified, or personified terms, whereas more literate and scientifically oriented Western cultures recognize abstract concepts and relationships. This is reflected, for example, in the frequently literal assumption of animal and spirit roles in religious ceremonies and the attempt to exert direct influence on natural events by ritualistic action and use of talismans. It is also signified by the frequently complete identification of the individual with the tribal group, which we have already related to concrete sensorimotor thinking. These differences in perception and conceptualization, Werner found, paralleled the assumed evolution of cognition from sensorimotor and concrete behavior to more abstract conceptualization along with the evolution of the human cortex. The differences also tended to provide gross parallels to the development of cognition from childhood to adulthood in more advanced societies. It is implied that there is something akin to an "arrested development" of cognitive differentiation in primitive cultures, which checks the cognitive development of its members. Although Werner's general theoretical framework is somewhat similar to our biosocial framework, the assumption of mental backwardness (underdeveloped cognition) in "primitive tribes" is probably unwarranted and is not necessary to the general theory. We have already mentioned that even preliterate tribes may make huge demands on the individual's power of abstract thinking in the learning of language, custom, and primitive religion. Werner's work was highly provocative, but we believe that he was too dependent on descriptive anthropology of an earlier era for his cross-cultural data.

Optical illusions. One of the more recent attempts to start from basic firsthand cross-cultural comparisons of perceptual processes was made by Segall and his co-workers (1966). These investigators tested the susceptibility of children and adults in a variety of cultures to the perceptual distortion conveyed by simple geometric figures. These familiar "optical illusions" were: the Müller-Lyer illusion, the Sander parallelogram, and the horizontal-vertical illusion in two versions (Fig. 8–4).

Data were collected from 17 different population samples in different parts of the world, from African and Philippine Islands tribes to residents and students in Evanston, Illinois. Data were also collected to determine gross differences in physical environment, such as "carpentered-world" types of homes (with rectangular walls, doors, windows, and furniture), versus thatched huts or makeshift shelters, and surrounding distant, rolling scenery or dense forest or city streets, etc. It was hypothesized that the carpentered-world environment of rectangles, squares, and parallel lines would facilitate perception of these illusions in certain cultural settings. A total of 1,030 adults and 848 children were tested by the investigators and

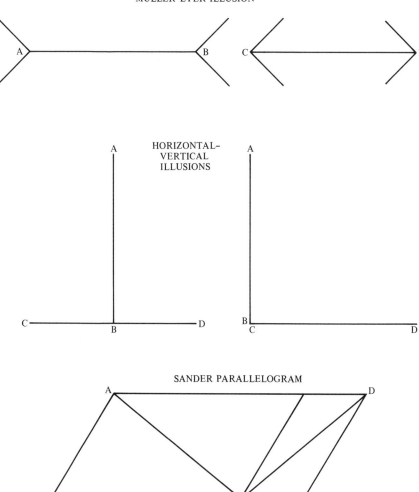

MÜLLER–LYER ILLUSION

HORIZONTAL–
VERTICAL
ILLUSIONS

SANDER PARALLELOGRAM

Figure 8–4. Standard optical illusions used by Segall *et al.* (1966) in their cross-cultural study of perception. *(Is AB longer or shorter than CD?)*

their assistants. The three types of illusions were presented in standardized format, using the psychophysical method of constant stimuli; that is, the pairs of test lines were presented in their respective figures with slightly varying lengths, and the subject picked the one in which they looked exactly equal. The actual discrepancy from equal length of the lines was the measure of illusory perception.

The results showed that the children in all cultures were generally more susceptible to these illusions than adults, though there were some consistent differences between some of the cultural samples as well. This did not unequivocally confirm the carpentered-world hypothesis, since perceptual modification by repeated environmental stimulation would have led us to expect increasing susceptibility to such illusions from childhood to adulthood. However, there was partial confirmation in the fact that both American and South African-European samples scored higher on the Müller-Lyer and Sander parallelogram illusions than did almost all of the other samples. These results suggest both an inherent tendency to perceptual differentiation in cognitive development, as Werner would express it, and a modification or adjustment of perceptual habits by environmental experience, as the investigators stress. The combination of the two is what one would expect from the general orientation of biosocial theory.

Inkblot figures. Somewhat more closely related to personality dynamics are studies in various cultures of individual and group differences in the perception of ambiguous figures such as the Rorschach inkblots. The mere fact that such ambiguous visual stimuli can be used to detect individual and group differences in personality variables is in itself a good illustration of the relationship of perceptual individuation to personality. The clinical applications of such projective tests will be discussed in Chapter 10. In cross-cultural research the application of such tests is frequently handicapped by the fact that no two test records are ever quite the same and standards of comparison for the largely qualitative analyses of the records are difficult to arrive at (cf. Lindzey, 1961; Holtzman *et al.*, 1968). However, some illuminating observations may be made even if they are incidental to the purpose of such studies.

The study of Holtzman *et al.* (1968) used the Holtzman Inkblot Technique (HIT) and a number of other tests on 417 American children and 443 Mexican children, ranging in age from 7 to 13, with test administration being repeated over a period of six years. An analysis of the HIT scores showed that

When taken together, these variables strongly suggest that the Mexican child is more passive in coping with the tasks set before him in the testing situation, more likely to respond in terms of his immediate sensory experience, and less likely to be highly differentiated in perceptual and cognitive structure than is the American child of the same age and social class. In the course of actively coping with inkblots, the American child puts forth more fantasy material involving high activity (movement) and fear-provoking images (anxiety) than does the Mexican with his more passive style. The American child appears to be more venturesome, more willing to risk failure, freer with his fantasies, more direct and forthright in his approach (Holtzman *et al.*, 1968).

These investigators found little by way of differences in general mode of perception in children, but the cultural differences were persistent throughout the age groups and the time-span involved in the study.

Another study by Gilbert (1959), however, showed increasing sex differences in inkblot perception from adolescence to later adulthood, reflecting the pronounced differences in the social role expectancies of Mexican men and women in a period of cultural turmoil.

This study of sex differences in mental health in a Mexican village employed a Rorschach examination of a 15 percent sampling of the population. It was found that males, particularly the older men, saw far more figures of a "morbid" variety in the inkblots than did the females, and far more than were typically encountered in United States middle-class and student populations. These responses included images of corpses, skeletons, decaying flesh, rotting vegetation, "bodies being devoured by worms," etc. Inquiry and free association revealed that these were the images associated with the revolutionary turmoil, death, and starvation of the childhood experiences of older men who had lived through the revolutionary period of 1910–1920, and who had been eking out a marginal existence from the soil ever since. A kind of immunity by virtue of sex role seems to have protected the women from the worst of these terrors, but for the men

Many had been orphaned and starved in the revolutionary and counter-revolutionary turmoil, as even the non-combatants were pillaged, tormented or killed by free-booting partisans on both sides. One 55-year-old man described the social turmoil of the time as follows:

"Before the revolution, it is true, the *campesinos* were treated like slaves by the *hacenderos* [landowners]. They were overworked, beaten, exploited, made to live like animals in pig-sties. . . . But for years during the revolution conditions were even worse. People starved or were killed right and left." There was no food, no work, no law enforcement, no school, no medical attention—just utter chaos. *"There was nothing, nothing, neither for animals nor for men!* How did we live? By the grace of God and the fruits and herbs in the field. Many died of starvation. Both the army and the rebels terrorized the people, living off the land, looting and murdering just as they pleased. . . . The only way to be safe was to live in the hills like an animal and live off the vegetation in the woods. When people starved or got sick there, they died and were buried without ceremony right in the ground where they dropped; if not, they were eaten by vultures and coyotes" (Gilbert, 1959).

Aside from its implications for mental health, this study illustrates why it is necessary to take cultural differences into account in their full historical perspective in order to understand how individuals perceive their world.

Culturally determined differences in the perceived content of Rorschach inkblot figures are so commonplace as to constitute an artifact that must be discounted in making personality interpretations (see Chapter 10). One would obviously expect more tropical plants to be seen on the colored inkblots by residents of tropical countries; more anatomical figures by biology and medical students, etc. More significant than the superficial content, however, are the cognitive styles and patterns of responses to such ambiguous visual stimuli in different cultures. Kaplan, who has studied many Rorschach protocols as editor of *Primary Records in Culture and Personality*, besides doing such research himself, comments:

> While many of the sets of data appear to seem so similar to each other that it is difficult to distinguish them as coming from different groups (see Kaplan, Rickers-Ovsiankina and Joseph, 1956), protocols from other cultures are so unique and dissimilar that they may be distinguished at a glance. The Rorschachs may be rich and expressive like those collected from the Hindu groups by G. M. Carstairs (1956), or sparse, stereotyped, and defensive like the numerous ones collected from the Ojibwa. They can involve the Pilaga children's responses to details so tiny that we have difficulty in seeing them at all (Henry, 1956) or the vagueness and diffuseness of many of the Melanesian records . . . (Kaplan, 1961, p. 302).

Thus there are cultural and subcultural "habits" of perception which help to determine both the content and style of perception by which individuals become aware of meanings in their environment. The more complex and ambiguous the stimulus configuration, the more susceptible it is to the biases of individual experience and cultural influences.

LONGITUDINAL STUDIES

We have already made use of Piaget's stages of growth of logical thinking and the psychometric criteria of mental growth on the Stanford-Binet to show the relevance of cognitive development to psychosocial development. These and other longitudinal studies of cognitive development deal only incidentally with perceptual development; indeed, it has not been customary to think of perception as undergoing any developmental process at all, except as a communication link between organism and environment in the development of thought, reasoning, and attitudes. Heinz Werner, however, gave central importance to the process of *perceptual differentiation*, as we have seen, in the ontogenetic, phylogenetic, and comparative cultural development of mental capacities and behavior. Witkin and his colleagues, after much productive research in detecting field-dependence versus field-independence as a variable in perceptual individuation, gradually came to the conclusion that such individual differences were but a special case of the general developmental process of perceptual differentiation already elucidated by Werner.

Witkin accordingly carried his line of research a great deal further into the realm of child development by relating maternal care and attitudes to the fostering of perceptual differentiation or articulation in children and

Personality Dynamics

adolescents. (Witkin *et al.*, 1962). His team obtained perceptual index scores from three groups of 10-year-old children, using procedures described earlier in this chapter. Data were then obtained independently by interviews with the children's mothers to determine whether their interaction fostered differentiation (IFD) or inhibited differentiation (IID). A total of 58 usable case records of children and their mothers was obtained. The general hypothesis to be tested was that fostering security, exploration, and independence in the child also tended to foster perceptual differentiation. Indicators included items such as: (1) maternal attitude toward child (approval-disapproval, possessive and anxious vs. affectionate and accepting); and (2) rearing procedures (encouraging independence vs. overprotection, permissiveness vs. coercion and punishment, or vacillation between indulgence and severe discipline). Correlations obtained between the perceptual index of differentiation and the IFD-IID scores of mothers in each of the three groups yielded biserial r's of .82, .85, .65, all significant at the .01 level. Strange as it may seem—but not so strange from a biosocial point of view—a boy's ability to distinguish figure and ground and to orient himself with respect to vertical position is dependent, to some extent, on his mother's ability to give him a sense of security in exploring his physical world and satisfying efficacy and psychosocial needs in infancy and early childhood.

The fact that even physical well-being in infancy may influence a function like the development of cognitive clarity was illustrated in a longitudinal study by Lois Murphy and her co-workers (1962) as well as in a follow-up study by the Witkin group (1962). Data obtained by Sibylle Escalona and Grace Heider (1959) on 31 infants during the first seven months of life were followed up by observations by the Murphy team during the preschool nursery period (age three to five) and during the prepuberty period (about 11 to 13). However, the investigators were not given access to the original infancy data until the follow-up study was completed. The data on "oral gratification" in infancy (pleasure in feeding, freedom from colic or diarrhea, etc.) were then correlated with uncontaminated psychiatric observations on cognitive clarity made at the later ages. Positive correlations were obtained between good vegetative functioning (or "oral gratification") and perceptual clarity at both the preschool and the prepuberty age levels. The implication is clear that good cognitive functioning in childhood requires good physiological integration and physical well-being in infancy. This literally determines whether the child will perceive its world as benign or threatening or just plain dull. Cognitive development is necessarily affected.

In another follow-up study of the same 31 subjects in preadolescence, Heider (1966) showed that both vegetative functioning and mother-child interaction in infancy were crucial in determining a child's vulnerability to stress. Some of the children rated high in vulnerability to stress at the preschool age managed to come through stronger in preadolescence by the successful use of "coping devices" (defensive strategies) against threats to security. More often, these more vulnerable children were having difficulties in interpersonal relationships in preadolescence and showing greater disturbance in reacting to traumatic social events, such as the assassination of President Kennedy. The relationship between cognitive-affective differentiation and integration, on the one hand, and anxiety and defense on the other, remains to be more fully explored.

In none of these studies were the subjects from families experiencing severe deprivation; yet the differences in satisfaction of early "caring" needs could be detected throughout childhood. In cases of severe neglect, we know that there are instances of childhood marasmus that leave children dull and retarded in their entire cognitive-affective responsiveness and inevitably dull and constricted as growing personalities. Unfortunately, we lack definitive longitudinal research which ties together all of these developmental factors, but the hypothesis is neither far-fetched nor hard to formulate. From a biosocial point of view, we would expect that depressed, unloving, neglectful, or unstimulating environments would tend to produce dull, unresponsive, and unsociable personalities. This is not because these children fail to learn the social amenities, but because cognitive-affective differentiation and integration have been retarded, empathy and efficacy needs stifled, and psychosocial development consequently handicapped to begin with.

The social as well as developmental implications are rather clear and far-reaching. The real deprivation involved in a "deprived childhood" or in the "culture of poverty" is not the mere absence of material comforts or luxuries, or even adequate food, but the starvation for affection and intellectual stimulation that often accompanies such conditions; the restrictions on social interaction and communication when broken homes and abandonment are involved; and the very dulling of the senses, which makes it impossible for a human organism to become a well-developed human being. That is the real import of studies such as the Moynihan report (1965), which show the disintegration of the Negro family in metropolitan slums and the need for projects which seek to overcome the educational handicaps of slum children before they even start school. Individuals who grow up in more stimulating, challenging, and affectionate environments, even though they may be economically underprivileged, are more likely to achieve their individual potentials as participating members of society with such satisfactions as motivation and circumstances may afford. At least they may be expected to show the cognitive differentiation and cognitive-affective integration which make a more discriminating response to the environment and normal psychosocial development possible.

Personality Dynamics

Summary Perception of self and environment in behavioral interaction is described as a very complex process involving selective attention, sensory reception, test of meaning in context, cognitive-affective screening, restructuring of meaning, and a restimulation of the entire sequence in the continually changing context. These circular and selective responses invariably reflect and ultimately influence personality differences and changes.

Studies of cognitive styles reveal that some people habitually perceive themselves and their environment in a highly articulated or differentiated manner, while others respond in a rather unarticulated (or field-dependent) manner. Some researchers refer to "levelers" and "sharpeners" in the articulation of successive experiences. These styles have been found to have some relevance to such personality variables as "sense of separate identity" and the use of defense mechanisms. Studies of cognitive dissonance confirm the basic need of cognitive clarity and consistency. They also have relevance to such behavioral variables as susceptibility to propaganda and communication, profit and prestige incentives, health habits, group affiliations, and a wide range of behavior-belief inconsistencies. Research on cognition under altered states of consciousness includes conditions of drug use and addiction, dream analysis, sensory deprivation, hypnosis, and suggestion. One result that seems to come through all of these studies by various investigators is the ability of the individual personality to maintain a certain degree of individual identity under very diverse states of stimulation and consciousness.

On the developmental side, cross-cultural and longitudinal studies show that early environmental influences have a decided effect in determining perceptual content, styles, clarity, and enrichment. It is pointed out that the most serious aspect of "cultural deprivation" may be the poverty of cognitive experience it affords, along with the starvation for affection, which seem to go hand in hand.

9

Attitudes,
Values,
Traits,
and
Character

Personality Dynamics In the last few chapters we have shown that
one kind of learning runs through the entire process of personality development, adjustment, and role assumption. That is the learning of attitudes and values that shape and give expression to individual character
as much as anything one could single out for special analysis. Representing an integration of both cognitive and affective reaction to the environment, and usually giving impulse to action, they provide expressions of
personality at the psychological level of integration, frequently involving
the psychosocial as well. Attitudes may be defined simply as learned but
individually characteristic ways of thinking or feeling about anything:
individuals, groups, objects, activities, ideas, even one's own worth and
relationships to society. Values are the learned standards by which such
attitudes are formed, usually reflecting the standards of the culture or
situation in which the learning takes place. Attitudes can often be verbalized, but it is not necessary that they be. It is possible to have a vague
aversion toward, or preference for, a particular person, idea, behavior,

or object, and hardly be aware of it, much less be able to express it in words. One can even have a pronounced aversion or preference and still not be able to articulate it in words, much less explain why. However, most adults do have attitudes which are sufficiently clear-cut and conscious to be communicated to and analyzed by an observer. Underlying values may not be so readily or correctly articulated, since it takes a good deal of social sophistication and self-insight for the ordinary individual to formulate such concepts. The psychologist can often infer these values from a study of the subject's expressed attitudes and evident behavior in relevant social contexts. In some simple contexts, an outright expression of opinion or preference suffices to signify both attitude and value system.

PSYCHODYNAMIC APPROACH

In recent years, the personality psychologist's interest in attitudes has shifted from the study of categorical opinions on given issues at a given moment (the opinion-polling technique) to their value as indicators of personality structure and dynamics. This involves a study of the way in which attitudes and values take shape in individual development, the motivational purposes and conflicts they serve, and the way in which they change or resist change under various communication influences. We have already seen how attitudes toward self and environment begin to form in earliest primary group interaction and start to become generalized into value systems during secondary socialization and adult role anticipation stages. They are intimately involved in defense mechanisms and defensive strategies. They serve as media through which social ego needs are channeled into social role preferences, and through which aspirations, interpersonal relationships, and ego defenses are maintained. Attitudes are, therefore, of central interest to the study of personality dynamics.

Among the proponents of the more psychodynamic approach to the study of attitudes and values, which relates such study, at least by implication, to personality theory, are: Gordon Allport, Daniel Katz, M. Brewster Smith, Theodore Newcomb, Muzafer Sherif, Leon Festinger, Milton Rokeach, and a host of others. We shall refer to some of these investigators' work in the appropriate places in the course of our discussion. Katz (1960) perhaps most clearly articulated the psychodynamic approach in contrast to the traditional verbalized-response-to-stimulus, by citing at least four psychodynamic functions served by attitude formation:

1. *The adjustment function.* Essentially this function is a recognition of the fact that people strive to maximize the rewards in their external environment and to minimize the penalties. The child develops favorable attitudes toward the objects in his world which are associated with the satisfactions of his needs and unfavorable attitudes toward objects which thwart him or punish

him. Attitudes acquired in the service of the adjustment function are either the means for reaching the desired goal or avoiding the undesirable one, or are affective associations based upon experiences in attaining motive satisfactions. . . .

2. *The ego-defensive function.* People not only seek to make the most of their external world and what it offers, but they also expend a great deal of their energy on living with themselves. The mechanisms by which the individual protects his ego from his own unacceptable impulses and from the knowledge of threatening forces from without, and the methods by which he reduces his anxieties created by such problems, are known as mechanisms of ego defense. . . . Many of our attitudes have the function of defending our self-image. When we cannot admit to ourselves that we have deep feelings of inferiority we may protect our egos by attitudes of superiority toward this underprivileged group. . . .

3. *The value-expressive function.* While many attitudes have the function of preventing the individual from revealing to himself and others his true nature, other attitudes have the function of giving positive expression to his central values and to the type of person he conceives himself to be. A man may consider himself to be an enlightened conservative or an internationalist or a liberal, and will hold attitudes which are the appropriate indication of his central values. Thus we need to take account of the fact that not all behavior has the negative function of reducing the tensions of biological drives or of internal conflicts. Satisfactions also accrue to the person from the expression of attitudes which reflect his cherished beliefs and his self-image. . . .

4. *The knowledge function.* Individuals not only acquire beliefs in the interest of satisfying various specific needs, they also seek knowledge to give meaning to what would otherwise be an unorganized chaotic universe. People need standards or frames of reference for understanding their world, and attitudes help to supply such standards. . . .

We would agree in general with all of the above, but would not be inclined to regard the functions cited as representing four separate functions. The adjustive (or utilitarian) function is really the same as the ego-defensive, once we recognize a relationship between adjustive-defensive *mechanisms* and adjustive-defensive strategies (see Chapter 7). Similarly, values should not be regarded as something that is essentially different from attitudes, but rather as a higher order of attitude integration; both are used interchangeably in the adjustive and goal-directed behavior of the individual in social interaction. We would summarize the *psychodynamic function of attitudes and values* by saying that they *serve to structure the individual's adjustment of social ego needs to the realities of the environment and daily experience.*

Smith *et al.* (1956) agree in general with this functional or psychodynamic approach and illustrate it in their research. They conducted an extensive series of tests, opinion polls, and depth interviews with 10 men of varying backgrounds in order to obtain information about their attitudes toward Communist Russia as well as material on their personalities.

The investigators then analyzed the results in terms of the dimensions of the attitude object ("Russia-as-it-exists-for-him"): *differentiation, saliency, time perspective, informational support,* and *object value,* and related these items to the personalities, needs, and defenses of each of the 10 men. Since the approach was essentially clinical and involved an understanding of the case histories and psychodynamics of each of the 10 personalities, the results cannot be expressed in a simple table. However, the general conclusions readily illustrate the importance of opinions and attitudes for the study of personality:

In considering the nature of opinions, their functions in an ongoing personality, and the conditions under which they may change, we have been impressed again and again by three things—and it is appropriate that we reiterate them in this closing paragraph. The first is that there is no rigid or one-to-one relationship between the opinions a person develops and the underlying needs or dynamics of his personality. Two men, both characterized by strong and unacceptable aggressive urges, may develop opinions that are at polar extremes: the one displacing his aggression by channeling it into feelings of bitter enmity toward Russia, the other avoiding the issue by urging the course of isolation from the world. The opinions that develop in a man are multiple in their determinants. They reflect his needs, his characteristic way of coping with these needs, his expressive style, his striving for social adjustment, and the manner in which through contact with the environment his values have been engaged by events about him. . . . A second and closely related conclusion is that opinions serve several functions for their holder: they aid him in appraising the value-relevance of the events he encounters; they serve his adjustments to the groups in which he participates and give him a badge of identity with his significant reference groups; and they provide an occasion for coping externally with analogues of still unresolved problems. In any given instance, an opinion or a fabric of opinions may serve one function more than another, but it is our impression that virtually always they serve all of them in some degree. Finally, it is only when we recognize the embeddedness of opinions in the functioning of personality that we can begin to understand the significance of an opinion and the condition of its change.

Implication for the Study of Personality . . . The first conclusion is that one gains rich insight into the functioning of personality by considering not only the deep dynamics but also the level that is closely in contact with events in the world. . . . One may learn much and go deep into the consistency of a personality without searching for basic hostility or underlying latent homosexuality.

The manner in which a person copes with his problems is the most revealing thing about him. The solutions to his problems are conserved in the form of values: ways of looking at and evaluating himself, the people about him, and the world around him. Those values represent a resultant of the contacts and struggles between a motivated individual and the surrounding world. From them one can infer much about the kinds of underlying problems with which the person has had to deal.

One's attitudes, examined for their consistencies and patterning, provide an excellent basis for inferring such values. In this sense, the student of personality cannot overlook the study of sentiments and opinions as an approach to his subject matter. To know the manner in which ego functioning proceeds, one literally must examine the attitude-value patterns of his subjects . . . (Smith *et al.*, 1956, pp. 278-281).

ATTITUDE MEASUREMENT AND ANALYSIS

Since attitudes and values are intrinsic to character and personality, any methods generally used for personality study may be applied to attitude measurement and value formation (cf. Chapters 1 and 10). To be more accurate, we should speak of the categorical classification of attitudes and values, since these cannot in any strict sense be "measured." Some of these rating and description devices have more special relevance to attitude study or are used in more specific forms than in the general investigation of personality dynamics. We shall briefly review some of these here.

Direct inquiry. Whether written or oral, direct inquiry is the simplest and most direct approach. It merely solicits a direct answer to a direct question or series of questions, on how one feels about a certain issue or object. This is the typical opinion-polling technique, but it may be used to elicit individual attitudes for personality study, as in the previously cited works of Smith *et al.* The question may be stated in "open-ended" form or in categorical form. The open-ended question allows the respondent to state his attitude or opinion in whatever terms he chooses, and is therefore more likely to elicit spontaneous reactions that accurately reflect his own feelings on the subject. The methodological problems involved in using open-ended questions are: the difficulty of avoiding "leading questions" and of summarizing the results into meaningful categories. The categorical question gives limited alternatives, such as: yes, no, don't know; preference for candidates A, B, or C; choosing which of two or three designs or packaged products is more appealing; stating "which side you favor" in any public contest or issue.

Psychologists have probably underestimated the utility of the direct question in the study of attitudes, because of the known pitfalls of suggestibility, defense mechanisms, hidden motives, conforming tendencies, and self-deception which tend to distort expressed attitudes. But attitudes may be elicited as consciously expressed, and their distortions or use in ego defense analyzed at a deeper level, if need be. Achieving insight into the discrepancies between expressed attitudes and repressed or suppressed conflicts is actually one of the chief aims of psychotherapy; but it is not necessary to psychoanalyze the "hidden meaning" behind every word, gesture, or food preference to judge a person's "true feelings." As Gordon Allport so cogently put it, "Doesn't the subject *ever* have a right to be believed?" There are times when it is both necessary and appropriate to "take him at his word" in studying attitudes and values, at least as a starting point in understanding the individual's own conception of his relationship to his environment.

Rating scales and inventories. These are written, more formal and impersonal forms of inquiry, and presuppose a degree of literacy and familiarity with paper-and-pencil rating procedures. They are scarcely adaptable to the limitations of the illiterate and untutored masses in many parts of the world. Rating scales may be either of the numerical rating or the checkpoint type. The numerical rating assigns *an arbitrary value to a subjective judgment* of one's position or degree of favorable-unfavorable disposition toward a given issue. It has been found by Likert and others that in constructing an attitude scale, more than five degrees of discrimination is usually superfluous. The checkpoint type of scale attempts to achieve the same effect visually. In both cases, the extremes of the scale are usually specified, and sometimes the neutral midpoint, or all five or more points are specified. This provides a frame of reference for the rater to make his subjective judgment, but it should not be assumed that this constitutes objective measurement in any real sense. This type of scale has been refined and called the "semantic differential" technique by Osgood and his co-workers (1957). Originally designed to test the structure of concepts for the purpose of semantic analysis (i.e., the analysis and communication of meaning), it was readily applied to the analysis of attitudes. An example of this type of rating would be the following rating of "what *mother* means to you." The subject checks the point on each dimensional scale which represents his estimate of how he conceives of mother on each dimension:

Mother

Active						Passive
Soft						Hard
Good						Bad

If some of the basic dimensions seem rather odd to apply to a concept like mother, it is only because semantic analysis often requires applying the same basic dimensions to a variety of concepts. The descriptive terms can, of course, be selected to suit the object of the attitude being analyzed. This has been done successfully in the analysis of stereotypes and other attitudes.

Other attitude scales are more of the questionnaire or inventory type. A large number of statements are made about a particular object, group, or issue, and the subject indicates his agreement or disagreement. The pro and con scores are added up and a scale score arrived at, which indicates the subject's rating on the type of attitude being measured, or the values or personality traits implied by the scale as a whole. The California E (ethnocentrism) scale is of this type. This simple pro and con summation has the disadvantage of requiring straight agree-disagree answers, so that an extraneous factor of acquiescence or conformity in test-taking attitude complicates the results. Another form of inventory is a check list of a large number of traits or descriptive adjectives from which the subject may choose whichever descriptions fit his attitude toward the object of the inquiry. This allows a great deal more freedom in expressing the subject's real attitude, if sufficient care has been taken to determine in advance all the possible characteristics that might apply to that particular kind of object. Examples of the use of this technique are the studies of stereotypes held by college students that were conducted by Katz and Braly (1933), Gilbert (1951), and Karlins *et al.* (1969).

Projective techniques. Unlike the direct inquiry or rating scale, projective techniques attempt to elicit attitudes indirectly through some imaginative interpretation or creation by the subject, which allows his attitudes to influence his response in a way that can be interpreted by the investigator. Although originally devised to detect underlying conflicts and maladaptions or basic orientations to reality in personality dynamics, such a test may be used to reflect an attitude toward a specific object or the introception of a specific value. This type of technique is most effectively used in getting indirect evidence of attitudes which a subject would be reluctant to express openly, or may not even have admitted to himself. This would include such sensitive areas as sexual indulgence or deviance, racial prejudice, antisocial impulses. A typical device is to show pictures of a situation involving key subjects and then asking the subject of the examination to describe the picture from memory or to answer a number of questions about it. In one classical example, a picture was shown in which a white man and a Negro were confronting each other, with the white man carrying a knife. In recalling the picture, some white subjects shifted the knife to the hand of the Negro in the picture, reflecting their prejudice against Negroes. Pictures of individuals may also be used to elicit attitudes by establishing ethnic identities for the portrayed individuals and then asking the subjects to describe their character. The attitudes are revealed when certain group identities are found to evoke different characterizations from others, and these attitudes are double-checked when the reversal of labeling enables the examiner to elicit a reversal of characterizations. Drawing pictures of people in particular roles or representing particular nationalities is another projective device. Though it might seem that this device depends on the drawing skill of the subject, this is greatly overshadowed by the biases revealed in the drawings. The way in which a rural American Negro child draws a white man from the city, or a German child draws her conception of an American sheriff, certainly reveals their attitudes and stereotyped conceptions of the objects represented (cf. Dennis, 1966).

A somewhat more elaborate technique is the use of the "incomplete story" to reveal the subject's basic values. The investigator presents, usually in written form, a series of problem situations in the form of short, incomplete stories. The subject must tell how the story ends, i.e., what the person in the conflict situation does (or should do). Presumably the subject projects his own values into the situation and tells how he would react on the basis of his values (e.g., whether to lie to escape punishment, etc.).

DIMENSIONS OF ATTITUDES

While recognizing the complex and qualitative nature of attitudinal psychodynamics, many researchers find it useful to give a little structure to the analysis of attitudes by thinking of these qualities as being variable along a few simple dimensions. Even the highly qualitative psychodynamic approaches of Smith *et al.* and Katz, which were previously quoted, made reference to certain dimensions of the attitude. In the former study it was the object-as-perceived (Russia) that was subjected to analysis in six dimensions. Usually it is the attitude itself, rather than its object, that is analyzed in terms of a few basic dimensions. There is partial agreement among various authorities on what these dimensions are, and we would suggest the following three basic dimensions as representing a fairly cogent and logical consensus:

Evaluative position. This tells us "where one stands" along the range of possible positions on an issue or attitudes toward an object. Some authorities call it the direction of the attitude (pro or con, like or dislike) and add another dimension of degree when necessary (how *far* would you go pro or con; how *much* do you like or dislike the object). Evaluative position covers the entire ground (in one dimension) with respect to "where one stands." This is usually all the opinion pollster wants to know: Are you for or against the bill before Congress? How far would you go in enforcing desegregation, as expressed in the following four measures . . .? Do you like "pop art" a great deal, a little, or not at all? This evaluative position dimension may also be applied to values and value-systems, which are more indicative of character than an isolated opinion on an isolated issue is likely to be.

Intensity of feeling. The strength of feeling that accompanies the attitude or is part of it may vary independently from the actual position taken by different people, and may in time change with the same person. There is some tendency for people who take an extreme position (on either side of an issue) to feel more intensely about it, but this is not necessarily so. It is quite possible to feel strongly about a moderate position or candidate, or value.

Action set. This refers to the readiness of the individual to act on his attitudes, values, or beliefs and not just think about them. It represents a test of the degree of sincerity or conviction in the attitude itself. This is often highlighted by such comments as: "practice what you preach," "just a parlor pink," "same old pious platitudes." Presumably those with the strongest feelings on any issue would be the most ready to act, but this is not necessarily so. Some individuals may feel very strongly about an issue and still be unwilling to back up their words with action, or they may suddenly find themselves not feeling so strongly about it. That is where the reflection of character comes in.

It should be pointed out that these three dimensions of attitudes are but special applications of the three classical dimensions of personality at the psychological level of analysis: (1) the *cognitive* (evaluative position); (2) the *affective* (intensity of feeling); and (3) the *conative* (action set). Such analysis may serve on occasion to help analyze and compare attitudes or values as attributes of character.

We can illustrate this by applying the three-dimensional scheme of analysis to that highly significant sphere of social orientation, political attitudes. While each culture has its own political structure and therefore its own range of political attitude positions, most of Western political party structures can be plotted on a simple four-position scale from "extreme left" to "extreme right." We have suggested that extremists are more likely to have more intense feelings and those with more intense feelings are more likely to be active in their advocacy of their positions, but we can still treat these three dimensions as being somewhat independent variables. Figure 9–1 attempts to convey a three-dimensional framework for the analysis of political attitudes. We chose a prismatic rather than a cubic form for this three-dimensional space, as a concession to the fact that the conative (action-set) dimension is not completely independent of the intensity dimension and, therefore, should not be represented at right angles to it, but at an acute angle.

In actual practice, some of the position-intensity-action locations in the three-dimensional space would not be occupied as much as some others, because of the characterological inconsistencies they imply or the role availabilities they require. It would be difficult to find a merely convinced

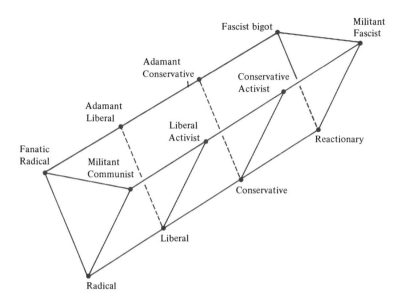

Figure 9–1. Three-dimensional variability of political attitudes; (evaluative position, intensity of feeling, action set).

reactionary in our culture who did not display some degree of active bigotry and an eagerness at least to support reactionary candidates and causes. The same goes for the radical, whose convictions are likely to find social facilitation by affiliation with some left-wing groups like the Communist party or one of its "fronts," if indeed the attitude were not formed by such association in the first place. Such association scarcely allows for being a nonactivist—but it is possible. There are "intellectual radicals" who shrink from violence and even consider activist organizations a travesty on their radical ideas. There are others to whom the term "parlor pink" would apply, since they talk a good game of radicalism, but are neither very intense in their convictions nor inclined to do anything about them. As for the "adamant liberal," that is almost a contradiction in terms, because the liberal philosophy is essentially one of reason and tolerance of differences. Nevertheless, there are some who are intensely liberal and express their liberal convictions through active support of liberal causes (e.g., freedom of speech, equalitarianism, and social legislation). This does not rule out affiliative strategies for purely ego-defensive purposes at any point in the three-dimensional attitude space. The dimensional analysis merely provides a basis for comparison; it does not explain anything. Only a detailed analysis of the individual's channeling of motives during his life history will give the true psychodynamic explanation of what purpose these attitudes serve and how susceptible the person is to attitude change.

Social Values and Character

We have deliberately chosen political attitudes and values as an illustration of dimensions of analysis, because these seem to us to be fraught with particular significance for character structure—a significance that greatly transcends the machinations of any local politics.

MAN AS A ''POLITICAL ANIMAL''

It is appropriate here that we pause to consider the true meaning of Aristotle's oft-quoted dictum: "Man is a political animal." Since we are already alert to the importance of semantic definition, we may as well begin by clarifying Aristotle's literal meaning. The word *politikos* in ancient Greek (adjective form of *polis*, the organized social community or city-state) actually meant *communal* or *social*, and that is how Aristotle actually characterized man. The Anglo-Saxon-European usage of "politics," along with the growing complexity of government in recent centuries, has given the term a connotation of partisan political affiliation and activity, usually with ulterior motives. That connotation of the term "political" scarcely seems like anything that could seriously be considered inherent in the nature of man or significantly related to personality and character, save on a purely "incidental learning" basis. But we have already made clear and now reiterate that political values and attitudes constitute but one medium through which the social ego drive or "communal" nature of man is canalized. It is in that broader sense that we speak of political attitudes, and it is for this reason that we consider the subject of more than passing interest in personality theory. Sociopolitical attitudes and values are particularly germane to the study of that aspect of personality called character, because it has definite ethical implications in structuring one's relationship to his fellowman.

If we examine the three-dimensional spectrum of political attitudes represented in Fig. 9–1, we must ask: On what issues in general is the individual taking an evaluative position? What is it that he feels strongly or not so strongly about? What kinds of action is he supporting or shunning? In general, these issues are ones that concern human welfare in his community or society. The evaluative position, the intensity of feeling, the action set, may all be said to be oriented toward the general issues of social reform or progress—that is, progress in the direction of more equality and self-government and the use of economic resources for the common good. The radical wants more drastic and immediate reforms and a greater sharing of the wealth than the liberal, and he is more inclined to favor radical measures of revolution and social upheaval to gain these ends. The reactionary favors the opposite extreme, going back to "the good old days" of rugged individualism, class privilege, and a laissez-faire position of government except for the protection of property rights. He is also more extreme in both his objectives and the action he favors than the conservative is. The conservative merely wants to conserve traditional values and social stability; he feels that society is a lot healthier if people are rewarded in proportion to their effort and not merely supported by government subsidy. The reactionary would abolish all of the "new-fangled social(istic) legislation" altogether, and use the authority and power of the state to keep the rabble in their place and to combat—by force, if necessary—any challenge to free, private enterprise. That does not mean that every person's social attitudes can be pinpointed on this three-dimensional scale. Sherif, *et al.* (1965) have properly pointed out that it is more appropriate to speak of ranges or "latitude of acceptance," "latitude of rejection," and "latitude of noncommitment" toward various positions or stands along the political spectrum.

But does everyone *have* to take a stand on political issues? Isn't there such a thing as being completely apolitical in one's interests and orientation? In the popular sense of political involvement, yes; in the biosocial or Aristotelian sense of social awareness, no! The individual who shows complete unconcern for the welfare of those around him and the social regulation that controls their relationship is not merely apolitical; he shows a type of character that might be judged as defective in biosocial terms. The etiology (developmental causes) of such asocial orientations is just as much a question of character formation as is the radical, conservative, liberal, or reactionary character formation.

The reason for this is that it is impossible to escape the ethical implications of such basic sociopolitical orientations or the lack of them. Attitudes and values that involve basic orientations toward one's fellow-man, as we pointed out in Chapter 4, inevitably involve the ethical implications of adult role behavior. These implications become clear at once if we but sample some of the issues that are typically used as objects of sociopolitical attitudes in contemporary American society, some of which are universal, some just regional: What, if anything, should be done for the economically underprivileged to soften the hardships of unemployment, ill health, and old-age dependency? Should racial or ethnic discrimination be allowed in public facilities, in housing, or in education? Should obedience to authority be stressed more than freedom of expression and the right of dissent, and at what point should the law draw the line? To what extent should limits be set on the freedom of entrepreneurs to exploit the labor and commodity markets for profit, or conversely, on the power of the State to control the life of the individual? These are, of course, historic issues over which wars and rebellions have been fought, and over which great social upheavals are still taking place. They involve vast and complex socioeconomic and geopolitical forces which have brought about numerous conflicts and resolutions at different times and places in history. We would not be so naïve as to claim that they are basically the result of an aggressive instinct in man. They do, however, involve the aspirations, attitudes, and values of people. They involve social-interaction by activists who bring about changes or precipitate and resolve conflicts by certain combinations of people and circumstances. Social conditions do not bring about revolutions or reforms; only people do. And people do so because man is a sociopolitical animal, and it behooves us to study him as such.

Very little attention was paid to such issues until World War II, when American and British psychologists, and a few from other countries, began to study the implications of the world-wide confrontation between democracy and fascism. We have already seen one example of the use of the clinical and participant-observer method in the study of the leaders of a revolutionary fascist dictatorship. In the case of Ribbentrop, the use of compensatory aggression and affiliative manipulation to satisfy status needs entered prominently into his motivation, while he suppressed insight into the incompatibility of his values. Other cases in our study showed more pathological need for aggression for aggressive ascendancy's sake (Goering), paranoid compensation and projection of inferiority feelings to a scapegoat group (Hitler), and rigid conformity to in-group values and prescribed role behavior (the militarists). All of these character structures played their parts in foisting a disastrous reactionary social movement on a culture just emerging from authoritarianism. It was stressed (Gilbert, 1950) that there was no isomorphic correspondence or one-to-one relationship between the characters of the leaders and the historical events that took place. Nevertheless, it was shown that reactionary authoritarianism and pathological cruelty do not exist in the abstract, but derive their character from the character of leadership. When placed in such stark perspective, the ethical or characterological implications of political attitude study are inescapable. Unfortunately, firsthand clinical studies of major leaders of the radical left have not yet become available, but certain autobiographical accounts give insight into the characterological processes involved (e.g., Crossman, 1950).

At the level of the attitudes of the common man, extensive studies have been made of authoritarianism of the right by Adorno *et al.* (1950); of dogmatism by Rokeach (1960); of English political attitudes by Eysenck (1955); of political attitude involvement and change by Sherif *et al.* (1965); of American voting behavior by Campbell *et al.* (1960); and of some European political attitudes by Cantril (1958) and by Christiansen (1959).

All of the above studies relate personality variables to sociopolitical attitudes. We shall take as illustrative the general area of authoritarianism-ethnocentricity, partly because so much research has been done in that area and partly because it has such obvious implications for character differentiation.

AUTHORITARIANISM AND ETHNOCENTRISM

On an a priori basis, authoritarianism and ethnocentrism might be considered to be two independent variables which may be measured separately, either as attitudes or as value systems. One deals with relations to authority figures and introcepted attitudes toward the idea of authority; the other deals with attitudes toward ethnic groups. However, a close relationship between the two has long been known to exist at the "far right" of the political spectrum, and research has confirmed this close relationship. The connecting link between these two attitude systems in what might be called the "fascist syndrome" is the basic attitude or value orientation that favors class privilege—that is, the right of the privileged in-group to rule, to retain privileged social status, and to dominate other ethnic or social class groups. This may or may not involve pseudoscientific rationalizations of "racial superiority" or ethical ones such as noblesse oblige, but a basically ethnocentric attitude is coupled with a basic belief in the right to use authority or power. The left-wing radical, on the other hand, believes in an equalitarian philosophy and a broader sharing of wealth and power. He, therefore, cannot advocate ethnocentrism or class privilege, but he may advocate a class struggle to bring about his equalitarian utopia. Both radicals and reactionaries would favor obedience to "party line" dogma and central authority (and are, therefore, authoritarian by definition), but the right-wing extremist is more likely to couple ethnocentrism with his authoritarian values.

Because of this close relationship, the most extensive psychological investigation of authoritarian attitudes undertaken in the 1940s proved to be just as much a study of ethnocentrism as of pure authoritarianism. This can be understood in view of the preoccupation of American psychologists with the problem of fascism during World War II. In the course of this investigation, several attitude scales were developed to measure authoritarianism of fascist attitudes (F scale), anti-Semitism (A-S scale), and general ethnocentrism (E scale), as well as politicoeconomic conservatism (PEC scale). All of these scales yielded high intercorrelations, as might be expected from the fact that agreement with the various test items was generally designed to indicate agreement with attitudes at the conservative-reactionary end of sociopolitical spectrum. The results have, therefore, been criticized as being subject to the "acquiescence artifact." Nevertheless, the use of a variety of projective and interview techniques to provide confirmation-in-depth of the test scores yielded some evidence of a character syndrome which the investigators called "authoritarian." The main features were the following:

exploitive power orientation
conventional values and moralistic condemnation of others
hierarchical conception of human relationships
distrustful-suspicious attitude
self-glorification or rationalization of faults
pseudomasculinity (for men)
diffuse and depersonalized aggression
externalized conscience or moral authority
rigid thinking and intolerance of ambiguity
preoccupation with "toughness," rejection of "softness"
(Adorno *et al.*, 1950)

The tendency to score high on each of these attitudes by various criteria was found to occur reliably more frequently among those scoring high on the E scale than those who scored low. These results serve to show how closely related attitudes are to defense mechanisms and strategies, to social values, and to character formation.

Character interpretation on the basis of attitude-value syndromes must take account of social norms as well as individual needs, however. Anti-democratic attitudes may have a different characterological connotation in a democracy than in a society that is traditionally authoritarian. One might hypothesize that in a democracy such attitudes are more likely to signify a *need* for authority and ethnocentric identification to resolve feelings of insecurity. On the other hand, such cultural norms may actually shape the "national character" of a society, so that one person's neurotic need is another person's norm (in another society). The probability, we would suggest, is that extreme and inflexible deviation from the norm in any society usually indicates individual need for anxiety resolution.

This brings us to the interesting question of whether there are attitudinal characteristics that transcend the "fascist syndrome" and apply to extreme authoritarianism of *any* ideology. An interesting approach to this problem has been made by Rokeach (1960) in his investigations of dogmatism. Among other things, Rokeach found that rigid and dogmatic thinking could be found among Englishmen and Americans of all political persuasions and could also be influenced by religious affiliation. Sherif *et al.* (1965) likewise found that individuals of any political affiliation differed in their "latitude of commitment" to a political position. Both sets of studies show that individuals differ in the rigidity of their convictions on sociopolitical issues and, therefore, differ in their susceptibility to attitude change. The subject of attitude change has a host of significant applications for ideological character structuring, ranging from Communist indoctrination and "brain-washing" to influencing the voting behavior of an electorate in a democracy. Authorities differ on the effect of discrepant communications on the political attitudes of an individual, which does not seem to follow the simple rules of conformity to suggestion. Sherif and his co-workers offer the clue that attitude change depends not so much on the size of the discrepancy between the subject's attitude and the influencing information offered, as it does on the individual's *ego-involvement* in his particular ideological stand. It may be that the degree of ego-involvement is reducible to the two other dimensions of intensity of affect and action set, but it apparently also involves a latitude of commitment. The more ego-involved one is in a particular "party line" (or religious dogma, or way of life, or any ideology), the less tolerant one will be of any deviation from that position. Attitude change will, therefore, not be merely a cognitive accommodation to reduce an apparent discrepancy (as Festinger and his co-workers are inclined to argue, on the basis of "cognitive dissonance" theory), but will be a function of the degree of commitment (in Sherif's terms) or of rigidity of thinking (in Rokeach's terms). Thus a fanatic Communist may be more hostile to a moderate socialistic viewpoint than a more tolerant liberal or even conservative might be.

The question of what *makes* a person rigid or intolerant of small deviations from his own ideological position is the crux of the psychodynamic aspect of attitude change. Only the studies that go into individual case histories provide evidence on that score (e.g., Adorno *et al.*, 1950; Gilbert, 1950; Smith *et al.*, 1956; White, 1952). In such case histories, we find that ideological fanaticism *at either extreme* of the political spectrum represents a neurotic ego-involvement and defensive affiliations which serve the purpose of: (1) enhancing the individual's sense of acceptance of self-justification and (2) giving clarity to social meanings and guidelines for decisions (reducing ambiguity). These are two of the functions we have assumed that attitudes and values serve to begin with. We merely suggest that they serve a more neurotic need in the cases of extremist fanatics. (We must make allowance, of course, for those social crises which clearly call for extreme measures to correct intolerable injustice or threats to survival. In such crises, it is not necessarily the perpetual extremist who most effectively rises to the occasion.)

Attitude studies, nevertheless, yield useful data in analyzing the influences involved in ethnocentrism and prejudice, although interpretation is frequently limited by the nature of the population surveyed. There is, for example, the still-current controversy over whether race prejudice is really *race* prejudice or merely prejudice against those who *think differently* (i.e., have different value systems) from those who hold the prejudice. Rokeach (1960) has suggested that it is more a matter of rigidity of belief systems than any natural aversion to members of a different race. Since prejudice is a question of belief systems in the first place, the controversy need never have arisen if it were not for the contention of some racists that people "naturally prefer their own kind"—the term *kind* meaning race of ethnic group. Rokeach has maintained that congruence of belief systems is the real determining factor in prejudice, not racial aversion as such. When stated in such either-or terms, it is easy enough to find evidence to support the belief-congruence theory.

However, Stein *et al.* (1965) showed that *both* kinds of attitudes may be found among teen-agers. Stein (1966) further elaborated this line of study with a larger sample and an attitude survey that gave clearer delineation of attitude congruence between subjects and described objects. Using 930 ninth-grade Ss in a northeastern suburban high school, he found that when belief systems of Negro and white Protestant, Catholic, and Jewish teen-agers were described, prejudice correlated inversely with similarity of S's beliefs, rather than with difference in race. The flaw in this kind of "test" of the belief-prejudice hypothesis lies in the limitations set by the sample population used. The results can be just as readily interpreted to mean that when race prejudice is not very strong (as would presumably be the case in a northeastern American suburban high school population long indoctrinated to shun blatant race prejudice), there might still be prejudices or preferences for association with people whose belief systems are congenial to one's own. We would predict that a similar study undertaken in a more traditionally prejudiced community, where racial segregation is still practiced and prejudice openly advocated, would find such prejudice relatively immune to congruity of belief systems. After all, congruity of belief has existed on many fronts in such communities for a very long time—e.g., belief in God, democracy, property rights, the rewards of virtue and honest toil, etc.,—but that has not prevented the prejudiced from twisting these very beliefs to rationalize their prejudices.

This phenomenon is a good example of how history may provide far more impressive evidence of operational forces in human relationships than a limited sampling of attitudes at a given time and place can hope to provide. The history of racial, religious, and class relations in different regions of the United States and other parts of the world bear massive witness to the virulence of ethnic bigotries with or without incompatible belief systems. We know that Southern Baptists have long refused to worship in racially mixed congregations, although their belief systems were supposedly fundamentally (and in true Fundamentalist tradition) much the same. Overcoming this racial bias is currently an arduous task of the Southern Baptist Church. Older contemporary Europeans witnessed the horror of Jewish persecution and extermination for *imagined* racial inferiority even when the nationalistic-authoritarian belief systems of the victims was originally quite congruent with the belief systems of the persecutors in their own countries. The bigoted American racist did not make allowances for the congruity of the Negro's Christian-American belief system any more than the Nazi made allowances for the Jew's patriotism. In short, it is always a belief, attitude, or value that is involved in prejudice, or in ethnocentrism, but that belief may be a racial one just as well as any other. These attitudes, when prevalent in the community, are inculcated during the secondary socialization stage of psychosocial development, and generally become crystallized as secondary ethnocentrism during the adult role anticipation stage. They also reflect the individual need for such defense by the extent to which the cultural value system is exaggerated or distorted to suit that need.

OTHER VALUE SYSTEMS

Sociopolitical ideologies represent one of the principal ways in which social attitudes are selectively organized into value systems that give expression to individual character. These value systems are, of course, inherent in the culture and are learned by the individual; but it would be an extraordinarily homogeneous culture that would provide neither the diversity of value systems nor the latitude of individual commitment to allow for such individual character formation.

This diversity of cultural value systems within and among different societies has generally been studied much more assiduously by sociologists and anthropologists than it has been by psychologists. Their approach has generally been to describe *uniformities* of behavior and cultural values within each culture or subculture, in order to emphasize the importance of the cultural environment in shaping personality. In some cases, anthropologists have been able to detect patterns of value integration around a central theme, so that the way of life and value-motivations of different ethnic groups could be generalized and contrasted. Thus Ruth Benedict (1934) compared the "Apollonian" way of life of the Pueblo Indians of Arizona and New Mexico with the "Dionysian" way of life of the Kwakiutl of Vancouver Island. The Apollonian way of life valued sobriety and moderation, appreciation of beauty, indulgence in the reflective life, and self-restraint. The Dionysian way of life represented unrestrained indulgence in sensual pleasures or aggressive impulses.

This "way-of-life" approach, reminiscent of Adler's style-of-life concept in character formation, has been amplified by Charles Morris (1956), who detected thirteen such ways of life as common variants of value systems around the world. These "Ways" were briefly described as follows:

13 Ways to Live

Way 1: preserve the best that man has attained
Way 2: cultivate independence of persons and things
Way 3: show sympathetic concern for others
Way 4: experience festivity and solitude in alternation
Way 5: act and enjoy life through group participation
Way 6: constantly master changing conditions
Way 7: integrate action, enjoyment, and contemplation
Way 8: live with wholesome, carefree enjoyment
Way 9: wait in quiet receptivity
Way 10: control the self stoically
Way 11: meditate on the inner life
Way 12: chance adventuresome deeds
Way 13: obey the cosmic purposes

These "Ways" were more fully described and preferential ratings obtained on them from college students in the United States, Canada, India, Japan, China, and Norway. The well-rounded life represented by Way 7 was the most highly valued by United States and Canadian students, while Indian students showed a preference for the tradition-oriented Way 1 and the stoic self-control of Way 10. Way 13 was the least valued by American students and most by Chinese, but this may have been partly due to an artifact of semantics. Wide individual differences were found, and there were also subcultural differences reflecting religious and socioeconomic status within each country. This approach to cultural values may have some utility in establishing cultural and subcultural norms, though it is limited by the choice of value-systems presented and the population sampling used. It is, of course, the individual position with respect to the norm, the intensity of affect accompanying it, and the action set with respect to living in accordance with that value system that gives meaning to the value as an expression of individual personality.

Recognizing that no discrete selection of "ways of life" could do justice to all the possible variations of value systems, Kluckhohn and Strodtbeck (1961) explored the possibility of setting up a five-dimensional system of value-orientations, which might have universal applicability to the analysis of cultural values. The five dimensions were conceived of as basic questions which man seeks to answer, usually implicitly, in orienting himself to life:

(1) What is the character of innate human nature? (*human nature* orientation)
(2) What is the relation of man to nature? (and supernature?) (*man-nature* orientation)

(3) What is the temporal focus of human life? (*time* orientation)
(4) What is the modality of human activity? (*activity* orientation)
(5) What is the modality of man's relationship to other men? (*relational* orientation)

The five value-orientations could be described on a scale of variations which was different for each value, thus:

Human Nature:				
	Evil	Neutral	Mixture of Good-and-Evil	Good

Man-Nature:			
	Subjugation-To-Nature	Harmony-With-Nature	Mastery-Over-Nature

Time:			
	Past	Present	Future

Activity:			
	Being	Being-In-Becoming	Doing

Relational:			
	Lineality	Collaterality	Individualism

On the basis of their knowledge of five ethnic cultures in the American Southwest (Spanish-American, Texan, Mormon, Zuni, Navaho), the investigators predicted what the consensus of attitude or value-orientation would be by members of these ethnic groups to questions eliciting preferences on these value orientations. For practical purposes, the Human Nature Orientation was omitted, and no predictions were made for the Zuni group, whose culture was believed to be in a state of transition. In almost all cases, the consensus of value-orientations on the questionnaire turned out just as predicted on the basis of previous study. Thus Texans were confirmed as being oriented toward mastery-over-nature, individualism, and doing things for future benefits. The Navaho, on the other hand, confirmed their orientations as being more in harmony with nature, collateral in human relationships, and doing things for present rather than future needs.

The student of personality will be gratified to note that the study of cultural values does stand up to the test of predictability, though prediction of actual behavior under comparable circumstances would be more convincing. He will naturally ask, however, how much such value analysis can tell him about the personality of an *individual* Navaho or Texan. To be sure, there are individual differences in the preferred value orientations within any culture, but the probability is great that value discriminations intended to differentiate between cultures are not fine enough to differentiate between individuals. Psychologists have found the activity-interest type of inventory more fruitful in revealing individual values within a given culture, although these instruments do not lend themselves readily to cross-cultural comparison and are subject to all the limitations of any questionnaire approach to personality assessment.

A favorite instrument for such investigation among more or less educated American Ss is the Allport-Vernon-Lindzey Study of Values. This is essentially an attitude-interest-activity inventory that elicits the subject's preferences on a variety of choices which reveal his basic values. The rationale of the test or inventory was adopted from Spranger's suggestion that people in Western civilization could be classified according to their degree of adherence to six basic value orientations: theoretical, religious, aesthetic, social, political, and economic. Those who had cultivated the scientific quest for truth were the *theoretical* type. Those seeking "higher truth" and moral principles more than anything else would be designated as *religious* in a sense that transcends sectarian affiliation. Those who found aesthetic satisfactions their most absorbing interest in life would be the *aesthetic* type. An interest in human welfare and social betterment was indicative of the *social* value orientation. The pursuit of and respect for power was indicative of the *political* value, and interest in material things, indicative of *economic* value orientation. The A-V-L Study of Values enables the individual to express his preferences and attitudes on a number of alternatives which reflect these values. Since the total number of choices is always constant, the resulting profile of scores reflects only the *relative* strength of each of these values *for that individual* (see Fig. 9–2). It is thus more useful in determining the most salient features of an individual's value-system within this framework than in comparing groups on any absolute scale. Not unexpectedly, it has been found that occupants of certain social roles reflect characteristic patterns of values. Scientists generally place higher value on theoretical pursuits, businessmen on economic, etc. The question of which is cause and which is effect need not be resolved, since our presentation of role assumption has already made the continual interaction process clear. The predictive value of such an inventory is almost self-evident in such areas as occupational interests that reflect clear-cut social value preferences.

An interesting sidelight on the use of such tests for personnel selection in industry is the allegation by W. H. White (1956) that these tests can be faked by anybody who wished to get the particular job. White presents the A-V-L Value profile preferred by Sears, Roebuck & Company in hiring its salesmen (p. 214), and adds a chapter on "How to Cheat on Personality Tests." The profile shows that the company prefers men who are low on aesthetic values and high in economic values, as one might expect. There is no doubt that anyone could figure this out for himself and "fake" the test, if he wants to. But White overlooks one basic principle

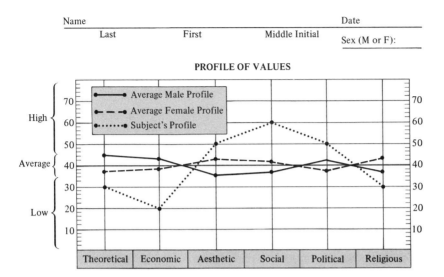

Figure 9–2. A male social science major's profile of values superimposed on average male and female college students' profiles on the Allport-Vernon-Lindzey Study of Values.

which we have stressed in this chapter. A person's values are a real expression of his character and personality, and his choice of roles in life is largely determined by those values. White does not explain why in the world an esthetic soul, who cares little for the pursuit of corporate and personal profits and shudders at the thought of devoting his life to the sale of merchandise in a chain store, should want to fake the test and violate his own sense of purpose and identity!

Traits
and
Character Types Once we recognize the relevance of social attitudes and values to character structure, the consideration of personality traits follows almost as a matter of course. This is so if for no other reason than the fact that many generalized attitudes and enduring values may be indistinguishable from character traits. If we speak of a fanatic radical or a dogmatic reactionary, we are referring to both an attitude-value syndrome and a fairly well-defined trait cluster. Some traits may be peculiar to a given individual; others may be of a more general or generic variety, permitting comparison among members of a given population. G. W. Allport long ago made the distinction between *ideographic* (unique) and

nomothetic (general) traits. More recently, he pointed out the close relationship between attitudes and traits:

It is not always possible to distinguish between what should properly be called a trait, and what an attitude. Is *patriotism* a trait or an attitude toward one's native land? Is *extraversion* a trait or an attitude toward life? Does one have an *authoritarian* trait or attitude? . . .

But ordinarily there are two distinctions between the two concepts: (1) An attitude always has an object of reference. One has an attitude *toward* parsnips, communism, or Arctic exploration. A trait is aroused by so many objects that we do not attempt to specify them. Therefore, a trait is ordinarily considered to be more general (a higher level of integration) than an attitude. A person is conforming, expansive, shy, ascendant in so many situations, that we do not, as in the case of an attitude, name them. (2) Attitudes are usually pro or con, favorable or unfavorable, well disposed or ill disposed; they can lead one to approach or withdraw from their object (Allport, 1961, p. 347).

Personality traits may involve any dimensions, functions, or levels of personality organization other than that of specific attitudes. All that is implied by "trait" is a consistency of some aspect of behavior or constitution of a given individual. This may also be extended to a consistent aspect of the impression an individual makes on others, provided that there is reason to assume that this consistent impression results from some intrinsic characteristics of the individual making the impression (otherwise, it would be prejudice or projection—but, admittedly, it is often hard to tell the difference). When generalized traits or trait-clusters are found to apply to a large number of individuals, thus creating a *mode* in the population, we may speak of a personality "type" or syndrome. These types may be of various kinds, some involving attitude-value clusters, some referring to temperamental dispositions, and some referring to generalized prototypes of social roles.

POSSIBILITIES OF CHARACTER TYPING

Biosocial theory allows for at least three levels of integration at which motivated behavior takes place. They might conceivably provide the basis for analysis of traits and syndromes that would differentiate character types.

At the psychophysiological level are organically determined traits and what might be called biotypes of personality. This would include behavioral variables directly attributable to endocrine balance, body build, nervous system functioning, such as: hyperthyroid excitability versus hypothyroid lethargy; muscular activity versus nervous sensitivity versus visceral self-indulgence. Consistent glandular-based syndromes have thus far defied systematic formulation because of the internal interaction of the endocrine system and the external interaction of the whole psychosomatic system with environmental experience. As for the muscle-brain-viscera clas-

sification, a promising attempt by Sheldon (1942) to correlate temperament with tissue development does not seem to have produced clear-cut
results—probably for similar reasons.

At the psychological level, we can include a host of traits referring to
attitudes and values, modes of perception, characteristic mood and affect,
etc. Much of what we discussed by way of individual differences in perceptual styles, sociopolitical attitudes, and values in this and the preceding
chapter might provide the basis for such character typing. The chief
difficulty here seems to be that individual differences are usually distributed in a normal distribution curve and lend themselves only arbitrarily
to type designations at the extremes. Examples would be Jung's Introver-
sion-Extroversion types, the A-V-L Study of Values, and most other personality inventories such as those we shall consider in the next chapter.
Some of them, of course, blend into the psychosocial level of analysis.

At the psychosocial level, we have already discussed social roles and
their effect in defining as well as selecting appropriate behavioral traits.
These social role prototypes are, in effect, culturally prescribed personality types, though the mode of role assumption and adjustment will
differ with the individual. These role traits and types rest on the biosocial
reality of the interdependence of role and personality. Every culture and
subculture tends to develop certain characteristic trait-patterns and "types"
in the roles that form its particular social structure. Thus, many upper-
middle-class American exurbanite businessmen may exhibit a pattern of
traits in common and one might then refer to the "exurbanite businessman syndrome." Is such a designation scientifically justifiable? Only to
the extent that a preponderance of individuals in that category exhibit
more behavioral characteristics, values, style of life, and interpersonal relationships in common with each other than they do with other social-role
types—such as "migratory laborer," "Oriental mystic," or even "pseudo-
intellectual hippie."

A somewhat ambitious attempt to designate the principal character
types in a capitalistic society was made by Erich Fromm (1947). With a
sort of Marxist adaptation of Freudian psychodynamics, Fromm laid great
stress on man's *alienation* from nature, from the fruits of his own labor,
and from his fellowman in the midst of our mass production, mass consumption, and mass media of communication. The problem of growth
and adjustment in modern society is not so much repression of psychosexual urges, says Fromm, as it is self-fulfillment in our alienated social
relationships. It is man's orientation to his social milieu that determines
his character.

These orientations, by which the individual relates himself to the world, constitute the core of his character; character can be defined as the (*relatively
permanent*) *form in which human energy is canalized in the process of assimi-*

lation and socialization. This canalization of psychic energy has a very signifi-cant biological function. . . . The character system can be considered the human substitute for the instinctive apparatus of the animal. Once energy is canalized in a certain way, action takes place "true to character" (Fromm, 1947, p. 58).

Fromm then goes on to delineate four nonproductive (in the sense of noncreative) orientations to (Western) society, and one productive (crea-tive) one. The nonproductive ones are the *receptive,* the *exploitative,* the *hoarding,* and the *marketing* orientations, each with a set of traits that may vary from positive to negative in each individual. The *productive orientation* is something of a creative ideal, which is possible in this or any other society, but is constricted in some social systems more than in others.

Unfortunately, little has been done to follow through on this provoca-tive approach to psychosocial personality typology by means of psycho-metric studies, as was done for Spranger's social value types. Some recent thinking along these lines may provide avenues for reexamination and investigation. Fromm's concept of the productive orientation seems to be highly congruent with Maslow's (1962) exposition of self-actualizing personalities, and has points of contact with McClelland's Achieving Society (1961).

DEVIANT PERSONALITY TYPES

The practical necessity of providing a framework for clinical diagnosis plus the easier identifiability of deviant trait syndromes have conspired to produce a more comprehensive and tested roster of deviant personal-ity types than of normal ones. Since maladjustment is at best a matter of degree, and very few adults in our society can be said to be perfectly well-adjusted, perhaps such a roster would be more widely applicable to the general population than might be offhandedly assumed. The task of preparing a diagnostic manual which includes not only all known mental diseases (especially psychoses and neuroses) but also fairly comprehensive coverage of deviant personality syndromes is truly a formidable one. After much criticism and deliberation, the American Psychiatric Association in 1968 published a revised edition of its *Diagnostic and Statistical Manual of Mental Disorders.* This Manual includes a revised section on "Person-ality Disorders," previously listed as "Personality Pattern Disturbance," and "Personality Trait Disturbance." These categories merit our attention as the most authoritative and comprehensive set of descriptions of deviant personality syndromes emanating from the psychiatric profession. Ten behavioral syndromes are described, as follows:

Paranoid Personality. This behavioral pattern is characterized by hypersen-sitivity, rigidity, unwarranted suspicion, jealousy, envy, excessive self-importance, and a tendency to blame others and ascribe evil motives to them. These characteristics often interfere with the patient's ability to maintain satisfactory interpersonal relations. Of course, the presence of suspicion of itself does not justify this diagnosis, since the suspicion may be warranted in some instances.

Cyclothymic Personality. (Affective Personality) This behavior pattern is manifested by recurring and alternating periods of depression and elation. Periods of elation may be marked by ambition, warmth, enthusiasm, optimism, and high energy. Periods of depression may be marked by worry, pessimism, low energy, and a sense of futility. These mood variations are not readily attributable to external circumstances. If possible, the diagnosis should specify whether the mood is characteristically depressed, hypomanic, or alternating.

Schizoid Personality. This behavior pattern manifests shyness, over-sensitivity, seclusiveness, avoidance of close or competitive relationships, and often eccentricity. Autistic thinking without loss of capacity to recognize reality is common, as is daydreaming and the inability to express hostility and ordinary aggressive feelings. These patients react to disturbing experiences and conflicts with apparent detachment.

Explosive Personality. (Epileptoid Personality Disorder) This behavior pattern is characterized by gross outbursts of rage or of verbal or physical aggressiveness. These outbursts are strikingly different from the patient's usual behavior, and he may be regretful and repentant for them. These patients are generally considered excitable, aggressive, and over-responsive to environmental pressures. It is the intensity of the outbursts and the individual's inability to control them which distinguishes this group. Cases diagnosed as "aggressive personality" are classified here. . . .

Obsessive-Compulsive Personality. (Anankastic Personality) This behavior pattern is characterized by excessive concern with conformity and adherence to standards of conscience. Consequently, individuals in this group may be rigid, over-inhibited, over-conscientious, over-dutiful, and unable to relax easily. This disorder may lead to an *Obsessive-compulsive neurosis* (q.v.) from which it must be distinguished.

Hysterical Personality. (Histrionic Personality Disorder) These behavior patterns are characterized by excitability, emotional instability, over-activity, and self-dramatization. This self-dramatization is always attention-seeking and often seductive, whether or not the patient is aware of its purpose. These personalities are also immature, self-centered, often vain, and usually dependent on others. This disorder must be differentiated from *Hysterical neurosis* (q.v.).

Aesthenic Personality. This behavior pattern is characterized by easy fatigability, low energy level, lack of enthusiasm, marked incapacity for enjoyment, and oversensitivity to physical and emotional stress. This disorder must be differented from *Neurasthenic neurosis* (q.v.).

Antisocial Personality. This term is reserved for individuals who are basically unsocialized and whose behavior pattern brings them repeatedly into conflict with society. They are incapable of significant loyalty to individuals, groups, or social values. They are grossly selfish, callous, irresponsible, impulsive, and unable to feel guilt or to learn from experience and punishment. Frustration tolerance is low. They tend to blame others or offer plausible rationalizations for their behavior. A mere history of repeated legal or social offenses is not sufficient to justify this diagnosis. *Group delinquent reaction of childhood (or adolescence),* (q.v.) and *Social maladjustment without manifest psychiatric disorder* (q.v.) should be ruled out before making this diagnosis.

Passive-Aggressive Personality. This behavior pattern is characterized by both passivity and aggressiveness. The aggressiveness may be expressed passively, for example, by obstructionism, pouting, procrastination, intentional inefficiency, or stubbornness. This behavior commonly reflects hostility which the individual feels he dare not express openly. Often the behavior is one expression of the patient's resentment at failing to find gratification in a relationship with an individual or institution upon which he is overdependent.

Inadequate Personality. This behavior pattern is characterized by ineffectual responses to emotional, social, intellectual, and physical demands. While the patient seems neither physically nor mentally deficient, he does manifest inadaptability, ineptness, poor judgment, social instability, and lack of physical and emotional stamina.

Summary Attitudes and values are recognized as having considerable psychodynamic significance in signaling the direction and structure of canalized motives, orientation to society and reality, prescribed role behavior, self-concept and defense, interpersonal relations, and character in general. Three basic dimensions of attitude are: evaluative position, intensity of feeling, and action set. These dimensions may be applied, for example, to political attitudes, in which evaluative position is represented on a scale from radical to reactionary; intensity of feeling is represented by degree of fanaticism or bigotry; and action set is represented by degree of militancy. Studies of authoritarianism and ethnocentrism show that these two attitude-value systems are closely related. Problems of prejudice and attitude change involve questions of rigidity, congruity, and latitude of commitment to the particular belief system. Attempts to evaluate cross-cultural and individual differences in value systems are discussed, as is the close relationship between attitudes, values, and personality traits.

Attempts to set up personality typologies on the basis of trait-clusters have not been particularly successful thus far, but a roster of "deviant personality types" is more or less recognized by the clinical professions.

I O

Evaluating the Individual Personality

The Clinical
Case Study
Method   In Chapter 1, we referred briefly to the clinical examination or case study as one of the methods psychologists use to study personality. This method is particularly adapted to the understanding or diagnosis of the individual case as an integrated, real, live person, engaged in the ongoing pursuit of individual goals and making adjustments to conflicts or handicaps that may be common to his group or to mankind, but which are, nevertheless, unique in their significance to him as an individual. The goal is to understand, perhaps to help the individual, perhaps to help him understand himself, rather than to prove a theoretical point or do a controlled experiment on some isolated variable of behavior in general. Nevertheless, cumulative data from many clinical studies can contribute to generalized principles of etiology, psychodynamics, and the diagnosis of normal and deviant personalities, as well as to principles of personnel selection and morale, public opinion, and social tensions. All of these applications have benefited from case studies and have in turn, along with experimental studies on relevant variables, contributed insights which have increased the sophistication of the clinical method itself. Now that we have considered some of the basic principles of personality develop-

ment, motivation and adjustment, and psychological processes involved in social interaction, we are in a better position to discuss the clinical approach to the understanding of the individual personality.

Interviewing and Observing

The clinical interview is so closely interwoven with direct observation that it would be futile to discuss one without the other. Indeed, an expert on the psychiatric interview, H. S. Sullivan (1954), regarded the interview as a special case of participant observation in an expert-and-client situation. Most behavioral scientists would regard participant observation as applicable to ongoing group social situations, but there can be no doubt that much observation of interpersonal interaction takes place while the clinician plays his role of expert in the examining situation.

Clinical interviewing is not a highly formalized technical skill like surgery or even diagnostic testing, but it does require experience, sensitivity and knowledge, and even a little "worldly wisdom" to do it successfully. Some general characteristics of clinical interviewing are perhaps best illustrated by comparing it with interviews in the profession of law.

When a lawyer interviews a client (let us say, a defendant in a criminal or civil suit), he is primarily interested in facts that will hold up in court or convince a jury of his client's innocence. This evidence must be strictly relevant and factual, preferably corroborated by documents, other exhibits, and witnesses. Feelings, thoughts, assumptions, and attitudes are considered to be largely immaterial and inadmissible, and so they are usually brushed aside. Even the client's motives or absence of motive is considered only insofar as it is relevant to the plausibility or implausibility of the defendant's guilt in this particular offense. As far as motivations developed in his past history and personality makeup are concerned, defense counsel is scarcely interested in how the client got along with his mother in childhood; how he made his adolescent sexual adjustments; and what he always dreamed of becoming when he grew up. As a partisan in an advocate system of jurisprudence, the defense counsel is obligated to prevent damaging testimony from being presented and to try to discredit it when it is presented, even if he suspects it is valid. Unless directly related to the case, the lawyer is not likely to probe into the client's personal habits, social values, cultural and recreational interests, or relations with family and friends.

The psychologist, on the other hand, is especially interested in all of the client's feelings, attitudes, emotional conflicts, ambitions, interpersonal relationships, and assumption of social roles. He is also interested in the childhood developmental pattern and the social interaction which brought about his client's present character structure and behavior patterns. To achieve a well-rounded clinical picture, he must not only take note of provable facts but also observe closely and "listen with the third ear," as Wilhelm Reich put it, to detect all the subtleties of accompanying affect, defensive distortions, suppressed desires, and hostilities that the client himself may be scarcely aware of. Even in the most casual conversation, the clinician is actively observing, interpreting, formulating impressions and hypotheses which become more and more structured as the interview progresses. It is quite in order if this includes clinical hunches and interpretations which would not hold up in court or even lend themselves to experimental verification. It is sufficient if it gives the clinician more insight into the subject's developing personality, experience, interests and skills, and motivational conflicts, so that he may better diagnose the case, make recommendations, or help the client gain self-insight. The interview is conducted in a sympathetic and confidential atmosphere, without witnesses or stenographers taking down testimony, and with no fear of imminent legal judgment and reprisal. Candor and confidentiality are, therefore, expected to be unlimited, even in the most sensitive areas of personal behavior and feelings. As in private dealings with a lawyer or a physician, the client's confidentiality is protected by both the professional ethics and legal sanctions of "privileged communication." That is, the psychologist cannot be compelled to reveal information obtained from the client if in his judgment it is confidential. The knowledge of this protected confidentiality, but even more, the client's confidence in the psychologist's professional integrity, greatly enhance the freedom of communication between the two. Not being involved in any partisan contest (for, even as an expert witness in a trial, the psychologist is supposed to be impartial), he attempts to assess and integrate *all* data, "with no holds barred" in his examination, to make as valid and unbiased an assessment of the case as he can.

CASE HISTORY

One of the most frequent uses of the clinical interview and observation is the construction of a case history of the individual being examined. This is different from an ordinary personnel record, because it goes into some depth to shed light on the etiology of a behavior disorder, the psychodynamics of the individual's values and motivational conflicts, and clues to the nature of the remedial measures required. It may even provide a background for an interpretive critique of qualifications for a position of responsibility, or a retrospective analysis of an individual's role in an historical episode. In other words, it not only establishes a sequence of historical facts but also lays the groundwork for the interpretation of those facts and reveals the individual as a living, unique personality with a past, present, and anticipated future. Psychological tests may give an immediate cross-sectional "x-ray" of a client's abilities and character structure, but only a case history can bring them to life in three-dimensional color and motion, with cause-and-effect relationships clearly indicated.

The amount of detail and type of focus of the case history will vary with the purpose of the interview or consultation. It may be extremely detailed if the examiner is attempting to explore all clues to the etiology of a behavior disorder with extensive psychosomatic, psychosexual, and psychosocial involvements. A psychoanalyst may use the case history as the beginning of his extensive therapeutic relationship with the patient, and probe deeply into childhood memories, fantasies, or dreams of psychosexual significance. A college counselor of the nondirective type would avoid all this probing, but would simply let the student tell what he wishes to tell about his background. If he is a counselor of more directive persuasion, he would at least want a thorough educational history and enough of the family background to illuminate the presenting problem of the student. (It usually turns out to be something much more intimate and emotional than the common presenting complaint of "study habits.") Yet, a psychiatric authority such as Sullivan (1954) would give short shrift to the educational history, because "Education is, so far as I am concerned, a clear index of the combination of foresight and blind ambition on the part of parents, wealthy relatives, and the patient." Most psychologists would not be so cavalier about such a vital aspect (in our culture) of secondary socialization and adult role learning and commitment.

If the psychologist is serving as personnel consultant for a private firm or a government agency, he might well have to be circumspect about the proprieties of probing into sensitive areas of personal experience and feelings (e.g., sex, religion, and politics). This severely restricts the scope of the case study, but it may be a necessary safeguard of the privacy of the individual in such settings. Some employers and government agencies require thorough examinations for responsible and sensitive positions, but leave it to the psychologist to safeguard the privacy and confidentiality of communication. In such cases, reliance is placed on the psychologist's final recommendation or evaluation, without submission of a detailed report. A detailed case history may still be kept in the psychologist's file, or in locked files in the consulting office of the institution, with no access given to the officials of the agency, firm, or school.

From the biosocial point of view, the case history should treat the developing personality as a continuing, dynamic integration of temperamental predisposition, basic generic drives, and the values and canalized motives that result in adult role commitments in social interaction. The following outline may be considered as being fairly typical of the range of information elicited in a moderately thorough case history, embellished, of course, by the nuances of affect and cognitive distortion detected by direct observation. It can be, and generally is, modified to suit the nature of the individual case and the purpose to which it is to be put.

Outline of Clinical Case History

Identifying data. Statement of age, occupation, and family status of client; source of referral and reason. Race, religion, nationality, and residence, if immediately relevant to the nature of referral or consultation.

Statement of problem and initial impression. Problem or purpose of consultation as seen by client; manner of presenting or acknowledging it; attitude toward interview situation. Physical appearance, poise, and affect; cooperation, candor, and insight displayed during interview; noteworthy behavior symptoms.

Family background. Order of birth and number of children in family; socioeconomic, occupational, and educational status of parents; marital harmony or discord between parents; age of client at time of any family disruption; surrogate or supplementary caring figures, if any.

Early developmental history. Any unusual aspects of motor, speech, or feeding development that client (or parent) is aware of; any disorders other than "usual childhood diseases." Awareness of parental treatment of him and siblings during early childhood. Any symptoms of emotional strain or instability, such as temper tantrums, bad dreams, periods of abandonment or hunger. Other primary group interactions: relations with siblings and playmates; relations with adult relatives and neighbors, particularly in giving or withholding affection. Secondary socialization experiences: reaction to school instruction, restraints, values, and any differential attitudes toward or from classmates, indicating social discrimination or acceptance. Growing awareness of social relations of family, and how that came about; effect on primary group relations and identification; inculcation of subcultural value system; hero figures; fantasies or ambitions of "what I wanted to be when I grew up." Early sex interests and habits— parental restraints, guilt feelings; inculcated moral and religious beliefs; other anxiety or guilt-provoking experiences. (Parent's version of all of above is desirable.)

Adolescence and adult role anticipation. Reaction to puberty; sex and romance in experience and fantasy; adolescent "crushes"; attitudes toward sex and marriage by example and indoctrination. Early learning, imitation, or practice of adult occupational role; how influenced by parents, teachers, public figures, or community. Influence of high school in preparing for adult roles or narrowing down expectations; study experience, dislikes and preferences; interpersonal relations, recreational and extracurricular activities. Further inculcation of social values through school, community, family interaction, and media of communication (press, TV, movies). Changes in relationships with parents, peers, or siblings. Romantic attachments or lack thereof. Frustrations or traumatic experiences; defensive reactions and strategies; influences on character formation or deviant tendencies. Signs of alienation or rebellion, experimentation with drugs or sex; reaction to such if encountered among peers.

Adult social role commitment and adjustment. If any college or graduate work, start with reasons for selecting area of specialization and success or frustrations in pursuing it. Significant college experiences, satisfactions, and frustrations. First job, age, and circumstances of employment, satisfactions or frustrations on job. Question of work and/or marriage (especially for woman), or timing of both (especially for man). History of employment; history of love affairs, courtship, marriage. Relations between marriage, occupational interests, social life. Sexual adjustment, temperamental adjustment, community of interests with spouse. Birth of children, delay or lack of children, and adjustments thereto. Progress of married and family life, occupational career or interests, social and recreational or further educational interests, particularly compatibility of all these between spouses if married, or in adjusting social and sexual needs if unmarried. Socioeconomic and health problems related to any or all of these. For more mature subjects: adjustment to children's growing up, becoming independent, leaving home, getting married. For man, success on job or in career. For woman, question of going to work or doing something useful with her time. Adjusting to older married life. If single: adjustment to prolonged bachelorhood. Widows and divorcees, ditto.

Present personal adjustment and mental health. Depending on nature of case and problems already encountered, focus on present adjustment, maladjustment, or psychopathology; interpretation of significance of deviant behavior as revealed by previous case history; problems and conflicts as seen by client, and as seen by clinician; practical considerations in confronting resolution, treatment, or choice of action. If no pathology involved, focus on character structure, qualifications, needs, as relevant to purpose of referral.

Diagnosis or recommendation. (As called for.) In case of clinical diagnosis, case will invariably be amplified by diagnostic tests; diagnosis offered, usually in terms of APA Diagnostic Handbook. In case of personnel selection or academic counseling, recommendation is usually made on basis of case history + aptitude tests.

Such outlines make it clear how much ground there is to cover in a moderately extensive case history, whether by direct questioning or volunteered information, usually a combination of both. It still leaves to the psychologist the task of focusing on the areas of particular conflict or salience in developing the character structure of the personality being examined, following the leads as they come to light in the course of the interview. He must be particularly alert to the significance of experiences which the client may wish to gloss over and the defense mechanisms which were called forth in living through certain experiences or in the telling about them. Above all, he must use his clinical perceptiveness and judgment to reconstruct the psychodynamic thread of cause and effect in personality development. This includes adjustments to the satisfaction of motivational needs at any and all levels—psychophysiological, psychological, and psychosocial, and at any stage of development. From the biosocial point of view, canalization and adjustment of needs or the provocation of anxieties may take place at any level of integration and may originate at any period of the life history. The interviewer may, therefore, not find it profitable to explore deeply into the circumstances of weaning and toilet-training and infantile sexuality on the assumption that all anxiety and character structure stems from repressed infantile sexuality. On the other hand, the early circumstances of being cared for, rejected, or neglected, may have a profound bearing on the individual sense of security developed early in life and the defensive patterns of interpersonal relationships that developed as a result. There are no pat formulas or guidelines for such clinical detective work. The interpretation and the very nature of the data elicited will depend in part on the clinician's theoretical orientation. More than that, however, they will depend on his sensitivity, empathy, and breadth of experience.

THE ASSESSMENT INTERVIEW

Many clinical or counseling settings do not call for such intensive interviewing and analysis or psychodynamics. They may require a rather summary or impressionistic evaluation of the subject's personality, qualifications, and motives for a specific purpose, on the basis of one extended interview, with or without test scores and background data. This would apply to many employment and placement situations, such as career and educational counseling of students, screening-out of deviant personalities in mass recruiting or college admissions, or selection for special assignments like the Peace Corps. The interviewing skill called for in such situations may be just as great as in the intensive clinical case history, but there is a premium on conciseness and relevance to the immediate purpose of the screening or summary assessment being undertaken. Here, for example, are brief personality descriptions written by an assessment psychologist on the basis of one-hour screening interviews with each of two female applicants to the Peace Corps, one accepted and one rejected. (This is part of a preliminary screening process sometimes used. More elaborate assessment procedures are provided during training.)

Candidate A. Pat is a bright, eager open-minded 23-year-old college graduate, who sees the Peace Corps as an opportunity for both a stimulating experience and a meaningful contribution. She is looking forward to involvement in community activities in addition to teaching English in a foreign setting. Her decision to enter the Peace Corps has the support of her family and is ideologically consistent with attitudes in the home, (mother is a member of the League of Women Voters), as well as her own belief in the importance of women utilizing their skills. Pat's approach is honest and flexible. She feels her concerns about professional inadequacy will be greatly reduced by the special training to be offered in this program. Sensitivity and awareness of psychological processes are evident.

Pat expresses no concern about future marriage possibilities, although no such plans exist now. She feels confident that she will ultimately marry and have a family. No pressure from home on this score. (Mother was 29 when she married.) She has never engaged in sexual relations and cannot see herself doing so outside of marriage, but has an open mind on the subject insofar as the conduct of others is concerned. She has also had a positive experience living away from home in a shared apartment with another girl, and enjoys travel.

She appears to be an outstanding candidate for an overseas teaching assignment after further training.

Candidate B. Vivian is a severely disturbed, isolated, desperate, very unhappy 25-year-old, who feels extremely thwarted in almost every way: sex identification and role acceptance, career, relationship with parents, etc. She feels that the avenues open to her have narrowed down to nothing and speaks as if living itself is a burden. She abhors teaching and any indoor confining environment. She has an active phobia of multi-legged organisms (lobsters, spiders, etc.). She feels people regard her as homosexual because of her masculine interests and behavior. She does admit that she would have been better off as a male, while her brother should have been a female, but says that she would be more properly described as asexual.

She has a keen sense of failure, having succeeded at nothing and not even being able to get along with her parents. She recently changed from their Baptist religion to the Lutheran, partly because the music and service were more appealing to her. She seems to have plunged into religious activity as a defensive affiliation, but was frustrated in her desire to undertake missionary work in Jordan. She tends to think of the Peace Corps as a last desperate resort to succeed at something, but does have a possibility of teaching in a Florida high school next fall. Although psychotherapy is clearly needed and has been suggested, she rejects it as something that would deprive her of her "individuality."

She is extremely ambivalent about volunteering and is a very poor risk for overseas assignment in any event.

Diagnostic

Tests   Psychological testing has long provided the psychologist's principal instrument for assessing individual differences in personality as well as one of the principal media for research in personality dynamics. The field of psychological testing or psychometrics covers a very broad range, including individual and group tests of intelligence, various kinds of achievement and aptitude tests for different skills and occupations, and a variety of tests of personality traits, symptoms, and behavior syndromes. The intelligence and aptitude tests, involving principally cognition and sensorimotor coordination, are clearly related to personality, as we have seen, because they are inevitably involved in the integration of personality and the determination of social role. However, it is customary to regard only those tests which expressly reveal attitudes, feelings, interpersonal relationships, or temperament, as personality tests in the stricter sense. These tests are generally of two kinds: the so-called objective or questionnaire type, and the less structured or projective type of examining instrument. The advantages of each type of test (which constitute disadvantages of the other type) may be summarized as follows:

Advantages of Objective Tests

Responses are definite, categorical responses to definite, direct questions, so may be scored objectively, at least categorically, to yield numerical ratings.

Standardization of scores or ratings readily achieved on basis of distribution of scores on representative population samples.

Reliability and validity of test may be computed by coefficients of correlations or by other statistical methods.

Scores on different tests may be easily compared if they test comparable variables or traits; "personality

Advantages of Projective Tests

Responses are spontaneous interpretations of ambiguous stimuli, reflecting subject's own feelings and thought processes; he is not aware of significance of his responses.

Subject not likely to be defensive or evasive in responses; has no way of deliberately creating favorable impression.

Clues to suppressed or repressed associations may be revealed implicitly or in disguised form, quite unwittingly.

Data not susceptible to direct questioning may be obtained (e.g., fan-

Advantages of Objective Tests (cont.)	*Advantages of Projective Tests* (cont.)
profile" may be constructed from a battery of subtests.	tasies, habits of perception and thinking).
Changes in individual subjects (e.g., improvement after therapy) may be readily measured.	Data reflecting uniqueness of individual personality come to light from unpredictable responses, since response possibilities are unlimited, all stemming from subject's imagination.
Group differences may be measured and significance computed; same for controlled experiments or changes over periods of time.	

In general, it can be seen from this sketchy list that the advantages of the objective tests lie principally in the examiner's ease of scoring and making comparative evaluations, while the advantages of the projective tests lie principally in the elicitation of more spontaneous and individually meaningful responses from the subject—with a heavier burden of interpretation left to the examiner. The advantages and limitations of each type predisposes them to somewhat different kinds of application, though either type can be used with any individual capable of taking a test.

PERSONALITY INVENTORIES

The objective or questionnaire type of test is essentially a highly structured and formalized interview which asks the same questions of all subjects and elicits categorical responses which can then be scored. Its objectivity and semblance of mathematical measurement rests on the arbitrary device of assigning a numerical value (usually 1) to each answer in each category and summarizing the categorical answers. The questions themselves are almost invariably of a subjective nature and so are susceptible to distortion and self-deception by the person being examined. Nevertheless, it does reflect *the way the subject sees himself*, which has a kind of face validity of its own. Some questionnaires are unidimensional in assessing a single trait (e.g., ascendance-submission, or masculinity-femininity), but the most popular ones are inventories that seek to establish a personality pattern or "profile" of traits or deviational tendencies.

The MMPI. One of the most widely used and thoroughly researched of these inventories is the Minnesota Multiphasic Personality Inventory, or MMPI (Hathaway and McKinley, 1951; Hathaway and Meehl, 1951). The test consists of 560 statements pertaining to a wide variety of functions: general health, psychosomatic symptoms, personal habits, familial relationships, religious and political attitudes, mood and emotional experiences, sex relations, ideational content, and fantasies, etc.—in addition to "catch questions" that detect the subject's tendency to systematic distortion of his answers. The subject is asked to indicate whether each statement is true, false, or "cannot say" with respect to himself. The 560 statements were intended to represent a pool of items in various categories, from which a comprehensive personality profile may be drawn in a variety of dimensions, based on empirical data. The nature and variety of items used may be seen from the following selection:

I have never felt better than I do now.
I have very few headaches.
I cannot keep my mind on one thing.
I have a great deal of stomach trouble.
I dream frequently.
I have used alcohol excessively.
I have very few quarrels with members of my family.
I have been disappointed in love.
I like to read newspaper editorials.
I am attracted by members of the opposite sex.
I believe there is a Devil and a Hell in afterlife.
I am a special agent of God.
I am easily embarrassed.
The future seems hopeless to me.
I often feel as if things are not real.
I like movie love scenes.
I am afraid of losing my mind.

Ten scales of diagnostic significance were developed, on the basis of responses by more than 800 patients in the neuropsychiatric division of the University Hospitals at the University of Minnesota and hundreds of normal subjects. These scales were based on the then-prevalent version of neuropsychiatric diagnosis plus the familiar masculinity-femininity and social introversion of previous psychological tests:

1. *Hypochondriasis* (Hs)
   Concern over health and bodily functions; complaints of pains and disorders difficult to identify and for which no clear organic basis can be found, in deliberate bid for sympathy.
2. *Depression* (D)
   Tendency to depressive mood, pessimistic outlook, worry, lack of self-confidence, narrowness of interest, and introversion.
3. *Hysteria* (Hy)
   Tendency to develop conversion-type hysterical symptoms, such as paralysis, contractures (e.g., writer's cramp), gastric or intestinal complaints, or cardiac symptoms, as means of solving problems confrontng him (without awareness, vagueness, or anxiety of hypochondriac).
4. *Psychopathic Deviate* (Pd)
   Tendency to antisocial and immoral or amoral behavior, lacking in deep emotional response or ability to profit from experience. Though potentially dangerous, they are outwardly normal and likeable; difficult to detect except when violating the social mores by persistent lying, stealing, alcoholsm, drug addiction, or sexual immorality.

5. *Masculinity-Femininity* (Mf)
   Tendency toward masculinity or femininity of interests, attitudes, habits, as established by social norms; high score does not necessarily imply homosexuality.
6. *Paranoia* (Pa)
   Tendency to suspiciousness, oversensitivity, and delusions of persecution, with or without expansive egotism, or of reference to self.
7. *Psychasthenia* (Pt)
   Presence of phobic or compulsive symptomatology, e.g., excessive hand-washing, repetitive ritualistic behavior, vacillation, unreasonable fear of things or situations or overreaction to them.
8. *Schizophrenia* (Sc)
   Disorientation (cutting off) from reality, with consequently inappropriate affect and irrational behavior, bizarre thoughts, delusions, erratic shifts in mood or impulse. (May refer to group of rather heterogeneous conditions.)
9. *Hypomania* (Ma)
   Overproductivity in thought and acton. Not manic, but impulsive, enthusiastic, and full of ideas.
10. *Social Introversion* (Si)
    Tendency to withdraw from social contacts; shyness, self-deprecation, uneasiness in social situations.

Although the correlation with psychiatric diagnostic terminology had some practical advantages in clinical work, the test was, unfortunately, standardized on a basic conceptual framework which was itself open to serious question, and continues to be revised. *Psychopathic deviate*, for example, had already become recognized as a rather meaningless wastebasket category for any type of antisocial or criminal behavior, which was changed to other diagnostic concepts in later editions of the psychiatric *Diagnostic Manual*. There is still much debate over whether *schizophrenia* is a unitary disease process or a collection of different ones. Nevertheless, the MMPI continues to be used as a screening device for signs of deviant behavior patterns, and its pool of question items has given rise to several other scales and inventories which are not committed to psychiatric diagnosis (e.g., Taylor Manifest Anxiety Scale).

A difficulty that is of greater significance for personality theory, and which apparently applies to all inventories, is the question of the subject's tendency to give socially desirable responses on such tests—the SD factor pointed out by Edwards (1957, 1964). Much discussion has ensued over whether SD effects are merely the result of having socially well-adjusted subjects like college students give SD responses because they are socially well-adjusted, or because most people tend to dissemble a bit in order to make a good impression on the examiner. (Both hypotheses would be consistent with biosocial theory.)

In an attempt to resolve this question, Megargee (1966) compared three groups whose motivation and adjustment could be surmised from the selective nature of each group and the circumstances under which the test was taken. A group of 21 Peace Corps volunteers was assumed to be well-adjusted (having been carefully screened in the selection process) and motivated to make a good impression just prior to final selection for overseas assignment. Another group of 41 college students were assumed to be well-adjusted but not especially motivated to make a good impression, because they took the test anonymously for research purposes only. A third group consisted of 65 disturbed criminals applying for probation. They constituted a group that was maladjusted but highly motivated to make a good impression. The MMPI responses of all three groups were scored on the Edwards SD Scale. The Peace Corps group scored significantly higher than both of the other groups, indicating that *both* adjustment and social motivation operated in raising SD scores. Other studies tend to minimize the SD effect, but Edwards' data (1964) are fairly definitive.

The Edwards PPS. Benefiting from his own criticisms of other personality questionnaire inventories, Edwards devised his own Personal Preference Schedule (PPS). This inventory was designed to reflect the relative importance of different motives for normal young adults, in somewhat the same manner as the Allport-Vernon-Lindzey Study of Values, largely bypassing the problem of choices that involve social desirability versus stigma. Nevertheless, the susceptibility of certain items to the SD factor was further minimized by pairing items of equal SD in the forced choices in the test construction. The motives that are weighed are derived from the Murray scheme of needs, developed in connection with the TAT, which we shall review in the forthcoming section on projective techniques. These needs, which represent largely psychological and partly psychosocial levels of integration, are as follows:

Achievement—to do one's best, to accomplish something very difficult or very significant.
Deference—to let others make decisions, to conform to what is expected of one.
Order—to have regular times and ways for doing things, to keep things neat and well-organized.
Exhibition—to be the center of attention, to say witty things or talk about personal achievements.
Autonomy—to be independent of others in making decisions, to avoid responsibilities and obligations.
Affiliation—to be loyal, to participate in friendly groups, to share or do things with friends.
Intraception—to analyze one's motives and feelings, to observe and understand the feelings of others.
Succorance—to receive help or affection from others, to have others be sympathetic and understanding.

Dominance—to persuade and influence others, to supervise others, to be regarded as a leader.

Abasement—to feel guilty when one has done wrong, to accept blame, to feel timid or inferior.

Nurturance—to help friends or others in trouble, to forgive others, to be generous with others.

Change—to do new and different things, to meet new people, to travel, to take up new fads and fashions.

Endurance—to keep at a job until it is finished, to avoid being interrupted while hard at work.

Heterosexuality—to go out with or be in love with one of the opposite sex, to tell or listen to sex jokes.

Aggression—to attack contrary points of view, to become angry, to make fun of others or tell them off.

The test norms were standardized on a census-representative sampling of 9,000 adults and a college sample of 1,500 from 29 institutions. Whether compared to his own occupational or student group, or simply analyzed by inspection, a subject's motivational profile on the Edwards PPS is likely to provide some interesting clues to "what makes him tick." In the usual kind of counseling or personnel selection situation, in which psychiatric diagnosis is not at issue, such a profile is likely to yield additional insights to the case history interview. Since the test is designed to elicit motivational patterns, rather than symptoms of disturbance, it is better suited to exploring the psychodynamics of normal personalities than the diagnosis of deviant types.

Other widely used self-report or questionnaire tests designed to elicit ratings on predetermined traits would include: the California Personality Inventory, the Gordon Personality Profile, the Allport-Vernon-Lindzey Study of Values, and the Omnibus Personality Inventory.

FACTOR ANALYSIS INVENTORIES

A somewhat different approach to personality inventory construction is represented by the factor-analysis technique. By the use of statistical analysis and the combination of appropriate test items, an attempt is made to construct a broad profile of characteristics with as little overlapping as possible. A leading example of the factor-analyzed inventory is the Guilford-Zimmerman Temperament Survey. This inventory consists of ten characteristics of personality or temperament, each tested by items, to which the subject may reply: "Yes," "?," or "No."

G   *General Activity:* Productivity, vitality, speed and efficiency vs. unproductive and dilatory activity.
R   *Restraint:* deliberation and persistence vs. carefree, impulsive excitability.
A   *Ascendance:* dominance vs. submissiveness.
S   *Sociability:* ability to make many friends, liking for social activity vs. being shy and friendless.

E   *Emotional Stability:* optimistic, even-tempered composure vs. pessimistic, excitable, fluctuating moodiness.
O   *Objectivity:* impersonal, accurate, somewhat insensitive observations vs. hypersensitive, self-centered suspicious tendencies.
F   *Friendliness:* warm and respectful acceptance of others vs. hostile, resentful, or domineering relationships.
T   *Thoughtfulness:* reflective, observant, mental poise vs. less reflective interest in overt activity.
P   *Personal Relations:* tolerance and faith in social institutions vs. fault-finding, uncooperative self-pity.
M   *Masculinity:* hard-boiled and unemotional activity vs. romantic sentimentality.

In view of the rather obvious social desirability of most of the above traits, the GZTS is regarded as somewhat susceptible to the SD effect. This is more easily detected, however, in an inventory of largely unrelated (low intercorrelation) factors.

R. B. Cattell (1956) extends the factor-analytic concept with a different set of factors which he called "source traits" in contradistinction to the usual "surface traits" of other inventories. The 16 Personality Factor inventory of Cattell (16 P.F.) contains 374 forced-choice items on two forms of an inventory, which permit ratings on each of the following 16 factors:

A.   *Cyclothymia vs. Schizothymia* (fluctuating vs. detached affect)
B.   *General Intelligence*
C.   *Ego Strength* (basic normality)
E.   *Dominance*
F.   *Surgency vs. Desurgency*
G.   *Super-Ego Strength* (susceptibility to social control)
H.   *Immunity* (or *Adventurous Cyclothymia*)
I.   *Sensitivity vs. Toughness*
L.   *Paranoid Trend* (suspiciousness, ideas of persecution or personal reference)
O.   *Free Anxiety*
Q_1 *Radicalism vs. Conservatism*
Q_2 *Self-Sufficiency*
Q_3 *Will Control*
Q_4 *Tension* (*Somatic Anxiety*)

PROJECTIVE TECHNIQUES

In Chapter 8 we discussed the various ways in which cognitive styles and content may be related to other personality variables such as motivation, attitudes, identifications, and value systems. In the foregoing discussion of personality inventories, we have also seen that complications affecting the "objectivity" of such tests are the subject's response-set tendencies—such as bias toward social desirability or to acquiescence. Projective techniques are expressly designed to elicit subjective reactions by the use of unstructured test material to which the subject reacts freely. Almost any kind of vehicle can be used, but such instruments all have in common the reliance on the subject's own interpretation of ambiguous stimuli, through which he "projects" his own perceptual styles and biases, attitudes, and emotional conflicts. Although such test material may be improvised for any given subject or situation, interpretation and comparisons are easier when a set of materials or stimuli has been selected by empirical sampling of a wide range of subjects whose personality patterns and deviations are already known.

Inkblot tests. The Rorschach Psychodiagnostic Test is the "grandfather" of all projective tests, having been introduced in 1921 by the Swiss psychiatrist, Hermann Rorschach. He noticed that differently diagnosed patients tended to make different kinds of interpretations and distortions of ambiguous visual stimuli like inkblots. Accordingly, he decided to systematize his observations on a set of ten large inkblot figures selected by trial and error to yield maximum discrimination among the various diagnostic categories. Although no two sets of figure interpretations could ever be quite the same, certain characteristics of these subjective cognitions were found to be either logically or empirically revealing of certain thought patterns.

Thus, for example, there was the habitual *mode of organization* of the perceptual field: some globally integrated; some meticulously detailed and compulsively complete; some orderly in proceeding from the general to the particular; some highly disorganized. There were different degrees of *accuracy* of perceptions reported (reality-testing): some with 100 percent accurate form criteria (all figures relevant to the form of the blots); some with very loosely structured and far-fetched interpretations, or even bizarre responses unrelated to the form of the inkblots. Then there was the extent of empathic *projections of human life* into some of these vague forms, which might reveal anything from empathic adult creativity to paranoid delusional preoccupations, depending on the propriety of the interpretations. The underlying *determinants* of the figures seen could vary from rigid adherence to the most obvious outlines of familiar objects to highly imaginative originality in structuring the percepts. Then there was the *content* of the figures seen. This, in conjunction with other signs, could distinguish the exuberant, highly responsive, warm and productive individual from the morbid, depressed, emotionally and intellectually constricted personality. The total pattern of responses, when analyzed on these and other criteria, could usually distinguish between major categories of mental diseases. It could also distinguish between the normal, healthy adult and the maladjusted individual whose anxieties kept him in a constant state of turmoil.

As refinements were developed on the basis of empirical studies by numerous investigators in America, the Rorschach inkblot technique was established as a useful diagnostic instrument in the hands of experts. Among many early studies, Benjamin and Ebaugh (1938) obtained complete agreement on diagnosis by Rorschach and by psychiatric examination in 39 out of 46 cases and rough agreement in 5 more. Krugman (1942) obtained an average of 84 percent correct matchings of Rorschach records against clinical descriptions of 25 problem children made by five judges. Subsequent studies (reviewed by Zubin, 1954) cast some doubt on the diagnostic reliability and validity of the Rorschach when analyzed by atomistic "signs," especially in blind analysis of the protocol alone. However, global content analysis and direct examination of the patient by the clinician generally yielded more valid results.

In clinical practice, the way in which the different figures seen by different people reflect their individualized perceptual worlds is often striking, indeed. Let us take, for example, two responses to Card II on the Rorschach test, elicited from two of the many hundreds of subjects examined by the author. One exuberant young college coed responded, "Oh, look! They're the most darling little clowns dancing around a fire with red dunce-caps on their heads—sort of dressed up for a Hallowe'en party. They're having a gay old time, playing patty-cake, dancing around a fire." The inkblot figures *can*, of course, look like dancing clowns, but it was her imagination that put them there. Another subject saw them quite differently—"Well, I don't know anything about these things . . . but the artist, whoever he is, painted some gruesome picture of two decaying corpses with broken legs and blood still dripping from the broken splinters of the leg bones—but I know nothing about these things. That's just what the artist painted." The subject who gave the latter response was an SS-Gestapo concentration camp officer, who had already been sentenced to hang for participation in the things he "knew nothing about." He was quite unaware that his own habitualized mode of perception had projected his sadistic tendencies into "that gruesome picture the artist painted."

Such vivid content revelations of cognitive-affective individuality are by no means the rule in Rorschach examination, however. The clinician must depend on a complex set of quasiquantitative scoring devices and formulas with more or less vaguely stated syndromes for different kinds of personality deviations and traits. Since the total number of responses is extremely variable, and the number of inkblots too few to tap a wide range of responses in all subjects, the application of such formulas is highly unreliable at best. Although the expert clinician with extensive experience in the use of the Rorschach may overcome these difficulties, as was achieved in the Benjamin and Ebaugh study, a better-standardized technique would be more easily applicable by the average clinician.

Accordingly, Holtzman and his associates (1961) developed a new set of inkblots that sacrificed some of the advantages of spontaneous and

Figure 10–1. Card II on the Rorschach inkblot test. (*Top details and lower center are colored red in the original.*) (*By permission of Huber & Co.*)

unlimited responses in favor of a better-standardized technique of testing and scoring. The Holtzman Inkblot Technique (HIT) consists of two equivalent sets of 45 inkblots, which may be used for retest purposes (e.g., before and after therapy). On each set, the subject gives just one interpretive response to each inkblot, or 45 responses in all. Each response is then scored on 22 variables such as: reaction time, location, form definiteness, form appropriateness, color, movement, pathognomonic verbalization (such as queer responses, incoherence, autistic logic), and human, animal, anatomical or abstract content, etc. Many of these variables were derived from the original Rorschach scoring categories, but were further refined; some were new, but all were made more easily scoreable according to definite criteria. The total score for each variable is arrived at by simple summation across all 45 inkblot cards, yielding a profile of 22 scores. Scoring reliabilities between two examiners on 40 schizophrenic patients ran about .92 to .99 on the 22 inkblot variables. The order of validity in diagnosis, once a pattern has been established empirically for a given mental disease, is indicated by a study by Mosely (1962), who was able to distinguish between 100 normals and 100 schizophrenics 90 percent of the time. Because this technique combines many of the advantages we have listed for both objective and projective tests, wider use and more extensive research applicability may be expected from this technique. It has already been found useful in cross-cultural longitudinal personality research (Holtzman *et al.*, 1968).

Picture story tests. Clues to cognitive-affective style and pathology may be detected in the interpretive responses to unstructured inkblot figures, but only indirect inferences may be drawn concerning the subject's social behavior. To elicit projection of personality characteristics at the psychosocial level, we must use media that allow for the projection of interpersonal relationships and social attitudes. Such a test is the Thematic Apperception Test (TAT), which is frequently used to supplement the findings of an inkblot test with data that are more amenable to the psychosocial level of analysis.

The TAT was developed at Harvard University in the late 1930s by H. A. Murray and his associates, as a medium for revealing individual motivational needs and conflicts, particularly in the interpersonal-social sphere. The subject is simply shown a series of cards with pictures of various kinds and asked to tell a story suggested by the picture. The complete series consists of two sets of 10 pictures for each sex, many of which are included for both sexes. Some of the pictures are readily suggestive of intrafamilial relationships; some merely show an individual in an undefined "mood"; and some are vague scenes without people.

The rationale of this technique is also based on the assumption that an individual perceiving the ambiguous situations presented by the pictures will unwittingly project his own feelings and attitudes into his interpretation of the pictures, and that he will identify with the leading figure in the story he constructs and thus reveal some clues to his personality. The stories woven around these pictures out of his own fantasy may reveal affection or hostility toward parental figures, emphasis on needs and frustrations, feelings of guilt or inferiority, and social attitudes and values that are really his own. Allowance must be made, of course, for stories based on stories read or scenes witnessed, but even here it is assumed that the subject's selective memory reveals his needs and attitudes. Lindzey (1952) has reviewed a number of these assumptions and the evidence supporting them—or the lack of such evidence. In general, subsequent research has proven them to be fairly plausible, though not infallible.

Thus, although the main character or "hero" in one story may not reliably reflect the feelings, goals, values, and conflicts of the storyteller, it is regarded as highly probable that any *persistent theme* running through many of his stories will be a projection of his own motivations. There is still some question whether these qualities appear directly, symbolically, or in overcompensated form (as in reaction formation, in which a selfish sadist will spin yarns about a sweet humanitarian idealist). On the basis of the frequency, intensity, and salience, each of the various emotional needs exhibited by the hero in each story can be rated on a scale of 1 to 5. A cumulative total may be obtained for each of the needs posited by Murray, in order to get a rough indicator of the relative strength of such needs. The same may be done for a list of environment stresses or pressures (called *press*) exerted on the heroes as perceived by the subject. The test manual lists 28 such needs and press (1943):

Needs	*Press*
(Motives and feelings of leading figures or heroes)	(Forces in the heroes' environment)
	Affiliation
Abasement	associative
Achievement	emotional
Aggression	Aggression
emotional & verbal	emotional & verbal
physical, social	physical, social
physical, asocial	physical, asocial
destruction	destruction of property
Dominance	Dominance
Intragression	coercion
Nurturance	restraint
Passivity	inducement, seduction
Sex	Nurturance
Succorance	Rejection
	Lack, loss
	Physical danger
	Physical injury

This is merely a suggested list of needs and stresses found by Murray and his collaborators to occur frequently in the stories of the many subjects they tested in the course of developing this test. As may be readily seen, the items deal principally with interpersonal relationships and so lend themselves to analysis at the psychosocial level of personality integration. In actual practice, many clinicians find it unnecessary to go through a systematic rating of all the listed needs and press on all the TAT cards. A scanning of the stories on a selected number of cards often gives the examiner the information he is looking for: clues to the filial origins of reactions to authority, problems of sex role or other social-role conflict, prevalence of depression or euphoria (exaggerated feeling of well-being) in outlook on life, dominant-submissive patterns of relating to peers, apprehension over stresses for achievement, and others.

Particularly germane to the psychodynamics of personality is Murray's list of motives. Many of the needs we have enumerated as being operant at different levels of integration (Chapter 2) are listed as needs by Murray or implicitly included under press. Thus associative and emotional affiliation may be thought of as more of an individual need than as a force in the environment. Rejection is a force in the environment only insofar as acceptance represents a universal need which is being frustrated in the individual concerned. On the whole, we would regard the distinction between need and press as somewhat artificial, since we are dealing fundamentally with interpersonal relations, which depend on reciprocal relations of generic and canalized drives. In such relationships, one man's environmental stress is another man's (or his own) drive. We would also question whether the four varieties of aggression are either needs or press per se, but would regard them as reactions to the frustration of needs. In any case, the analysis of TAT stories by a skilled clinician makes it possible to draw inferences about the subject's motives and interpersonal relations which are basic considerations in the evaluation of any individual personality structure.

Retest and interjudge reliabilities on rating TAT themes have been reported on the order of .7 to .9, which is quite satisfactory for a projective test. Validity remains a moot point, as usual, because it is difficult to define independent criteria and still more difficult to give predictive ratings to thematic productions which do not even have deviant personality types as their frame of reference.

Several other varieties of the TAT technique have been devised to facilitate projection: by children (Children's Apperception Test by Bellak and Bellak, 1950); by Negroes (Thompson Modification of the TAT, 1949); and by subjects in other cultures and countries, of which there are many versions. An interesting departure from the TAT technique is the Make-A-Picture-Story (MAPS) Test of Schneidman (1947). The MAPS test allows the subject (usually a child or adolescent) to participate more actively in the storymaking process by selecting his cast of characters from among 67 cardboard figures, placing them, stagelike, on the table against a cardboard background scene, and then telling a story about the scene he has created. The examiner may use a checklist of some 800 signs of selection and treatment of the figures, but basically must rely on his qualitative observation of the performance to interpret the subject's attitudes, motives, primary group relationships, and cultural adaptation.

Human Figure Drawings. The drawing of a human figure (usually both male and female), is sometimes used as a means of obtaining a projection

Figure 10–2. Material for a projective picture-story test. *The Schneidman Make-A-Picture-Story (MAPS) Test provides a number of cardboard figures which the subject may use to create a dramatic scene before one of several backgrounds. (Courtesy of The Psychological Corporation.)*

of a subject's self-concept or body image, social role, and relations with the opposite sex. The differences in the presentation of human male and female figures by different individuals seem to be independent of artistic ability and to yield signs which are somewhat indicative of maladjustment, gross pathology, retardation, or normality. Occasionally, they provide clues to the particular nature of the emotional conflicts and defenses of the subjects. Drawing a small, childish-looking man and a large, buxom woman may indicate a regressive sense of dependency and yearning for succorance if the subject is a man. Omitting or exaggerating sexual differentiation between the two figures may indicate homosexual tendencies. Leaving the hands off may be a clue to sadistic or masochistic tendencies or a feeling of impotence. Any one of these signs may at least be a clue to some emotional conflict, and all three of them would almost certainly be. However, it is dangerous to jump to conclusions in interpreting signs that seem to have an "obvious" significance.

To remove some of the conjecture from such interpretations, at least for children, Koppitz (1968) did a normative study of 1,856 American public school children, ranging in age from 5 to 13. The relative frequency of different signs were tabulated by age and sex for the standardization group, and comparisons were then made between matched normal and disturbed groups. In one such study, 12 of 30 "Emotional Indicators" were found to be significant at the .10 to .01 level. It is further noted that the presence of two or more such signs increase the discrimination between normal and deviant to the .001 level. Although it is not suggested that such "signs" should be used mechanically to discriminate between normal and maladjusted, they do provide a realistic baseline for interpretation.

Table 10-1 EMOTIONAL INDICATORS ON HFDS OF CLINIC PATIENTS (GROUP A) AND WELL-ADJUSTED PUPILS (GROUP B)
(After Koppitz, 1968)

Emotional Indicators	Group A	Group B	χ^2	P
Poor integration	9	0	7.07	.01
Shading of body, limbs	10	1	6.63	.01
Shading of hands, neck	5	0	3.36	.10
Asymmetry of limbs	5	0	3.31	.10
Slanting figure	11	0	9.80	.01
Tiny figure	10	0	8.67	.01
Big figure	7	0	5.55	.02
Transparencies	8	2	2.68	.10
Short arms	11	3	3.85	.05
Big hands	5	0	3.31	.10
Hands cut off	11	3	3.85	.05
No neck	7	0	5.66	.02

For the purpose of interpreting the psychodynamics of each case it is best, of course, to analyze the figure drawings in the light of the case history and other tests such as the Rorschach and TAT. This step is not just to confirm the fact that the child or adult *is* maladjusted—that may be the most obvious thing about the case, from the very fact of referral—but to round out the clinical picture and etiology of just what the nature of the emotional conflict is, how it came about, what defense mechanisms and defensive strategies are being used, and how these factors may be exploited or overcome in psychotherapy.

The use of such batteries of tests in conjunction with a case history and direct observation is far more revealing than any single test, but still leaves a great deal to the "clinical intuition" of the examining psychologist. That does not mean he must be possessed of some mysterious "sixth sense" to interpret and interrelate a variety of clinical data, but that his sensitivity as a person, refined by clinical training and experience, will enable him to make valid inferences the rationale of which he cannot easily verbalize or state in a mathematical formula. It is conceivable, of course, that with enough data of the sort collected by Koppitz for the HFD and by Holtzman for the HIT, one might eventually reduce psychodiagnostic testing to a computerized operation. But it is difficult to see how the qualitative and psychodynamic aspects of such evaluation, aside from diagnostic labeling, can ever be reduced to mathematical formulas. At any rate, until that scientific millennium arrives, clinicians will have to make the best use they can of that ultimate clinical instrument, empathic-sensitivity-refined-by-disciplined-judgment, with just enough anchoring to empirical data to provide a check on such judgments.

Such multifaceted evaluation by competent clinicians is often provided for in well-staffed mental hygiene clinics and mental hospitals, in sensitive governmental selection programs such as the Peace Corps, and in private or industrial consulting settings. However, it must be stressed that the accuracy and insightfulness of such personality evaluations depend on face-to-face examination of a reasonably cooperative and candid subject by a reasonably competent and experienced psychologist. Exercises in the "blind diagnosis" of case history data and test scores of individuals whom a group of judges has never even seen (e.g., Little and Schneidman, 1959) can scarcely discredit direct examination by competent clinicians who select their own instruments and methods of dynamic interpretation.

Summary Clinical examination for diagnostic or other evaluative purposes involves three basic techniques: interviewing, observation, and testing. Observation is usually carried out in conjunction with interviewing and testing in the face-to-face examining situation. One of the principal uses of interviewing is to establish the factual and psychodynamic background of the individual's personality development through the case history. Screening or summary assessment interviews seek to evaluate a candidate's suitability for a specific purpose.

Personality tests are of two general types: the questionnaire or "objective" type and the unstructured or "projective" type. The latter consists of material to be interpreted by the subject, such as inkblots, pictures to be made into stories, incomplete sentences to be completed, pictures to be drawn, etc. Clinicians generally prefer the projective type of test because it gives the subject free rein to reveal his own emotional preoccupations, it is more likely to yield clues to his own motivational dynamics, and is not as subject to self-deception or deliberate distortion. However, such tests have the disadvantage of not being readily standardized, scored, validated, or compared in "before and after" situations.

It is emphasized that the ultimate testing instrument is the trained clinician himself. Furthermore, the combined use of firsthand case history, test data, and observations by a sensitive clinician is likely to produce keener insight into the individual personality than games of "blind diagnosis" from records alone would indicate.

II

Antisocial
Behavior

Diagnosing
Criminal
Behavior   Although we stated that an explicit treatment of psychopathology was beyond the scope of the present volume, there are at least
two reasons why antisocial or criminal behavior warrants our attention
here. One is that the rather widespread and persistent violation of social
codes by some individuals in many societies around the world seems to
contradict the biosocial thesis that human beings generally tend to conform to their inculcated social mores—that it is this inherent tendency
in the emergent evolution of human nature that has made culture possible. How, then, do we account for the widespread phenomenon of
antisocial behavior on the part of juvenile delinquents and adult criminals and the fact that in varying degrees most individuals seem susceptible
to lapses from social conformity? The other is the oft-disputed question
whether antisocial behavior—even that of the confirmed criminal—represents a type of mental disorder in the usual psychiatric sense. The need
for clarification is evident when we consider that, on the one hand,
psychiatry has always provided some kind of diagnostic nomenclature for
habitual criminals, as though this constituted some kind of mental disease, while psychologists and sociologists have usually found crime to be
correlated with social conditions or the individual's environment and not
confined to any discernible personality type or pathology. Furthermore,

the designation of criminality is inescapably dependent on the nature of existing laws or mores in a given time and place, and it has never been quite clear how clinical diagnosis could be so dependent on circumstantial factors.

It is possible, of course, that only those with a particular type of deviant personality structure will indulge in behavior specifically proscribed by the culture, whatever that may be, so that we would be diagnosing an underlying personality defect rather than a proneness to a particular type of social offense. That was, in fact, the position implied by the old psychiatric diagnoses of the "criminal psychopath" or "sociopathic reaction." However, even that implied rationale foundered on the lack of evidence for any consistent pattern of psychopathology or character defect among habitual criminals.

The key to the problem of social nonconformity has already been hinted at in the paradox of the conforming nonconformist and the compensatory or alternative satisfaction of social ego needs (Chapter 7). The rigid codes of conduct of the juvenile delinquent gang, the adherence to an ideological "cause" by many revolutionists and counterrevolutionists, even the professed ideals of tyrant and assassin alike, as well as the "honor among thieves" and the camaraderie among the social misfits of any description all testify to the fact that some degree of social conformity is being observed even by the most violent and deviant of the nonconformists. As to the problem of psychiatric diagnosis versus atypical social behavior, it is best to review briefly the background and present status of the confusion.

RISE AND FALL OF THE "CONSTITUTIONAL PSYCHOPATH"

During the latter part of the nineteenth century and early part of the twentieth, as the theory of evolution gained ever wider acceptance, psychiatrists and criminologists placed a great deal of credence in the hereditary trait concept of the "born criminal." This was most clearly expressed in the Lombrosian theory (1911), in which the criminal type of personality was supposed to be an atavistic reversion or "throwback" to man's caveman ancestors in the hereditary endowment of an occasional unfortunate individual. Such an individual was presumably incapable of exercising normal self-restraint and moral judgment, because the primitive mentality he inherited failed to provide these necessary capacities for civilized living. Lombroso even held that such criminal types could be recognized by certain physiological or physiognomic "stigmata of degeneracy," such as a receding forehead, low forehead hairline, meeting eyebrows, receding lower jaw, or an ingrown earlobe, etc. Unfortunately for the theory, investigations showed that criminals could not be distinguished from noncriminal populations on the basis of such stigmata. Goring (1913), for example, showed that the so-called stigmata were just as prevalent among students at Oxford and Cambridge as they were among the inmates of the London prisons. Although this careful study went far toward discrediting Lombroso's theory and the general notion of the "born criminal type," the idea persisted in psychiatric diagnosis. First the diagnostic term *constitutional psychopathic inferior* was used to designate those who were thought to be (on the basis of their criminal records) "born criminals" (as popular usage had it), or "moral imbeciles" (as British law designated it). In any event, these people were supposed to be innately incapable of abiding by the rules of civilized living.

As it became clear in time that many habitual criminals were fairly normal intellectually and physically, the term *inferior* was dropped, and the diagnosis *constitutional psychopathic personality* applied. However, the constitutional basis for criminal behavior came more and more into disrepute as research advanced, so by the time of World War II the *constitutional* part of the diagnosis was fairly generally discarded and the vague designation of *psychopathic personality* was retained as a diagnostic term for persistent criminal and socially degenerate behavior.

This was the diagnosis that prevailed in psychiatric circles all through the 1940s and early 1950s to designate an assumed behavior disorder underlying persistent criminality and violation of the social mores. It was frankly recognized as a "wastebasket diagnosis" or ill-defined repository for a variety of social misfits who were not demonstrably psychotic, neurotic, or feeble-minded, but were nevertheless always in trouble with society. Unfortunately, there never was any clear-cut definition of just what a psychopathic personality was supposed to be, clinically speaking, except by exclusion of the other major syndromes and the checking of traits that could be assumed in anyone who had a record of repeated criminal offenses (e.g., shows lack of restraint of selfish impulses, does not profit by experience). Even so, the incidence of the psychopathic syndrome was found to be surprisingly low in delinquent and prison populations. Other psychological defects were found to be just as frequent (Healy and Bronner, 1939; Bromberg and Thompson, 1937), and the absence of any gross defect was even more frequent. To make matters worse from a clinical point of view, sociological and psychological research repeatedly showed that the incidence of crime was related to circumstances of social marginality and disorganization, as well as ethnic, ecological, and circumstantial factors.

The upshot of a losing battle to relate criminal behavior to psychiatric diagnosis has been the recognition, in recent years, that social and circumstantial factors play at least as important a part as deviant personality structure in determining antisocial behavior, and that no single syndrome predominates. As a result, a postwar revision of the APA's psychiatric *Diagnostic Manual* (1952) included *Sociopathic Personality Disturbance* in place of the former *Psychopathic Personality* as the proper diagnostic label for individuals whose behavior finds them in continual difficulties with society:

Individuals placed in this category are ill primarily in terms of society and of conformity with the prevailing cultural milieu, and not only in terms of personal discomfort and relations with other individuals. However, sociopathic reactions are very often symptomatic of severe underlying personality disturbance, neurosis, or psychosis, or occur as the result of organic brain injury or disease. . . .

This statement was correct as far as it went, but unfortunately left the question of psychiatric diagnosis as much up in the air as ever. Are we dealing here with an actual deviant personality syndrome or just another label for a wastebasket category for people who, for one reason or another, do not get along well with society? If individuals thus diagnosed are "ill primarily in terms of society and of conformity to the prevailing cultural milieu," is it society or the individual who is ill? On the one hand, is this disturbed social relationship not true of all mental disease? On the other, is personality disturbance or illness a proper concept to apply to amoral, immoral, or unconventional behavior per se, when this may or may not be symptomatic of commonly understood behavior disorders? In other words, may not the concept of a criminal type of mental disorder be entirely superfluous? Do we not have to distinguish between psychopathology and social pathology and then deal with the relationship between the two? The *Diagnostic Manual* of 1952 failed to give any independent criteria for diagnosing the sociopathic disturbance, but merely compounded the confusion by offering a kind of diagnostic breakdown by type of offense involved: *antisocial reaction, dyssocial reaction, sexual deviation,* and *addiction.*

Finally, to avoid the many pitfalls of diagnosis by type of social offense, the latest revision of the *Diagnostic Manual* (1968) merely falls back on the device of including a generalized *antisocial personality* among the ten "personality disorders" which it lists as being "characterized by deeply ingrained maladaptive patterns of behavior that are perceptibly different in quality from psychotic and neurotic symptoms." We have already quoted these descriptions under "deviant personality types" in Chapter 9. The question of whether there really is any distinguishable antisocial personality syndrome or type still remains. The problem of psychiatric diagnosis by social offense has not been entirely resolved, especially since social offenders manifestly cut across all types of personality disorders.

The evolution of diagnostic convention from the untenable *constitu-*

tional psychopath to the clinically confusing or irrelevant *antisocial personality* thus represents an advance from gross error to mere ambiguity. Some clarification is clearly called for if we are to understand this aspect of personality dynamics. Since there is as yet no commonly accepted resolution to the confusion surrounding antisocial behavior, we may present our own carefully considered viewpoint, based on years of experience with criminals and deviates of all varieties, and conceived within the comprehensive framework of biosocial theory.

PSYCHOSOCIAL LEVEL OF ANALYSIS

The principal source of ambiguity, as we see it, is the confusion of levels of analysis and the misapplication of diagnostic concepts at levels to which they do not apply. In other words, there must be a distinction between a sick individual and a sick society or the value judgments that society places on the social behavior which is symptomatic of this illness. Psychiatry, as a branch of medicine which is concerned with the behavior disorders of the individual, properly applies its concepts of psychopathology to the analysis of behavior at either the psychophysiological level or the psychological level of behavior. This may include a wide range of disturbances from neuroendocrine to cognitive-affective functions. Disturbances of behavior at the psychosocial level (e.g., interpersonal relations, role behavior, conformity or nonconformity to the social mores), may be predicated on such organismic disturbances, but psychiatric concepts are not necessarily appropriate, valid, or relevant at that level of analysis. Thus we may distinguish clinically the inadequate personality, the schizoid personality, the paranoid personality, the emotionally unstable personality, the passive-dependent personality, and a host of others. But it only confuses matters clinically to lump together all those individuals whose social behavior happens to violate the social mores as *antisocial personalities*, as though that really constitutes a definite type or syndrome unlike any of the others. Such pseudodiagnosis, which by-passes the psychodynamics and the essential characteristics of the individual case, is rendered highly inconsistent by virtue of the fact that a wide variety of deviant personalities, and some that are not so very deviant, may become habitual criminals.

By way of illustration: murderers, who surely exhibit a clear-cut type of antisocial behavior, have not been found to exhibit any one specific type of deviant personality. They include cool, insensitive schizoids who may kill as an incidental necessity in the course of armed robberies; emotionally unstable impulse or revenge killers; or a paranoid personality who kills out of a sense of persecution or ideological "mission" (like the murderer of Senator Kennedy). They include also sadistic-anxiety neurotics who kill for pleasure or the resolution of psychosexual or psychosocial frustrations, and they also include the passive-dependent personalities who "don't hate anybody," but perform the role of triggerman or intermediary for a patron gangster or dictator. What is more, the kind of murder indicated is by no means confined to the personality type specified in each case above. The matter is further complicated by the fact that similar personality types, under similar or somewhat different social conditions, may commit far less serious crimes or none at all. Certainly there are many schizoids, paranoids, neurotics, and passive-dependent personalities who have never murdered anybody and have never committed any more serious crime than being queer nonconformists or perpetual nuisances to their neighbors, fellow workers, or families. It is thus impossible to correlate deviant personality types with even so extreme and specific a form of antisocial behavior as murder.

In the realm of injury or death inflicted by participants in civil insurrection, war crimes, and genocide, the relationship is further complicated by the impersonal and mechanical nature of killing, the arbitrary distinction between murder and military necessity, and the obscured sense of individual responsibility for murders committed in the name of a mass movement or national security. Nevertheless, the example of Nazi Germany provided a clear and extreme illustration of a destructive social movement's leadership which was later subjected to psychological examination during the Nuremberg war crimes trials. If we may add Hitler, Himmler (the Gestapo chief), and Colonel Hoess (commandant of Auschwitz extermination camp) to the 18 convicted war criminals at Nuremberg, the writer would diagnose the top 21 Nazi war criminals[1] as follows:

2 paranoid neurotics
   (Hitler with additional obsessive-compulsive involvement; Hess with alternating dissociative states)
1 aggressive-egocentric personality
   (Goering, the No. 2 dictator and chief of the Air Force)
1 passive-dependent personality
   (Ribbentrop, the Foreign Minister)
1 emotionally unstable (hypomanic) personality
   (Hans Frank, minister of occupied Poland)
3 schizoid personalities
   (Himmler, Kaltenbrunner, Colonel Hoess, all of the SS-Gestapo network)

---

[1] Hitler and Himmler had committed suicide before they could be brought to trial, but the writer obtained sufficient data on them to permit an approximate diagnosis. Colonel Hoess was captured during the trial and was studied extensively in Nuremberg before being sent to Poland for trial and ultimate execution.

3 inadequate personalities
   (propagandists Rosenberg and Streicher; slave labor chief Sauckel)
10 without gross pathology
   (including all 4 military leaders)

While it cannot escape notice that a regime so grossly responsible for so much destruction, death, and misery was also deeply saturated with deviant personalities in high places, it is impossible to equate the type or extent of pathological leadership with the sheer enormity of the devastation visited by them on Western civilization. In a social structure that made it possible for one schizoid extermination-camp commandant (Colonel Hoess) to admit to the murder of 2½ million innocent men, women, and children, the nature of the deviant personalities can neither explain nor be inferred from the nature of their criminal behavior. Diagnosis at that level of analysis clearly involves the nature of the entire social system which made it possible, and goes far beyond the clinical organismic concepts of psychiatry. At all events, it was a wide assortment of personalities that made up the group known as Nazi war criminals, and there is little likelihood that the same men would have committed the same crimes or any crimes at all under different social circumstances, even though their behavior would in some way have proven "true to type."

Coming to the more commonplace petty crimes and unconventional behavior, much the same holds true. There is no particular type of deviant personality that accounts for any particular category of offenses. Thieves and prostitutes are sometimes passive-dependent individuals of subnormal intelligence who start to ply their trades during adolescence (the adult role learning stage) as the easiest way to make a living without studying for it. On the other hand, they may be comparatively normal members of underprivileged social groups and communities in which such behavior is commonplace and may be drifted into without the pressure of perverted social needs. Drug addiction and alcoholism are merely two avenues of toxic escape from social pressure and frustration or of conformity to group mores that only secondarily become addictive. Such victims range from the inadequate or neurotic to the brilliant and socially successful conformists. It obviously tells us nothing about their personalities to classify them as addictive sociopathic personality disturbance or as antisocial personality. Recent studies of limited samples of prostitutes (Greenwald, 1958), homosexuals (Hooker, 1957), drug addicts (Ausubel, 1961; Chein et al., 1964; Kolb, 1962), and alcoholism (Syme, 1957; Bier, 1962) tend to show a wide variety of personality types involved in such deviant adult role commitment, as well as the social and circumstantial factors which help determine their initiation and confirmation, regardless of "pathology."

It therefore appears that the traditional approach of clinical psychiatry, based on the diagnosis and treatment of mental disease, is really not directly applicable to the realm of antisocial or socially condemned behavior. Such behavioral syndromes cut across all clinical types of deviation, are too subject to cultural and circumstantial factors in their etiology and definition, and too often involve the normative and disintegrative processes of social pathology, which require a different set of evaluative concepts. This does not mean that psychopathology is irrelevant to social pathology, but rather that the two function at different levels of integration and that the criminal or pervert is caught somewhere in between. What is clearly needed is a diagnostic approach that makes allowance for the complexity of psychosocial pathology.

We suggest that this is most readily accomplished by retaining the *personality disturbances* described in the *Diagnostic Manual* (see Chapter 9) as deviant personality types, along with the psychoses, neuroses, and mental deficiency to constitute basic behavior disorders. The erstwhile *antisocial personality* would be eliminated as primary personality disorder per se. It would serve, instead, as a qualifying phrase to indicate the kind of psychosocial misbehavior that accompanies the underlying organismic psychopathology. This diagnostic scheme is already recommended in the *Diagnostic Manual* when a more primary personality disturbance is recognized. We merely point out that much confusion would be avoided if this procedure were always used. If the antisocial behavior in question is not sufficiently severe or persistent to betray an underlying personality defect, then there is not much reason for any psychiatric diagnosis at all. This implies, of course, that serious and persistent antisocial behavior or violation of the social mores invariably betrays an underlying personality defect—it is just not normal to make a career of incurring social disapproval and inflicting injury on others, even if such behavior cannot automatically be diagnosed as a mental disease. This brings us to the basic question of the psychodynamics of antisocial behavior, which is our main interest in this whole problem.

Psychodynamics:
The Psychosocial Needs
of the Antisocial
We have already referred to the paradox of the conforming nonconformist; the juvenile delinquent's obedience to the rules of the gang; the criminal code of "honor among thieves"; the revolutionist's dedication to the "cause." Having disposed of the constitutional psychopath and the sociopathic disturbance as explanatory concepts for antisocial behavior, we may now explore more fully the possibility that psychosocial needs and conflicts provide their own best explanation for the paradox of antisocial behavior in a manifestly social animal. We have

repeatedly stressed that every human being craves affection, acceptance, belonging, and social participation and that he tends to conform to the social mores and values of his culture more or less automatically in order to fill these needs. On that basis, we would hypothesize that any individual who persists in serious antisocial behavior or in defying the social mores is either betraying a deviant pattern of personality development or is conforming to some atypical subcultural pattern of behavior—perhaps both at the same time. In any case, both the cause of the behavior pattern and the form it takes would reveal persistence of social ego needs and a constant attempt to make adjustments or to prevent their frustration.

DRUG ADDICTS

Repeated evidence of this conclusion comes through, sometimes in an almost surprised manner, from research reports on social deviates. Thus, Chein *et al.* (1964, p. 6) report on their study of drug addicts:

It did not occur to us to ask how much drug-taking behavior would not take place were it not for the challenge of the risk; the attractiveness of the forbidden; the glamour of defying authority; the power of self-destructive needs given a socially validated channel of expression; the drawing power of an illicit subsociety to lonely individuals alienated from the mainstream, and the lure of its ability to confer a sense of belonging, interdependence of fate, and common purpose to individuals who would otherwise feel themselves to be standing alone in a hostile world.

Just how does this frustration of social ego needs originate and create a craving for compensatory affiliation, acceptance, and social participation (to which the use of drugs is initially only instrumental)? In much the same manner that most feelings of rejection, aimlessness, and unworthiness originate: defective primary group interaction and secondary socialization as a result of broken home life and family discord or negligence. The research data on the subjects' family life as compared with the control group shows far more frequent weak or hostile parent-son relationships, discord between parents, vague or inconsistent standards of behavior, unhealthy attitudes toward life and authority, and overindulgence or frustration of the boy's wishes (Table 11–1). Such pathogenic conditions of family life are the sort that render children susceptible to neurotic defense systems or to the acting out of their frustrated psychosocial needs through the substitute primary group of the street gang. Table 11–1 gives the data on a sample of boys who succumbed to drug addiction because that was part of the subcultural milieu and because their own character structures made them more susceptible. Those who did not succumb, like many of those in the control group who were brought up under similar conditions, did not necessarily go unscathed. The use of drugs is almost incidental to the frustration and maladaptive

Table 11-1 SOME DIFFERENCES IN FAMILY BACKGROUND OF DRUG ADDICTS AND CONTROL GROUP
(From Chein et al., 1964)

Item	Percentages	
	Addicts	Controls
1. Boy experienced an extremely weak father-son relationship	80	45
2. For a significant part of early childhood boy did not have father-figure in his life	48	17
3. Some father-figure was cool or hostile to boy	52	13
4. Father had unrealistically low aspirations for boy (late childhood & early adolescence)	44	0
5. Some father-figure was an immoral model (early childhood)	23	0
6. Marked impulse orientation in father-figure	26	0
7. Father had unstable work history during boy's early childhood	43	14
8. Father was unrealistically pessimistic or felt that life is a gamble	47	11
9. Lack of warmth or overtly discordant relations between parents	97	41
10. Mother-figure was more important in boy's life during late childhood period	73	45
11. Some mother-figure was cool or hostile to boy (early childhood)	23	0
12. Some mother-figure was cool or hostile to boy (late childhood)	37	3
13. Boy experienced extremely weak mother-son relationship	40	7
14. Mother did not trust authority figures	38	10
15. Mother had unrealistically low aspirations for boy (late childhood and early adolescence)	31	0
16. Mother was unrealistically pessimistic or felt that life was a gamble	31	7
17. No clear pattern of parental roles in formation of disciplinary policy (adolescence)	23	0
18. Parental standards for boy were vague or inconsistent (early childhood)	55	4
19. Parental standards for boy were vague or inconsistent (adolescence)	63	3
20. Boy was overindulged, frustrated in his wishes, or both	70	10

Addicts N=30; Controls N=29; not all items applicable to all Ss. All differences significant at .05 level of confidence.

resolution of psychosocial needs, but it eventually dominates the victim's life unless he "kicks the habit." Interestingly enough, one of the more successful techniques for this achievement is group therapy with other addicts who have kicked the habit, (Synanon, etc.). Here, a substitute primary group works on the same need for acceptance, belonging, and self-esteem to reverse the process of addiction, though it is by then working against heavy odds.

PROSTITUTES

A more frequent outlet for antisocial behavior in girls is prostitution. Though psychosexual needs are obviously involved, it is apparently an ironic twist in the psychosocial needs themselves that plays a large part in determining the choice of career after the initial break has been made with social convention. Greenwald (1958) reports the typical course of induction to the career of "call girls" (prostitute by appointment only, in contrast to streetwalkers) as follows:

Most women avoid friendships with girls who participate constantly in promiscuous sexual relationships. Therefore, these girls, to have any friends as they grew up and as they began to participate in promiscuous sexual behavior, had to find groups of people like themselves, to whom their sexually deviant behavior was acceptable. Such associations are formed in that gray area situated half-way between respectable society and full criminals—an area where drug addicts, shady businessmen of various kinds, bookmakers and large numbers of other people who seem to have lost their attachments to normal society form a society of their own. It was within this world that the girls made their first contacts with other call girls. None of the girls interviewed decided to become a call girl without having someone make the suggestion to her. By becoming call girls, they gave themselves some sense of belonging—in this gray world. . . . In this group she would find call girls, pimps, and madams. While she was sleeping with people in this group, someone would say: "What's the sense of giving it away, baby, when you can make so much money out of it?" Once she became a call girl she no longer felt like an outsider in this group; she felt as if she belonged; she had a place (Greenwald, 1958, pp. 143-4).

Greenwald reports that call girls are quite status conscious, looking down upon streetwalkers and amateur barflies with contempt and putting great value on their dress, the furnishings of their apartments, as well as the style in which they support their pimps. They also go to great lengths to keep their activities confined to a small circle of acquaintances in the gray-world environment, so that they will not risk embarrassment when out in polite society. (Apparently, a prostitute has pride and status needs, too.) In discussing their occupations, they frequently indulge in rationalizations and projections of their feelings of self-abasement, claiming that they are more honest and less hypocritical than many a respectable housewife or "high society dame," and certainly less hypocritical than their customers and most of the society that condemns them. The reader will recognize here some of the defense mechanisms and defensive strategies that the maladjusted and neurotic use to resolve the anxieties and insecurities of defective psychosocial development.

Interestingly enough, Greenwald describes the early family background of his subjects in much the same terms as Chein describes the backgrounds of his drug addicts.

There is an amazing similarity among the family atmospheres into which these girls were born. Of the entire group of twenty, I found not one example of a permanent, well-adjusted marital relationship between the parents. Not one of these girls reported growing up in a happy home where her parents got along well together. In fifteen, or three-fourths of the cases, the girls' homes were broken before they reached adolescence. This contrasts with about one-fourth of the general population which comes from broken homes. In the five cases where the home was not broken by the time of adolescence, where there was some attempt to maintain the home, the girls never saw any evidence of sympathy or affection between the parents (Greenwald, 1958, p. 107.)

The evidence of defective psychosocial development which these and other studies show to be common to prostitutes and drug addicts may not be surprising in view of the common world these people share as social outcasts in their adult role commitments. Many prostitutes become drug addicts and/or accomplices in racketeering, while many drug addicts become thieves, pimps, prostitutes, or racketeers to support their habit in conformity with the activities tolerated in their underworld. Their attempt to seek acceptance, recognition, affection, and a sense of belonging within that underworld, and to rationalize, camouflage, or deny their membership within it, all bears witness to the fact that social need has never been absent. It has become frustrated, perverted, or diverted, and has left a hunger which they still seek to satisfy within the limits and conflicts of their roles in that subculture.

CRIMINALS IN GENERAL

Similar defective psychosocial development (e.g., broken families, parental hostility and rejection, racial discrimination) and similar defenses were found among the general prison population by the writer while he served as consultant to the Michigan Department of Correction and did a study on prisoners' attitudes toward crime (Gilbert, 1958). Most prisons have their "social hierarchy" of crime, taking some comfort from the fact that they "never stooped as low as that"—a comment that usually referred to sex perverts and child rapists, while the sex perverts claim that unlike killers and armed-robbery convicts they never harmed anybody or even threatened to do so.

Antisocial reactions to the frustration of racial discrimination compounded by the prevalence of broken families and the underworld associations in the culture of poverty help swell the representation of minority groups. This is manifest in the high percentage of Negroes in the prison population of Michigan and many other states, which is several times the proportion of Negroes to the general population.

All kinds of cliques form on the basis of common interest, ethnic, regional, criminal, or occupational affiliations, or on the basis of congenial personality defects, much as they do in the outside world. The more aggressive vie for status and power, while the passive and weak cling to them for protection, sometimes even submitting to homosexual relationships as the price of their "protection." The distribution of personality types and defects ranges from the severely mentally deficient and psychotic (the "criminally insane" or nearly so) through the neurotic and mildly deviant personalities to the more or less normal but "indiscreet." There has as yet been no successful demonstration of a preponderance of any type of personality or psychopathology in any particular type of crime, although the distribution of personalities by offenses is probably far from a chance distribution. (Obviously, a mental retardate could scarcely become an embezzler of corporate funds, or a stock swindler. Similarly, a meek, passive-dependent personality would usually shrink from a career of armed robbery unless he was also a drug addict.) Regardless of the segment of the underworld, gray world, or open society they may come from, or the nature of the pathology they may exhibit, virtually all these criminals show some remnants of frustrated social drive and strive mightily to show that they still have some pride in themselves, some status among their fellows, or some rationalized self-justification in a world full of corruption.

Such studies and clinical impressions would justify the generalization that deviant personalities are frequently, but not always, found among criminals and social outcasts, but these deviations are not confined to any particular type. It is, therefore, futile to speak of a "criminal mind," or to make a diagnosis of *psychopathic personality*, or *sociopathic personality disturbance*, or even *antisocial personality* as if the disorder were a distinct mental disease. Furthermore, it is untenable to divide such a diagnostic category into subcategories by general type of offense, as if there were rather distinct kinds of pathology involved in each—or, indeed, any pathology at all. Finally, it is a mistaken notion to assume that habitual criminals, even the hardened ones, are completely devoid of social drive or sensitivity, as implied in the phrase "lacking in superego development," and therefore assumed to be totally incorrigible. We suggest that it is more often a maldevelopment or perversion of psychosocial needs themselves which takes place early in life and continues to seek resolution through antisocial behavior. Alternatively, it may be the influence of a socially unhealthy or deviant subculture that distorts the norms and values which the individual naturally adapts to in fulfilling his social ego needs. Since any but the insane are cognitively and affectively capable of recognizing right from wrong, as defined by society at large, and have no desire to become social outcasts, we are still confronted with the rationale that *some form* of deviant or perverted motivation must frequently underlie persistent antisocial behavior. Our discussion should, therefore, focus on which types of deviation are *most susceptible* to such antisocial role commitments, rather than on trying to diagnose antisocial behavior itself as a behavior disorder in the psychiatric sense.

DEVIANT PERSONALITIES SUSCEPTIBLE
TO ANTISOCIAL BEHAVIOR

If deviant personalities do not necessarily go in for grossly antisocial behavior, and those who do are not necessarily deviant in a clinical sense, we can nevertheless point to the patterns of motivation and maladjustment that make certain types of psychopathology more susceptible than others to persistent violation of the social mores. Even when social pathology creates conditions that are conducive to immoral, hostile, or self-destructive behavior, we still have to explain the selection of individuals who succumb to such influences and those who do not. We believe that the following personality defects and deviations are the most susceptible, each providing its own psychodynamic rationale, though not predicting which type of offense will be indulged in, or that any acting out against society will be indulged in at all.

mental retardation (mild)
paranoid personalities
schizoid personalities
inadequate or passive-dependent personalities
aggressive-egocentric personalities

In the case of *the mildly retarded* (generally speaking, IQ's of 70–85), we have a level of retardation sufficient to impair discrimination of the subtleties and abstractions of the social mores that are generally automatically learned by normal individuals during the secondary socialization stage of development, but not enough to impair concrete instrumental behavior for immediate purposes. Social needs remain pretty well confined to primary group interaction, which would include personal loyalties and the desire to please a protector, much as they did in early childhood. The lack of social discrimination, however, makes these people susceptible to corrupting influences and generally inadequate in coping with the various demands of adult social role behavior, especially with the sense of responsibility that is demanded of both sexes and the economic self-support that is generally demanded of all males. It is not surprising, therefore, that institutions of juvenile delinquency are disproportionately populated with mildly retarded boys and girls who have already committed offenses such as theft, vandalism, prostitution, and use of narcotics. Their desires for physical and social gratification are not essentially different from those of the normal juvenile population; but their ability to delay gratification for more long-range social acceptance, to anticipate the damaging effects of socially disapproved behavior, and to understand the proprieties of behavior in different social situations is sufficiently restricted to make them easy prey to corrupting influences. They require guidance to avoid careers as objects of criminal exploitation or as social outcasts eking out a marginal existence.

The *paranoid personality*, on the other hand, has developed a suspicious, hostile, or defensive attitude toward society or to some members of it, such as authority figures or members of some ethnic or other social group. He may be a political fanatic with a "mission" to fight certain kinds of evil as defined by him or his fanatic group, and believe that the end justifies any violent means. He may feel that he is being personally persecuted or threatened with harm, and then kill or harm his imaginary tormentor. He may be compensating for a deep sense of inferiority by professing superior accomplishments and condemning an "inferior race," until he commits overt acts of persecution and even murder. The political assassin, the racial agitator, the subversive who plots the violent overthrow of a supposedly (but not really) tyrannical government, may be this type of paranoid fanatic. But so may the jealous husband who shoots his wife because he suspects her of the infidelity which his own infidelity or suppressed adulterous urge has led him to project to her. In all of these cases, it may seem that we are dealing with just a "difference of opinion." Who can say if the political fanatic does not have some just cause for grievance; if the racist is not merely reflecting an attitude prevalent in his culture; if the jealous husband has not, in fact, detected the seductive signals broadcast by his wife. In all these cases, it is necessary to assess the subject's "reality testing," his realistic assessment of provocation and the extremes to which he is willing to go to act on such provocation. This necessarily involves differences of opinion; but it is not difficult to detect a pattern of behavior on the part of some people which always distorts reality because of these individuals' own emotional conflicts, so that they resort to antisocial or hostile behavior which is out of all proportion to any real offense. When the distortion of reality is indigenous to the culture —as is often the case with political, religious, or racial fanaticism—we have suggested that the term "cultural pseudoparanoia" be used, to distinguish it from self-generated clinical paranoia. The paranoid personality would still exaggerate and exploit for his own hostile social needs the existence of such a cultural distortion. Hitler was a classical example of this, and many racists in many countries bear conspicuous witness to the prevalence of such psychodynamics in modern civilization.

The *aggressive-egocentric personality* is usually intelligent enough and sufficiently stable emotionally to understand the social mores in a reality context, but his self-centered needs impel him to manipulate reality without the usual restraints or consideration for others. Inordinate greed, a need for dominance in interpersonal relationships, and notoriety and power in his social role are among the hallmarks of the aggressive-egocentric, while empathy and concern for morals seem to be lacking. In the underworld of rackets and vice, there is often an aggressive-egocentric character playing the role of entrepreneur, while others serve as "stooges" or small-time operators paying tribute to the racket-and-vice overlord. In the field of politics, such a character may occasionally gain a foothold because of his clever use of power and propaganda and his readiness to manipulate people without moral restraint, for the sake of his own self-aggrandizement. As individual criminals operating without benefit of organized crime or political corruption, they may pursue careers as confidence men, blackmailers, imposters, bigamists and seducers, or petty swindlers. Their frequently sharp assessment of reality and the selfishness of other people's motives, combined with superficial conformity to the social mores, make it possible for them to carry on their schemes of exploitation and self-aggrandizement without detection for long periods of time. They may, of course, be successful businessmen in a highly competitive society, who have kept within the law for utilitarian reasons.

For this reason, the original concept of *psychopathic personality*, which the aggressive-egocentric most closely resembles, could not stand scrutiny as the prototype of the "criminal mentality." However, we may hypothesize that, in any given case, one who persistently and deliberately violates the social mores and inflicts harm on others without concern for their rights or feelings may be either temperamentally insensitive or have undergone some trauma to his own psychosexual or psychosocial needs during childhood. Such trauma might have produced overcompensatory acting-out behavior. We shall present a case of this type at the end of this chapter.

In contrast to the paranoid or aggressive-egocentric personalities, the *schizoid personality* is somewhat remote and apathetic in his interpersonal relationships, with no strong motivation for either social or antisocial involvements. In his case, it may be suspected that empathy was blunted or underdeveloped in early childhood, and that he has remained a "loner" all his life as a result. He is likely to become a friendless isolate, rather than a criminal. However, the lack of craving for social interaction and approval can readily lead him into a "lone-wolf" kind of predatory behavior or life of a social outcast, as the course of least resistance. Since normal human empathy is blunted, he may also accept the role of "trigger-man" or "enforcer" of violent reprisal in a gang or racket, executing assignments for which the mob leader and other members have little stomach. The mass murderers of Nazi Germany were frequently of this type (Gilbert, 1950, Chapter 6), and many criminals in our own prisons are found to be either schizoid or borderline schizophrenics. Schizoids are not *necessarily* criminals, but they are susceptible to antisocial influences because of their blunted affect and empathy, and consequently reduced psychosocial sensitivity.

Finally, the *inadequate* or *passive-dependent personality* may find himself committed to the career of a criminal or social outcast for reasons somewhat similar to those that apply to the mentally retarded or schizoid, without his being either. Since he is inadequate, passive, dependent, and suggestible, he is more susceptible than the average person to the influence of more dominant personalities in his environment. He (or she) will "follow the leader" or go along with the group as the course of least resistance or as the easiest means of gaining acceptance, protection, and identification with a symbol of competence. Patterns of psychosocial gratification and security through dependence on an authority-figure are often established in childhood relations with the father and continue through life as surrogate father-figures enter the individual's life. If such an authority-figure should induce a particularly suggestible passive-dependent to indulge in immoral or criminal behavior, even to the violation of his own professed values, the seduced individual may find himself committed to complicity in crimes without quite understanding how he ever got there. In the political realms, we have seen such a case in that of Nazi Foreign Minister Ribbentrop (Chapter 7). In more commonplace antisocial behavior, such people are usually petty offenders and accessories to crime, but their offenses may range from sex perversion to crimes of violence, depending on the demands of their "protectors" and the sense of immunity they think they get from obeying him. Since we are not dealing with the lack of comprehension typical of the mentally retarded or the lack of concern of the aggressive or the schizoid, we may expect such cases to exhibit massive defense mechanisms and defensive strategies to overcome the emotional conflict and sense of guilt which their behavior engenders.

Summary The study of antisocial or criminal behavior has long been complicated by conceptions of psychiatric diagnosis which confused mental disorder with social disorder and nonconformity. Although diagnostic terms like psychopathic personality or sociopathic personality disturbance are no longer used, the current term, antisocial personality, still conveys the impression that there is such a specific personality type or syndrome. The author suggests that antisocial behavior cuts across *all* personality types, although some deviant personality types are more susceptible to such influences than others. These would include the mentally retarded, paranoid personalities, aggressive-egocentric personalities, schizoid personalities, and inadequate or passive-dependant personalities.

It is noted that the dynamics of antisocial behavior usually involves some frustration of social ego needs, which the affected individual over-compensates for by reactive hostility toward society. This is often facilitated by the defensive strategy of affiliation with an antisocial group, which provides a measure of acceptance, understanding, and identity. Studies of drug addicts and prostitutes, for example, show surprising similarities in their backgrounds, such as rejection, absence, or indifference on the part of their parents in childhood, even though their personalities may be radically different. Similarly, criminals in state prisons are found to be jealous of their social status in the criminal hierarchy, susceptible to group loyalties and codes of "honor among thieves." The biosocial viewpoint is that antisocial or criminal behavior represents a perversion of the generic social drive, rather than an absence of it.

Illustrative Case History

EARL WARD, HOMICIDAL IMPOSTOR, ROBBER, AND POLYGAMIST

Referral. Examination of this 28-year-old life convict was requested by the Warden of State Prison, as soon as the riot which this convict had led was brought under control. The prisoner is serving a life term for a second attempted murder, the first being a juvenile offense. Charges are now pending for kidnapping with attempted murder as a result of taking hostages and threatening their lives during the recent riot.

Initial impression. Earl Ward is a handsome, slender young man who looks and conducts himself for all the world like a matinee idol, if it were not for his prison garb and the residue of nervous tension from the riot experience. He acts greatly offended at being threatened with further charges after negotiating the surrender of the embattled prisoners "like a gentleman, without killing any hostages." Aside from that, he cooperated well during the series of five long examination sessions as a relief from solitary confinement and a chance to enjoy his notoriety. He related his life adventures—whether sexual conquests, petty crimes, or major brutalities suffered and inflicted—with a casual indifference and self-righteousness that betrayed a deeply ingrained moral depravity beneath his charming, boyish manner.

Case history. Earl states that he was the illegitimate son of a small-town eastern politician who forced his wife to assume Earl's parenthood immediately after his birth to another woman. He says this was done to avoid a scandal that would have damaged his father's career, implying that his father had sired him with the other woman. Earl did not learn of his illegitimacy until adolescence, but he says that his assumed mother hated him from the very beginning and he retaliated with equal hatred. There were no other children in the family, so his only primary group interaction in childhood was with a hostile mother and a guilt-evading father, to whom Earl was only a constant reminder of past mistakes which his wife would never let him forget. In this rejecting home environment, Earl displayed anxiety symptoms and overt hostility all through childhood. He was subject to nightmares, temper tantrums, and various psychosomatic complaints. In later childhood he began to act out his resentment of his rejection more and more, indulging in truancy, petty theft, vandalism, violent fights with his mother and teachers, and general malicious mischief in the neighborhood. By adolescence the anxiety symptoms had subsided in favor of a frankly delinquent pattern of acted-out aggression and selfish impulses, which made him a chronic problem to the community and to the police. He enjoyed showing off his new-found manhood to the local girls and hobnobbing with the local hoodlums, who admired his "spunk" and his precocity. They soon involved him in their car-theft operations and allowed him to hang around with the gang. This underworld gang affiliation apparently satisfied his hunger for acceptance and belonging which was denied him at home and failed to reach him at school. After several arrests for car theft and malicious mischief, he was sent to reform school at the age of 15. By that time he had already made one of his girlfriends pregnant.

Reform school only served to brutalize him still further. Engaged in a constant battle with the other inmates to prove who was the toughest among them and the most defiant of discipline, he suffered and inflicted many broken bones and bruises in fights with the other boys. He also received many severe punishments from the reformatory authorities, for whom he conceived a fierce hatred. His violent reaction to punishment culminated in an attempt on the life of the supervisor and his escape from the institution. He described this as something of a homicidal conversion experience. "I suddenly realized that the only way to stop being kicked around like a punk good-for-nothing kid was to *kill* if I had to." Recaptured by state troopers, he was sent to prison, where he again became involved in assaults on inmates and a guard. (He claims to have been goaded into stabbing a guard to death, but there is no confirmation of this in the records.) According to Earl, he barely escaped a life sentence on that occasion only by virtue of his father's political influence, which enabled him to be remanded to an institution for the criminally insane and ultimately released as "cured." This, at least, corresponds to the record.

By the time he was released from custody at the age of 19, World War II was in progress, but he was classified as unfit for military service. He took a job as a butcher, but defied parole restrictions and teamed up with his car-stealing cronies again. He used his charm and easy money to seduce older women, marrying one after another without bothering about the formality of divorcing the previous wives. In his craving for "respectability" and admiration, he forged a medical diploma and began to frequent medical clinics with "fellow medical internes" he ran into. To cover up his penchant for seducing older women, as well as his pose as a graduate M.D. while still in his early twenties, he assumed an age ten years older than his real age. Using his underworld connections, he teamed up with an abortion ring in Miami, where he enjoyed high living and "respectability" for a time with wife No. 4 or 5. His comment on this phase of his career was: "Boy, it's great to be looked up to as a doctor, ain't it, Doc? People treat you with respect, you belong to the best clubs. . . . I'll never forget those two years in Miami, even if I have to spend the rest of my life in the can. I showed them I wasn't no punk good-for-nothing little kid!"

Although Earl described the activities of the abortion ring in great detail, it is difficult to accept his claim that he personally performed many hundreds of abortions, with no medical training. Confirmatory interview with the assistance of two medical colleagues leads us to conclude that he was probably lying about performing all those abortions himself, but may very well have assisted with them, or performed some more amateur service as a contact man in the racket.

When his connection with the abortion ring (whatever it was) and the mounting suspicions of his numerous wives became too "hot" for him, he left Miami with spur-of-the-moment wife No. 5 or 6. He then set up a private medical practice in a Detroit hotel. Here, an attempt to do away with one of his patients with an overdose of prescribed drugs, in order to obtain a large sum of money being held for the victim, led to his arrest and conviction on a charge of attempted murder.

During this latest prison term he has already taken a leading part in two riots. The first was an attempted prison break which involved an attempt to kidnap the visiting governor. In the more recent disturbance, he took charge of the disorganized riot by thousands of prisoners, set up headquarters with

Figure 11–1. Negotiating end to Michigan prison riot of 1952. *Earl Ward (left) negotiates with deputy warden (right), while one of hostage guards awaits outcome. The perverted drive for recognition and acceptance which is commonly present in criminals is illustrated by the case history of Earl Ward. (Photo from the Detroit News).*

hostages in his cell block, held negotiations and press conferences through the outside cell bars, and ultimately forced the governor to accede to a list of terms to bring the riot to a halt. His reaction to all this is that he showed cool-headed leadership "while all them punks was running around like crazy." He is also proud that he proved he was a man of his word in high-level negotiations with the governor's spokesmen in bringing the riot to an end. However, he admits with a shrug that he might have had to give the word to slit the throats of the hostages if the state troopers had tried to "pull anything" to defy his authority, like trying to storm his cell block with riot guns.

Psychological tests. Examination showed Earl Ward to be fairly intelligent, but emotionally immature and somewhat unstable. A marked feature of both the intellectual and projective personality tests was a tendency to romanticize an antisocial ego ideal with little recognition of its basic lack of humanity. The IQ test yielded an IQ of 122 with above-average performance on all sub-tests, except those dealing with numbers. This seems to be a handicap of his sixth-grade education, which he never overcame. Many of his responses on the IQ test revealed a cynical contempt for the social mores, coupled with a deep sensitivity about his own mental capacity and sophistication. The Rorschach record was a highly productive but variable sequence of large and small details pertaining mostly to animals and human anatomy. It is significant that there is not a single well-integrated, live human figure in the entire record, which indicates an extreme degree of emotional immaturity or lack of empathy for one of his intelligence. His preoccupation with medical-anatomical figures probably indicates an intellectualization of actively sadistic impulses.

Of particular significance are some of his responses to the TAT pictures, which reflect a strongly persistent urge to romanticize and act out his childish fantasies of social ascendency and license. His association to Card 8 (boy imagining a surgical operation): "Ahhhh, this is it! There's a kid dreaming of life in the raw. He wants to be a man of character, intelligence, skill. He's decidedly a dreamer—a man of books, treasure, war, romance. He would want to be a surgeon that instant.—I know I would—to save a life, of course. I wouldn't want to be the guy on the table. There's a certain physical sensation too—the actual participation in the dream: the sudden maturity—no childish ideas. The realization is maturity. A lifetime between the thought and the actual environment." To Card 13 (man covering his face, standing beside nude woman on bed), he gave the following: "Hah—Jesus Christ! The guy's just killed her. Either that, or—if not, he's a man of means, out of place. Probably just woke up and saw what the hell was beside him. . . . Will get the hell out of there and save his position. I will not comment on the woman. She's 'indecently exposed.' I never comment on women and their nudity.— Keep it holy, damn it! (laughs)—Hope that's not a Gideon Bible on that table. Hell, you find them in all the hotel rooms." These are scarcely concealed projections of Earl's own reactions to being "kicked around as a good-for-nothing punk little kid"—that is, a defiance of social restraint by acting out one's own fantasies of prestigious social role assumption, even if one has to kill, seduce, or become an impostor in the process.

Interpretation and summary. Earl Ward's rejection as an illegitimate child and his reactive hostility produced a maladjustment from earliest childhood, which was bound to result either in neurosis or in antisocial behavior in adulthood. Because of his aggressive acting-out tendencies and the antisocial influences of his environment, the aggressive antisocial pattern became predominant even before he was sent to reform school. However, he became conscious of a deliberate decision to kill, rather than suffer punishment and humiliation, during one of his punishment sessions at the reform school, and it was then that he made his first actual attempt at homicide.

His acting out of aggressive childish fantasies of both a psychosexual and a psychosocial nature served to dissipate a good deal of the underlying anxiety generated by these conflicts. He resolved, in effect, to make others, rather than himself, suffer for his rejection, and to gain social ascendancy in the process, even if it was only by deceit and violence—the standards of the underworld. The psychodynamics of his criminal behavior in adulthood may thus be traced right back to the psychosexual and psychosocial trauma of his childhood. His rejection as an illegitimate child by a hostile mother-figure undoubtedly helps to explain his morbid interest in participating in the wholesale abortion of illegitimate offspring, his murderous defiance of male authority, and his compulsive seduction and marriage of older women. At the psychosocial level, his inordinate need for social acceptance and recognition prompted this aggressive-egocentric to act out prestige and notoriety-producing roles to prove to the world that he was not a "good-for-nothing punk little kid." This aggressive acting out of resolutions to his psychosexual and psychosocial conflicts, and their partially successful integration into antisocial adult role behavior, has already become so deeply ingrained at the age of 28 that rehabilitation is highly doubtful.

Clinical impression.   Aggressive-egocentric personality with pronounced antisocial tendencies.

12

Social
Change
and
the
Individual

Throughout this book we have sought to portray the growth and adjustment of the individual personality as a member of society, channeling his basic generic needs and potentialities into patterns of behavior that reflect both individual and cultural differences. Although the progressive circularity of interaction in this field of personality-culture forces has been assumed from the very beginning, the discussion has been couched largely in terms of the effect of the existing social mores on the personality of the individual. It is now time to take a broader view of these social mores, to consider the ways in which they themselves change in the course of social interaction, and the ways in which individual personalities may affect social change as well as being affected by it.

For it is the social mores that not only help determine society's influence on individual character formation, but also become the medium through which individuals may selectively and cumulatively improve, alter, weaken, or even destroy that society. The social mores that provide the growing child's first conception of the rules of living and need gratification must not be thought of as fixed environmental absolutes. They are but the residual prescriptions of cultural evolution in that particular society at that particular time, which successive generations have reacted to from youth to old age, and have modified and continue to modify in the constant process of social interaction.

In fact, it is probably one of the unsuspected historic functions of the youthful conformity-nonconformity paradox that it repeatedly tests the validity and relevance of traditional values and becomes an agency of social change for good or ill. When Cicero declaimed to the Roman Senate, "*O tempora, O mores!*" he was bemoaning the decline of solid Roman virtues which were inculcated in the Roman youth of his generation: physical bravery, civic pride as a Roman, respect for elders, and personal integrity. It is a commentary on the perpetual changeability of the social mores in any era that older folks of our own and previous generations have complained that "the younger generation is going to the dogs!" What is being perceived, evidently, is the conspicuous nonconformity of more audacious youth "testing the limits" in the adult role anticipation stage, along with the more general conformity to peer-group "nonconformity." The adult roles are often anticipated with an implied reservation that "Anything you can do, we can do better!"

But youth has no monopoly on initiation of social change. The canalized drives of efficacy-competence, social participation and recognition, hunger, sex, comfort, and even cognitive consistency, clarity, and novelty are quite sufficient to stimulate less complacent adults of all ages to dissent, social reform, invention, innovation, or even rebellion. Occasionally there are truly revolutionary outbursts against the traditional social mores; sometimes reactions to reestablish traditional institutions or modernized versions of them. There are also peaceful revolutions brought about by inventions and discoveries which set in motion drastic changes that not only alter social structure but that in time also change national character as well. In any of these slow or revolutionary changes it is not uncommon for one or a few individuals to have a profound effect on the social structure and its mores. In any case, it behooves us to study the psychosocial dynamics underlying the operation of such social changes as changing expressions of human needs that are brought about by human beings, rather than taking them for granted as fixtures of the environment.

Social Mores and Human Needs

From our broad biosocial perspective we may distinguish four main groups of social mores, overlapping and closely interrelated though they may be. First there are the politicoeconomic

self-maintenance mores that have to do with the organization and maintenance of the society as a "going concern." This includes the customs or
laws pertaining to the authority structure of government, the division of
labor, and the production and distribution of the necessities of life. Then
there are the *self-perpetuation mores*, in which the biological drive for
procreation is elaborated into a system of institutions and customs by
which courtship, marriage, child-rearing, and kinship relations form the
foundation for the continuation of the society with much of its mores
intact. Third, there are the *personal conduct mores*, which go beyond
politicoeconomic controls, but which involve ethical, legal, religious, or
just customary prescriptions for appropriate behavior of the individual in
his interpersonal and spiritual relations. Finally there is the system of
self-gratification mores, which go beyond the primary-need gratifications
of hunger, sex, and comfort already accounted for, and provide for aesthetic
satisfactions, intellectual pursuits, sport and amusement, and the social
amenities that characterize civilized man. Both of the last two imply needs
of a higher order in our hierarchy of drives.

CENTRALITY OF SELF-MAINTENANCE MORES

These four clusters of social mores are, as we have said, interdependent.
The self-perpetuation (sexual) mores are to a large extent dependent on
the religious and moral constraints of personal conduct. The religious and
moral sanctions which control the personal conduct mores have at times
also controlled the politicoeconomic self-maintenance mores. There is an
overriding consideration, however, by which the politicoeconomic self-
maintenance mores are more fundamental than any of the others. In a
practical sense, they set the limits and dictate the changes in all the others.
This may be so because man's cultural evolution had to provide for food
and shelter before it could provide for anything else.

Consider the effect of changing economic customs on the mores associated with marital and family life. New machines and new methods of
producing and distributing food and clothing may change the practicality
and the value of a woman's domestic labors. This drastically alters the
mother's role in the family and affects both the extent of household and
farmhand drudgery as well as the skills and other attractions that make her
a desirable wife. It may also, in the long run, determine the practicality of
polygamy or of equality in the status of men and women. If the economy
calls for heavy unskilled labor that women can do near the homestead,
wives may find themselves confined to lives of perpetual drudgery and
child-rearing. If the advances of invention, labor-saving devices, and mass
production and mass communication provide for broader socializing and
leisure, then the complexities of social life may require a sophisticated

mistress of the household and social companion. Enhanced social status, education, a voice in community affairs are all more likely to follow. But political and economic systems change because people make them change. The new inventions, labor-saving devices, mass production, and mass communication facilities are demanded and invented by people to fulfill human needs. The demand for escape from drudgery is rooted in the human drive for dignity and social participation. One does not have to conjure up an image of militant suffragettes demanding the vote in early twentieth-century America to understand the impetus for the liberation of women. Men of liberal dispositions have long recognized the benefit to society, to the marital institution, and to their own social ego needs to have well-informed, understanding, and helpful participating partners in life's endeavors and satisfactions, as well as its problems. At any rate, it represents a significant symptom or trait in the character structure of men whether they prefer mates who are subservient, domineering, or companionable on mutually considerate terms. The example of liberal innovators inevitably helps shift the social norms of marital relations.

Much the same may be said of the racial issue. Racial equality in fact is dependent on the equal opportunity of a society's ethnic groups to participate in its politicoeconomic "power structure." No amount of pious platitudes about the equality of all men in the eyes of the law or in the eyes of the Lord can make men truly equal unless that piety is translated into economic opportunity. Both human dignity and the orderly perpetuation of society itself revolve around this key issue of "civil rights." But the resolution or polarization of this widely recognized need for social reform depends very largely on the wisdom and good will of leaders of both the in-groups and the disadvantaged minority group themselves. The repercussions of social lag or social reform in this sector can be far-reaching indeed, but there can be no doubt that the outcome will be largely determined by the quality of leadership on all sides, as we can see in the vacillation between cooperative reform and defiant confrontation or backlash before our very eyes. Even the self-perpetuation mores of a race can be affected by leadership in correcting unequal opportunities in the politicoeconomic sphere. This is the clear implication of the Moynihan report (1965) and the efforts of government and industrial leaders to restore the bread-winning, head-of-the-family status of the father in under-privileged Negro families.

Even the self-gratification mores, as expressed in the arts, reflect man's preoccupation with the social structure that regulates his economic needs. The earliest examples of prehistoric art give evidence of man's basic preoccupation with his hunting economy (Leroi-Gourhan, 1968) and probably reflected a similar concern of his first gropings toward religion. Ancient mythology, poetry, and drama, as well as the plastic arts and architecture of ancient civilizations, are replete with the sagas and symbols of man's struggle for politicoeconomic power and freedom. Much of modern literature and art has likewise been concerned with individual and social ramifications of the struggle for existence, or is heavily dependent on the economics of leisure, education, and mass communication for its own existence.

This is not to deny that there has always been a perfectly valid "art for art's sake" expressing man's aesthetic inclinations, his generic efficacy drive, and even his need for the communication of ideas for sheer self-expression. While such "pure art" may not be demonstrably necessary for survival, artistic self-expression and communication does unquestionably enhance social cohesion, and *that does* have survival value, as pointed out in Chapters 1 and 2. But even so, the fine arts do not escape a certain dependence on the realities of the socioeconomic order. Their very existence is often predicated on the value placed on pure artistic expression by the mores of the society in which such expression is attempted. In a social order given over to the grinding struggle for the mere necessities of life, some representational forms of art may be tolerated; but a life devoted to the expression of esoteric artistic urges is hardly possible. Even in a more advanced society, if ideologically dedicated to materialism and concrete social progress, as in Russia, there is precious little tolerance of and no encouragement for art that strays far from representing "the worker's heroic struggle to build a better socialistic society." Such a goal may be laudable, but it does set limits on self-gratification through artistic expression.

Even the personal conduct mores, as guided by religion, law, and custom, give evidence of serving the purposes of self-maintenance as well as self-perpetuation mores. We have mentioned previously that primitive religion may have emerged simultaneously with primitive art as an attempt to seek magical aid in eking out subsistence from the hunt, protection from dangers, and victory in the competitive struggle for existence. Freud offered the fanciful conjecture in *Totem and Taboo* (1913) that religion may have begun as a ritualistic repentance for the murder of the father of a primal horde (the original Oedipal guilt complex) and a pledge never to practice incest thereafter. Granted that the religious regulation of the self-perpetuation mores universally proscribes incest and regulates marriage and sex relations in various ways, it is still believed by many anthropologists that exogamous family formation had more of an economic basis to begin with. Mating with the offspring of other families enhanced the self-maintenance possibilities of the extended family or tribe in its increasingly socialized way of life.

As Tylor has shown almost a century ago, the ultimate explanation [for incest taboo] is probably that mankind has understood very early that, in order to free itself from a wild struggle for existence, it was confronted with the very simple choice of "either marrying-out or being killed-out" (Levi-Strauss, 1960, p. 278).

Nevertheless, it cannot be denied that religion has served, all through history, as a principal instrument of man's cortical control of his sexual propagation functions.

There is also some possible validity to the theory that conceptions of the deity frequently represent idealized images of parental figures. That is, "man creates gods in his own image"—or at least the idealized image of mothers and fathers. In that connection, Lambert et al. (1959) studied the religious beliefs of a number of societies and came to some interesting conclusions. Those religions that were dominated by aggressive and punitive gods tend to have strict child-rearing practices. Those societies which had more permissive child-rearing practices tended to have more benevolent and indulgent gods. It is not surprising that the very nature of the gods or God people worship both reflects and influences their ideals of authority and self-maintenance mores. The ancient Greeks worshiped warlike gods and goddesses like Zeus and Athena, but also had room for a noble aesthete like Apollo. You do not have such majestic Olympian gods holding sway over the superstitious minds of primitive savages. They must personify something of the power and dignity and aesthetic ideals of a civilization with a cultivated leisure class sufficiently advanced to produce the sculptures of a Phidias and the epics of a Homer. When leading exponents of Greek democratic philosophy advanced to the point of making moral criticisms of cruel and arbitrary authority, the gods who represented such authority in their mythology tended to be discredited.

In our own time, personal conduct mores based on faith in supernatural authority are being severely challenged by the values of a world in which self-maintenance mores are increasingly dominated by science and economics. The criticism of "materialistic decadence" by some of the clergy does not convince better-informed modern generations. People can look back on centuries of religious wars and struggles for temporal power and compare them with the efforts of the modern "democratic welfare state" to relieve the hazards of economic disadvantage and its assaults on human dignity. Such comparisons can, of course, be oversimplified. There is also competence and achievement motivation to be considered in the economic base for human dignity; but here, too, religion is being challenged to prove its relevance. Indeed, the call for a redefinition of moral values comes from laymen and clergymen alike.

Thus even if self-maintenance needs of the species are central to the entire system of social mores in any culture, and even if traditional moral authority is subordinated to this categorical imperative, it must still be recognized that ethical value judgments permeate all such behavioral prescriptions. It has repeatedly been pointed out that the very word *mores* is not far removed in derivation or meaning from *morals*—that which society considers right, proper, or appropriate in the behavior of its members toward each other in given situations. Although behavioral scientists properly refrain from making dogmatic pronouncements about good and evil, it is impossible, in our opinion, to deny the ethical implications of voluntary choice behavior in maintaining, modifying, and defying the social mores in any category. We must not forget the basic biosocial thesis that it is only because man developed, in the course of evolution, the capacity and need to create and abide by social values favoring mutual cooperation for survival, that social systems exist at all. What we are cautioning against here is the assumption that social institutions and values are fortuitous and independent characteristics of a particular culture in a particular time and place, which one-sidedly influence individual character formation all through life, so that moral conceptions can only be relative to the culture in which they are conceived. We object to this "cultural relativism" on two grounds: (1) the very nature of social cohesiveness as a factor in human survival precludes unlimited and capricious variation of ethical values and (2) the inevitable interaction between individual and society means that individuals must also have some influence in modifying values, institutions, and the course of history itself.

Let us take the matter of the individual's influence on society and history first. Social institutions and values change constantly in all societies— rapidly in some, slowly in others. When they do change, it is not merely because changing ecology or technology has brought about altered living conditions in the abstract. It is usually because some individuals have made adaptive behavioral changes to accommodate the altered living conditions and others have chosen to conform to the changing mores. Such changes, whether of ideas, technology, or ritual, may be initiated by imaginative innovators, inventors, reformists, or exploiters of labor, power, or material wealth. They may be motivated by social competence and achievement; by rebellion against suppressive authority or satisfaction of ascendancy needs; by secondary humanitarianism or ethnocentrism; by aesthetic, sexual, or safety needs; or merely represent change for the sake of change. Eventually a residue of such social changes becomes incorporated into the social mores and values of the culture, because more and more people find it responds to their needs. If it does not, other innovators will introduce new changes. These changing mores and values of the culture influence succeeding generations of individuals in a seemingly impersonal institutionalized manner, but the process still involves a two-way personality-culture interaction every step of the way.

In a more dramatic fashion, individuals and their individual quirks of ethical values may actually influence the course of history. The study of the leaders of Nazi Germany provided a unique opportunity to observe the influence of individual personalities and their individualized ideologies on the course of mid-twentieth-century history (Gilbert, 1950). Contrary to the widely held thesis among sociologists that wars come about by the force of socioeconomic imbalances, our analysis showed that a handful of neurotic and militaristically inclined leaders tipped the scales of ideological conflict and international relations, and deliberately precipitated a war that might never have come about under a slightly different leadership constellation. More shocking still was the conclusion that one dictator's neurotic obsession with anti-Semitism determined the mass murder of millions of innocent Jews in the extermination camps of Europe. To be sure, the ethnocentrism and authoritarianism of an entire culture was involved. But Hitler and his propagandists inflamed and rigidified those very cultural tendencies as a precondition to achieving the realization of his destructive fantasies. We have even suggested that World War II and mass extermination might have been averted if Hitler had been eliminated earlier in his rise to power.

Such historic catastrophes might be written off as the aberration of social turmoil incidental to the competitive struggle for existence (or testing of self-maintenance mores); but such socioeconomic determinism fails on two counts. It can by no means be established that World War II and the extermination of the Jews were socioeconomically inevitable; nor does the evidence support the notion that any of the other leaders who might have assumed the dictator's role would have so doggedly pursued a policy of war and extermination. As for the underlying social mores of the nation that allowed it all to happen, Germany has to a large extent repudiated those secret machinations by a handful of power-hungry men, denied knowledge of much of it at the time (with some justification), and prosecuted many of the guilty participants while seeking to compensate some of the surviving victims. One cannot properly regard this as the cynical cover-up of a national viciousness that misfired, but rather a repudiation by the vast majority of a society that had seen its social mores grotesquely distorted by a deceptive demagogue and his unconscionably ambitious cohorts. The question, therefore, is not what happened to the social structure of Germany under Nazi rule, but what happened to the conscience and social awareness of individual Germans who disapproved of war and would have found extermination unthinkable. The answer, on the basis of the evidence, seems to lie more in the inhumanitarian values and obsessions of the dictator and those around him than in any cultural inevitability.

On a more constructive note, history is replete with the names of charismatic leaders who founded religions, led rebellions or passive resistance movements against tyranny, liberated slaves, restored the rights of ethnic minorities or women, and opened up new frontiers of adventure and discovery. Less dramatically, but often with more far-reaching impact on society, many artists, scientists, inventors, educators, and civic leaders have had their cumulative effect in gradually changing the social mores of their contemporaries and those who came after them. It would require an extraordinary application of socioeconomic determinism and historic fatalism to say that all wars and social reforms, inventions, discoveries, and artistic or technical innovations would have happened *anyway* when they did, because of the antecedent social conditions. At the very least, we must credit individual human ingenuity and perversity for the timing and manner of introduction of such changes, and in some cases at least, the credit (or blame) for creating such changes altogether.

On our own contemporary scene in America, social change is taking place every day on the technological and human relations fronts. Thanks to modern mass communication—itself a social product of the inventive genius of a limited number of individuals—we are able to see and read about many of these changes literally taking place before our eyes. We can also see and hear and read about the individuals who are helping to effect these changes, so there is no mystery about the cause-and-effect relationships involved.

This book is being finished just as America's astronauts have returned from their first landing on the moon, while civil rights and peace demonstrations are jarring college campuses from coast to coast and ethnic conflicts flare up around the world. It is easy to show that there are far-reaching changes in our social mores and new challenges to our value-systems involved here, as the result of the direct action of individuals. These innovators and activists are not only the ones most conspicuously associated with the actions in question; we must include the planners, the political decision-makers, the inspired instigators, even the researchers behind the scenes, who bring action to a head.

Let us take the case of the struggle for implementation of Negro civil rights in America, since it illustrates both the effect of individual action on social change and the persistent ethical issue of human dignity in our social mores. It is common knowledge that the U. S. Supreme Court rejected the "separate but equal" doctrine in its historic reversal of decision in the case of *Brown vs. Board of Education of Topeka* in 1954. Though far from settling the issue all at once, that historic decision continues to have far-reaching effects on the social mores of this country and has lent great impetus to the whole civil rights movement. It might be said that this doctrine would have been reversed sooner or later anyway, because of the changing climate of public opinion. But that would be overlooking those who influence public opinion as well as the opinions of courts. In this case, three psychologists submitted a summary of research on the effects of segregation, which formed the basis of an appendix to the appeal to the Supreme Court. This appendix stated in part:

> The report indicates that as minority group children learn the inferior status to which they are assigned—as they observe the fact that they are almost always segregated and kept apart from others who are treated with more respect by the society as a whole—they often react with feelings of inferiority and a sense of personal humiliation. Many of them become confused about their own personal worth. On the one hand, like all human beings, they require a sense of personal dignity; on the other hand, almost nowhere in the larger society do they find their own dignity as human beings respected by others. Under these conditions, the minority group child is thrown into a conflict with regard to his feelings about himself and his group. He wonders whether his group and he himself are worthy of no more respect than they receive. This conflict and confusion leads to self-hatred and rejection of his own group. . . .
>
> The report indicates further that confusion, conflict, moral cynicism, and disrespect for authority may arise in majority group children as a consequence of being taught the moral, religious and democratic principles of the brotherhood of man and the importance of justice and fair play by the same persons and institutions who, in their support of racial segregation and related practices, seem to be acting in a prejudiced and discriminatory manner (Quoted in Clark, 1963).

Largely on the basis of such research-based arguments by the psychologists who summarized the evidence (Clark, Chein, and Cook), the U. S. Supreme Court issued its historic reversal and called for desegregation of all American schools "with all deliberate speed." There has been progress, reaction, backlash, and renewed effort since then; but no one can deny that the American social mores are changing as a result of the efforts of men and women to make them change.

ETHICAL UNIVERSALS

If we thus return some of the credit or blame for historic events and social change back to individual personalities as a focal point and initiator of personality-culture interaction, just what aspect of this interaction determines the kind of influence that personalities will have on social change? We would suggest, as our illustrations have shown, that usually it is the ethical value systems of individuals interacting with the mores of the culture that determines the nature of social change, the course of history, the ultimate survival of the species itself. This hypothesis finds its operational basis in the biosocial thesis that social cohesion through cooperation, consideration, and sympathy were indispensable to man's survival as *Homo sapiens socialis*; that a sense of responsibility is the hallmark of mature adulthood in the species.

Returning now to the first of our objections to cultural relativism of morals, we may well ask whether there are ethical universals that transcend cultural variations—a kind of "categorical imperative" imposed by human nature itself. Anthropologists, who have given these problems much more thought than psychologists, are of divided opinions, with the idea of "ethical universals" slowly gaining the upper hand over extreme cultural relativism. Kluckhohn (1962) expresses his viewpoint as follows:

The first point to note is the universality of moral standards in general. Morality is as genuine a human universal as is language. All cultures have moral systems—that is, standards for conduct that go beyond temporary circumstances or special situations and standards that are not infrequently obeyed in the face of conflicting personal needs of the moment. . . . Not only is *human* social life inevitably a moral life in theory and to a large extent in practice, but ethical principles are the fundament of most of the rest of the culture. Fortes remarks: "Every social system presupposes such basic moral axioms . . . these axioms are rooted in the direct experience of the inevitability of the interdependence between men in society. . . . The focal field of kinship is also the focal field of moral experience."

Every culture has a concept of murder, distinguishing this from execution, killing in war, and other "justifiable homicides." The notions of incest and other regulations upon sexual behavior, of prohibitions upon untruth under defined circumstances, of restitution and reciprocity, of mutual obligations between parents and children—these and many other moral concepts are altogether universal (Kluckhohn, 1962, p. 276).

Kluckhohn agrees with Asch (1952, p. 374) in rejecting a radical cultural relativism which makes all behavior subject to the circumstances of instrumental conditioning of animal drives (cf. Chapter 6). That means that normal individuals react selectively to the moral alternatives presented to them, or that cultures present variations that are fundamentally not so different after all. We contend that the key to the selectivity as well as the transcendence of cultural variation lies in the universality of inherent social ego needs and the inevitable emergence of moral sensitivities in the course of normal personality development. It is, therefore, appropriate that we finally review and synthesize our views of the moral development of the individual as the crux of what we have been saying about human adjustment to and influence on social change.

Moral

Development We touched but briefly upon some conceptions of moral development in the course of our presentation of developmental stages of personality from a biosocial point of view (Chapters 3, 4, and 5). We confined ourselves to pointing out implications of unfolding cognitive-affective capacities for interpersonal relations, and more or less glossed over other points of view on moral development. In view of our recognition of the importance of individual initiative and the personal conduct mores (morals) in influencing human relationships and history itself, it is best that we fortify the notion that there is such a thing as a developing moral sense in *Homo sapiens socialis*. This does not mean that all men are born moral by some preconceived standard, but that man's evolution and development as a social creature includes and implies a development of moral sensitivity.

THE COGNITIVE APPROACH

The pioneering work of Piaget (1932) dealt primarily with the development of moral judgment as a significant aspect of cognitive development in childhood and adolescence. Using little anecdotal stories that raised questions about misbehavior and punishment or guilt, Piaget and his collaborators sought to illustrate that moral judgment, like all social behavior, was dependent in the first place on the cognitive maturity of the individual. This is a sound biosocial principle which does not deny that a great deal of cultural and situational learning enters into the formation of such judgments; nor does it deny that behavior is frequently at variance with one's better judgment. According to the data presented by Piaget and his collaborators (1932) there is a gradual shift in normal children from defining wrong as that which is punished in one way or another (the predominant mode of middle years of childhood), to conceptions of equality, formal rules, and authority (the predominant modes of preadolescence), to more equitable conceptions of fairness and of individual responsibility (the predominant modes of adolescence). These changes correspond roughly to the modes of reasoning which progress from preoperational intuitive classifications of middle childhood, to concrete operations of preadolescence, and finally to the formal operations (hypothetical reasoning) of adolescence. Various studies have partially confirmed Piaget's results on American children, while emphasizing individual and cultural differences (Boehm and Nass, 1962; Johnson, 1962; MacRae, 1954).

Since different operational criteria are involved in the sequential stages for different kinds of moral judgments in Piaget's scheme, Kohlberg (1963) sought to formulate a generic sequence of moral judgment stages on the basis of his own empirical data. Applying Piaget's techniques to American children from 7 to 16 years of age, Kohlberg discriminated three levels of moral judgment, divided into six types or stages (Table 12–1). These categories could be applied to 10 different kinds of moral choices, varying from simple obedience or conformity to the personal conduct mores or to judging the value of a human life. These results are somewhat more refined than Piaget's, but are consistent with them and agree with the basic rationale of a developmental sequence that has a large component of cognitive maturation. The sequential nature of these six types or stages of moral judgment has been confirmed by Turiel (1966), who found that a sample of seventh-grade boys could be induced by a role-playing technique to accelerate one stage beyond their current stage more easily than two stages beyond or one stage back. Children at any stage of moral development always understood the principles implied in earlier stages of moral choices. There were, of course, individual differences in development rate of moral understanding.

Table 12–1   STAGES OF MORAL DEVELOPMENT AND SOME EXAMPLES
(After Kohlberg, 1964)

Levels of Morality	Example of "Motivation for Obedience or Moral Action"	Example of "Basis for Worth of Human Life"
Level I. *Premoral*		
Type 1. Punishment and obedience orientation	Obey rules to avoid punishment	Confused with value of physical object & based on social status
Type 2. Naive instrumental hedonism	Conform to obtain rewards, have favors returned, etc.	Seen as instrumental to satisfaction of individual's needs or needs of others
Level II. *Morality of Conventional Role-Conformity*		
Type 3. Good-boy morality of good relations, approval of others	Conform to avoid disapproval, dislike by others	Based on empathy & affection of family members & others
Type 4. Authority-maintaining morality	Conform to avoid censure by legitimate authority & resolve guilt	Conceived as sacred in categorical moral or religious order of rights & duties
Level III. *Morality of Self-Accepted Moral Principles*		
Type 5. Morality of contract, individual rights	Conform to maintain respect of impartial judge of community welfare	Valued both in terms of community welfare & universal human right
Type 6. Morality of individual principles of conscience	Conform to avoid self-condemnation	Belief in sacredness of human life as universal value of respect for individual

The Piaget-Kohlberg approach seems to be very promising in providing a cognitive-developmental basis for increasing moral discrimination in the individual. We are also inclined to agree with the implication that the development of moral standards, while partly learned and culturally relevant, also represents the canalization and maturation of an inherent "moral sense" in *Homo sapiens socialis*. However, we would maintain that a great deal more than cognition is involved in this inherent moral sense, if there is such a thing, and that moral behavior involves more than the application of logic and cognitive discrimination. We are dealing here with the most profound dimension of man's relation to his fellow man, the very basis for viable human relations in the interpersonal and the cultural sphere. We see it, in a sense, as the epitome of man's evolution as a social animal, the ingredient that makes social cohesion for survival work. It is also the ingredient that largely determines the individual's sense of security in fulfilling and balancing the whole hierarchy of basic needs. This certainly involves the developmental integration of organismic functions—cognition, affect, and action—into a *way of life* in dealing with one's fellow human beings. It is not that there is any independent special moral sense bred into the species in some specific way, but rather that the process of natural selection for social cohesion inevitably demanded selective integration of capacities for some kind of *mutually considerate* behavior in thought, feeling, word, and deed. For this reason we have sought to call attention to emerging landmarks of interpersonal-ethical relations with each succeeding stage of personality development. We offer in Table 12–2 a tentative sequence of emerging levels and landmarks of human relations as a somewhat more global and psychodynamically integrative scheme of moral development.

According to this scheme, an individual may suffer arrested moral development with or without arrested cognitive development, but mental retardation does in general imply moral retardation. One cannot assume adult roles if one is mentally retarded, and by the same token one cannot assume adult responsibilities or appreciate the ethical subtleties of group relations. On the other hand, emotional retardation or insensitivity may cause arrested development at the infantile primary egocentric level, even if cognitive development is normal. We might also hypothesize a degree of moral immaturity in rigidly circumscribed primary group identifications or ethnocentrism, provided the culture provides other alternatives. The rationale would be that primary sympathetic altruism normally facilitates the development of more humane attitudes and social relations when the culture offers a widening range of social identifications. But individuals,

Table 12–2 HYPOTHESIZED SEQUENCE OF ETHICAL-INTERPERSONAL-RELATIONS
POTENTIALITIES ACCOMPANYING STAGES OF PSYCHOSOCIAL DEVELOPMENT

Modal age range	Stage of psychosocial development	Ethical-interpersonal (human relations) landmarks
1st to 3rd year	Ego emergence and dependency	Primary egocentricity
3rd to 7/8th year	Primary group interaction	Primary (sympathetic) altruism; nominal primary group identifications and reciprocal situational relationships
7/8th year to puberty	Secondary socialization	Differentiated and reciprocal true altruism; ethnic awareness with incipient ethnocentric, defensive, or humane bias
Adolescence	Adult role anticipation	Emerging sense of responsibility; structured reference group attitudes & practices, reflecting ethnic-humane bias and anticipated reference group interests
Early adulthood	Social role assumption	Full social responsibility of assumed role complex; structured reference group relationships and style of life; explicit moral code and defenses for interpersonal and social role behavior

especially those achieving leadership and influence, will always help to determine the direction of such changes in the personal conduct mores.

Moral Dilemmas and

Survival   It may seem at this stage that we are suggesting a reversion to ancient concepts of the struggle between good and evil in man, merely adding new scientific arguments which make Good the odds-on favorite, because inherent social cooperation has increasingly favored survival up to now. If it were that simple, we would need only to preach the gospel of the brotherhood of man and use the sanctions of law and custom to punish or ostracize the occasional offender against the public welfare. Unfortunately, the realities of social life in most parts of the world and in some aspects of the most congenial social settings require a more sophisticated approach.

Though we do not accept the argument of cultural relativity to explain away morality, we also know that no society divides itself into good guys and bad guys like the leading roles in a TV western. Even if man's emergent evolution required a preponderance of cooperative tendencies over the destructively aggressive, neither the blessings nor the catastrophes of human history have generally been initiated by majority vote. Especially in an age of fantastically increasing technology and mass communication, the use of power and influence in directing social change and in determining historic events seems to us to place a high premium on humane adaptive initiative for man's continued survival. What we seem to be approaching here is the question whether the choice of moral values, especially in the use of power and influence by leaders who can affect social change, is not a decisive factor in modern life and the future of man.

This is not to advance a simplistic virtue-will-triumph philsophy backed by biosocial theory, but to call for a more sophisticated analysis of moral values implicit in man's behavior as a social animal. Indeed, the most telling argument against such a simplistic view would be, we think, the moral dilemmas posed by the very basic functions making for social cohesion, when impulsively or indiscriminately applied to changing social contexts. We suspect that this has always been true, and that evolution is essentially a series of trial-and-error experiments in which more and more discriminating behavior was required to meet the exigencies of the very social life that man's emerging capacities brought about. We may well pause to ask ourselves whether the social complexities man has created for himself do not in fact call for far more discriminating use of some of the socially cohesive functions which have stood him in good stead in his primitive past.

We have already suggested that latent ethnocentrism, an outgrowth of primitive primary group identification, may already be a mode of interpersonal relations that has to be outgrown in both ontogenetic development and in social evolution, if man is to survive. Fortunately, primary sympathetic altruism and secondary humanitarianism provide positive influences for survival with dignity. That is not to say that a little pride of heritage or ethnic identification is an evil that threatens human survival. Denying that pride of identity by stigmatizing any group may be the very paradoxical problem at issue. In other words, man's social organization into reference groups in an all-inclusive humanity with mass communication and highly developed technology requires a more discriminate use of ethnic identification and mutual regard.

OBEDIENCE, CONFORMITY, OR REBELLION

Another dilemma revolves around the problem of handling individual responsibility with respect to authority. Undoubtedly, compliance to suggestion and obedience to socially sanctioned authority have served man well in the course of his evolution as a socially responsive animal. But thinking men have recognized for centuries that blind obedience to authority, however sanctified, and compliance with the pressure of public opinion, no matter how united, does not necessarily serve social needs, especially in a time of social change. Even rebellion against the social order has been found at times to be the best way of serving longer-range humanitarian needs and ultimate survival. Compliance with tradition or public opinion may be a considerate or a cowardly thing to do, depending on whose needs are served and whether social change is in order. Obedience may be a responsible exercise of social role commitment or a violation of one's own principles. Both kinds of conformity may even, on occasion, violate primary empathy, which is at the very root of humane behavior.

Psychologists have begun to turn their attention to such problems of conflicting motives, ever alert for concrete experimental evidence on which to base speculations about man's adaptive social behavior. A series of studies of obedience to instructions requiring the apparent inflicting of pain by each subject on another subject was conducted by Milgram (1963, 1965). Milgram originally tested 40 male Ss of varying ages and occupations in the Yale laboratory in an ostensible "learning experiment." The subjects were instructed to administer successively more severe shocks for each wrong answer given by a "learner" (actually a confederate) strapped to an "electric chair" inside a booth. The naïve S, or "teacher" in the experiment, operated a simulated shock generator panel with keys labeled *slight shock* (15 v to 60 v), *moderate shock* (75 v to 120 v), *strong shock* (135 v to 180 v), *very strong shock* (195 v to 240 v), *intense shock* (225 v to 300 v), *extreme-intensity shock* (315 v to 360 v), DANGER: SEVERE SHOCK (375 v to 420 v), and finally just XXX (435 v to 450 v). The "teacher" S's task was to flash certain words to the "learner" in the booth and administer an increasingly severe shock every time the learner gave a wrong answer. By prearrangement, the learner responded with a succession of right and wrong answers, receiving successively more intense shocks after each wrong answer. When 300 v. of "intense shock" was reached, the learner kicked at the door of the booth in apparent agony and failed to respond to the learning experiment thereafter. If the teacher S balked at continuing the experiment, he was given increasingly insistent instructions to go on with the experiment, no matter how the learner felt, counting each failure to respond as a wrong answer.

Of the 40 Ss, 16 refused to go on with the experiment within a few trials after the kicking at the door and cessation of responses occurred, which signified pain or agony on the part of the learner. The rest, while showing various signs of discomfort and misgivings, proceeded to the very end, obeying the instructions to inflict increasingly painful shocks to a man already apparently immobilized by intensely painful shocks.

These results have been widely interpreted as signifying the common man's willingness to obey authority blindly, even to inflict pain on his fellowman under mildly mandatory conditions. There was no apparent penalty for disobedience, and nothing to be gained by compliance. Many people seemed to obey just because obedience is the habitual course of least resistance, no matter how painful the consequences for others. How much more, the reasoning goes, can one expect from soldiers under orders, or civilians with much to gain from another's mistreatment? Does this experiment not illustrate man's basic inhumanity to man? The issue raised is a very profound one and is worth clarifying from our humanistic-biosocial point of view.

In the first place, these studies do not illustrate a basic depravity of human nature, as some of the criticisms seem to imply, but rather a confirmation of primary empathy. The significant overriding fact revealed by the data is that almost all subjects showed various signs of empathic reactions to the learner's sufferings, from agonized expressions of misgivings to outright refusal to go on. The question is not one of basically depraved insensitivity to suffering, but the willingness of a majority to *act contrary to their better judgment and humane feelings*. The only explanation for such action seems to be the superior motivating power of conformity to social expectations or to transitory role commitment. It is indeed startling to many observers (as shown by data predicting greater resistance to such obedience) that such a trivial pressure of conformity should in many cases overrule such a fundamentally humane tendency as sparing the suffering of a fellow human being. It is this tendency to act contrary to one's better judgment and feeling under authoritative sanction or suggestion that poses a major paradox in man's social evolution. It is not a question of primitive sadistic impulses being stronger than "learned humanitarian" behavior, but of one basic social impulse being stronger than another for some people under some circumstances.

The obvious resolution of this dilemma lies in strengthening independent value judgment and action with "the courage of one's convictions" to determine the limits of obedience and conformity. This is in keeping with our conception of responsible adult role commitment as the hallmark of maturity in *Homo sapiens socialis*.

Unfortunately, independence of thought and action—this implicit readiness to rebel against the social mores, the social pressure of the moment, or the established order if need be—cannot be qualified as unadulterated virtue either. Given free rein, such rebellion tends to displace social cohesion with caprice and anarchy—a direction of social change contrary to the demonstrated survival advantages of cooperative and culture-maintaining behavior. Moreover, the lust for unsocialized self-assertion of the antisocial character structure is often unleashed by the heady wine of self-righteous rebellion against any and all established order. History has witnessed many such exploitations of holy causes for sheer self-aggrandizement, and we can see symptoms of it even today. Social change and social lag are inevitable in the scheme of man's technological and social development. Social reform is, by definition, a constructive adaptation to such change. But rebellion for rebellion's sake, or defiance of all authority for irresponsible anarchy's sake, is likely to prove maladaptive for both social and individual needs.

Erich Fromm has repeatedly stated that "History is a graveyard full of corpses of would-be revolutionaries who turned out to be merely petty rebels." The distinction is worth noting. There is room and great need for dedicated humanitarian reformers to guide social change into constructive channels; there is little need and much danger of an excess of immature rebels seeking only the self-indulgent abrogation of the very restraint and mutual consideration that transformed the hominids into social human beings, or that makes a mature adult out of an impulsive child.

Here, as elsewhere throughout this book, it is difficult to find much clear-cut laboratory evidence to prove a point or even to formulate an easily testable hypothesis. Perhaps the continual participant observation of historical personality-culture interaction will provide predictive clues to the future, from the successes and failures in terms of human adjustment of the present and past. Psychology will have to cope more effectively with these abundant sources of data from real life. There is one general hypothesis resulting from the biosocial study of the human personality that we think is constantly being subjected to such an historical test: Man is not only the only animal capable of controlling and altering his environment at will but also of determining his own survival and future evolution. Much of this depends on his manipulation of the politico-economic self-maintenance mores, but the ultimate determining factor in his own personality is his capacity for moral judgment and action.

References

Adams, J. S., and Rosenbaum, W. B. The relationship of worker productivity to cognitive dissonance. *J. appl. Psychol.*, 1962, 46, 161-164.

Adorno, T. W., Frenkel-Brunswick, E., Levinson, D. J., and Sanford, R. N. *The Authoritarian Personality*. New York: Harper & Row, 1950, (also paper, New York: Wiley, 1964).

Allport, G. W. *The Nature of Prejudice*. Reading, Mass.: Addison Wesley, 1954.

Allport, G. W., *Pattern and Growth in Personality*. New York: Holt, Rinehart & Winston, 1961.

American Psychiatric Association. *Diagnostic and Statistical Manual of Mental Disorders*. Washington, D. C.: American Psychiatric Association, 1952; 1968.

Ardrey, R. *African Genesis*. New York: Atheneum, 1961.

Ardrey, R. *The Territorial Imperative*. New York: Atheneum, 1966.

Aronson, E., and Carlsmith, J. M. Performance expectancy as a determinant of actual performance. *J. abnorm. soc. Psychol.*, 1963, 65, 178-182.

Aronson, E., and Cope, V. My enemy's enemy is my friend. *J. Pers. soc. Psychol.*, 1968, 8, 8-12.

Asch, S. E. Effects of group pressure upon the modification and distortion of judgment. In Guetzkow, H. (ed.) *Groups, Leadership, and Men*. Pittsburgh: Carnegie Press, 1951.

Asch, S. E. *Social Psychology*. Englewood Cliffs, N. J.: Prentice-Hall, 1952.

Ausubel, D. P. Causes and types of narcotic addiction: a psychosocial view. *Psychiat. Quart.*, 1961, 35, 523-531.

Baldwin, A. L. *Theories of Child Development*. New York: Wiley, 1968.

Bandura, A., and McDonald, F. J. Influence of social reinforcement and the behavior of models in shaping children's moral judgments. *J. abnorm. soc. Psychol.*, 1963, 67, 274-281.

Bandura, A., and Walters, R. H. *Social Learning and Personality Development*. New York: Holt, Rinehart & Winston, 1963.

Barber, T. X., and Calverly, D. S. An experimental study of "hypnotic" (auditory and visual) hallucinations. *J. abnorm. soc. Psychol.*, 1964, *68*, 13-20.

Barber, T. X. "Hypnotic" phenomena: a critique of experimental methods. In Gordon, J. E. (ed.) *Handbook of Clinical and Experimental Hypnosis.* New York: Macmillan, 1967.

Barry, H., Bacon, M. K., and Child, I. L. A cross-cultural survey of some sex differences in socialization. *J. abnorm. soc. Psychol.*, 1957, *55*, 327-332.

Bellak, L., and Bellak, S. S. An introductory note on the Children's Apperception Test (CAT). *J. proj. Tech.*, 1950, *14*, 173-180.

Benedict, R. *Patterns of Culture.* Boston: Houghton Mifflin, 1934, (also paper, New York: Penguin Books, 1946).

Benjamin, J. D., and Ebaugh, F. G. The diagnostic validity of the Rorschach test. *Amer. J. Psychiat.*, 1938, *94*, 1163-1178.

Berkowitz, L. *Aggression: a Social Psychological Analysis.* New York: McGraw-Hill, 1962.

Berkowitz, L. *The Development of Motives and Values in the Child.* New York: Basic Books, 1964.

Berlyne, D. E. *Conflict Arousal and Curiosity.* New York: McGraw-Hill, 1960.

Berlyne, D. E. Curiosity and exploration. *Science*, 1966, *153*, 25-33.

Bettelheim, B. *Children of the Dream.* New York: Macmillan, 1969.

Bier, W. C. (ed.) *Problems of Addiction: Alcohol and Drug Addiction.* New York: Fordham Univ. Press, 1962.

Boas, F. *The Mind of Primitive Man.* New York: Macmillan, 1938.

Boehm, L., and Nass, M. L. Social class differences in conscience development. *Child Developm.*, 1962, *33*, 565-575.

Bordes, F. *The Old Stone Age.* New York: McGraw-Hill, 1968.

Boring, E. G. *The Physical Dimensions of Consciousness.* New York: Appleton-Century-Crofts, 1933.

Bowlby, J. *Attachment and Loss.* New York: Basic Books, vol. 1, 1969, vol. 2, 1970.

Brackbill, Y. Extinction of the smiling response in infants as a function of reinforcement schedules. *Child Developm.*, 1958, *29*, 115-124.

Brehm, J. W., and Cohen, A. R. *Explorations in Cognitive Dissonance,* New York: Wiley, 1962.

Bridges, K. M. B. Emotional development in early childhood. *Child Developm.*, 1932, *3*, 324-334.

Bromberg, W. G., and Thompson, C. B. The relation of psychosis, mental defect, and personality types to crime. *J. crim. Law Criminol.*, 1937, *28*, 1.

Butler, R. A. Discrimination learning by rhesus monkeys to visual exploration motivation. *J. comp. physiol. Psychol.*, 1953, *46*, 95-98.

Butler, R. A. Effects of deprivation of visual incentives on visual exploration motivation in monkeys. *J. comp. physiol. Psychol.*, 1957, *50*, 177-179.

Butler, R. A., and Alexander, H. M. Daily pattern of visual exploratory behavior in monkeys. *J. comp. physiol. Psychol.*, 1955, *48*, 247-249.

Butler, R. A., and Harlow, H. F. Persistence of visual exploration in monkeys. *J. comp. physiol. Psychol.*, 1954, *47*, 258-263.

Campbell, A., Converse, P., Miller, W. E., and Stokes, D. *The American Voter*. New York: Wiley, 1960.

Cantril, H. *The Politics of Despair*. New York: Basic Books, 1958.

Casler, L. Maternal deprivation: a critical review of the literature. *Child Developm. Monog.*, 1961, 26, No. 2.

Cattell, R. B. Validation and intensification of the Sixteen Personality Factor Questionnaire. *J. clin. Psychol.*, 1956, 12, 205-214.

Chein, I., Gerard, D. L., Lee, R. S., and Rosenfeld, E. *The Road to H: Narcotics, Delinquency, and Social Policy*. New York: Basic Books, 1964.

Chomsky, N. *Language and the Mind*. New York: Harcourt, Brace & World, 1968.

Chotlos, J. W., and Deiter, J. B. Psychological considerations in the etiology of alcoholism. In Pitman, D. J. (ed.) *Alcoholism: an Interdisciplinary Approach*. Springfield, Ill.: Thomas, 1959.

Christiansen, B. *Attitudes Toward Foreign Affairs as a Function of Personality*. Oslo: Oslo Univ. Press, 1959.

Clark, K. B. *Prejudice and Your Child* (2nd ed.). Boston: Beacon Press, 1963.

Cohen, A. R., Brehm, J. W., and Latané, B. Choice of strategy and voluntary exposure to information under public and private conditions. *J. Pers.*, 1959, 27, 63-73.

Cooley, C. H. *Social Disorganization*. New York: Scribners, 1902 (also in *The Two Major Works of C. H. Cooley*. New York: Free Press of Glencoe, 1956).

Cowan, P. A., Langer, J., Heavenrich, J., and Nathanson, M. Social learning and Piaget's cognitive theory of moral development. *J. Pers. soc. Psychol.*, 1969, 11, 261-274.

Crossman, R. (ed.) *The God That Failed*. New York: Harper & Row, 1950.

Dart, R. A. The predatory transition from ape to man. *Int. Anthrop. & Ling. Rev.* 1953, 1, 201-208.

Dart, R. A., and Dennis, C. *Adventures with the Missing Link*. New York: Harper & Row, 1959.

Darwin, C. *The Descent of Man*. New York: Modern Library (orig. pub. 1871).

Day, M. *Guide to Fossil Man*. New York: World Pub. Co., 1965 (also paper, 1968).

Dennis, W. *Group Values Through Children's Drawings*. New York: Wiley, 1966.

Deutsch, M., Katz, I. Jensen, A. R., (eds.) *Social Class, Race and Psychological Development*. New York: Holt, Rinehart & Winston, 1968.

Dollard, J., and Miller, N. *Personality and Psychotherapy*. New York: McGraw-Hill, 1950.

Edwards, A. L. *The Social Desirability Variable in Personality Assessment Research*. New York: Holt, 1957.

Edwards, A. L. The assessment of human motives by means of personality scales. In Levine, D. (ed.) *Nebraska Symposium on Motivation*. Lincoln: Univ. Nebraska Press, 1964.

Epstein, R., and Komarita, S. S. Childhood prejudice as a function of parental ethnocentrism, punitiveness, and outgroup characteristics. *J. Pers. soc. Psychol.*, 1966, 3, 259-264.

Erikson, E. H. *Identity and the Life Cycle.* New York: International Univ. Press, 1959.

Erikson, E. H. *Childhood and Society.* New York: Norton, 1950 (2nd ed., 1963).

Escalona, S. and Heider, G. M. *Prediction and Outcome.* New York: Basic Books, 1959.

Etkin, W. Social behavior and the evolution of man's mental faculties. *Amer. Naturalist*, 1954, 88, 129-142. Also in Montagu, M. F. A. (ed.) *Culture and the Evolution of Man.* New York: Oxford Univ. Press, 1962.

Eysenck, H. J. *The Psychology of Politics.* New York: Praeger, 1955.

Festinger, L. *The Theory of Cognitive Dissonance.* New York: Harper & Row, 1957.

Festinger, L. *Conflict, Decision, and Dissonance.* Stanford: Stanford Univ. Press, 1964.

Festinger, L., Riecken, H. W., and Schachter, S. *When Prophecy Fails.* Minneapolis: Univ. Minn. Press, 1956 (also paper, New York: Harper & Row, 1964).

Festinger, L., and Bramel, D. The reactions of humans to cognitive dissonance. In Bachrach, A. (ed.) *The Experimental Foundations of Clinical Psychology.* New York: Basic Books, 1962.

Flapan, D. *Children's Understanding of Social Interaction.* New York: Teachers College Press, 1968.

Fowler, H. *Curiosity and Exploratory Behavior.* New York: Macmillan, 1965.

Freud, A. *The Ego and the Mechanisms of Defense.* International Univ. Press, 1946.

Freud, S. *Three Contributions to the Theory of Sex.* (Orig. pub. as *Drei Abhandlungen zur Sexualtheorie*, 1905). New York: Dutton, 1962 (paper).

Freud, S. *Totem and Taboo.* (Orig. pub. Vienna, 1913.) In Brill, A. A. (ed.), *The Basic Writings of Sigmund Freud.* New York: Modern Library, 1938.

Freud, S. *The Problem of Anxiety.* New York: Norton, 1926.

Freud, S. *An Outline of Psychoanalysis.* New York: Norton, 1949.

Freud, S. *Civilization and its Discontents.* London: Hogarth, 1930.

Fromm, E. *Man for Himself.* New York: Holt, Rinehart & Winston, 1947.

Gardner, R. W., Holzman, P. S., Klein, G. S., Linton, H. B., and Spence, D. P. Cognitive control: a study of individual consistencies in cognitive behavior. *Psychol. Issues*, 1959, Vol. I, No. 4.

Gardner, R. W., and Moriarty, A. *Personality Development at Preadolescence: Explorations of Structure Formation.* Seattle: Univ. Wash. Press, 1968.

Gesell, A., and Ilg, F. L. *Infant and Child in the Culture of Today.* New York: Harper & Row, 1943.

Gesell, A., and Thompson, H. Twins T and C from infancy to adolescence: a biogenetic study of individual differences by the method of co-twin control. *Genetic Psychol. Monog.*, 1941, 24, 2-121.

Gilbert, G. M. *Nuremberg Diary*. New York: Farrar, Straus, & Giroux, 1947 (also paper, New York: New American Library, 1962).

Gilbert, G. M. *The Psychology of Dictatorship*. New York: Ronald Press, 1950.

Gilbert, G. M. Stereotype persistence and change among college students. *J. abnorm. soc. Psychol.*, 1951, 46, 245-254.

Gilbert, G. M. Crime and punishment: an exploratory comparison of public, criminal, and penological attitudes. *Ment. Hygiene*, 1958, 42, 550-557.

Gilbert, G. M. Sex differences in mental health in a Mexican village. *Intl. J. soc. Psychiat.*, 1959, 3, 205-212.

Gilbert, G. M. Toward a comprehensive biosocial theory of human behavior. *Int. J. soc. Psychiat.*, 1963, 2, 85-93.

Goode, W. J. Illegitimacy in the Caribbean social structure. *Amer. sociol. Rev.*, 1960, 21-30.

Goring, C. *The English Convict*. London: H. M. Stationery Office, 1913.

Greenacre, P. *Trauma, Growth, and Personality*. New York: Norton, 1952.

Greenwald, H. *The Call Girl, a Social and Psychoanalytic Study*. New York: Ballantine Books, 1958.

Grinker, R. R., and Spiegel, J. P. *Men Under Stress*. New York: McGraw-Hill, 1945.

Guilford, J. O., and Zimmerman, W. S. The Guilford-Zimmerman Temperament Survey. Beverly Hills, Calif.: Sheridan Supply Co., 1949.

Hall, G. S. *Adolescence*. New York: Appleton-Century-Crofts, 1916 (also reviewed in Muuss, R. E., *Theories of Adolescence*, New York: Random House, 1968).

Hall, C. S., and Lindzey, G. *Theories of Personality*. New York: Wiley, 1957.

Harlow, H. F. Learning and satiation of response in intrinsically motivated complex puzzle performance by monkeys. *J. comp. physiol. Psychol.*, 1950, 43, 289-294.

Harlow, H. F. Mice, monkeys, men, and motives. *Psychol. Rev.*, 1953, 60, 23-32.

Harlow, H. F. The nature of love. *Amer. Psychologist*, 1958, 13, 673-685.

Harlow, H. F., Blazek, N. C., and McClearn, G. E. Manipulatory motivation in the infant rhesus monkey. *J. comp. physiol. Psychol.*, 1956, 49, 444-448.

Harlow, H. F., and Harlow, M. K. Social deprivation in monkeys. *Scient. Amer.*, 1962, 2-10.

Hathaway, S. R., and Meehl, P. *An Atlas for the Clinical Use of the MMPI*. Minneapolis: Univ. Minn. Press, 1951.

Hathaway, S. R., and McKinley, J. C. *Manual for the MMPI* (rev. ed.) New York: Psychological Corp., 1951.

Havighurst, R. J. *Human Development and Education*. New York: Longmans Green, 1953.

Healy, W., and Bronner, A. *Treatment and what happened after*. Boston: Judge Baker Guidance Center, 1939.

Hebb, D. O. Drives and the C.N.S. (conceptual nervous system). *Psychol. Rev.*, 1955, 62, 243-254.

Heider, G. *Vulnerability in Infants and Young Children: A Pilot Study*. *Genet. Psychol. Monogr.*, 1966, 73, 1-216.

Helson, H. Some problems in motivation from the point of view of the theory of adaptation level. In Levine, D. (ed.) *Nebraska Symposium on Motivation*. Lincoln: Univ. Nebraska Press, 1966.

Henry, W. E. The business executive: a study of the psychodynamics of a social role. *Amer. J. Sociol.*, 1949, 54, 286-291.

Herskovitz, M. J. *Economic Anthropology*. New York: Knopf, 1952.

Hess, E. H. Imprinting. *Science*, 1959, 130, 133-141.

Hilgard, E. R. Pain as a puzzle for psychology and physiology. *Amer. Psychologist*, 1969, 24, 103-113.

Hill, W. F., Activity as an auronomous drive. *J. comp. physiol. Psychol.*, 1956, 49, 15-19.

Hodge, R. W., Siegel, P. M., and Rossi, Ph. H. Occupational prestige in the United States, 1925-1963. *Amer. J. Sociol.*, 1964, 70, 286-302.

Hofstadter, R. *Social Darwinism in American Thought*. Philadelphia: Univ. Pennsylvania Press, 1944 (also paper, Boston: Beacon Press, 1955).

Holt, E. B. *Animal Drive and the Learning Process*. New York: Holt, Rinehart & Winston, 1931.

Holtzman, W. H. Inkblot perception and personality: the meaning of inkblot variables. *Bull. Menninger Clinic*, 1963, 27, 84-95.

Holtzman, W. H., Diaz-Guerero, R., Swartz, J. D., and Laria Tapia, L. Cross-cultural longitudinal research on child development: Studies of American and Mexican school children. In Hill, J. P. (ed.) *Minnesota Symposium on Child Psychology* Vol. II. Minneapolis: Univ. Minnesota Press, 1968.

Holtzman, W. H., Thorpe, J. S., Swartz, J. D., and Herron, E. W. *Inkblot Perception and Personality*. Austin: Univ. Texas Press, 1961.

Hooker, E. The adjustment of the male overt homosexual. *J. proj. Tech.*, 1957, 21, 18-31.

Horney, K. *Our Inner Conflicts*. New York: Norton, 1945.

Howell, F. C. *Early Man* (rev. ed.) New York: Time-Life Books, 1968.

Howells, W. *Mankind in the Making* (rev. ed.) Garden City: Doudleday, 1967.

Inhelder, B., and Piaget, J. *Growth of Logical Thinking from Childhood to Adolescence*. New York: Basic Books, 1958.

Inkeles, A., and Rossi, P. H. National comparisons of occupational prestige. *Amer. J. Sociol.*, 1956, 61, 329-339.

Johnson, R. A. A study of children's moral judgments. *Child Developm.*, 1962, 33, 327-354.

Kaplan, B., Rickers-Ovsiankina, M., and Joseph, A. An attempt to sort Rorschach records from four cultures. *J. proj. Tech.*, 1956, 20, 172-180.

Kaplan, B. (ed.) *Studying Personality Cross-Culturally*. New York: Harper & Row, 1961.

Karlins, M., Coffman, T. L., and Walters, G. On the fading of social stereotypes: studies in three generations of college students. *J. Pers. soc. Psychol.*, 1969, 13, 1-16.

Katz, D. The functional approach to the study of attitudes. *Pub. Opin. Q.*, 1960, *24*, 163-204.

Katz, D., and Braly, K. W. Racial stereotypes of 100 college students. *J. abnorm. soc. Psychol.*, 1933, *27*, 280-290.

Kinsey, A. C., *et al. Sexual Behavior in the Human Male.* Philadelphia: Saunders, 1948.

Kinsey, A. C., *et al. Sexual Behavior in the Human Female.* Philadelphia: Saunders, 1953.

Kluckhohn, C. *Culture and Behavior.* New York: Free Press of Glencoe, 1962.

Kluckhohn, F. R., and Strodtbeck, F. L. *Variations in Value Orientations.* New York: Harper & Row, 1961.

Kohlberg, L. Moral development and identification. In Stevenson, H. W. (ed.) *Child Psychology:* 62nd Yearbook, Nat. Soc. Study of Ed. Chicago: Univ. Chicago Press, 1963.

Kohlberg, L. The development of children's orientations toward a moral order. *Vita Humana*, 1963, *6*, 11-33.

Köhler, W. *The Mentality of Apes.* London: Kegan Paul, Trenck, Trubner, 1925 (also paper, New York: Vintage Books, 1959).

Kolb, L. *Drug Addiction.* Springfield, Ill.: Thomas, 1962.

Koppitz, E. M. *Psychological Evaluation of Children's Human Figure Drawings.* New York: Grune & Stratton, 1968.

Krugman, J. I. A clinical evaluation of the Rorschach with problem children. *Rorschach Research Exch.*, 1942, *6*, 61-70.

Kuppuswamy, B. A statistical study of attitudes to the caste system in South India. *J. Psychol.*, 1956, *42*, 169-206.

Lambert, W. W., Triandis, L. M., and Wolf, M. Some correlates of belief and malevolence and benevolence of supernatural beings: a cross-cultural study. *J. abnorm. soc. Psychol.*, 1959, *58*, 162-169.

Lawlor, E. E. Effects of hourly overpayment on productivity and work quality. *J. Pers. soc. Psychol.*, 1968, *10*, 306-314.

Leroi-Gourhan, A. *Treasures of Prehistoric Art.* New York: Abrams, 1968.

Leuba, C. Toward some integration of learning theories: the concept of optimal stimulation. *Psychol. Reports*, 1955, *1*, 27-33.

Levi-Strauss, C. The family. In Schapiro, H. L. (ed.) *Man, Culture, and Society.* New York: Oxford Univ. Press, 1956 (also paper, 1960).

Lewis, O. *Five Families: Mexican Case Studies in the Culture of Poverty.* New York: Basic Books, 1959.

Lewis, O. *La Vida: a Puerto Rican Family in the Culture of Poverty.* New York: Random House, 1966.

Lindzey, G. Thematic Apperception Test: Interpretive assumptions and related empirical evidence. *Psychol. Bull.*, 1952, *49*, 1-52.

Lindzey, G. *Projective Techniques and Cross-Cultural Research.* New York: Appleton-Century-Crofts, 1961.

Lindzey, G., and Aronson, E. (eds.) *The Handbook of Social Psychology.* Vol. III: The Individual in a Social Context. Reading, Mass.: Addison-Wesley, 1969.

Linton, R. *The Study of Man.* New York: Appleton-Century, 1936.

Little, K. B., and Schneidman, E. S. Congruences among interpretations of psychological tests and anamnesic data. *Psychol. Monogr.*, 1959, 73, No. 6 (Whole No. 476).

Loevinger, J. The meaning and measurement of ego development. *Amer. Psychologist*, 1966, 21, 195-206.

Lombroso, C. *Crime and its Causes and Remedies*. Boston: Little, Brown, 1911.

Lorenz, K. *On Aggression*. New York: Harcourt, Brace & World, 1966. (Orig. pub. as *Das Sogenannte Böse*. Vienna: Borotha-Schoeler, 1963.)

MacRae, D. A test of Piaget's theories of moral development. *J. abnorm. soc. Psychol.*, 1954, 49, 14-18.

Malinowski, B. *The Father in Primitive Psychology*. New York: Norton, 1927.

Malinowski, B. *Sex and Repression in Savage Society*. New York: Harcourt, Brace & World, 1929 (also paper, New York: Meridian Books, 1955).

Marshall, H. R. Relations between home experiences and children's use of language in play interactions with peers. *Psychol. Monogr.*, 1961, 75, No. 5.

Maslow, A. H. *Toward a Psychology of Being*. Princeton, N. J.: Van Nostrand, 1962.

Maslow, A. H. *Motivation and Personality*. (rev. ed.) New York: Harper & Row, 1970.

McCarthy, D. L. *Language Development. Monogr. Soc. Res. Child Developm.*, 1960, 25, No. 3.

McClelland, D. C. *The Achieving Society*. Princeton, N. J.: Van Nostrand, 1961.

Mead, M. *Male and Female*. New York: Morrow, 1949 (also paper, New York: New American Library, 1955).

Megargee, E. J. The Edwards SD Scale: a measure of adjustment or dissimulation? *J. consult. Psychol.*, 1966, 566 (also in Megargee, E. J., ed., *Research in Clinical Assessment*. New York: Harper & Row, 1966).

Milgram, S. Behavioral study of obedience. *J. abnorm. soc. Psychol.*, 1963, 67, 371-378.

Milgram, S. Some conditions of obedience and disobedience to authority. *Hum. Relat.*, 1965, 18, 57-76.

Miller, N. E. Liberalization of basic S-R concepts: extension to conflict behavior, motivation, and social learning. In Koch, S. (ed.) *Psychology: A Study of a Science*, Vol. 2. New York: McGraw-Hill, 1959.

Miller, N. E. Some reflections on the law of effect produce a new alternative to drive reduction. In Jones, M. R. (ed.) *Nebraska Symposium on Motivation*. Lincoln: Univ. Nebraska Press, 1963.

Miller, N. E., and Dollard, J. *Social Learning and Imitation*. New Haven: Yale Univ. Press, 1941.

Montagu, M. F. A. *The Human Revolution*. Cleveland: World Pub., 1965.

Montagu, M. F. A. *Man: His First Two Million Years*. New York: Oxford Univ. Press, 1969.

Montagu, M. F. A. (ed.) *Culture and the Evolution of Man*, New York: Oxford Univ. Press, 1962.

Montagu, M. F. A. (ed.) *Man and Aggression*. New York: Oxford Univ. Press, 1968.

Morris, C. *Varieties of Human Values*. Chicago: Univ. Chicago Press, 1956.

Mosely, E. C. Psychodiagnosis based on multivariate analysis of the Holtzman Inkblot Technique. Unpublished doctoral dissertation, University of Texas, Austin, 1962.

Mowrer, O. H. *Learning Theory and the Symbolic Process*. New York: Wiley, 1960.

Moynihan, D. P. *The Negro Family: the Case for National Action*. Washington, D. C.: Office of Policy Planning and Research, U. S. Dept. Labor, 1965.

Murphy, G. *Personality: A Biosocial Approach to Origins and Structure*. New York: Harper & Row, 1947.

Murphy, G. *In the Minds of Men*. New York: Basic Books, 1953.

Murphy, L. B. *Social Behavior and Child Personality: an Exploratory study of some roots of sympathy*. New York: Columbia Univ. Press, 1937.

Murphy, L. B. Coping devices and defense mechanisms in relation to autonomous ego functions. *Bull. Menninger Clin.*, 1960, 24, 144-153.

Murphy, L. B., et al. *The Widening World of Childhood: Paths Toward Mastery*. New York: Basic Books, 1962.

Murphy, L. B. Some aspects of the first relationship. *Int. J. Psychoanal.*, 1964, 45, 31-43.

Murray, H. A. *Thematic Apperception Test Manual*. Cambridge: Harvard Univ. Press, 1943.

Muuss, R. E. *Theories of Adolescence*, 2nd ed. New York: Random House, 1968.

Osgood, C. E., Suci, G. J., and Tanenbaum, P. H. *The Measurement of Meaning*. Urbana: Univ. Illinois Press, 1957.

Papageorgis, D. Repression and the unconscious: a social-psychological reformulation. *J. Indiv. Psychol.*, 1965, 21, 18-31.

Peck, R. F., and Galliani, C. Intelligence, ethnicity, and social roles in adolescent society. *Sociometry*, 1962, 25, 64-72.

Peck, R. F., Havighurst, R. J., et al. *The Psychology of Character Development*. New York: Wiley, 1960.

Piaget, J. *The Child's Conception of the World*. London: Kegan Paul, Trench, Trubner, 1929 (also paper, Paterson, N. J.: Littlefield, Adams, 1963).

Piaget, J. *The Moral Judgment of the Child*. New York: Harcourt, Brace & World, 1932 (republished, New York: Free Press of Glencoe, 1948; also paper, 1965).

Piaget, J. *The Origins of Intelligence in Children*. New York: International Univ. Press, 1952 (paper, New York: Norton, 1965).

Piaget, J. *The Construction of Reality in the Child*. New York: Basic Books, 1954.

Pribram, K. H. Reinforcement revisited: a structural view. In Jones, M. R. (ed.) *Nebraska Symposium on Motivation*. Lincoln: Univ. Nebraska Press, 1963.

Proshansky, H., and Newton, P. The nature and meaning of Negro self-identity. In Deutsch, M., Katz, I., and Jensen, A. R. (eds.) *Social Class, Race, and Psychological Development*. New York: Holt, Rinehart & Winston, 1968.

Rapaport, D. A historical introduction to psychoanalytic ego psychology. In Erkson, E. H., *Identity and the Life Cycle*. New York: International Univ. Press, 1959.

Razran, G. The conditioned evocation of attitudes (cognitive conditioning?). *J. exp. Psychol.*, 1954, 48, 278-282.

Reiss, I. L. *The Social Context of Pre-marital Sexual Permissiveness*. New York: Holt, Rinehart & Winston, 1967.

Research Center for Mental Health, New York University. *Biennial Report, 1963-1965*. New York: New York Univ., 1967.

Rheingold, H. L. The modification of social responsiveness in institutional babies. *Monogr. Soc. Res. Child Developm.*, 1956 21, No. 2 (Whole No. 63).

Roe, A. *The Psychology of Occupations*. New York: Wiley, 1956.

Roe, A. A psychological study of eminent physical scientists. *Genet. Psychol. Monogr.*, 1953, 67, 121-239.

Roe, A., and Simpson, G. G. (eds.) *Behavior and Evolution*. New Haven: Yale Univ. Press, 1958.

Rokeach, M. *The Open and Closed Mind*. New York: Basic Books, 1960.

Schachter, S., and Latane, B. Crime, cognition, and the autonomic nervous system. In Levine, D. (ed.) *Nebraska Symposium on Motivation*. Lincoln: Univ. Nebraska Press, 1964.

Schaffer, R. H. Job satisfaction as related to need satisfaction in work. *Psychol. Monogr.*, 1953, 67, No. 14.

Schneidman, E. S. Make a Picture Story Test. New York: Psychological Corp., 1947, 1952.

Scotch, N. A. A preliminary report on the relation of sociocultural factors to hypertension among the Zulu. *Annals N. Y. Acad. Sci.*, 1960, 84, 1000-1009 (also in Smelser and Smelser, eds., *Personality and Social Systems*, New York: Wiley, 1963).

Sears, R. R., Rau, L., and Alpert, R. *Identification and Child Rearing*. Stanford, Calif.: Stanford Univ. Press, 1965.

Segall, M. H., Campbell, D. T., and Herskovits, M. J. *The Influence of Culture on Visual Perception*. New York: Bobbs-Merrill, 1966.

Shapiro, H. L. (ed.) *Man, Culture, and Society*. New York: Oxford Univ. Press, 1956 (paper, 1960).

Sheldon, W. H. (with S. S. Stevens) *The Varieties of Temperament*. New York: Harper & Row, 1942.

Sears, R. R. Dependency motivation. In Jones, M. R. (ed.) *Nebraska Symposium on Motivation*. Lincoln: Univ. Nebraska Press, 1963.

Sherif, C. W., Sherif, M., and Nebergall, R. *Attitude Change*. Philadelphia: Saunders, 1965.

Shirer, W. L. *The Rise and Fall of the Third Reich*. New York: Simon & Schuster, 1960.

Shor, R. E. Physiological effects of painful stimulation during hypnotic analgesia under conditions designed to minimize anxiety. *Int. J. clin. exp. Hypnosis*, 1962, 10, 183-202.

Skinner, B. F. *Walden Two*. New York: Macmillan, 1948.

Smith, M. B., Bruner, J. S., and White, R. W. *Opinions and Personality*. New York: Wiley, 1956.

Solley, C. M., and Murphy, G. *Development of the Perceptual World*. New York: Basic Books, 1960.

Spence, J. T. Learning Theory and Personality. In Wepman, J. M. and Heine, R. W. (eds.) *Concepts of Personality*. Chicago: Aldine, 1965.

Spitz, R. A. Hospitalism: an inquiry into the genesis of psychiatric conditions in early childhood. In *Psychoanalytic Study of the Child*, Vol. 1. New York: International Univ. Press, 1945.

Spitz, R. A. The smiling response: a contribution to the ontogenesis of social relations. *Genet. Psychol. Monogr.*, 1946, 34, 57-125.

Stein, D. D. The influence of belief systems on interpersonal preference. *Psychol. Monogr.*, 1966, 80, no. 8 whole no. 616.

Stein, D. D., Hardwyck, J. A., and Smith, M. B. Race *and* belief: an open and shut case. *J. Pers. soc. Psychol.*, 1965, 1, 281-289

Stone, L. J., and Church, J. *Childhood and Adolescence*. New York: Harper & Row, 1968.

Sullivan, H. S. *Interpersonal Theory of Psychiatry*. New York: Norton, 1953.

Sullivan, H. S. *The Psychiatric Interview*. New York: Norton, 1954.

Syme, H. Personality characteristics and the alcoholic: a critique of recent studies. *Q. J. Stud. Alcohol.*, 1957, 18, 288-302.

Tart, C. T. (ed.), *Altered States of Consciousness*. New York: Wiley, 1969.

Tax, S. (ed.) *Evolution After Darwin: The Evolution of Man*. Chicago: Univ. Chicago Press, 1960.

Taylor, G. R. *The Biological Time Bomb*. New York: Harcourt, Brace & World, 1968.

Terman, L. M., and Merrill, M. A. *Stanford-Binet Intelligence Scale: Manual for the Third Revision*. Boston: Houghton Mifflin, 1960.

Thompson, C. E. *The Thematic Apperception Test: Thompson Modification*. Cambridge, Mass.: Harvard Univ. Press, 1949.

Thompson, G. G. *Child Psychology*. Boston: Houghton Miflin, 1962.

Thorndike, E. L. *The Psychology of Learning*. New York: Teachers College, Columbia Univ., 1913.

Turiel, E. An experimental test of the sequentiality of developmental stages in the child's moral judgments. *J. Pers. soc. Psychol.*, 1966, 3, 611-618.

Vaughan, G. M. Concept formation and the development of ethnic awareness. *J. genet. Psychol.*, 1963, 103, 93-103.

Veblen, T. *The Theory of the Leisure Class*. New York: Macmillan, 1899 (also paper, New York: New American Library, 1953).

Watson, J. B. *Behaviorism*. New York: People's Inst. Pub., 1924.

Watson, J. B. *The New Behaviorism*. New York: Norton, 1930.

Watson, J. B., and Maynor, R. Conditioned emotional reactions. *J. exp. Psychol.*, 1920, 3, 1-14.

Werner, H. *Comparative Psychology of Mental Development* (rev. ed.) New York: International Univ. Press, 1957.

White, R. W. Motivation reconsidered: the concept of competence. *Psychol. Rev.*, 1959, 66, 297-233.

White, R. W. Competence and the psychosexual stages of development. In Jones, M. R. (ed.) *Nebraska Symposium on Motivation.* Lincoln: Univ. Nebraska Press, 1960.

White, R. W. *Lives in Progress.* New York: Dryden Press, 1952.

White, W. H. *The Organization Man.* New York: Simon & Schuster, 1956.

Witkin, H. A., Dyk, R. B., Faterson, H. F., Goodenough, D. R., and Karp, S. A. *Psychological Differentiation: Studies of Development.* New York: Wiley, 1962.

Zubin, J. Failures of the Rorschach Technique. *J. proj. Tech.*, 1954, 18, 303-315 (also in Megargee, E. I., ed., *Research in Clinical Assessment*, New York: Harper & Row, 1966).

Index

Adams, J. S., 232
Adaptation, human, to environment, 29, 39, 53, 56, 190. *See also* Evolution, human; Environment
Adjustment and defense, Chap. 7. *See also* Defense mechanisms; Defensive strategies
Adler, Alfred, 202, 208, 266
Adolescence, Chap. 4
adjustment problems in, 112 f., 114 f.
attitudes toward sex, 121 f.
biosocial significance of, 102 ff., 111–124, 127–132. *See also* Behavior, psychosocial integration in
character formation in, 127–130
cognitive-affective integration in, 115–125, 126, 131 f.
definition of, 102–105
developmental tasks of, 125 ff., 131
moral development in, 337. *See also* Society and social mores; Values
pregnancy in, 108 f.

role anticipation in, female, 104 f., 108–114, 131 f.; male, 105–115, 132. *See also* Behavior, role; Roles
sexual maturation in, 102–115, 120 f., 121–125. *See also* Behavior, sexual; Sex drive
value learning in, 111–115, 116 f., 120 f., 127–130, 132, 150, 264. *See also* Attitudes; Society and social mores; Values
See also Adulthood; Child and adolescent development; Preadolescence
Adorno, T. W., 260, 262, 263
Adulthood, biosocial integration in, 133 ff., 157 f., 161 ff., 163 f. *See also* Behavior, psychosocial integration in; Personality, integration of
definition of, 133 ff.
reference group identification in, 150–157, 202 ff. *See also* Child development, reference group identification

70 71 72 73   7 6 5 4 3 2 1